The New Financial Order

The New Financial Order

RISK IN THE 21ST CENTURY

Robert J. Shiller

Princeton University Press · PRINCETON AND OXFORD

In the United Kingdom:
Princeton University Press
3 Market Place
Woodstock, Oxfordshire OX20 1SY

Library of Congress Cataloging-in-Publication Data

Shiller, Robert J.
    The new financial order : risk in the 21st century /
Robert J. Shiller.
        p.   cm.
    Includes bibliographical references and index.
    ISBN 0-691-09172-2 (alk. paper)
    1. Risk management.   2. Information technology.   I. Title.
HD61 .S55   2003
368—dc21   2002042563

British Library Cataloging-in-Publication Data is available

Book design by Dean Bornstein

This book has been composed in Adobe Galliard and Formata
by Princeton Editorial Associates, Inc., Scottsdale, Arizona

Printed on acid-free paper. ∞

www.pupress.princeton.edu
Printed in the United States of America

10 9 8 7 6 5 4 3 2

I returned, and saw under the sun, that the race is not to the swift, nor the battle to the strong, neither yet bread to the wise, nor yet riches to men of understanding, nor yet favor to men of skill; but time and chance happeneth to them all.

—ECCLESIASTES 9:11

Contents

CONTENTS

Preface

Economic gains achieved through technological progress do not themselves guarantee that more people will lead good lives. Just as enormous economic insecurity and income inequality pervade the world today, worsening conditions can develop even as technological advances mark greater levels of economic achievement. But new risk management ideas can enable us to manage a vast array of risks—those present and future, near and far—and to limit the downside effects of capitalism's "creative destruction." Application of these ideas will not only help reduce downside risks, but it will also permit more positive risk-taking behavior, thereby engendering a more varied and ultimately more inspiring world.

The New Financial Order proposes a radically new risk management infrastructure to help secure the wealth of nations: to preserve the billions of minor—and not so minor—economic gains that sustain people around the world. Most of these gains seldom make the news or even evoke much public discussion, but they can enrich hard-won economic security and without them any semblance of progress is lost. By radically changing our basic institutions and approach to management of all these risks both large and small we can do far more to improve our lives and our society than through piecemeal tinkering.

Just as modern systems of insurance protect people against catastrophic risks in their lives, this new infrastructure would utilize financial inventions that protect people against systemic risks: from job loss because of changing technologies to threats to home and community because of changing economic conditions.

If successfully implemented, this newly proposed financial infrastructure would enable people to pursue their dreams with greater confidence than they can under existing modes of risk management. Without such a means to greater security, it will be difficult for young people, whose ideas and skills represent the raw materials for a growth-oriented information society, to take the risks necessary to convert their intellectual energies into useful goods and services for society.

Historically, economic thinkers have been limited by the state of relevant risk management principles of their day. Recent advances in financial theory, information technology, and the science of psychology allow us to design new inventions for managing the technological and economic risks inherent in capitalism—inventions that could not have been envisioned by past thinkers. Karl Marx, the instigator of the communist movement, had no command of such risk management ideas when he published *Das Kapital* in 1867. Nor did John Maynard Keynes, the principal expositor of modern liberal economic policy, when he published the *General Theory of Employment, Interest and Money* in 1936. Nor did Milton Friedman, the chief expositor of economic libertarianism, when he published *Capitalism and Freedom* in 1962.

Ultimately, *The New Financial Order* is about applying risk management technology to the major problems of our lives. That is, it depicts an electronically integrated risk management culture designed to work in tandem with the already existing economic institutions of capitalism to promote wealth. The book does not promise utopia, nor is it a solution to all of our problems. It is not motivated by any political ideology, nor by sympathies with one or another social class. It does offer steps we can realistically take to make our lives much better. By presenting new ideas about basic risk management technology, this book does not propose a finished blueprint for the future. Instead, it describes a new direction that will inevitably be improved by future experimentation, innovation, and new advances in financial theory, in the manipulation of relevant risk-related information, and in the ability of social scientists to draw on psychology to design user-friendly techniques to help people manage income-related risks.

I began working on this book in 1997 as a culmination of years of thinking and writing about how to improve institutions for dealing with risks, both to individuals and to society. In 1993 I published a technical monograph, *Macro Markets: Creating Institutions for Managing Society's Largest Economic Risks,* accompanied by a series of scholarly articles on the general topic of risk management with Allan Weiss, Karl Case, Stefano Athanasoulis, and others. But these pieces neither drew the big picture nor addressed the big issues that I thought needed to be stressed to a broad audience.

At that time I had planned to use this book to integrate my thinking about risk management into a broader picture of our society and economy. I had hoped to correct the egregious public misunderstanding of technological and economic risks, and convey a clearer, more accurate picture of the actual risks people face. Also, I had hoped to explain how the presence of various forms of risk, many hidden in plain sight, prevent us from achieving our highest potential.

But I was interrupted in 1999 by the increasingly impressive evidence of an enormous boom in the stock market, a boom that proved of historic proportions. On the advice of my fellow economist and life-long friend Jeremy Siegel, I decided to set aside the work on this book to write a book about the stock market boom—a classic example of the very kind of misperception and mismanagement of long-term risks that I had written about in the scholarly literature. With the help of Princeton University Press, I managed to get *Irrational Exuberance* into bookstores in mid-March 2000, precisely at the peak of the market and of the tech bubble.

Irrational Exuberance concluded by saying that not only was the level of the stock market exaggerated but society's attention to the stock market, and the importance we attach to it, were also exaggerated. The stock market will not make us all rich, nor will it solve our economic problems. It is foolhardy for citizens to pay attention to the world of business only for the purpose of picking stocks, and even more foolhardy to think stock prices will go nowhere but up.

The New Financial Order picks up where my earlier research and *Irrational Exuberance* together leave off. By showing how we misconstrue risk and by bringing significant new ideas to bear on this problem, I hope to explain how we can fundamentally resolve the economic risk predicament. We are indeed entering a new economic era, robust stock market or not, and we need to think about the implications of emerging technologies—the real drivers of global economic change—not just on individual companies and their stock prices but on all of us. We need to understand how the technology of the past has shaped our institutions. And we need to change our thinking in a vigorous, creative way to navigate this new environment. *The New Financial Order* outlines critical means of making this ideal a reality.

As an aid to critical readers of this book, I have also assembled a number of technical and background papers as well as news clips relating to the themes of this book. They are on the web site http://www.newfinancialorder.com.

Acknowledgments

My style of writing has changed over the years. I now make use of as many minds as I can to filter existing ideas, to suggest new ones, to search out the facts, and to discover what I really need to know. Sometimes it seems I spend more time talking to others than writing, but I feel that it has been time well spent. And so for this book I owe an unusual debt to others.

Of all the people who have collaborated with me on this book, Allan Weiss, my former student at Yale and president of the firm we founded in 1991, Case Shiller Weiss, Inc. (now a subsidiary of Fiserv, Inc.), stands out. He has been a brilliant originator of ideas. Allan and I worked together to develop our concepts of regional real estate futures markets, home equity insurance, and a macro-market instrument we call macro securities.

My editor at Princeton University Press, Peter Dougherty, has helped form my thinking in fundamental ways, and I owe a deep debt to him. His genius stands behind this book, and I never would have done it without his help and ideas. I have also developed a close intellectual relationship with Henning Gutmann, until recently an editor at Yale University Press, and have spent many hours talking with him about the ideas in this book.

Stefano Athanasoulis, a former student of mine at Yale, is another close collaborator. For five years now we have worked to develop a mathematical theory of optimal market definition that has helped refine some of the ideas in this book, particularly that of a market for claims on the combined national incomes of the world, an idea that we first published together.

Many of the ideas in this book ultimately derive from a tradition here at Yale, where I have now been immersed for twenty years. The late James Tobin was a formative influence. His fundamental development of the mathematical theory of diversification, his innovations in practical risk management, such as the Yale tuition postponement option that he created, and his sincere concern for the unlucky in our society, have all been inspirations. Work that he and William Nordhaus have done on accurately measuring economic welfare has also encouraged me to think that genuine improvements in our society can result from quantitative research. Work that William Brainard did with Trenery Dolbear on management of life's risks was a direct precursor to the macro markets that I discuss here. John Geanakoplos's work on information and incomplete markets and Martin Shubik's work on trading systems have also been an influence.

Other colleagues at our firm Case Shiller Weiss, Inc., were important to this book. Karl Case helped develop the idea of real estate futures markets. He led me to appreciate the importance of devising good indexes for measurement of core concepts and provided the first impetus to this research. Howard Brick, David Costa, Jay Coomes, Neil Krishnaswami, Linda Ladner, Terry Loebs, James Mealey, and others at Case Shiller Weiss, Inc., have also been involved in the discovery process.

Allan Weiss and I have founded a second firm, Macro Securities Research, LLC, now being led in its early stages by Chief Operating Officer Sam Masucci. Its purpose is to create new risk management vehicles. Neil Gordon, Larry Hirshik, Julius Levin, Tom Skinner, and others have been helpful in getting our enterprise started. Our advisory committee, including John Campbell, Franco Modigliani, and Jeremy Siegel, has been helpful as well.

Earlier drafts of portions of this book were presented as the Spruill Lecture at the University of North Carolina in February 1998, as a public lecture at the London School of Economics in November 1998, as the McKenna lecture at St. Vincent College in January 1999, as the Jundt Lecture at Gonzaga University in March 1999, as the Samuel Levin Lecture at Wayne State University in April 2001, as the Kenneth Arrow Lecture at Stanford University in May 2001, as the Henry George lecture at the University of Scranton in September 2001, as an "In the Company of Scholars" lecture at Yale University in January 2002, as a public lecture at the European Central Bank in Frankfurt in May 2002, at the Finance Seminar at the University of Chicago in October 2002, and finally at the Hong Kong Economic Association meetings in December 2002. The feedback from people at these various lectures has been very helpful.

I am indebted to Luiz Abreu, Kenneth Arrow, Aleksander Askeland, Sohrab Behdad, Amar Bhide, Murray Biggs, Michael Boozer, David Bradford, Diane Coyle, David Darst, Brad DeLong, Keith Dengenis, Mohamed El-Erian, Herb Gintis, Nader Habibi, Robert Hall, Henry Hansmann, Robert Hockett, Jeeman Jung, Stephen Kaplan, Michael

Krause, Stefan Krieger, David Laster, Gil Mehrez, Felipe Morandé, Stephen Morris, Jessica Paradise, Mats Persson, Andrew Powell, John Quiggin, Tano Santos, Ian Shapiro, Jeremy Stein, Lars Svensson, James Tobin, Robert Townsend, Andrei Ukhov, Salvador Valdés-Prieto, Marek Weretka, and Janet Yellen for helpful comments, discussions, and suggestions along the way.

Many Yale students have worked with me on this book, including Claudio Aragón Ricciuto, Marlon Castillo, Michael Cheung, Chian Choo, Peter Devine, Peter Fabrizio, Sunil Gottipati, Makiko Harunari, Monali Jhaveri, Fadi Kanaan, Jay Kang, George Korniotis, Lingfeng Li, Adrienne Lo, Junzhao Ma, Nicola Mok, Gaye Mudderisoglu, Patrick Nemeroff, Steven Pawliczek, Michael Pyle, Virginia Raemy, Isabel Reichardt, Kira Ryskina, Zaruhi Sahakyan, Philip Shaw, Bjorn Tuypens, Michael Volpe, and Maxine Wolfowitz. I have spent hours talking with most of them about the book, and each of them has individually helped me carry the ideas further with their own thoughts and research.

I also owe much gratitude to Carol Copeland, a loyal and dedicated assistant, who has constantly provided help in my research efforts. Glena Ames provided technical assistance in making this book a reality.

Most of the research that over my academic career has led to this book was supported by the U.S. National Science Foundation. For over ten years the Russell Sage Foundation has been supporting the conferences on behavioral economics that Richard Thaler, George Akerlof, and I have been organizing, and that have kept me involved with and abreast of some of the latest work on psychology in economics. The Smith Richardson Foundation gave me a research grant specifically for writing this book.

My wife Virginia Shiller, a clinical psychologist at the Yale Child Study Center, has been a lifelong inspiration to my work on human behavior for economics. Her support of my work on this book was exceptional, especially given that she was also writing a book of her own at the same time. She also read the entire manuscript and suggested some fundamental changes. Our sons, Ben and Derek, are now old enough to engage me in intellectual discussions; both have signed on as research assistants and have made their own contributions.

I also acknowledge my debt to the many others in the university, business, legal, and government communities who have thought seriously about our economic institutions. I have had the pleasure of being in the economics profession for decades and of observing the parade of theorists who have presented their models over the years. Listening to them can be frustrating at times. I am tempted sometimes to dismiss much of their work as overly academic and irrelevant. But later, I realize that my thinking has been fundamentally changed by understanding their models. I have also had the opportunity, with Case Shiller Weiss, Inc., and Macro Securities Research LLC, to observe the financial world as a participant, which has enabled me to watch this immense ferment of ideas in action. Hearing excitingly new or different financial ideas proposed is also often frustrating because they often turn out to be very hard to implement. Like pipe dreams, they seem far from reality, which rudely seems to place obstacles in their way. But, again, I recognize later that much of this thinking represents progress that eventually accumulates, over many years, into real and practical financial technology with genuine social utility.

The New Financial Order

The Promise of Economic Security

WALL STREET, along with the City of London and other world financial centers, has served as the liveliest laboratory for new ideas in all of capitalism. Modern finance—not only securities and banking but also insurance and public finance—grows out of powerful theories, both mathematical and psychological, and has produced economic inventions of the greatest utility. Despite some awful financial scandals that surface from time to time, these inventions *really work,* most of the time. The inventions work because the fundamental ideas are sound and because finance professionals have learned to apply them effectively to real people, with all their psychological biases and quirks.

The primary subject matter of finance is the management of risks. Finance looks at the various forms of human disappointments and economic suffering as risks to which probabilities can be attached. Finance poses arrangements that reduce these disappointments and blunt their impact on individuals by dispersing their effects among large numbers of people. Finance helps us realize our dreams by enabling creators and innovators to pursue their ideas without bearing all of the risks themselves and encourages them to take great risks for good purposes, as when entrepreneurs start new companies financed by venture capitalists.

Unfortunately, the insights of finance have been applied in only a limited way. Risk sharing has been used primarily for certain narrow kinds of insurable risks, such as stock market crashes or hurricanes, or for managing the risks of conventional investments, such as diversifying investment portfolios or hedging commodity risks, benefits that often accrue mainly to the already-well-off members of our society. Finance has substantially neglected the protection of our ordinary riches, our careers, our homes, and our very abilities to be creative as professionals.

We need to democratize finance and bring the advantages enjoyed by the clients of Wall Street to the customers of Wal-Mart. We need to extend finance beyond our major financial capitals to the rest of the world. We need to extend the domain of finance beyond that of physical capital to human capital, and to cover the risks that really matter in our lives. Fortunately, the principles of financial management can now be expanded to include society as a whole. And if we are to thrive as a society, finance must be for all of us—in deep and fundamental ways.

Democratizing finance means effectively solving the problem of gratuitous economic inequality, that is, inequality that cannot be justified on rational grounds in terms of differences in effort or talent. Finance can thus be made to address a problem that has motivated utopian or socialist thinkers for centuries. Indeed, financial thinking has been more rigorous than most other traditions on how to reduce random income disparities.

Equipped with modern digital technology, we can now make these financial solutions a reality. Right now we are witnessing an explosion of new information systems, payment systems, electronic markets, online personal financial planners, and other technologically induced economic innovations, and consequently much in our economy will be changed within just a few years. Almost all of our economy will be transformed within just a few decades. This new technology can do cheaply what once was expensive by systematizing our approach to risk management and by generating vast new repositories of information that make it possible for us to disperse risk and contain hazard.

Society can achieve a greater democratization of finance and stabilization of our economic lives through radical financial innovation. We must make this happen, given the economic uncertainty of our future at a time of global change and given the problems and inadequacies of today's financial arrangements. This book presents ideas for a new financial order, a new financial capitalism, and a new economic infrastructure, and further describes how such ideas can realistically be developed and implemented.

Incentives for Great Works without Moral Hazard

Financial arrangements exist to limit the inhibitions that fear of failure places on our actions and to do this in such a way that little moral hazard is created. Moral hazard occurs when financial arrangements encourage people to engage in destructive rather than productive acts, such as phony work done only to impress investors, wanton spending, or accounting malfeasance.

An entrepreneur may feel discouraged from starting an exciting new business because the risk of failure is too high. Modern financial arrangements can often solve this problem. For instance, this entrepreneur might find a venture capital firm that will agree to bear the risks, paying the entrepreneur a salary yet providing the entrepreneur some incentive for inspired work by offering shares in the upside if the company does well. The risk that might have prevented the entrepreneur from ever launching the business seems to disappear. Actually, the risk does not disappear, but its *effects* virtually disappear as the risks to the individual business are blended into large international portfolios where they are diversified away to almost nothing among the ultimate bearers of the risk, the international investors. International portfolio managers from Kabuto-Cho to Dalal Street to Piazza Affari to Avenida Paulista each take on some of this entrepreneur's risk, but as less than a millionth of their total portfolio—so small a part of their portfolios that they do not feel any of this entrepreneur's risk. The entrepreneur is now protected, at virtually no cost to anyone, and can launch an exciting new business without fear. Thus do financial arrangements foster individual creativity and achievement. This is the essential wisdom of finance and its principle of diversification.

As noted above, this inspirational effect of risk management on the entrepreneur can work very well if the venture capital firm is careful to avoid moral hazard, that is, incentives for the entrepreneur to burn down the plant or to pursue flashy opportunities that have only the *appearance* of potential for success, to postpone dealing with problems for fear of revealing them to others, or to continue too long in an enterprise that is clearly failing.

Finance has not been perfect in containing moral hazard—witness the recent Wall Street scandals in the United States. But it would be absurd to junk the system because of a few failures. We should instead adapt and extend finance's insights by applying its essential wisdom to the management of economic risks faced by everyone, and similarly spread the payoffs to everyone. Financial institutions can be strengthened to short-circuit fiascoes like that at Enron Corporation, where moral hazard escaped the controls, where top management, using some clever financial innovation as a foil, dishonestly ran off with the money at the expense of their employees.

Six Ideas for a New Financial Order

In this book I present six fundamental ideas for a new risk management infrastructure. The first three are intended primarily for the private sector: insurance, financial markets, and banking, respectively. The risk management concepts in these three ideas are the same, but they are applied to different risk management industries. Each industry—insurance, financial markets, and banking—has evolved its own methods of dealing with moral hazard, defining contracts, and selecting clients. At a time of fundamental innovation in risk management, it is prudent to build on these methods, respecting each industry's unique body of knowledge and extending and democratizing finance through them.

The next three ideas are designed primarily for development by the government, both through taxation and social welfare and through agreements with other countries. Government has a natural role in risk management because long-term risk management requires the stability of law, because most individuals have limited ability to construct appropriate long-term risk contracts, because fundamental institutions must be managed in the public interest, and because major international agreements require coordination with an array of government policies.

The first idea is to extend the purview of insurance to cover long-term economic risks. *Livelihood insurance* would protect against long-term risks to individuals' paychecks. In contrast to life insurance, which was invented at a time when deaths of young adults with dependents were much more common than they are today, livelihood insurance would protect against currently very significant risks—the uncertainties in our livelihoods that unfold over many years. *Home equity insurance* would protect the economic value of the home but would go far beyond today's homeowners' policies by protecting not just against specific risks to homes such as fires but also against all risks that impinge on the economic value of homes. In the form offered here, first proposed by my colleague Allan Weiss and me in 1994, the problem of moral hazard is dealt with by tying the insurance contracts to indexes of real estate prices.[1]

The second idea for a new financial order is for *macro markets,* which I first proposed in my 1992 Clarendon Lectures at Oxford University and in my 1993 book, and that has been a campaign of mine ever since.[2] It envisions large international markets for long-term claims on national incomes and occupational incomes as well as for illiquid assets such as real estate. Some of these markets could be far larger in terms of the value of the risks traded than anything the world has yet experienced, dwarfing today's stock markets. Even a market for the combined gross domestic products (GDPs) of the entire world, a market for the sum total of everything of economic value, should be established.[3] These markets would be potentially more important in the risks they deal with than any financial markets today, and they would remove pressures and volatility from our overheated stock market. Individual and institutional investors could buy and sell macro securities as they do stocks and bonds today.

The third idea is *income-linked loans.* Banks and other lending institutions would provide loans that are contingent on incomes to individuals, corporations, and governments. The loan balance would automatically be reduced if income falls short of expectations. Income-linked loans would effectively allow borrowers to sell shares in their future incomes and in income indexes corresponding to their own incomes. Such loans would provide protection against the hardship and bankruptcy that afflicts so many borrowers today.

The fourth idea is *inequality insurance,* which is designed to address definitively, within a nation, the serious risk that income in the future will be distributed among people far less equally than it now is, that the rich will get richer and the poor poorer. It reframes the progressive income tax structure so that over time it fixes the amount of inequality rather than fixing arbitrary tax brackets.

The fifth idea is *intergenerational social security,* which would reframe social security to be more truly a social insurance system, allowing genuine and complete intergenerational risk sharing. Intergenerational social security's defining characteristic would be a plan to pool the risks that different generations hold, risks that today are primarily dealt with only informally and then only to a limited extent within the extended family.

The sixth idea is *international agreements* to manage risks to national economies. These unprecedented agreements among governments of nations would resemble private financial deals, but they would surpass such deals in scope and horizon.

Beyond these six ideas for risk management, this book proposes components of a new economic information infrastructure: new *global risk information databases* (GRIDs) to provide the information that would allow effective risk management, and *indexed units of account,* new units of measurement and electronic money for better negotiating risks.

Some Scenes from the New Financial Order

Picture vast international markets that trade major macroeconomic aggregates such as the total outputs of countries such as the United States, Japan, Paraguay, and Singapore, or indexes of single-family home prices both in cities—from New York to Paris to Sydney—and in regions, such as shoreline properties on the Riviera or agricultural property in the corn belt or the rubber plantations of Indonesia. Portfolio investors will be able to take positions in a wide array of such markets with little cost. International markets for human capital will emerge as well for occupations from medical and scientific professions to the careers of actors and performers to common labor. These markets will facilitate the creation of livelihood insurance policies on every major career and job category, and home equity insurance policies on the value of everyone's home. Massive electronic databases made accessible by user-friendly designs will enable people everywhere to engage these markets to manage their real risks.

As these markets transform our appreciation of risks, our concepts and patterns of thought will change accordingly. People will set prices in light of the prices in these markets; countries will make international agreements that parallel some of the risk management afforded in these markets and will similarly revise their welfare and social security systems. Our economies will run more efficiently because these markets provide the means to control our risks. The presence of these new markets will make it easier for firms to offer livelihood insurance, home equity insurance, and income-linked loans to individuals.

Our fundamental risks will thus be insured against, hedged, diversified, making for a safer world. By lightening the burden of risk, a new democratic finance will encourage all of us to be more venturesome, more inspired in our activities.

As a thought experiment, consider a young woman from India, living in Chicago, who wants to be a violinist. She finds it worrisome to borrow the money for her training given that her future income as a musician is so uncertain. But new financial technology enables her to borrow money online that need not be fully repaid if an index of future income of violinists turns out to be disappointing. The loan makes it easier for her to go into her favored career by limiting her risk because if it turns out that musicians' careers are not as lucrative as expected, then she will not need to repay as much of the loan. Her risk over the years would be measured by indexes of occupational incomes maintained by networks of computers. A good part of the risk of her career is ultimately borne by portfolio investors all over the world, not by her alone.

This same woman worries about members of her extended family in a small town in India, many of whom work in an industry in danger of closing rendering their special skills obsolete. But their company buys a newly marketed livelihood insurance contract intended to protect its workers in the event of untoward economic developments. The insurance company then sells off the risk on the international markets. Moreover, the Indian government makes an agreement with other countries to share economic risks, further protecting her family.

Our young woman worries, too, about the neighborhood in a small industrial town in the United Kingdom where her parents live, a neighborhood that is undergoing economic and social change. She worries that her parents may lose the remains of their savings if their house loses value. But in a new financial order, her parents' mortgage comes with an attached home equity insurance policy, protecting them against such an unfortunate outcome; paying a claim if the resale value of their home declines. Moreover, an intergenerational social security system and an inequality insurance system will further protect them.

New digital technology, with its millions of miles of fiber optic cable connections, can manage all these risks together, offsetting a risk in Chicago with another in Rio, a risk for violinists' income with an offsetting risk in the income of wine producers in South Africa. The result will be the stabilization and enhancement of our economies and our lives.

Risk Management Today

Most long-term economic risks that people face are actually borne by each individual or family alone.[4] Social welfare exists primarily for the very poor but is limited even for them. In today's world we cannot insure against risk to our paychecks over years and decades. We cannot hedge against the economic risk that our neighborhoods will gradually decay. We cannot diversify away the risk that economic and societal changes will make our old age difficult, and our elderly are left vulnerable to the risk that a stock market crash will wipe out their retirement savings. Many people live in relative poverty today because of a failure to control these risks.

To the extent that we are aware of these ever-present risks, we tend to be overcautious with our decisions, sometimes avoiding opportunities because we justifiably fear having to bear the consequences of failure. We may tend to work cynically instead, treading water, staying in an unsatisfactory job, pretending to achieve, fearing to venture out into the rapids where real achievement is possible.

Under present conditions, the woman in Chicago thus postpones her career as a violinist, waiting for some better time that may never come. She lacks information about the prospects for such a career and has no way to protect herself economically except to choose an uninspiring career.

Her uncle in India is laid off from his job and is unable to secure a comparable job; he goes into unwanted early retirement with only a meager income. Her parents in the United Kingdom see the value of their house fall as their neighborhood declines. At the same time, the economy in their region slows, and the value of the U.K. stock market where they had stashed their other savings drops. As a result, they lack the wealth to support themselves well in their remaining years. Worrying about the risks to other members of her family can make the young woman's own life more difficult, and dreams of a career as a violinist even more remote.

The risks we face today are substantial, even if we do not easily measure them from day to day because they either unfold only slowly over the course of our lives or descend sometimes quickly but rarely as part of rare cataclysmic historical events. World economic growth over the past century has been terribly uneven, rewarding some extravagantly and leaving others far behind. As a result, the distribution of world income is astonishingly unequal. For example, while per capita real GDP in the United States was $31,049 in 1998, it was only $2,464 in India that same year.[5] This inequality itself causes further social disruptions that can in some circumstances generate even more risks through the forces of resentment, despair, and lost ambitions, which in turn create problems of fear, crime, and social degeneration.

We cannot properly control our most important risks since they are not dealt with by any existing financial institutions. Until now, the focus of almost all financial innovation has been found in traditional stock markets and other financial markets. Only a small percentage of our true aggregate wealth—only that portion represented by the corporate business sector—is tradable in the stock markets around the world. The corporate income flows that are represented in the stock markets are not as large as people imagine. In the year 2000, a record year, total after-tax corporate profits (the income left over after companies pay all their employees, their bills, and their taxes, and that is theoretically available to pay out as dividends to shareholders) per person in the United States were only a little over $2000, only about half the money that state and local governments in the United States spent in that year. Corporate profits represented by the stock exchanges in other countries are even smaller per capita than in the United States. The stock markets are big and important, but not as big and important as we think. Financial perturbations such as the dot-com and tech-stock bubbles suggest that investors have far too much enthusiasm for chasing far too few risk management vehicles.

Far more important to the world's economies than the stock markets are wage and salary incomes and other nonfinancial sources of livelihood such as the economic value of our houses and apartments. This is where the bulk of our wealth is found.

Achieving massive risk sharing—that is, spreading risk among many individuals until it is negligible to any one person—does not mean that the world will live in harmony. History shows, however, that long-term financial arrangements for risk sharing have often been useful despite wars and disruptions of government authority. Indeed, those events themselves are risks that the financial arrangements addressed.

Massive risk sharing can carry with it benefits far beyond that of reducing poverty and diminishing income inequality. The reduction of risks on a greater scale would provide substantial impetus to human and economic progress. Indeed, the progress that our society has achieved to date would not be so magnificent were it not for the kinds of risk management devices that evolved over time. If, for example, insurance did not exist, a vast variety of vital enterprises would have been considered too risky to even consider. Without our capital markets, we would not have many of the corporations and partnerships, large and small, that produce so much of value for us. Again, their work would often have been considered too dangerous to embark upon. Without existing financial technology, we would be living in a much less inspired world.

While we can be thankful for the applications of finance and insurance that make today's level of economic activity possible, great risks still inhibit us from greater levels of achievement. Brilliant careers go untried because of the fear of economic setback. The educations that people undertake, the occupational specialties they choose, the ventures they set out on, are all limited by the knowledge that economically we are on our own and must bear virtually all of the losses we incur.

Imagining the social and economic achievement that could come from a new financial order is difficult because we have not seen such an alternate world. We have not yet seen what remarkable things can happen if we remove all unnecessary fear of loss and enable people to embark on the pursuit of their greater potential.

Information Technology

In the past, complex financial arrangements such as insurance contracts and corporate structures have been expensive to devise and have required information that is costly to collect. With rapidly expanding new information technology, these barriers are falling away. Computer programs, using information supplied electronically in databases, can make complex financial contracts and instruments. The presentation of these contracts and instruments, and their context and framing, can be fashioned by this technology to be user friendly. Financial creativity can now be supplied cheaply and effectively. It is critical to pursue such a transformation.

The implementation of some of our most important existing personal risk management devices, including life insurance, health insurance, and social security, was made possible for the broad public by improvements in information technology in the nineteenth century. The information technology that was new then embodied simpler things: cheap paper on which to keep records, printed forms, carbon paper, typewriters, and filing systems, as well as an efficient postal service and more effective business and government bureaucracy.

Consider the old age insurance of social security, which was first implemented by Germany in 1889. That plan, like most modern social security plans today, made payouts to retirees that depended on lifetime contributions, and hence required reliable records for millions of individuals for many decades. The German social security administrators needed to add to the records regularly, retrieve records reliably without losing them, and communicate with retirees around the country while managing a large payment system. The information technology available in the nineteenth century—the paper, the forms, the filing systems, the government bureaucracy—made this possible without prohibitive cost. It converted social dreamers into implementers. This particular risk management innovation has long since drastically reduced the problem of poverty among the elderly.

Today's new information technology is orders of magnitude more powerful than that of Germany in 1889. I have seen the kinds of changes our newest technology can make. The new digital technology has made vast amounts of data about people's homes available electronically. Karl E. Case, Allan Weiss, and I founded our company, Case Shiller Weiss, Inc., in 1991 to create new measures of price appreciation by zip code and home-value tier in the United States to facilitate devices to manage the risks to our homes.[6] Since then, we have witnessed the proliferation of electronic databases about single family homes and have been able to exploit these new measures in ways that we could not have imagined when we began our company.

The emerging information technology in 1990 made it possible for us to launch our campaign to create home equity insurance. We saw then that it was important to base insurance claims in terms of indexes of prices rather than on the selling price of the individuals' homes; otherwise, we would face a moral hazard. Our campaign probably would not have been feasible before the 1990s because no electronic databases on home prices existed to allow computation of neighborhood home price indexes. Now the opportunities for such insurance, and many other financial innovations, are even better: Our data resources are growing at astounding rates.

Financial Theory and Practice

While finance has been progressing for centuries, it has made stunning progress in the second half of the twentieth century, both in theory and in practice. Theoretical finance was advanced to a high level of mathematical sophistication by such scholars as Fischer Black, Eugene Fama, Harry Markowitz, Merton Miller, Robert Merton, James Mirrlees, Franco Modigliani, Stephen Ross, Paul Samuelson, Myron Scholes, William Sharpe, and James Tobin, and by their successors.

An outcome of this research is a comprehensive theory showing how rational individuals ought to decide on their lifetime investments taking account of all the parameters of their uncertainty and the statistical properties of all risk management tools.[7] No longer is the optimal allocation of people's assets to various investments just an intuitive call or tradition-based rule of thumb. Specific outcomes of this research include computerized financial planning services—some particularly advanced examples being esplanner.com, financialengines.com, morningstar.com, and riskgrades.com—that will improve in the future as theoretical finance and econometrics continues to advance.

Academics have had their counterpart among numerous innovators in real markets. Practical finance has seen many innovations created by exchanges, such as the American Stock Exchange and the Chicago Board of Trade, and electronic communications networks (ECNs), such as Instinet and Island. Dramatic innovation has also come from investment banking firms such as Bank of America, Barclays, Bear Stearns, Citigroup, Deutsche Bank, Goldman Sachs, Hongkong and Shanghai Banking Corporation, JP Morgan Chase, Merrill Lynch, Morgan Stanley, Société Générale Group, and Wasserstein Perella.[8] More innovation has come from insurance and reinsurance companies such as ACE Group, Aegon Insurance Group, AIG, Munich Re, Skandia, Swiss Re, and XL; from mortgage and consumer finance firms such as Fannie Mae, Freddie Mac, and GE Capital; from pension funds and mutual funds such as CalPERS, Fidelity Investments, TIAA-CREF, and the Vanguard Group; from settlement firms such as the Bank of New York, Depository Trust, and State Street Bank; and from brokerage firms such as Charles Schwab and E*Trade. Central banks, such as the Federal Reserve and the European Central Bank, and development organizations, such as the World Bank, the International Monetary Fund and the Grameen Bank, have contributed as well.

Their strides have made the last few decades the most compelling period in world financial history. We have seen the development of vast varieties of new futures, options, swaps, and other risk management vehicles, new forms of mortgages and consumer credit, new forms of health insurance, and innovative ways of making development loans. Finally, insurance has been extended to cover a wide variety of specific risks, even including weather disasters and other such catastrophes.[9] Conferences sponsored by professional organizations such as the Association for Investment Management and Research (AIMR), the Global Association of Risk Professionals (GARP), International Association of Financial Engineers (IAFE), and the Risk Waters Group have become major international events.

The 1980s saw the beginnings of a rapid rate of experimentation with financial forms in countries formerly committed to Marxian communist ideologies, notably China and Russia, but also in numerous developing countries. This experimentation is potentially valuable for the world at large because it proceeds in varied environments and traditions and is supported by an eagerness to try different approaches. Such experimentation is likely to inform new innovations that will someday be copied elsewhere.

Psychology, Behavioral Finance, and Framing

If society is truly to democratize finance, business must make financial devices and services easy to use by ordinary people and not just by financial experts. People are not computers; they are not capable of doing endless calculations and pinpoint analysis of self-interest, despite what conventional economic theory has said for many years. Practical finance has always known this, but academic finance is only just coming to grips with the facts of human nature.

Most people are not comfortable with financial risk management principles or the contraptions needed to apply these principles. Moreover, many people do not have a solid appreciation of their risks, nor do they even know that they ought to reduce their risks. Gratuitous income inequality is hard to control since many people may not take basic steps to control it, even when they can.

In light of these realizations, the theory of finance underwent a fundamental transformation starting around 1990 with the development of behavioral finance, the application of principles of psychology and insights from other social sciences to finance. Behavioral finance corrects a major error in most mathematical finance: the neglect of the human element.[10]

A particularly important lesson from behavioral finance is that psychological framing matters enormously for risk management. *Framing*, as used by psychologists Daniel Kahneman and Amos Tversky, refers to well-documented patterns of human reactions to the context, reference points, mental categories, and associations that influence how people make decisions.

In designing new financial products, appearance and associations not only matter but are fundamental. Some of the ideas for a new financial order that follow have framing at their very core, and our understanding of the power of psychological framing is an important part of the reason to expect that real progress in risk management can be achieved in the future.

Potential Problems with Financial Innovation

Financial progress has repeatedly encountered several significant problems in the past, which might frustrate our efforts to innovate in the future. First is the problem of excessive speculative activity, which can induce great volatility in financial markets. Notably, as I discussed in *Irrational Exuberance,* the stock market boom in the late 1990s, peaking in early 2000, encouraged wasteful corporate investments, accounting trickery, and risky investment decisions by individuals. After this boom, most of the stock markets of the world fell dramatically. The real inflation-corrected Standard & Poor's Index fell by half by mid-2002. Some other countries' markets fell even further. The amount of wealth that was wiped out in the stock market declines between 2000 and 2002 is measured in the trillions of dollars. In the United States alone, the dollar value of this economic loss from this stock market crash is roughly equivalent to the destruction of all the houses in the country or the razing of many thousands of World Trade Centers. Even though the stock market loss may one day be restored by another bull market, the markets generate ever-present risks.

I have been frequently asked, when giving talks, what should be done about such stock market volatility. I have always been at a loss to give an answer that satisfies my questioners. In fact, the best thing that we can do to reduce such risks is to expand our financial technology so that we can use this technology to cushion against unnecessary instability.

Despite the volatility we observe in speculative markets, no one should conclude from any of my or others' research on financial markets that these markets are totally crazy. I have stressed only that the *aggregate stock market* in the United States in the last century has been driven primarily by psychology and fads, that it has shown massive excess volatility. But many markets for subindexes relative to the market do not show evidence of excess volatility, and the market for individual stocks shows substantial evidence supporting the notion that prices in these markets do carry genuine information about future fundamentals.[11]

A second problem is that financial innovation sometimes encourages secret dealings, deception, and even fraud. Secretive firms such as Long-Term Capital Management have misled investors and then blown up, mismanaged firms such as Metallgesellschaft have pursued perilous financial strategies at the expense of shareholders, and unethical firms, such Enron, have committed malicious fraud that harmed many people.[12] But this should not be viewed as evidence against impressive progress in the field of finance. New technology, with all its power, is always dangerous, and accidents will happen as our society learns how to control it. In the early age of steam, many people were killed by boiler explosions, in the early age of air travel, by airplane crashes. Eventually, technological advances sharply reduced such accidents. So too the challenge in economics is to advance and democratize our financial technology, not reverse progress.

Third is the problem of disruption of government authority. Financial arrangements can be simply canceled or otherwise frustrated by changing governments, and history suggests that long-term financial arrangements have to confront political instability. But financial contracts have usually survived changes in governments. Indeed, they have usually survived the complete transfer of power to hostile forces as a result of war and revolution. The Hague Regulations, adopted at an international peace conference in 1899, specify that victors in war must respect the property and rights of individuals.[13] And, indeed, even after World War I, despite Germany's total defeat and such anger on the part of the Allies and Associated Powers that extensive reparations were required from her government, German nationals were allowed to keep their investments in Germany and abroad as well as their insurance and pensions.[14] In Iran, after Ayatollah Ruhollah Khomeini displaced the shah in 1979, the new radical Islamic government, despite its profoundly revolutionary rhetoric, made good on the pensions that government employees under the shah had earned.[15] In South Africa in 1994, after a fundamental turnover of the government from whites to a black majority at a time of great bitterness due to a history of repression and apartheid, financial securities, insurance, and pensions were not confiscated.

Of course, one can also find examples of broken financial contracts. Although the world is no longer so impressed by the socialist theory that allowed Vladimir Lenin, Lazaro Cardenas, Mao Tse-Tung, Mohammed Mossadegh, Gamal Abdul Nasser, Indira Gandhi, and other leaders to justify major confiscation of property and nullification of financial arrangements, theories justifying such irregularities have not been forgotten. Financial contracts will not always survive disruptions. But history suggests that they usually will and that risk sharing contracts usually are upheld.

15

The Moral Dimension

Throughout this book, I apply the concepts of finance to issues that sometimes provoke moral outrage, such as economic inequality, and to issues of fairness, such as how well society should treat its elderly. The reader may find this application of finance rather odd. Finance is widely viewed as an amoral field, even as an occupation for the selfish and grasping. Indeed, financial deals often seem to highlight the most self-ish aspect of humanity, simply because they are so explicit about who gets what. These deals respect property rights through time, and they provide incentives for great work and risky ventures whose rewards come much later. Afterward, when the work is finished and risk suc-cessfully navigated, people who did the work and who now demand their contracted recompense may appear selfish and grasping to others who are not aware of the risk and efforts.

But financial theory does relate directly to the problem of achieving distributive justice without creating economic inefficiency or bad in-centives. Moral judgments cannot be made without reference to our underlying economic theory.

Philosopher John Rawls, in his influential 1971 book *A Theory of Jus-tice,* developed a theory of distributive justice by reinterpreting con-cepts of justice advanced by philosophers through the ages.[16] In partic-ular, Rawls reinterpreted Immanuel Kant's Categorical Imperative. And as I reinterpret Rawls, along lines originally advanced by econo-mist John Harsanyi, his philosophical theory ought to help bring the field of finance to the fore as we make moral decisions about our eco-nomic institutions.[17]

Rawls's theory requires that we consider questions of distributive justice from a viewpoint that he calls the "original position," that is, the point at which our economic status is unknown and hence subject to risks. In other words, society should make ultimate distributive justice judgments as if we were setting up rules and principles before we were born, before we knew which person we would be. Then our judgments will be essentially fair, even if they do not require absolute equality for everyone. Use of Rawls's theory can make justice a principle of risk management by centering on the risk of being born into, and living out, bad circumstances.

Rawls is a philosopher, not a financial theorist, so it is not surprising that he rounded out his theory in a way that would be considered rather primitive from the standpoint of finance. He proposed that our moral judgments should follow the "difference principle," which asserts that our economic institutions should be designed to maximize, considering all issues of economic incentives and possible inefficiency, the minimum possible economic position of people, that is, to make the most disadvantaged class of people as well off as possible, all things considered. The difference principle asserts that we accept rules that allow inequality only insofar as these rules help improve the situation of the least advantaged class. This "maximin" (maximize the minimum human condition) solution is hardly the most natural way to define our goal of risk management. After all, we care about all individuals, not just the most disadvantaged.

I intend to adopt a principle of justice from a "picture window view" of Rawls's original position. I ask what kind of world, in the broad picture, we would like to live in if we could choose before we were born, assuming we had an equal probability of being born as anyone. We are thus concerned about all people's lives, not just those of the poorest. In asking this question, we will use our broad sense of tastes for equality and opportunity and the emotional significance of life's experiences, looking at the whole picture of such a world. Then income inequality, rather than being automatically a bad thing in moderation, becomes an aspect of the picture window view. We will tolerate substantial income inequality. What we surely do not want is gratuitous, random, and painful inequality. [18]

Rawls's theory of justice is important to my argument because it shows that the intuitive sense that many philosophers have had about achieving justice is in fact amenable to an application of financial theory. We will broaden the scope of this financial theory to relate it more deeply to society at large.

Outline of This Book

Part 1 of this book describes the basic parameters of the problem that financial technology is designed to address—the risk of sharp declines in economic status for many individuals. These risks are very real even if we confidently expect dramatic world economic progress overall. We will see that economic risks are much more substantial than many of us seem to realize—technological innovation is itself an important source of individual economic risks, and many other sources of risk threaten individual prosperity as well.

Part 2 discusses how technological progress promises to alter risk management in the future. Modern information technology offers opportunities to improve risk management that we can only begin to grasp today. Part of this technological progress lies in the science of psychology, which is changing our understanding of how people can interact with risk management devices.

Part 3, the heart of the book, presents the six ideas for a new financial order, one per chapter.

Part 4 discusses other devices to deploy the new financial order: global risk information databases, new units of measurement, and electronic money. Moreover, it describes the kinds of research and advocacy that are needed to implement the ideas for a new financial order.

Part 5 provides an analysis of the history of financial markets and of social insurance, revealing a slow, ongoing process of changes analogous in some ways to those I am proposing. Innovators who achieved similar changes over the last two centuries were cognizant at least at an intuitive level of basic principles of finance and of basic human psychology and made effective use of the new information technology of their day. It is natural to expect that we can carry on such fundamental progress in the future.

The epilogue rounds out a model of radical financial innovation, a view of how our lives can be fundamentally improved by financial institutions that are sharply different from the ones we have today.

Part One

Economic Risks in an Advancing World

ONE

What the World Might Have Looked Like since 1950

VISUALIZING THE MAJOR economic risks of the future is difficult. Because such risks are only hypothetical—at least until we have concrete evidence of their imminence—most people do not feel easily convinced of the benefits of any new measures against them. We tend instead to be distracted by little day-to-day problems that are already clearly revealed. We seldom think about how we should be dealing with deep and fundamental risks.

In contrast, the dangers that have dominated the past are well known to us. Thus, let us consider, as a thought exercise, risks that have already come to pass. Let us imagine how history since 1950 might have been different if it had somehow been possible to implement some of the new financial ideas that are developed in this book. This exercise will lend some concreteness to our evaluation of the potential for financial innovation.

We will assume for this exercise that the relatively undeveloped state of information technology in 1950 had imposed no obstacles to the adoption of radical financial innovations. We will also assume quite a bit more financial sophistication among governments, businesses, and the public than was in fact common in 1950. And we will ignore the complexities of the changing world political situation since 1950: We will focus on the possible benefits of risk management technology, assuming that they could have been applied.

This is an exercise in alternate history, which seeks to illustrate what might have happened from a given date forward if some crucial fact of history were changed. Alternate history has been criticized by some mainstream historians: The complexity of history is such that any conclusions are highly conjectural. Other historians, however, believe that alternate history is useful as a mental exercise, alerting us to significant facts and details about our world that might otherwise have escaped notice.[1]

Reconstructing History since 1950
with Better Risk Management

In 1950 the Marshall Plan (the European Recovery Program authorized by the U.S. Congress) was in full swing, helping to offset the devastation and disruption caused by World War II. The total sum transferred during the life of the program, from 1948 until 1951, from the United States to European countries (Austria, Belgium, Denmark, France, Germany, Greece, Iceland, Ireland, Italy, Luxembourg, The Netherlands, Norway, Portugal, Sweden, Switzerland, Turkey, and the United Kingdom) was thirteen billion dollars, most of which was transferred as outright gifts. This would appear to be an impressive example of spontaneous charity.

From another perspective, however, this magnanimous gesture still amounted to only 1.3 percent of U.S. GNP for those four years. While the Marshall Plan is widely regarded as a significant factor in European recovery, in fact it amounted to a relatively small sum of money. If one considers the situation in Europe, where in some places the population bordered even on starvation after the war, thirteen billion dollars would not seem an adequate amount of assistance envisioned from Rawls's original position.

Nor was the Marshall Plan really charity. Secretary of State George C. Marshall's proposal for a costly plan to repair Europe initially received a skeptical reception from the U.S. Congress, until it was pointed out that the dollar value of the Marshall Plan would be no more than 5 percent of the amount that the United States spent for all of World War II, and that unless this additional expenditure were made, all of the war effort might have been for naught and Europe could yet fall to fascist, communist, or other unwanted influences (as had happened after World War I).[2] The supporters of the Marshall Plan framed it as the successful completion of the war effort. There is a natural human urge to complete tasks that have been started, and the psychological framing of the Marshall Plan tapped into this urge.[3] Had it not been framed this way, the United States might have left war-damaged Europe almost entirely to its own resources. Hardly an example of altruism, the Marshall Plan at best showed that the United States could summon the political will to make substantial payments abroad when it deemed them important.

Now comes the thought experiment: Let us imagine that most European people and governments had made fundamental risk management contracts before World War II to protect their livelihoods: *livelihood insurance, macro markets, income-linked personal loans,* and *international financial agreements between governments* (mentioned in the introduction and developed later in this book). The reader may still be puzzled by these terms at this point, but for now suffice it to say that these contracts reduce major risks to incomes and that if they were understood before 1950, many of them would not have cost much to set up.

Had these arrangements been made before the war, then they might well have transferred much more money than did the Marshall Plan. In other words, it is quite possible that the United States (and other countries) could have turned 10 percent of GDP or even more to damaged countries after the war in fulfillment of their financial obligations as defined by risk management contracts signed before the war. The benefits would have been enormous: To the undamaged United States, a 10 percent loss in income would have had relatively modest impact, while the effect on war-battered Europe of these same resources would have been huge.

What about the doubts that risk management contracts can survive war? In this case, it seems clear that most of the Marshall Plan countries would have had their contracts honored, since most of the damaged countries were not antagonistic to the United States or its allies during the war. Beyond that, the very fact that even conquered Germany and Italy received Marshall Plan support after World War II shows that the bitterness of war does not necessarily obviate responsible actions. Most likely, Germans and Italians would have benefited from their risk management contracts, had they been arranged earlier.

During the same post-war period, nothing comparable to the Marshall Plan was authorized for Asian countries, even though many areas were also devastated by World War II. U.S. President Harry S. Truman's Point Four Program for the rest of the world (so-called because it was the fourth point in his 1949 inaugural address), as implemented between 1952 and 1954, appropriated only 6 percent of the total spent in the Marshall Plan.[4] Why did the United States favor Europe for its beneficence? Presumably, this decision reflects the same pattern of foreign aid that we see today: feelings of kinship mixed with a sense of political expediency. The United States saw Asia differently from Europe.

But if we can imagine that governments and individuals understood risk-sharing opportunities well enough before the war to take some of these steps to manage income risks in Asia, then it is reasonable to surmise that many Asians would have been successful in protecting their interests. As a result, Asia would not have remained so economically devastated after the war. Finance is impersonal—unlike foreign policy. It seeks out the highest return wherever it can be found, regardless of nationality. Asia would then have received substantial help after the war through the macro markets, livelihood insurance, or other contracts arranged before the war. If such risk management measures had been undertaken, the Japanese economic miracle of the 1960s and the economic miracle of many of the Asian countries might have been moved forward into the 1950s, and similar advances might have occurred in yet other countries that are only emerging today.[5] An entire generation might have led better lives.

Even if no such risk management had been in place before 1950, in Europe or Asia, the immediate tragedy of the war could have been reduced after the war if the war-damaged countries around the world had sold claims on their own future GDPs to raise money for recovery. Rather than borrowing in U.S. dollars, they might well have raised more money through macro markets—massive claims on national income, occupational income, or other income indexes—because the risk properties of such debt would have been more advantageous for both sides. U.S. investors who were optimistic about a European economic recovery might well have been attracted to making such loans, seeing a chance to make a lot of money with risk that they could have limited by diversifying it among the rest of their investments. European borrowers needing development funds might have been more inclined to borrow, since they would not have to worry about the risk that an anemic European recovery would have made it difficult to pay the debt back. Had risk management contracts been available in Europe in 1950, they would have helped offset the effects of uneven recovery from the war.

Now suppose that economic risk management treaties had been undertaken by African countries and their European patrons when Africans received their independence beginning with Ghana in 1957. Governmental agreements could have been written to exchange unexpected African-country per capita GDP growth for unexpected European-country per capita GDP. The relationships between these African countries and their European patrons were strained at that time, but one can still imagine that a sense of self-interest might have prevailed among these countries if the financial concepts of risk sharing had been firmly established at the time.

Governmental risk-sharing contracts negotiated in 1960 would have forced European countries to think in risk management terms that would have been utterly uncharacteristic of the time. In designing the international agreements, they would have had to talk openly about the expected prospects of the African economies. In addition to the possibility that the African economies would do worse than expected and receive payment from the European countries, parties would have had to consider that the African economies might also have done better than expected, and thus would have had to pay their European patrons according to the terms of the agreements.

In fact, the history of much of Africa since 1960 has been quite disappointing. For example, Nigeria's real per capita income at the time of its independence in 1960 was $1,054. Thirty-eight years later, in 1998, its real per capita GDP had in fact declined slightly to $1,025.[6] One might have expected greater success for the newly independent oil-rich country. Nigeria could not have paid with cash for insurance in 1960, but it could have agreed to pay in the future out of these expectations, agreeing to pay substantially if its economy did better than expected. It might seem hard-hearted for the other country in the agreement to require payments from such a poor country under any circumstances, but such an agreement would have been enormously beneficial to Nigeria. As we now know, the outcome would have been that Nigeria would not have paid at all and would have obtained a great deal of money to offset its disappointing performance.

If Europe and Africa had made such risk management contracts in 1960, then many countries in Africa today that today are suffering enormously from poverty and resulting problems of crime, ethnic warfare, and disease would instead be getting large financial payments from their colonial patrons. Millions who died from AIDS and other afflictions might be alive today. Medical researchers studying such tropical diseases as malaria, Nile fever, and sleeping sickness might have had the greater economic impetus to find solutions. Moreover, with the higher living standards made possible by these risk management contracts, a better response to the African problem of high birth rates and consequent high increase in population might have been possible.

25

Suppose also that similar risk management contracts had been made between the developed countries of the world and the nations of the former Soviet Union when it dissolved in 1991. The economic near-disaster that we saw in the 1990s in the poorer regions of these former-Soviet countries would have been automatically ameliorated by large payments from the developed countries. If these payments had been contractual, they might well have been vastly larger than the meager foreign help that flows to these countries today.

Had former Soviet Bloc countries done all of their borrowing in terms that were linked to their GDPs, then these countries might not have found themselves in such economic doldrums after independence. We might not have seen the 1998 financial crisis, marked by the fall, far away in the United States, of Long-Term Capital Management because the feared default in Russian debt would have been prevented.

By the same token, suppose that less-developed country (LDC) debt to foreigners could have been indexed to a country's own GDP starting in 1950. We can then reasonably suppose that events like the LDC debt crisis of the early 1980s, the Mexican crisis of 1994, the Asian crisis of 1997, the Argentine crisis of 2001, or the Brazilian crisis of 2002 might have been less severe. The real value of these countries' debts would have fallen at the time of the crisis. Because investors and bankers would have known that this safety valve was in place, they would have been less likely to exacerbate the crisis by betting against these countries in financial markets.

Suppose that we had created *home equity* insurance contracts on the market values of individual homes in major U.S. cities, protecting homeowners against declines in the market value of their homes and thus eliminating the panic selling that sometimes devastates housing values. We might not have seen the collapse of home values in major cities undergoing racial change, and the transition could have been smoother and gentler than the "white flight" that ensued. The economic destruction of parts of cities such as Detroit, Washington, and Philadelphia might not have happened. Had city centers stayed vital, industry might have been more inclined to remain there, further supporting their vitality.

Suppose that we had created *inequality insurance*. Such insurance would have protected society against any serious increase in the extent of income inequality over time. If we had such insurance, then the deterioration in the income distribution in most advanced countries at the end of the twentieth century might not have happened at all. The spectacle of large mansions being built amidst tiny homes, of some driving flashy big cars while others make do with very little, may not have happened to such a degree.

Suppose that we had adopted genuine *intergenerational risk-sharing social security*. In the United States in the early 1980s, elderly people would not have experienced the windfall caused by inflation indexing of their benefits, at the expense of younger people. The debate about "fixing" social security today would be cast in entirely different terms—about sharing risks between generations.

Suppose we had had, by 1950, the *indexed units of account* (described in part 4). The reader cannot be expected to understand this idea yet, but the important thing to know is that these institutions would make indexation to inflation much more widespread, protecting people against the ravages of unexpected inflation. Contracts such as long-term bonds and mortgages would have been effectively indexed to inflation. Thus the enormous increase in inflation around the world that built up more and more force until around 1980, and the decline in inflation around the world afterward, might have had a much diminished effect.

Since 1950, major inflations have harmed many countries in the world—in most Latin American countries, in the Middle East, and in Africa. An unexpected rise in inflation occurred in almost all major countries between around 1960 and 1980. If contracts had all been indexed, long-term bond holders might not have seen their real wealth decimated by 1980. People who retired on fixed pensions in 1960 and lived thirty more years might not have seen their real value pension income reduced by two-thirds as the years went by. Homeowners who bought near the beginning of this period might not have received the tremendous windfall they did due to the inflation because their mortgages would have been fixed in money terms. Of course, the actual windfall came at the expense of bondholders and savings accounts holders, especially those who were not homeowners. With indexed units of account in use, younger people looking forward to buying their new home might not have found themselves so sharply disadvantaged.

Since the mid-1990s we have seen substantial *deflation* in Japan. With inflation falling far short of earlier expectations there, the real value of debts have turned out to be far higher than the borrowers expected, often making it impossible for them to repay, compromising the banking system, and stagnating Japan's economy. If they had made widespread use of indexed units of account, the so-called lost decade of Japan might have turned out very differently.

And if we had set wages in proper terms instead of currency (as the *indexed units of account* also facilitate), we might not have seen the vicious cycle of anticipated wage increases leading to more actual wage increases and to the structural inflation, or stagflation, that we then saw. The intensity of recessions would probably have been less severe because wages would have tended to fall automatically in recessions, thus likely reducing the impact on unemployment and, without the shock to confidence and to the stock market, the feedbacks of recessions to other aspects of the economy might have been less.

Hardest of all to gauge is how the world would have been different as the result of positive opportunities that advanced risk management arrangements would have provided. If the impulse to conservatism, to sameness around the world, to copying others' modest successes rather than launching exciting ventures, had been significantly reduced, then the outcome might have been full of innovation that we can only guess at today. For example, today's LDCs might now have major centers for technology. In advanced and less-developed countries alike, we may have seen more geographic specialization of economic activity and more personal specialization of expertise. Economically insular LDCs, notably India, might long ago have opened their borders to foreign competition, taking the chance that the new competition would damage key industries in their own country and harm important segments of their population since they could have protected these using a democratized finance. The standard of living all over the world might have been enhanced by more venturesome and diverse human initiatives.

The forgoing discussion has been a thought experiment, only that. One can never be sure what would have happened differently had the world implemented the tools of democratized finance. The Cold War, the arms race, the ideological and military confrontations, and the political corruption that marked the second half of the twentieth century might still have undone much of the economic progress imagined in this chapter. Still, it would appear that a risk management infrastructure might have had substantial potential to lessen the impact of serious problems.

The Shortage of Information Technology in 1950
and the Thought Experiment

The risk management contracts between nations and the macro markets to trade such risks could not have been used reliably to hedge national income risk in 1950 because of the primitive state of information technology. Methods of calculating Gross National Product and National Income were not then well established, and their definitions were in flux. The United Kingdom did not begin publishing National Income until 1941, after the economist Richard Stone gave the United Kingdom an accounting model. The United States did not begin publishing its National Income and Product Accounts until 1942. Even as late as 1950, the relevant definitions were not well established. Stone published *Input–Output and National Accounts* in 1961. Many developing countries published no national income figures then, and the data available were too unreliable to be meaningful.

The macro markets for single-family homes could not have been established because no accepted indexes of existing single-family home prices existed. By 1950, economists published single-family home price indexes based on asking prices in newspapers, but these were not ongoing projects; rather they were one-at-a-time index calculations based on historical data. The National Association of Realtors (NAR) did not consistently publish its median price of single-family homes for an array of cities until the 1980s, and even then some of the numbers were so choppy and implausible that it was impossible to use the index to settle any risk management contracts. The NAR numbers were, and continue to be, affected by a change in mix of houses sold from time to time. It was not until 1991 that Chip Case, Allan Weiss, and I founded our firm to publish the first statistically reliable index of single-family home prices on an ongoing basis.

The very limited computer technology available in 1950 would have hampered a number of other details of implementation of the inventions. Instead of computers, we would have had paper and pencil, paper and typewriter, and paper and printing press. These devices would have made computation, to say nothing of communication, slow and expensive. Standards of presentation could not be as easily changed as they are today by computer programmers.

The absence of detailed information on incomes would have made a number of the ideas difficult, and in some cases probably impossible.

29

We could not have easily had effective livelihood insurance, macro markets, international agreements for risk control, or income-linked personal loans because we would not have had the kind of detailed indexes of income that these presuppose. Designing effective inequality insurance or intergenerational social security would have been difficult because they would have been hampered by the absence of detailed information about the economic well-being of individuals.

The Urgency

Our review of history since 1950 shows that some of the most difficult problems of these years might have been dealt with substantially better if we had earlier been able to make appropriate risk management contracts. Now, at a time of tremendous advance in information technology, it is urgent to get such technology to work to prevent such problems in the future.

Thinking about risks as we have just done may help us to appreciate the likelihood that the next half-century will have its upheavals, too. There is no reason to think it will have fewer vicissitudes than the last. In fact if we consider the nature of the rate of advance of new information technology and robotic technology, we have every reason to expect that change will continue apace, and that there will be even more risks in the future, with more people eventually impoverished by a sequence of unexpectedly adverse shocks, while some other people become unexpectedly wealthy.

There is a peculiar fact about risk management contracts: They must be signed and sealed before a crisis arises, before the information that would create a sense of urgency arises. One must buy life insurance before one shows the first symptoms of a grave illness. One must buy fire insurance before one sees the flames lapping at one's house. With economic risks that evolve gradually through time, the public has no vivid sense of risk, and so is not impelled to action.

Management of risk of sudden disaster has a long history. Fire insurance began after the fire of London in 1666, and life insurance soon thereafter. For gradually unfolding economic risks for which there is no sudden time of crisis, however, there are still few avenues for risk management.

A realistic timetable does exist for the adoption of new advanced technological measures like those that will be described here. The important first step is to adopt prototypes of the new measures and to get them working in some measure or on a small scale to establish their feasibility and to present them as viable options. More ambitious programs could spread gradually from these initial experiments, gaining impetus from whatever new mini-catastrophes come our way in the future. These financial innovations would then eventually become linked in people's minds as obvious ways to prevent real losses. Once demonstrated, widespread application of new technology may be unstoppable.

TWO

The Hidden Problem of Economic Risk

FOR ALL THE TALK about risk and finance, the critical economic risks that we face remain substantially hidden, almost as if they did not exist. We do not fully perceive the risks to individual careers, to the opportunities of the next generation, to our neighborhoods, to local industries, or to the economic success of countries. Individuals are aware of the economic risks facing *themselves* and their *own* families, but only intermittently and imperfectly. They do not really understand the nature of these risks or their breadth.

Gaining basic perspectives on our long-term economic risks is essential if we are to control them. In this chapter I will provide a broad initial overview of the economic risks that people face and will suggest some of their complexity and some of the reasons why risks are often hidden. Subsequent chapters in part I will refine this picture.

The Variability of Living Standards

Public figures in business and government often suggest that a capitalist free-market economy naturally makes *everyone* best off, not just the average person. "A rising tide raises all boats," so spoke President John F. Kennedy. Unfortunately, today's reality suggests that this is not necessarily the case, and that living standards vary greatly among individuals, and also within an individual's span of life. This is due to the essential variability of income.

In fact, people's ability to earn income by selling their own labor in a free market is ultimately determined by what they can contribute to the production process. Changes in their ability to earn income from their efforts are thus fundamentally tied up with changes in the technology of production. In a time of rapid advance in the economy, when technology is changing quickly, individual risks are especially large.

Standard economic theory asserts that labor's income is approximately their "marginal product," that is, their contribution after all others' contributions are taken into account to the output of their employer. The theory states that employers will generally pay this amount, no more and no less, because of competitive pressures on them in the goods marketplace where they sell their products and in the labor marketplace where they hire their employees. The theory says that one gets paid only if one can produce, and one gets paid only as much as one can add above and beyond the contributions already made by others. While there are other considerations that affect employee compensation, as for example the bargaining of labor unions, to a first approximation and in most circumstances it is useful to think of the labor income of any individual as equal to that individual's marginal product.[1]

An individual's ability to contribute to a larger enterprise depends on how that person's abilities interact with the abilities of everyone else, with the other available inputs to production, and with available technology. This interaction can have varied and complex forms because the nature of value sources are complex. Technology is constantly changing, the application of the technology is changing, and the prices of other inputs to production are changing. Thus, economic theory suggests that the determinants of our livelihoods are ultimately tenuous and can be changed by factors that we will never understand, even long after the fact.

An individual, without taking part in a larger enterprise and without combining efforts with others, may be able to produce little or nothing of value. An enterprise usually requires a variety of skills supplied by many different persons and requires other factors of production: machinery, equipment, commercial real estate, and raw materials and other inputs for production. Setting up a business also requires time and patient investors to see it only gradually become profitable. A one-person enterprise without these other contributing factors can succeed only in the most unusual circumstances.

Anyone of suitable talents can in principle access these other factors by borrowing money from banks, raising money in capital markets, and persuading others to work for him or her. But only persons of exceptional talents, energy, and work ethic will succeed in doing so. For almost everyone else, earning an income means joining an ongoing enterprise as an employee.

The dilemma people face—that their labor is essentially worthless when not combined with other factors and thus that their incomes are at the mercy of others who have access to these factors—was a key motive behind Karl Marx's theory of communism. The very name *communism* comes from Marx's conclusion that the means of production should be owned communally. Under communism, individuals' ability to earn would no longer be tied to their individual ability to contribute to an enterprise. But Marx's solution ran into problems in application, problems of moral hazard and perverse incentives. Hence, Marxian communism has been abandoned practically everywhere. Throughout most of the world, people must sell their labor on free markets to ongoing businesses. Thus, the dilemma that Marx deplored is still with us.

Little Public Talk about Personal Economic Risks

Until quite recently, people didn't discuss marital or sexual problems, and especially not in public forums. Because of the lack of discourse, they had little information and subsequently naive ideas about their problems. They suffered alone, each person or couple imagining that the problems were rare or even unique. So too is it with the problem of long-term economic risks, even though the reasons we talk so little about them are different.

Given this lack of discussion of our long-term and most important economic risks, most of us have some difficulty maintaining a proper perspective on our own and others' economic risks, especially because the ultimate reasons for our economic strengths and weaknesses are entangled in an ever-changing and complex economy. Our difficulties in understanding our risks may make us skittish about them, prone to ignoring the biggest risks altogether while overreacting to only vaguely held fears. With so little discussion of long-term risks, the public ultimately suffers. Individuals must deal haphazardly with risk of their own initiative, and with little help.

It is not surprising we talk so little about major risks. The causes are too abstract, un-newsworthy, complex, and hypothetical. Instead, we tend to talk about vivid risks—catastrophes that we see in the newspapers—rather than the complex long-run factors that affect our livelihoods. Changes in standards of living that happen gradually over time, and for obscure reasons, to some but not all of us are just too intangible for us to have much of a conversation about outside of economic theory seminars.

Beyond this, most public figures actively avoid talking about long-term economic risks. Business leaders, when they speak publicly, do not like to focus on major economic risks unless they are selling a specific insurance product for the risks. Publicly dwelling on bad things that may or may not happen to people is not considered good business practice—better to focus on the positive. Similarly, politicians rarely talk about potential future economic risks because it is just not good politics. They rather prefer to be oracles that confidently predict shining futures for everyone.

When government leaders do talk about our risks, they focus on solutions—swift actions that they can take with the stroke of a pen and that will yield great immediate benefits. When can such stroke-of-the-pen actions really be justified? Usually, when the actions are part of a consistent risk management policy. But to try to justify their actions in risk management terms, political leaders would have to talk explicitly about risks, which they prefer to avoid.

When a president or governor decides to sign a bill to help certain distressed groups—the elderly, the farmers, or whomever—they tend to speak as if they were the distributors of manna from heaven, rarely mentioning the source of funding. But that money is coming from other people, through their taxes. Politicians seem to be playing a zero-sum game, taking money from one group of people and giving it to another, with no net effect. But even though a proposed income transfer is a sort of zero-sum game in terms of government budgets, it need not be a zero-sum game in terms of risk management—not if it systematically takes money from people who are not currently in distress and gives it to others who are in distress unexpectedly. Whenever the government is following a consistent policy of risk management, effectively creating government insurance for all elements of society, then such stroke-of-the pen actions can create great benefit in terms of human welfare.

But social policy arguments are rarely couched in such terms. Politicians generally eschew explicit risk management justifications for their actions, preferring instead to talk only of those who benefit from government largesse and ignoring the costs of that same largesse to others. Politicians often speak such nonsense because they know that the public has no understanding of our economic risks and no sense of the rational division between public and private risk, of the role of government in risk management as opposed to welfare, of the large picture of risk management, public, private, and familial.

If politicians were to argue that a proposed policy that helps distressed groups has potential to benefit any group in society, including *yours*, because of the risk management principles now at society's service, they would have to argue that there is a risk to *your* group that the government policy could someday relieve, and they would have to justify why this is a matter for government, not private insurance, to handle. Public understanding of such issues, and acceptance of risk management principles, is usually too poor to allow politicians to use such justification.

People Avoid Risks by Forgoing Opportunities

Despite the lack of public discussion of long-term economic risks, people naturally focus on their *own* risks—their job, career, neighborhood, and so on, and make costly individual decisions to mitigate these perceived risks. Our economic risks are substantially hidden from view in large measure because people avoid doing things that subject them to economic risks, so the problem of risk is partly transformed into a less visible problem of lost opportunities. If people are left to their own devices to manage their poorly understood lifetime economic risks, they will deal with them as best they can, usually by making conservative decisions. This avoidance reduces the impact of risky outcomes but at a significant cost of lost opportunity. The effects of the risks become hidden from view, and we are left only with less success for people over all.

Education provides a telling example. The desire to avoid risks typically encourages college students towards the "safest" majors, avoiding specific majors that would develop their talents in unusual (but potentially risky) ways. Students are more likely to major in business or law rather than in theoretical physics or music, which are less versatile and hence more risky. Even within business or law they will seek to pick out the safest specialty, avoiding more focused training for fear that it will turn out not to have a ready market. Students are less likely to choose majors in area studies that focus on individual foreign countries or in narrow scientific specialties, even if such specialized knowledge could possibly be highly lucrative and beneficial to society in future years. In fact, demand for such majors is so small that most colleges seldom offer them. Imagine how our colleges would be different if students could manage their livelihood risks better.

This problem besets not only college education but also vocational education, where choosing a specialty or an apprenticeship program means launching into a lifetime career specialty whose payout will be discovered only through time. Lacking any way to insure the risks of such a choice, young people will naturally tend to choose specialties that are less risky, even if less potentially valuable.

The inability to insure lifetime risks can also cause people to avoid opportunities for advancement in mid-career. Advancing in one's career typically means acquiring highly specialized knowledge and skills, often knowledge about a specific business environment or about specific trends—trends that might later be reversed. Acquiring this knowledge can result in spectacular careers—but not without risk. The outcome could be unfavorable in later years if the specialized knowledge eventually becomes irrelevant.

Risk-avoidance behavior can also have undesirable consequences in our decisions about where we work and live. Unable to insure the risks inherent in our choice of geographical area, people may tend to choose jobs in big metropolitan areas, where a wide variety of opportunities is available, rather than small rural communities or towns far from city centers, where the job market is more specialized. Thus, we tend to be more dependent on big cities and their suburbs than we may want to be. We may also tend to purchase homes that are standardized and unexciting, avoiding new and creative design ideas for fear that such homes will not do well in resale if the style turns out not to have an enduring market. Developers anticipate these consumer attitude, and tend to build generic designs and "McMansions" instead of creative designs.

Risk-avoidance behavior also has an impact on the behavior of city, regional, and even national governments. Fearing the uncertainties associated with new economic development initiatives, these governments typically choose to play it safe and model themselves along conventional lines. They slavishly imitate other successful entities when they ought to be cultivating their locale as a vital center for some kind of emerging technology.

The result of all this avoidance behavior is a depressing uniformity and lack of adventure in our society. People should avoid essential risks—risks to society at large—but not insurable risks, which can be spread out across many people and thereby blunted. But people tend to avoid both kinds of risks, draining society of much of its ability to be creative.

The upshot of this is that while most people may seem to be meeting the status quo in terms of objective standards of living, the average of achievement for society as a whole has suffered. Moreover, the psychic benefits that people derive from their work, home, and neighborhood have also suffered.

Seeing the Outcome of Economic Risks

Judged by media accounts, many people think that the broad middle class, the bulk of society, are all quite comfortable economically. But this is in substantial measure an illusion, even in the most advanced countries. This illusion comes from the relative invisibility of personal economic failure.

People in the economic mainstream usually do not see economic failures up close and often blame those they do see on personal shortcomings. Novels such as Victor Hugo's *Les Misérables* in 1862 and George Orwell's *Down and Out in Paris and London* in 1933 tried to to make the suffering of the poor more visible. Social commentaries such as George Sims *How the Poor Live* in 1889 and Michael Harrington's *The Other America* in 1962 did the same. These books helped improve social policy and thereby helped reduce the incidence of poverty in advanced countries, but none of these authors was really successful in changing public impressions for very long. The personal suffering caused by randomness in economic outcomes continues today and continues to be mostly invisible except, of course, to those harmed.

Barbara Ehrenreich dropped out of her privileged life as a journalist to learn about low-income life by working at relatively low-wage jobs around the United States. She took a variety of unskilled jobs, working as a waitress, a cleaning woman, a nursing home aide, and a sales clerk at Wal-Mart, that paid six to seven dollars an hour, well above the minimum wage. Since she had no children to care for and no health problems, it would seem that she should have been able to get by all right. On the contrary, she discovered that she could hardly afford to live indoors on a full-time income. Even some of the most Spartan mobile homes in the worst neighborhoods were often beyond her reach. She learned that working two jobs left her exhausted, and she marveled at the courage of the people who live such lives year in and year out. In 2001 she published *Nickel and Dimed: On (Not) Getting by in America* about her experiences.[2]

We are talking about working people, not the unemployed, in America, arguably the richest large country in the world. According to the U.S. Department of Labor, the fraction of the U.S. working population aged 35 to 64 in 2000 that earned less than $15,000 a year (that is, under $7.50 an hour for a full-time two-thousand-hour year, or roughly the outer limit of what Ehrenreich was able to earn in routine jobs) is 24.5 percent. Nearly half (48.3 percent) of the population aged 35 to 64 in United States in 2000 earned less than $30,000 a year, which leaves much to be desired, as people who live below that level will attest.[3]

The vividness of her experience left Ehrenreich wondering why "nobody puts all these stories together and announces a widespread state of emergency."[4] She was struck by the fact that she and her suffering were almost totally invisible to anyone else. While working in these jobs, almost no one showed any sympathy for her plight, not even so much as to offer her a drink of water when she was thirsty. (She had various bosses who tried to regulate things such as drinking water or going to the toilet, but showed little understanding of her condition.) Many people who do such menial jobs put on a cheerful face and do not complain.

Those who fall sharply in economic status must share experiences something akin to Ehrenreich's, but they rarely look for sympathy. Usually, they try to conceal their newfound hardship. In her study of downward mobility, *Falling from Grace,* Katherine Newman details the concealed psychological trauma faced by formerly middle-class people who suddenly discover that they are no longer really middle class. She writes

> The downwardly mobile managerial family jealously guards its public face, even if this means that everyone must eat a dreary diet so that the children can have some stylish clothes for school. They cherish central symbols of family belonging, like the family home, and families make considerable sacrifices in other domains to hold on to these valued possessions.[5]

Just as often, people in developed countries to see to it that the nation's borders are closed to free immigration and to block from view the desperately poor people living in less successful countries. Even within developed countries, more successful people increasingly tend to live in enclaves of other such people. Ensconced in gated communities, with expressways that allow us to move swiftly through poorer neighborhoods, we are able to more and more easily isolate ourselves with new means of social control. We in the middle and upper classes have created a world in which we can often avoid seeing low-income living, except for occasional fleeting images on our television screens. And these, confined as they are to an artificial medium, seem unreal. Looking at the poor through the media is like seeing the earth from an airplane window. One feels no fear at the height and the little people down there do not seem real. Just as we can easily forget these people's experiences, we can also forget—or ignore—the magnitude of economic vulnerability that everyone faces.

Those of us who are economically successful like to imagine that success is proof of our own intrinsic self worth, and hence to feel that no risk threatens to reduce our incomes. George Katona, the economic psychologist who wrote the classic *Psychology of Economics* in 1975, asked people in interviews in the early 1970s how much their income had changed over the preceding five years.[6] Because this was a time of high inflation, the great majority of his interviewees had of course seen substantial increases. When he then asked them why their income had gone up, however, almost none of them mentioned the inflation. Instead, they tended to congratulate themselves on their own individual work quality, foresight, and willingness to work hard.

Underestimating the riskiness of our economic system seems natural, as does underappreciating the role of chance in our own successes. We tend to imagine that we live in such a just world that people get what they deserve.[7] From time to time we are aware of our own risks because they stare us in the face, but we do not understand the general character of our risks.

Families Help Cushion and Conceal Risks

While very imperfect public understanding of economic risks prevails, the risks can at times be highly visible within the family. And, within the family, the need to share risks can be painfully obvious.

Barbara Ehrenreich tried to live alone on her wages, but she noted that none of her coworkers lived alone. In fact, most people, especially lower-income people, partially insure their economic risks by retaining family ties. Family members help protect one another. If one member of the family is unable to earn an effective income, others will take up the slack. Family ties as insurance mechanisms are in fact the oldest risk management device and are endemic to our culture and to our thinking. They comprise a fundamental existing social institution, one that must be considered when any new risk management institution is considered.

Often in discussions of inequality and the institutions needed to combat it, family ties are disregarded. The U.S. Welfare Reform Act of 1996 imposed a lifetime five-year limit on cash payments of welfare. This act has been called the "granny tax." What happened to single women with children when they were cut off from welfare? Many of them did go back to work, but others moved in with the children's grandmother, who must assume the economic burden of their care.

A major problem with the family as a mutual insurance compact, however, is that it is too small and unstable a group to be reliable. Family members may die or move away or they may become irresponsible. Even if no such problems exist, entire families may suffer economic misfortune through geographic or occupational proximity.[8] Relations within a family can and often do break down, leading to an atmosphere that can be deeply depressing and even destructive. In the United States and many other countries, roughly half of all marriages end in divorce. The economic function of the family can help keep families together, and in many cases survive temporary bad periods that would have otherwise led to divorce. On the other hand, reliance on the economic function of the family can keep some people in terrible marriages for decades.

Still, despite all of its imperfections, the family is likely to continue to be a major institution for risk sharing. In pursuing innovations for risk management, we must respect the family and design around it to augment and regularize its functions.

Society Redistributes Income in Major Ways

Our society, our cities and nations, and our churches and charitable organizations, are a little like a family in reducing the impact of economic risks. Such help for people who find themselves in poor economic circumstances represents another important reason why we do not see the full impact of the economic risks that our free-market economic system generates.

Some critics think that society's efforts to redistribute income from rich to poor are ineffective. While they acknowledge that our progressive tax system is supposed to tax the rich at higher rates and use the proceeds to help the poor, they point out that the rich hire tax advisors who find loopholes for them and lobbyists who create even more loopholes. Moreover, these critics may note that emergency aid and welfare may be more token or short run than substantial. In the United States, for example, unemployment benefits last for only twenty-six weeks, and, as we have noted, the welfare act of 1996 placed a five-year limit on receiving welfare. Moreover, welfare benefits only the really down-and-out, not those who have jobs, however ill paying.

However, society's success in redistributing income has actually been an important part of the reason why we do not see more economic distress among our population. Those with higher income in the United States really do pay more taxes, despite all the efforts of wealthier people to exploit tax loopholes. High-income people even pay a higher proportion of their income as taxes; that is, the U.S. tax system truly is progressive. A 1998 study by the U.S. Congressional Budget Office found that families with children younger than eighteen, two parents, and cash incomes less than $10,000 paid on average a personal income tax at an effective rate of a *negative* 17.0 percent. Other taxes, social security, excise, and the indirect incidence of the corporate income tax, reduce the impact of this negative tax, but the total federal taxes paid by these families remain slightly negative. In contrast, families with incomes over $200,000 paid on average 22.9 percent of their adjusted gross income in federal personal income taxes. The combined effect of this and other federal taxes means that their total federal tax bite was about a third of their adjusted gross income.[9]

Whether higher income people pay taxes at higher *percent* of their income, higher income people, in the United States and other countries, do pay more taxes measured in dollars or other currency. The government takes more money from higher income persons so that governmental services and benefits can be maintained for the poorer citizens for free.[10] The combined effect of the taxation system and the governmental services strongly benefits lower income people, even in countries that have had less progressive taxes overall than in the United States. In Sweden, for example, the higher level of taxes and the higher level of public services have made for an unusually egalitarian system, even though the tax system has been by some accounts less consistently progressive than the United States'.[11]

A fundamental aspect of income redistribution is the provision of basic services to all citizens, including health care, law enforcement, and public roads and parks. Most notable among these services is education; all developed countries provide free public education for children. Providing such education from early childhood through the teen years is an expensive proposition but is of enormous value in helping equalize incomes. It benefits people at a time when they most need it, in the years when they are starting their lives, and, moreover, it provides not only education but shelter, community, sports events, entertainment, facilities for parties and club activities, and mentoring and establishment of connections to others in society. Parents have more money for themselves since these needs are taken care of for their children.

Also, in many countries a charitable income tax deduction encourages people to give to charities. This tax deduction is an implicit government grant to charity, even though the gifts are technically defined as gifts from individuals. Tax relief to charitable, nonprofit, and religious organizations helps to provide many services to lower income people.

Historically, this system of redistribution has been extremely important, and we must consider its established function when thinking of any new initiatives to manage people's risks. But we should not take such redistribution for granted. We cannot be assured that society will offer the same distribution of income across society as it has in the past. Shifts in the economic condition, the political climate, and interpretations of responsibility for others means that government support might not be as great in the future as it has been in the past.

The Lucky Twentieth Century

We tend to think of century-long trends as facts of nature that can never be reversed. People are impressed with a century's worth of data and imagine that it is evidence enough to prove any point. But a century is a short time in the span of human history, and there have been both good centuries and bad.

The standard of living in virtually every advanced country of the world has increased substantially since 1900. Real per capita income in the United States has quadrupled. Even slow-growing India has shown substantial real income growth during the twentieth century. In the less developed world almost every country has witnessed an increase since 1950. The increase has been so prominent and uniform among most countries of the world that one is perhaps inclined to want to extrapolate the trend and to regard it as certain that we will all be better and better off as time goes by.

This view stems in part from our faith in progress, in new inventions, procedures, and methods. One may regard a reversal of the trend as an impossibility. But to place such assurance in the to new technology, or on continuation of historical trends, is simply wrong.

We must not forget that even the successful twentieth-century economy was seriously disrupted at certain times. World War I, the Great Depression, and World War II are notable examples. At his Harvard commencement address in 2002, Daniel Patrick Moynihan, after reviewing the animosities and ambitions that exist in the world today, concluded that "now we have to ask if it is once again the summer of 1914."[12] Further major disruptions are likely, if hard to describe in advance.

There are serious questions, too, whether the pace of technological progress seen in advanced countries in the twentieth century can be sustained and extended to all the peoples of the world. Peter Raven, in his presidential address before the American Association for the Advancement of Science in 2002, pointed out that "the world has been converted in an instant of time from a wild natural one to one in which humans, one of an estimated 10 million or more species, are consuming, wasting, or diverting an estimated 45% of the total net biological productivity on land and using more than half of the renewable fresh water. The scale of changes in Earth's systems . . . is so different from before that we cannot predict the future."[13]

The mere fact that so many countries have shown overall income growth since 1900 means that the twentieth century has been a good one, but not that the next century must be also. During some centuries, standards of living in a country improve, and during others they retract. The economic growth of the last century is the result of certain kinds of technological and social progress that may not be repeated again in the same forms or to the same degree. The fundamental fact is that the future is unknown. We are complacent if we think otherwise.

Putting Ourselves and Our Risks in Perspective

In this chapter we have seen that the basic free-market capitalist system is capable of doling out some spectacularly risky outcomes. This system does not automatically make everyone well off. The capitalist system itself can be unforgiving, mercilessly tossing out people when they are no longer productive.

Nor do we see, for various reasons, the full ravages of this system. It takes some mental effort to appreciate the risks that ultimately are faced by people throughout society. It is difficult to appreciate the losses that different social classes have incurred and to understand the existing institutions that limit those losses, institutions that themselves may have weaknesses and undesirable consequences. But it is important to undertake this effort, as we shall do later in this book.

In the absence of such an effort, we tend to go around day to day with a feeling of invulnerability, interrupted only occasionally with sudden concerns. In church, one may hear read aloud the verse about time and chance from the Book of Ecclesiastes (the epigraph of this book). At such a reflective moment, surrounded by and at one with a broad community of rich and poor, successful and unsuccessful alike, one may momentarily accept the idea that "I am just a buffeted mote in God's vast swirling universe." But that feeling usually does not last long.[14]

Overcoming the false sense that each individual's fate is fully deserved is vital, not only because it inures us to our own risks but also because it prevents us from appreciating the kinds of policies that society needs to adopt to deal with these risks and blinds us to the arbitrariness and absurdity of the misfortunes that others face. Only then can we really confront these risks and take timely action against them. Only then can we design economic institutions that encourage people to take more risks that can be spread through society while also providing greater levels of security.

We need to confront risk systematically. We need a new set of modern institutions that allow us to take action against these risks—institutions that will provide the building blocks of a new financial order.

THREE

Why New Technology Creates Risks

FEW ADULTS who lived through the building and bursting of the "Nifty Fifty" technology bubble of the early 1970s or the dot-com bubble of the late 1990s would argue against the claim that our economic destinies, for better or worse, are tied to technology. But technology has even more fundamental economic impacts than these examples would suggest. To the extent that technology is ubiquitous in economic activity, any consideration of our future must take into account the risks associated with evolving technology, both for good and for ill.

To secure and advance our economic prospects, we must work to enhance the positive, productive power of technological advancements while at the same time reducing the downside "revenge effects" of new technology. What matters now is a greater understanding of how technology poses risks for us, of the economic implications of these risks, and hence of the ways that financial innovations can mitigate or control these risks. It is popular to say that there are no economic risks to new technology. But the risks are real.

People who worry about the economic risks associated with new technology are often labeled "Luddites." The real Luddites, a nineteenth-century group of workers named after their (apparently imaginary) leader King Ludd, was formed at a time when jobs were being replaced by machines. They launched a campaign of machine breaking in England from 1811 until 1816 to try to halt technological progress.[1] It is correct to describe the Luddites as fundamentally misguided; breaking machines was indeed a futile action. The Luddites, however, were unquestionably suffering economic distress and were hardly misguided in their estimation that the new machines played a role in their travails. Handloom weavers were being replaced by steam looms and were not readily finding new jobs.[2]

During the Great Depression, the idea that technology could harm anyone was further denounced. Because many people seemed to believe that technological progress was the cause of the rampant unemployment, which had reached as high as a quarter of the labor force in the United States. The American Institute of Physics, fearing a backlash against scientific research, launched a publicity campaign in 1933 against this idea and enlisted the support of technological luminaries Orville Wright, Charles Lindbergh, Amelia Earhart, and Henry Ford in their efforts.[3] Their authoritative campaign succeeded in discrediting the story of technologically-induced unemployment. The scientists were right that the Great Depression was not caused by technological progress. But they never presented any arguments that technological progress could not in principle cause serious problems for many.[4]

The idea that technology creates economic risks has also been wrongly discredited by its association with the "lump of labor fallacy," and by the tendency to describe the risks caused by new technology in terms of job loss, of higher unemployment. The "lump of labor fallacy" is the idea that the number of jobs in an economy is fixed, so that if a machine replaces any single job, one more person is perpetually unemployed. This is an obvious fallacy: We certainly expect most people displaced from their jobs to find other jobs, and sometimes they will be blessed and find even better jobs. There is no fallacy, however, in the idea that machines replacing jobs on a large scale creates the risk of lowering some people's incomes. People who are replaced at a time of major, wide-ranging technological changes may indeed be able to find other jobs, but a risk exists that they will have to take much less pay.[5]

Notwithstanding arguments to the contrary, technological progress can certainly create serious challenges for our society.[6] Four basic aspects of technology pose important risks today. The first is the consummation of cybernetics. Over the next few decades, the full development of this science of computerized control could mean the replacement of many kinds of human labor by automated technology. The second is an exaggeration of the winner-take-all effect by new technology. The ability of the most talented people to marginalize even slightly less talented people, to monopolize wages and profits, could be further abetted through mass communications and digital replication. The third is increased globalization. The weakening of international economic barriers can make possible the replacement of highly paid people in one country by lower paid people in another. The fourth is the destabilizing effects of new technology on military strategy. Devastating wars or major terrorist activities constitute serious risks not only to political and social, but also to economic, welfare.

47

The Consummation of Cybernetics

Cybernetics, the science of computer control systems, analogues to human neurocircuitry, has seen exponential growth over the last half century. Scientists and engineers have spent decades searching out the fundamentals of cybernetics, with relatively limited economically important applications to date. But the accumulated knowledge in this field is now beginning to have real economic impact. If this exponential growth continues for the next few decades, cybernetics will almost certainly have a truly revolutionary impact, replacing much present-day human labor and thereby dramatically altering the distribution of economic power.

In 1947, the very dawn of both the computer age and atomic age, the mathematician Norbert Wiener in his book *Cybernetics* spoke of the "ultra-rapid computing machine" and of the automatic devices it would make possible:

> Long before Nagasaki and the public awareness of the atomic bomb, it had occurred to me that we were here in the presence of another social potentiality of unheard-of importance for good and for evil. . . . There is no rate of pay at which a United States pick-and-shovel laborer can live which is low enough to compete with the work of a steam shovel as an excavator. The modern industrial revolution is similarly bound to devalue the human brain at least in its simpler and more routine decisions. Of course, just as the skilled carpenter, the skilled mechanic, the skilled dressmaker have in some degree survived the first industrial revolution, so the skilled scientist and the skilled administrator may survive the second. However, taking the second revolution as accomplished, the average human being of mediocre attainments or less has nothing to sell that is worth anyone's money to buy.[7]

Over fifty years after Wiener wrote *Cybernetics,* the worst fears of the long-run effects of automation have not been realized. Many jobs are still done by manual labor, if at low wages. Until now, machines that displace some people from their jobs have not been general enough in their abilities to displace all people in all such jobs. For example, we still do not have mechanized replacements for fruit and vegetable pickers. The technology to distinguish ripe berries from the unripe, to pick only the ripe without bruising them, and to place them safely in a container is still not practicable mechanically.

Not only do manual labor jobs remain; the new technology in some cases has even created new such jobs. For example harvesting machines create new manual jobs by encouraging the development of more diverse and difficult-to-manage agricultural products that require human attention even as harvesting is mechanized. But the point is that we do not know what the effect of new technology will be for everyone. Technology creates fundamental uncertainty. We will have to wait and see whether it helps or harms low-income workers. Either is a real possibility.

An extreme economic disaster for low-income workers may seem remote. To destroy the incomes of low income workers, machines will have to progress to the point at which they can accept simple instructions of varied sorts, visually recognize varying situations, exercise simple common sense, and show some versatile manual dexterity. They would have to do all that before they really exhaust the value of human labor. That technology seems a long way off. But substantial risks are not so remote; technology may *reduce* workers' rate of pay long before that.

Already, automatic control systems do some of the most routine of human tasks. For example, Robotics of Danbury, Connecticut, has sold its HelpMate robot to over one hundred hospitals. This robot makes pickups and deliveries to rooms throughout the hospital, navigating with sonar sensors and infrared cameras. It even uses public elevators to change floors. The company is developing versions of this robot to provide help around the house, for example, by following and watching a feeble elderly person for falls or other abnormal activity and calling for help if necessary. The CareBot robot can vacuum floors unattended, and the Robomower can navigate itself around and cut a lawn while unattended. The InteleCady robot is a caddy that tracks the golfer at a comfortable distance, avoiding bunkers, water hazards, and tees, and responds to the golfer's commands. Even the automatic fruit-picking machines appear to be almost here. A robotic melon-harvesting machine has been demonstrated by Purdue University in collaboration with three Israeli organizations, Ben Gurion University, the Weizmann Institute of Science, and the Agricultural Research Organization.[8] The list of abilities that unskilled labor offers that cannot be simulated by robots continues to grow shorter. While most of these robots are currently expensive, technological progress ought to bring their costs down, so we can expect to see many of these robots in the future. While robotics will not destroy jobs on a one-to-one basis, it will destroy some jobs while creating others and it is likely to reduce the wages of the remaining similar jobs. The only predictable variable is the uncertainty that will affect the lives of many workers.

In addition to the spread of cybernetics, the advent of "ubiquitous computing," in which computers are installed in just about every device we use, and "wearable computers," which people carry around with them wherever they go, may make great inroads in the service professions by eliminating the need to have people around to operate equipment and explain what to do. A single program may direct the robots that have replaced service personnel, or a single person may be able to direct a "staff" of robots.[9]

It has long been apparent that digital devices can achieve the same objectives as human labor without necessarily duplicating the actions of the human labor it replaces. For example, a system that detects cars running through red lights, using digital cameras that automatically photograph the license plates of the offending cars, or a system that measures cars' speeds using a global positioning system, can replace certain enforcement activities of traffic police. The new technology is much more effective than traditional human enforcement, for it can make it a virtual certainty that running a red light or speeding will be detected and can send out a ticket automatically. Someday it may even be possible automatically to add the ticket to the offender's income tax bill or debit his or her savings account.

Recall that in a free market an individual's pay tends to be related to what he or she can contribute at the margin, after all others' contributions are taken into account, to the hiring firm. That is, the individual tends to be paid roughly in line with his or her marginal product. The marginal product that people offer to their potential employers is the difference between their ability to carry out productive activity under normal conditions and the hazards and obstacles that they also inadvertently tend also to create for their employers. Some employees are forgetful or careless and may even damage things, others are troublesome or otherwise unpleasant, others demand the valuable time of managers. When firms make hiring and firing decisions one person at a time, in each case a dominant consideration must be how much that person is contributing to the firm after all these costs are considered.

If machines can do their jobs, even less well, then the marginal product could become negative for many individuals. The fraction of the population for which this marginal product is negative has never been accurately estimated but may be quite substantial even today. And so a risk exists that this fraction could rise substantially in coming years with increasing technology.

Unskilled laborers are not necessarily the only people who are most likely to find their work replaced by machines. Those who develop specific skills over many years—translators or stenographers, are obvious examples—may find that they have been replaced by machines. Workers whose particular talents are in learning complex but routinizable tasks are clearly at risk of competition from non-human "workers."

Technological progress can also create random opportunities for some workers to adapt to the new technology, opportunities that set them on a different career trajectory than those who were not lucky enough to have the opportunity. Thus, technological progress can create disparities in income even among people who start out with identical skills and talents.[10] We do not know today who will be harmed and who helped by the new technology. Technological progress is thus generating risk, uncertainties whose outcome will become known only through time.

Winner-Take-All

The more one voice can be heard by many others, the greater the ability of listeners to hear only the best. Before the advent of technology for the reproduction of sound, the market for singers was much broader. Now a few stars with very high incomes tend to dominate. Before the advent of the motion picture, demand for actors in stage plays was much larger. Now here, too, only a few actors dominate in terms of incomes.[11]

Today, even deceased singers and actors can sometimes out-compete living ones, through use of their recordings or movies. New technology seemingly even enables dead artists to create new works. When the actor Oliver Reed died near the end of the filming of *Gladiator,* the producers were able to finish the movie using a body model for the filming of a crucial two minutes of the movie and then superimposing an image of the head of the actor.[12] There are new ways also of reproducing the speech of a deceased person: New speech software from AT&T Labs is reportedly simulating individual voices with only "a few robotic tones and unnatural inflections."[13]

Improved presentation and teleconferencing systems are allowing stars in other walks of life to similarly extend their reach, thus raising demand for their services and displacing the need for others. Education provides an important example. In education, new technology is making it easier for a star teacher to access more and more students. Improvements in lecture technology, such as PowerPoint and mobile microphones that allow the lecturer to walk amidst the classroom, make large lectures more attractive to students. E-mail technology allows a teacher to handle the requests and demands of more students than could personally visit the teacher. On-line education allows an individual teacher the means to reach thousands of students.

Many students will always demand small classes and traditional personal teacher-student interaction, but the total demand, and willingness to pay for it, may be significantly diminished. Moreover, even such an interpersonal experience can be supplied much more efficiently with online technology. With the virtual classroom, professors and students seated at video camera–equipped terminals in diverse locations can see one another through postage stamp–sized pictures of their faces arrayed on their monitors, and the professor can click on the picture of a student who has a question to transform it into a full-screen live video image for all in the class to see. The system could be designed to encourage a more satisfying interaction between students and professors and among students by storing and replaying past interactions so that both professor and students will better remember each other. The system could also replay salient classroom moments. Such technology, combined with programmed learning technology, can economize on the use of teachers by reducing their need to do other things and using their direct interpersonal contact more intensively. Education may improve, but fewer professors will be needed—only those with strong interpersonal skills that suit the new technology—and so many professors may face significant economic risks.

The same technologically induced changes in demand that we are likely to see with traditional teachers could easily, by extension, apply to doctors, lawyers, bankers, and a thousand other professions. Where and how this will happen will only become clear with time. Meanwhile, the uncertainty about the effects on future income constitutes a risk that can still be dealt with using financial methods.

Globalization: Breakdown of Geographic Barriers

Constantly improving technology is making it easier for businesses to use the services of people who are not on site, who in fact may be in a different city in the country or on the other side of the planet. Bit by bit, new technological advantages may take away at the advantages that on-site office workers have over off-site workers.[14] The effect may be to lower their marginal product and ultimately the wages of some, and to raise the marginal product and wages of others. The anti-globalization protesters are right about these risks, though generally wrong about the solutions.

E-mail technology has made the cost of a long-distance communication virtually nil. E-mail eliminates paper filing, and the subsequent search through voluminous files, that used to be a significant activity of on-site office workers. Now, electronic files can be backed up in an instant, searched quickly and easily, and shared at great distances.

Instant-messaging technology allows immediate real-time communication. Computer users can engage one another in a written conversation, receiving and responding to messages with no perceptible delay and without disrupting another meeting or phone conversation. Communication with a person on the other side of the world is as easy as communication with a secretary just outside one's office.

Teleconferencing allows interaction among people at a distance almost as if they were in the same room. This is important partly because our ancient communications patterns involve looking into the face of another person, judging that person's feelings, and experiencing an emotional reaction of one's own that in turn stimulates thought and conversation. Already, some teleconferencing services, such as PlaceWare, Polycom, and WebEx, allow integrated teleconference and visual presentations, and they allow convenient sharing of files on line. We might speculate on how teleconferencing may develop as its cost declines. A parallel development of technology and businesses that apply the technology could someday allow meetings to work even better than they do among people together in a room, for instance, by allowing individuals to better hear and see presentations, communicate more effectively in pairs without disturbing others, and record these and other communications. Indeed, forms of teleconferencing might be a considerable improvement upon the business lunch and the cocktail party.

Improved physical delivery technology, facilitated by improved computer tracking services, and by improved routing and networking of warehouses, have decreased the importance of physical location in business activity. Now parts of the physical surroundings of a work place can be shipped around the world in hours.

These technological advances have already begun to create a global workplace. For example, India has so many plans to offer office services around the world that *The Economist* predicted India might soon be "back-office to the world."[15] Indeed, with a large population of educated people who speak perfect English, many of whom are currently very poorly paid by world standards, the possibilities appear to be enormous. Similar trends are observed in other countries. Low-income regions of China perform telephone answering services for Hong Kong, and Ghana processes paperwork for the New York City Police Department.

These changes may offer large opportunities for developing countries or areas within countries. At the same time, these opportunities may work against the pay of currently employed office workers in higher income countries.

At this time, the actual size of these back-office operations in such places as India remains relatively small by world standards, and forecasts for the near term are not for very large increases. But the spectacular growth of such services in coming decades must rank as a real possibility. Part of the uncertainty comes from the difficulty predicting the development of new technology that will further foster such electronic dissemination of basic human services. Some new technology that fosters everyday contact, that improves a shared virtual desktop, or that simply lowers communications costs might make a dramatic difference.

In fact, we are seeing the beginnings of both "work at a distance" and "groupwork," in which people in far distant locations collaborate as if they were working together in the same room, and there will be many more improvements, allowing various kinds of work to be done together that could not before. For example, workers in two factories in different cities on opposite sides of the globe can collaborate to make some difficult-to-produce specialty steel product, giving verbal suggestions or instructions to each other and pointing out work to be done on various phases of the project; these are presented twelve hours later (when it is again day on the other side of the world) in an orderly and seamless way as if they were in the same workroom together at the same time. Such a facility will diminish the advantage held by businesses that are geographically close to major economic centers. According to some scientists, doctors in two different cities may someday jointly perform an operation on a single patient in a third city, assisted by local personnel and by remotely operated equipment.[16] Such technology will permit international collaboration as never seen before and will change the advantage that physicians in high-income areas currently enjoy.

All of these changes create risks to high labor incomes enjoyed by people in favored regions. They also create risks to real estate values in these regions. But it is important to stress that these are *risks* to incomes and values, not certainties. While we can be confident that the technology will advance, the economic outcome is uncertain. The possibility exists that advances in communications and transportation technology will raise, rather than lower, the incomes of people in favored regions, if the increase in electronic communications generates even more regional opportunities or a demand for even more face-to-face communications. This outcome is not implausible; indeed, urbanization has actually increased, not decreased, over the twentieth century when the telephone became widespread.[17] It remains to be seen what the economic effects of the new technology will be.

Advances in Military and Terrorist Technology

Advances in military technology have always lent instability to the balance of power in the world. These risks are not confined to nuclear weapons, nor to the many forms of germ or chemical warfare that have been so much discussed recently. Information technology and robotics can also play a significant role.

Advances in control and information technology often have the consequence that the control of large amounts of power is concentrated in a very small, and often fragile, center, making possible sudden shifts in power and misuses of this power.

55

In the 2001 war in Afghanistan, advances in information technology were highlighted for the world. The potential power of robotics was seen with the unmanned Predator drones that the United States used for reconnaissance. These drones are capable of recognizing an individual target from the air and are equipped with Hellfire antitank missiles that can destroy that target. The drones were instrumental in killing central figures in Osama bin Laden's organization. As this robotic military equipment proliferates, it could change the entire character of warfare since it may make it possible to wage war in a less savage way, avoiding collateral damage and without putting one's own soldiers at risk.

These highly expensive weapons are not easily obtained by terrorists. But there are some aspects of technological advance that make the potential terrorist threat more worrisome. The terrorists who attacked the World Trade Center and the Pentagon on September 11, 2001, were able to inflict such horrible damage because of the development of very large aircraft, carrying many tons of highly flammable fuel, that can be piloted by a single person. Both Boeing 767 aircraft that crashed into the World Trade Center was capable of carrying 13,900 gallons of fuel, compared to the mere 800 hundred gallon capacity of the Army Air Corps B-25 aircraft that accidentally crashed into the Empire State Building in dense fog in 1945, causing only relatively minor damage.[18] Moreover, the advanced control technology for the modern aircraft is designed to minimize the need for specific human skills and is relatively standardized across different types of aircraft to reduce the risk of pilot error, thus inviting abuse by unauthorized parties.

The technology for delivery of deadly power has in some dimensions outpaced the technology for defense. This situation invites exploitation by some nations or terrorist groups willing to bluff a country into submission by feigning willingness to use nuclear weapons, even despite the possibility of retaliation.

When lethal technology can be operated by a small group of people, without the cooperation of larger groups, their chance for success increases. Moreover, when technology facilitates doing such damage very quickly, the probability that such a group will be interrupted decreases. The general principle is that the proliferation of many more types of advanced technology may itself raises the uncertainty about the extent of malicious damage.[19]

Confronting Our Risks

Most of the economic risks caused by new technology discussed in this chapter are collateral risks or systemic risks, not the kind of risks that the engineers who design the new technology see it as their mission to avoid. If cybernetics replaces human labor with machines, if the massive reproduction of individuals' voices and actions allows first-place winners to replace the runners up, if the massive communications around the globe allow distant foreigners to replace local workers, and if advances in military technology destabilize the balance of power in the world, it is not the engineers' problem. It is instead a challenge to risk management experts, and to our financial system.

We can do much using modern financial risk management techniques to mitigate these risks. New technology is never unambiguously a good thing, and we must be vigilant with it and apply it broadly and creatively, considering carefully all of its unanticipated consequences.

The risks that are directly related to new technology are not the only risks that we must consider. They interact with other sources of economic uncertainty. Let us now turn to a broader analysis of economic risks to give us a better understanding of the issues that a new order of risk management must confront.

FOUR

Forty Thieves: The Many Kinds of Economic Risks

DEALING INDIVIDUALLY with all of our separate risks is impossible because there are too many of them to comprehend. We can buy insurance policies on our house's burning down, on having our laptop stolen, and on contracting a deadly disease. But if we imagine that such a piecemeal approach to risk management works well by itself, we are mistaken. Economic risks pervade life. Hence, we instead need to insure against risks to some comprehensive measures of economic well-being such as income itself—a theme of a number of the ideas for fundamental risk management to be discussed later in this book. In the present chapter, I demonstrate this important principle of risk management.

The risks posed by technological progress (discussed in chapter 3) are manifold, and, moreover, these are not our only economic risks. Each considered alone may appear to be insubstantial or to have low probability or to be hard to quantify. But the sum total of the effect of all these risks in the long term can be downright staggering.

Imagine forty thieves, each with a small probability—say a 10 percent chance—of taking some of your money—and each taking about 10 percent of the total money. Each thief, therefore, poses an expected loss of only 1 percent of your money (10 percent of 10 percent), seemingly negligible. Rounding down each of these 1 percents to zero and ignoring the thieves altogether, ignoring the risk, would be easy. But you do so at your own peril. If there really are forty thieves, the expected loss is 40 percent of one's income, and the uncertainty about the loss quite substantial. If the risks are not independent of one another, if the thieves tend to gang up on already weakened victims, then the danger can be quite large.[1]

When it comes to our economic security, it is hard to count the "thieves." Who are they? The major demographic and socioeconomic variables—age, years of schooling, years of job experience, parents' level of schooling, occupation, and income—predict very little of the variations of incomes across individuals.[2] Many other factors must be at work in propelling some to riches and others to privation.

When so many sources of risk threaten, we naturally tend to neglect most of them and to be overconfident of our future. An extensive psychological literature confirms a human tendency toward overconfidence. Part of the reason for overconfidence is a human failure in judging the complexity of risks, the lack of an ability to consider how many different ways our understanding or construal of the situation may be wrong.[3]

We have to get beyond this overconfidence and our tendency to compartmentalize our thinking about risk into little boxes, each of which looks small. This means we must summon the imagination to think of the many different kinds of risks that we really face.

Risks to Whole Countries

Some of the factors that account for the economic successes or failures of individuals are factors that affect entire countries. These factors are very hard to disentangle and identify. Historically, when a country's standard of living has declined, experts inconclusively debate for years the reasons for the decline, disagreeing about the multiplicity and complexity of the causes long after the fact. For example, the ultimate causes of the Great Depression, the greatly disappointing performance of Argentina in the second half of the twentieth century culminating in a deep economic crisis in 2001–2, the surprising stumble of the Japanese economy since 1989, and the terrible growth rate in the 1990s of the Russian economy when compared with, for example, that of the Chinese economy, remain the subject of ongoing debate.

Some of the proximate reasons for bad economic performance in such extreme cases are well known, but an accurate accounting of the ultimate reasons is unavailable. Too many details, too many tiny factors that cannot be accurately measured conspired to produce these unfortunate economic outcomes.

The difficulty in comprehending these risks in recent history confounds our appreciation of the potential losses to our livelihoods. One would think that with the aid of a century of data, we ought to have a good idea about the potential risks to livelihoods. One reason that we do not is that we have only observed a few of the many possible random outcomes, and we have observed a certain mix and distribution of outcomes that will never be repeated again in the same way.

Economic theory offers little agreement as to what ultimately causes differences in national income from year to year or decade to decade or country to country. Economic theorists like to tell simple stories because only then can we prescribe safe and simple policies. But the number of contradictory simple stories that have been offered by these theorists is revealing of the multitude of risk factors that we face and of our poor accounting of them.[4] For instance, real business cycle theorists have argued that the fluctuations in national economic growth are due to technological shocks, new productive technologies, or new technologies that make obsolete investments we already have.[5] We have stressed such technological shocks here, but there are many other shocks to national incomes.

Other economists have argued that fluctuations in national income are due primarily to changes in monetary policy,[6] or to changes in desired savings for the future,[7] or to structural shifts such as changes in the demand for produced goods relative to services,[8] or to changes in the price of energy, such as oil-price shocks that have been in turn caused by factors such as the political maneuvers of OPEC.[9] Still others have traced changes in national income to shifts in population growth rates,[10] or to breakdowns in the process of borrowing and lending,[11] or to fluctuations in the strength of cartels,[12] or to changes in public support of labor unions,[13] or to changes in social capital, the sense of trust and cooperation and willingness to participate in networks.[14]

Some others have stressed changes in the legal enforcement of long-term property rights that influence people's willingness to work for the future,[15] or changes in the decisions of nations to invest in education and other forms of human capital,[16] or increasing returns to capital, which may favor countries that can invest heavily in certain industries.[17] And others have stressed that the dynamics of "learning by doing" can generate important differences through time, giving advantages to those societies who start development earlier,[18] or that changes in public confidence for the economy may generate self-fulfilling prophecies that convert these psychological changes into actual economic fluctuations.[19]

There are also other potential causes of national income fluctuations that have not been stressed by economists because they did not clearly manifest themselves in the past, especially the recent past that they tend to study, but that could appear in the future. These include such things as unanticipated social, environmental, or international problems, problems that we cannot delineate now but that we nonetheless may yet discover to be very real.

As such, there are too many possibilities to allow any clear consensus on the sources of risk to nations. Most likely, all the different theories have elements of truth to them. But it is futile to consider writing insurance policies individually against each such ill-defined and ill-measured risk.

Risks across Individuals within a Country

On top of these shocks to whole countries, one must remember that each individual incurs the combined effect of country risks, of occupational risks within a country, and of individual career risks within an occupation. Even if no one of these risks is alarming, the sum may be. Each of them matters since it contributes to an overall pattern of individual risk, and these risks go far beyond the disability risks that are currently insurable. Careers provide a helpful window on this problem.

Individual careers are the cumulative effect, over a lifetime, of many small victories and disappointments. A positive career break may be an opportunity to take a challenging position, a random event that puts one in a position that includes training for yet another important job or that puts one in the public eye and creates an impression of authority—"being in the right place at the right time." Negative career breaks include being passed by for such opportunities, or encountering illnesses or disabilities or reputation diminishing mistakes.

Those of us who are successful may imagine that our own hard work and intrinsic worth accounts for our success. A good part of this feeling is just that—imagination. Barbara Ehrenreich, during her sojourn among the low paid, was surprised at how easily she could have been stuck in such jobs. No one recognized her considerable talents, the talents of a best-selling writer. She even tried talking about the book she was writing to her co-workers but got no reaction. Everyone knows someone who is writing a book. If Ehrenreich were really stuck in those jobs without her reputation and contacts, she might have found it difficult to climb out.

The role of such career breaks, both positive and negative, in forging one's lifetime income and position are hard to quantify, but histories suggest that such events inject a great deal of randomness in one's lifetime income. We do not generally have data on the vicissitudes that affect individual careers, nor do we generally know whether these vicissitudes were really exogenous shocks to careers or whether they are possibly brought on by the individuals themselves. For example, missing a positive career break may result from a lifestyle decision hampering monetary success, as for example when a lawyer eschews the private sector for government office or teaching.

But there are some hard data on the effects of random and unexpected career breaks. Labor economist Joshua Angrist found a clever way to estimate the effect of one such random event, being drafted into the U.S. military during the Vietnam War.[20] Normally, finding out the effect of such conscription is difficult because we do not know whether the conscription is random. Some people, perhaps the more resourceful, well-connected, self-centered, talented, or educated, may have found ways to avoid the draft. But at one point during the Vietnam War, the U.S. government created a draft lottery, constructed to be random. Each U.S. male subject to the draft was assigned a number from 1 to 366, a Random Sequence Number (RSN), based solely on his birth date. The birth dates were drawn randomly in public ceremonies, the first of which was on December 1, 1969, and the numbers corresponding to birth dates announced. The lower the number, the sooner one would be drafted, and most of the men with high numbers were never drafted.

Angrist looked at the effect of the number drawn on individual earnings in the early 1980s, long after the war was over. By looking at the effect of the individual's RSN on earnings, and not at all on whether the individual actually served in the military, he was able to eliminate any possible biases in his estimate from the fact that more resourceful people might somehow evade the draft. He concluded that the effect of military service was to reduce income by 15 percent as much as ten years after discharge from the military. This conclusion does not mean that a stint in the military necessarily is bad for everyone, but it does show the possible long-term effect of having one's career interrupted and assigned randomly to some other task. His results suggest the importance of career breaks in our lives.

I can personally testify to the importance of the draft lottery. I received the RSN 362 in the 1969 lottery, which essentially ruled out my being drafted and allowed me to go on with plans for a career in economics with no concern about interruptions or of being forced to participate unwillingly in a war I regarded as immoral. I am inclined to think that my relative success in life is not unrelated to that draw.

Income Changes in Times of War and Social Upheaval

An important reason why the multiplicity of economic risks creates so much uncertainty is that the risks are not independent of one another. Even though the different risks that we have discussed have no logical relation, they do tend to reveal themselves together. For example, during the Asian financial crisis of 1997–98, a number of Asian countries experienced exchange rate crises and stock market crises and labor crises and foreign lending crises and political crises all at the same time. And at times of national crisis, individual careers also take their own individual ups or downs. Thus, the cumulative effects of the risks can be much better or worse than one imagines thinking of them separately.

Some of the biggest changes in people's income occur at these times of social upheaval, for instance at times of war. War has been, and will probably continue to be, a regular feature of human life. At a time when terrorists are trying to use advanced technology to create massive loss of human life, the possibility of a serious war can seem imminent. Wars are times of great redistributions of wealth, even in victorious countries and countries where fighting is far away. The war creates profit opportunities for some, economic hardship for others.

At times of war, people naturally feel great concern about the inequity of the distribution of the burdens of war, with some giving their lives in an effort to defend the country and others becoming rich from war profits. But for any society to escape from such inequity is difficult. The national economy must operate substantially on the basic principle of economic incentives as dictated by wartime need; the government cannot order the economy as it does the army. Given this fact, some people will make a lot of money, while others will miss out. That is the nature of incentives. If the incentives are real, they must have an effect. This is not to say that the effects of the war on the income distribution cannot be ameliorated, but it is difficult to do so.

During World War I, there was great concern in the United States about the inequity of the burden of the war within the country, and the War Industry Board was empowered to monitor corporations. Prices were set that were supposed to allow only a normal margin of profit.

Moreover, the government penalized profitable firms with an excess profits tax. Still, these measures came too late, and during the years of World War I, before the United States actually declared war in 1917, real after-tax corporate profits soared, reaching levels not seen again until the mid 1950s.[21]

During World War II, the memory of the wartime profits of World War I was much on the minds of U.S. citizens and lawmakers alike, and the Roosevelt administration was bent on preventing the appearance of such inequity. But it faced the fundamental problem that the private sector must be given incentives to function efficiently. The outcome was high profits, but they were disguised. Companies were forced to price on a cost-plus basis, but the definition of cost is always ambiguous. Companies could also invest in the future, retooling and rearranging their production, as well as doing research and development, which would yield them greater profits in the future, after the war was over. Companies were not allowed to pay abnormally high salaries or hourly wages, for that would be too conspicuous a way to consume profits. But companies were allowed to grant employees generous expense accounts, and so World War II became a period of expensive business lunches and unnecessary business trips. It was also a time when craftspeople or other workers who did war-related work saw unusual opportunity to work long hours at full pay, and many of those people used the occasion to pay off their debts, upgrade their homes and small businesses, and sharpen their skills. Those who were connected to the business world during the war were well positioned to prosper after the war, in contrast to those who were off fighting.[22]

In countries where the war was being fought, the shocks to personal income caused by the war were even greater, creating great opportunities for some, disappointments to others. In Japan after World War II, for example, the Allied authorities, who resented the role of the wealthy Zaibatsu families in the war, forced them to exchange their holdings for yen-denominated bonds, which were then made nearly worthless by postwar Japanese inflation. Only those among the Zaibatsu who kept their former business connections, and astutely used them take to advantage of postwar opportunities, remained wealthy.[23] Opportunities abounded for new wealth. Some in Japan managed to get control of wartime stocks of goods at low prices and sold at a time of postwar scarcity, or some bought real estate at temporarily distressed prices. In 1946, alert Japanese could buy choice downtown properties in Tokyo for a pittance. Among other, more terrible results of the war, World War II also produced a profound shakeup of the distribution of wealth in Japan.

Financial Innovation and the Multiplicity of Risks

We have seen in this chapter that the list of possible risks is so large and ill defined that no one expert can describe them all in detail. Thus, it would be impossible to write insurance policies against all specific risks. Ultimately, our insurance is most effective if it is against some measure of outcome of economic well-being, such as income itself. That is why some of the most important risk management institutions of the past, such as progressive taxes and social security, manage the risks of incomes themselves, not just individual shocks to incomes. Hence, in the ideas for a new financial order presented in this book, much of the attention will be focused on managing risks measured in terms of large national aggregates, such as national incomes or GDP. These values summarize the impact of all risk factors on the economy of a nation at any given time.

We must still pay attention to the separate sources of risk, and we must try to understand them insofar as this is possible. Leaders must pay attention to risks below the national level because individuals' risks are the sum of the risks to the nation they live in and other risks that impinge on groups within a nation or on single individuals. Even if the total risk to a nation could be considered tolerable, if borne equally by all people within a nation, the total risks that each individual faces are much larger. The unit of analysis should not be the nation alone.

At times of national crisis such as war, well-designed instruments of incentive must be used to do the work required to deal with the crisis at hand while at the same time reducing as far as possible the random shocks to individual incomes. Achieving this requires some financial techniques that did not exist at the time of World War I or World War II. A risk management infrastructure should be in place before a crisis, so that we will be prepared to apply modern principles of financial management that preserve high incentives while they manage the unusual risks.

At all times, whether in crisis or not, the project of managing risks involves dealing with risks represented by many different levels of aggregation, from the nation down to the individual. Managing these risks is therefore inherently information intensive and requires massive information technology properly directed at these multiple risks. In part 2 of this book, we will consider some of the changes in information technology and our associated technology for human-computer interaction that make effective risk management possible.

Part Two

How Science and Technology Create New Opportunities in Finance

FIVE

New Information Technology Applied to Risk Management

ADVANCES IN INFORMATION TECHNOLOGY promise to serve us very well in achieving radical financial innovation. As hardware capabilities steadily advance, so too do software capabilities, and, with them, the structure of our human organizations. At any time of fundamental technological change, our concepts, our units of measurement, and our framing of issues change. With such technological and cultural ferment afoot, fundamental transformations in the nature and quality of our lives are possible through financial progress.

Past Information Technology Progress
Related to Financial Progress

Consider the development of some important information technology that has been around for quite a while that we generally take for granted—very simple technology, such as paper and pens, that nonetheless underwent some critically important advances in the last couple of centuries. The importance of such technology in our lives today illustrates the potential importance of new technology that will be discussed later in this chapter. The gradual progress in the improvement of information management and storage—over a couple centuries—offers a suggestion of the slow and steady pace that we can expect from progress in information technology and its pervasive consequences.

The last two centuries saw highly significant advances in information storage technology, advances that allow vast stores of records to be kept, processed, and relied upon. Consider advances in the manufacture of the paper. A machine to make paper automatically was developed in 1800, and a method of making paper from wood pulp was developed in 1865. These and other advances in paper making dramatically lowered the cost of paper, and hence the cost of record storage. A newspaper in London in 1799, which consisted of only four pages, cost sixpence, or more than 10 percent of the daily wage of a carpenter or bricklayer.[1] In contrast, newspapers today cost a fraction of 1 percent of a worker's daily wage, and use vastly more paper. This progress over the centuries in reducing the cost of record storage was a small but important part of the reason that humans were able to achieve a dramatic increase in financial complexity. Today, looking forward to a fully electronic office, we are in the process of eliminating the cost of paper altogether.

Nineteenth-century advances in technology dramatically lowered the cost of sending a letter. Standardized envelopes appeared by 1849, street addresses proliferated in the late nineteenth century, and modern postal services soon appeared. In the United States in 1850 postage for letters sent between cities in the United States ranged (depending on distance) from five cents to ten cents, or about $1.50 to $3.00 in today's dollars, then a high fraction of personal income for most people. Because of these costs, the average person in the United States in 1850 received only four pieces of mail a year. In contrast, by 1990 the average person received 670 pieces of mail a year. These advances, too, have to be connected with the increasing financial complexity we have witnessed over the last centuries. The flow of information by mail dramatically increased, and today it is in the process of increasing rapidly faster with electronic mail.

Copies are essential to reliable record keeping because they provide backups, reducing the probability of loss of records to virtually zero and speeding the accurate transmission of information. The earliest practical method of making copies mechanically was the letter press, invented by James Watt (the inventor of the steam engine) in 1780, but it had important limitations.[2] Crude carbon paper was invented in 1806. A photographic document-copying machine was invented in 1900. By 1911, the Photostat could copy a page a minute, though at a price of ten cents a copy, or nearly two dollars per copy in today's prices. This machine was an important advance, though unless speed or perfect accuracy were an issue, having secretaries retype a documents by hand was generally cheaper. Copying prices eventually became much lower when xerography was invented after 1950.[3] Once again, this steady progress in copying technology was inevitably connected to increased financial technology over these years. Today, we have automatic backup systems that copy with virtually zero cost, another step with the potential for yet more complexity in our financial dealings.

The invention of the typewriter in 1868 was significant not only for the increased speed of data entry but also for the increased reliability of typewritten records, which eliminated the errors of deciphering handwriting. In the nineteenth century printed forms—and subsequently business form companies—came of age.[4] Filing cabinets improved too, culminating in the vertical file of the end of the nineteenth century.[5] Methods of filing improved substantially then.[6] The common uniform standard for file folders was a sort of achievement in itself.[7] Computing machines and automatic data processing systems improved dramatically in the nineteenth century, and of course on into the twentieth and twenty-first centuries.[8] Progress in all of these devices facilitated financial progress, and their electronic counterparts today promise to do so again.

Over these years bureaucracies advanced to create more efficient human organizations for improved management of records, though these are harder for us to remember for the lack of physical evidence. The management of the people who handled information improved. In modern Europe, government administrative service outside the military still remained a "hotbed of nepotism and venality, cavalier independence and professional ignorance" until the first modern civil service was developed in eighteenth- and nineteenth-century the German states.[9] In 1770 Prussia reformed the civil service by introducing a system of examinations for hire in government service that ensured a professional staffing of government jobs. This civil service eventually became a model for the whole world, slowly adopted by one country after another over the centuries.[10] Important bureaucratic innovations, associated with our new physical information technology, can be expected in the future.

These improvements in information infrastructure were essential for plans for modern finance. Tens of millions of records must be kept reliably for use decades later. They must be available for use systematically and must not be damaged or lost by such use. They must be protected from hazards such as fire, bookworms, and becoming brittle. The records must be backed up, and the copies must be kept at a separate site, so the cost of storage is multiplied by the number of backups. The system must be highly reliable on such a large scale so that people can trust that the information in the records is accurate and is used as intended. The cost of achieving such results must be low enough to be acceptable. Improvements in all these directions kept apace with our financial progress, and will yield yet more progress in the future.

Products of Today's Database Technology

The same functions that were advanced in the nineteenth and twentieth centuries by cheap paper, copying methods, effective postal services, typewriters, and filing systems are being advanced much further by compact discs, CD burners, electronic mail, laptop computers, and electronic filing systems. All of these functions are now orders of magnitudes better than in the nineteenth century, and the result is a plethora of databases at our disposal and associated development in concepts and methods to use the databases.

We have begun to see the advantages of this progress. In the early years of the twentieth century, almost none of the regular data on economic quantities that we today see flashing across our monitors or television sets was regularly available. Notably, governments did not then even regularly publish the consumer price index, the GDP, or the unemployment rate.[11] The proliferation of data-processing equipment and the attendant advance in econometric methods of analyzing economic data over recent decades have made it possible for us to see the magnitude of many economic quantities that had gone unobserved. Indexes that measure factors highly relevant to the risks of individuals and firms and even of countries are now commonplace. The ability to measure these values makes possible the creation of institutions to improve the management of risks. The trend to more and more data sources is likely to continue unabated.

In 1993 the World Bank created a System of National Accounts, allowing national incomes to be calculated on a consistent standard around the world. The World Bank has missions in developing countries that deal with the agencies that report national incomes. These missions may sometimes catch errors, or prevent fraud, in the accounts. The European System of Accounts has also helped standardize national income measurements.

The World Bank and the International Monetary Fund now collect detailed national income data electronically. The rapid advance of digital communications makes the information about any economy more readily available so that there are more and more ways for people to verify a country's national income as time goes on, and eventually to use such figures as a basis for risk management contracts.

Index number theory has shown important developments over the decades in allowing us to define the level of prices in a national economy. Economic theorists in the first half of this century studied the derivation of an optimal consumer price index and became aware of certain biases that can be caused by simple index number formulae.[12] Similar advances in asset price indexes have also been made.[13]

We still do not have reliable data on many significant economic variables, for instance, a reliable price index of commercial real estate that is based on actual transaction prices; the best available indexes are based only on appraisals. There are no reliable published indexes on occupational income based on repeated measures of individual incomes, analogous to the repeat sales indexes we developed for home prices. Nor are there personal income indexes based on other personal characteristics. But extrapolating from recent progress, we may expect to see these and other useful indices of economic data before long.

New Electronic Money

Historically, systems of risk management have functioned only to the extent that a means of exchange—a currency—has been available. Currency provides the medium in which risk management contracts are transacted. The more fluid and adaptable the currency, the greater the possibilities for covering a broader range of risks.

Hand-to-hand currency has been a prominent institution in human society for over two thousand years, but it is now gradually being replaced by various forms of electronic money as well as credit cards and debit cards. Automatic payment systems require little human intervention beyond the use of the item or service to be paid for. For instance, in some hotel mini-bars, merely removing the item from the shelf automatically sends an electronic signal that causes the item to be charged to the room account.

In 1997 Hong Kong introduced a contactless smartcard called Octopus that allows people to pay for items (including convenience store purchases and transportation services) by merely swiping one's wallet over a sensor; one does not need to remove the card from the wallet.

Tolls on highways are increasingly being collected by transponders, small boxes installed in the car, that connect to a computerized accounting system. As the car passes a sensor on a toll highway, the account is automatically charged the fee for the use of the highway. These systems allow more complex setting of prices, allowing for peak-load pricing that is higher in times of congested traffic, thereby encouraging people to use the highways at less crowded times. Singapore, where every car has a transponder and toll use extends far beyond the expressway system, has shown great creativity with such systems, suggesting what we can expect around the world eventually.

Computers continually manage peak-load pricing, making it responsive to more and more information. The system does not have to adhere to fixed peak-load hours as has been the case with most similar systems. It can respond to the traffic situation in real time, varying over time and place in complex ways, since the system has continuous data about the use of roads in different places. In the future, the system can provide people with useful information about current and expected future peak-load pricing of various routes. People will be able to program in their alternate routes to work, knowing the expected costs (in terms both of user fees and of time in heavy traffic) of the routes.

Transponders are already beginning to be used to pay for goods and services other than highway tolls. McDonald's restaurants have experimented with charging automobiles using existing transponder systems (E-ZPass in New York, Speedpass in Chicago, and FasTrak in Los Angeles) for meals purchased at the drive-through windows. People carrying a personal transponder could in the future have the convenience of walking out of any store with whatever they want, seeing the items automatically charged to their account.

Payments without coins or currency can now be made for any person to person transactions. The advent of person-to-person (P2P) payment systems has made it easy for individuals to pay other individuals electronically. The Silicon Valley firm PayPal, which is used on eBay and on about twenty thousand other Web sites, makes it easy to e-mail money to others.[14] With the use of handheld e-mail devices such as the Palm VII, one can stand on a street corner and instantly pay another person without using any cash. The European firm Paybox has also made such payments possible using mobile telephones.

New payment-system technology will also make it commercially feasible for businesses to charge very small prices for correspondingly small online services by lowering the difficulties of making payments. While efforts to establish micropayment systems by such firms as Digicash, Cybercash, Gemplus, and Mondex have not yet been very successful, they or their counterparts eventually will be.

Such convenience may sometimes seem inconsequential. But in fact it is fundamental. With convenience come possibilities for the future. Any reduction in transactions costs means that we can make more transactions. The systems will allow businesses to profitably offer services with very small prices to very large numbers of customers, which will enable them to pursue some business models never before seriously considered. Moreover, there are profound positive consequences if payment systems have the ability to interact in a sophisticated way with individuals, clarifying the real cost or real benefit of a given transaction, taking account of their circumstances at that moment and allowing payments in terms of formulas instead of fixed cash amounts.

New Technology for Exchange of Risks

Just as risk management systems depend on money as a medium of exchange, so too do they depend on markets as a means of transaction. As time goes on, the cost of trading declines, and with that, the scope of risks that can be traded increases.

Online trading dates its origin with the creation of the NASDAQ (National Association of Securities Dealers Automated Quotations system) in 1971. Until that time, small stocks prices were quoted on paper "pink sheets." The National Association of Securities Dealers hired Bunker Ramo, Inc., to figure out how to string wires linking far-separated brokerages to provide up-to-date information on members' screens. Bunker Ramo's achievement set the stage for advanced electronic trading. A fully electronic system was adopted by the London Stock Exchange in 1986, and many other exchanges around the world have followed. Many derivatives exchanges outside the United States, such as Eurex, Euronext, and the Sydney Futures Exchange, have become electronic, and U.S. exchanges are likely to rely increasingly on electronic systems in the future.[15]

The use of a "trading floor," where stock traders meet to buy and sell in person, is rapidly declining. The trading floor survives at the New York Stock Exchange, but even there small orders are now filled using an electronic system called SuperDot. In addition to electronic exchanges, we now have a variety of electronic communications networks (ECNs), such as Instinet, Island, Archipelago, REDIBook, and Bloomberg. The advent of online trading systems has drastically lowered the costs of trading and hence expanded the menu of items that can ultimately be traded.

New techniques have been developed for trading many assets at once. Exchange-traded funds (ETFs) allow investors to trade whole portfolios of stocks on the regular stock market as if they were individual stocks. ETFs began with the Standard & Poor's Depositary Receipts (Spiders) on the American Stock Exchange in 1993 and their use has exploded since.

Auction theory, a domain of mathematical economics and game theory, has over the last two decades developed ideas on how we can achieve new and more efficient ways of matching buyers and sellers.[16] These changes have had substantial impact. Led by economic theorists, much of the capital stock of the Soviet Union was auctioned off in the early 1990s with an innovative voucher system.[17] Now frequencies on the radio spectrum are auctioned off, young doctors find their residencies through a sophisticated market mechanism, electricity is produced by many different sellers in an electronic market, and on eBay and other auction sites huge exchanges allow individuals to trade a million goods.

Market microstructure theory,[18] a branch of mathematical finance, has offered new ideas on how to use electronic technology to make trading more efficient, advances that have paid off with some important financial products, such as the parimutuel digital call auction developed by Longitude, Inc., in 2002.[19]

These advances in technology for exchange of assets will make it possible to trade more and more kinds of financial assets. The richness of our financial markets will increase, and with them the possibilities for risk management.

Identification Devices Tied to Databases

For critical risk management purposes, we must keep track of who is who, so that the right person receives benefits and the right person pays claims. Since ancient times human society has kept track of who is who on the basis of inborn human facial recognition abilities and social networks, as well as props such as books of record, letters of introduction, identification cards, and passports. The ability to identify specific individuals is so fundamental a tool for social organization that birds and fish have this ability; even some social insects do.[20] Human society is at a historic moment where our computers will be able to recognize us individually and couple that recognition to vast databases of information.

Computer systems have evolved for biometrics, that is, identification through such biological identifiers as fingerprints, handprints, facial features, and irises, retina, and voice patterns. All of these systems have been improving in accuracy through time. In the future some of these systems will be nearly perfect at identifying individuals. Even identical twins will be reliably distinguished. Some of these systems can be operated at the keyboard of personal computers, while others can be operated without the individual's consent or knowledge, for instance, via video cameras as they pass through an airport.

The cost of such technology is steadily falling. The incorporation of such technology into an information infrastructure that provides easy and standardized access to the data will stimulate critical new technologies for financial risk management.

As identification technology develops, it will be necessary to ensure individual privacy. Fortunately, modern digital technology can be discriminating about what it makes public and selective about what it makes available. Concerns about privacy should not lead us to try to stop progress in identification systems tied to databases. The challenge is to design these systems correctly. Proper design of systems needs also to attend to the issues of fraud and identity theft.

Identification systems are gradually developing around the world. According to Privacy International, roughly one hundred countries have compulsory national identification cards with unique numbers for each person. For example, Finland has adopted a national smart card with 16 kilobytes of memory that functions as a passport, and allows individuals to file their tax returns and to register as a job seeker. South Africa plans to adopt a national identification card with fingerprint templates supporting a smart card. Estonia plans to issue a smart card that will include biometrics. China has a plan to issue seven hundred million smart cards that would identify every adult there.

The United States has come close to creating a national identification system. In 1993 President Bill Clinton proposed that each American be given a health-care identifier to allow tracking of medical records and to help prevent fraud. With the 1994 health care bill Congress allocated funding for the identifier, but the cards have never been issued. Over the years, many other countries have been weighing issuing smart identification cards for their citizens.[21]

Despite public opposition to the identification inventions in some countries, their eventual adoption is quite likely after they are modified to address particular concerns about privacy and possible government and corporate abuse.[22] Recently, Larry Ellison, the founder and chief executive officer of Oracle Corporation, argued that a national ID system is necessary to prevent terrorist attacks like those of September 11, 2001, and offered to "provide the necessary software for free."[23] Providing a safe and reliable identification system for hundreds of millions of people may have been a daunting technical challenge a few years ago, but no longer.

Identification systems should be designed so that an individual has a lifetime identity that can be accessed by others for legitimate purposes without revealing personal secrets, which is essential to upholding contracts. Electronic identification today, which involves a hodgepodge of passwords and computer cookies, has to be replaced with something more comprehensive and orderly.

Sometimes great hopes are expressed for identification systems integrated with other basic systems of our society. For example, the Malaysian government has built from undeveloped jungle a "multimedia Super Corridor" (MSC) called Putrajaya, a city of the future, an "intelligent capital."[24] Putrajaya has been a major site of investment in digital hardware, and Malaysia is the first country to embark on a program to give each citizen a multipurpose smart card. The Malaysian smart card identifies that person, serves as a driver's license, passport, and medical record, and will eventually allow access through their electronic network to a wide variety of governmental, banking, transportation, and health services. The prime minister of Malaysia, Mahathir Mohamad, sees great inspiration in their new system of identification and networks.

> We are not just upgrading. We are talking here about something much more far-reaching. We are talking about changing the way we live and work in the MSC. . . . The MSC will be the R&D center for the information based industries, to develop new codes of ethics in a shrunken world when everyone is neighbor to everyone else, where we have to live with each other without unnecessary tension and conflicts.

The actual implementation of the Malaysian system, however, has been very slow. The plans are ambitious for a developing country, and it is too soon to say what will come of them.

But their inspiration is solidly based: The new technology is very powerful, and we must all think how we can use it well. We will have to consider carefully how the new power to identify people and link them to databases can serve our purposes, and not create opportunities for exploitation or oppression. Clearly, identification systems are fundamental to any far-reaching hopes for risk management, for only through these can there be a human-computer interaction that is capable of transforming the economic basis of an individual's life. We will need to integrate such identification systems into these visions for the future if they are ever to succeed.

Decline of the Underground Economy

The underground economy, the shadow economy where transactions are informal and made in cash to evade taxes, has apparently been growing in many countries in the last half century. But there is reason to expect that it will decline in the future.

The new world of digital information networks can make it increasingly difficult for people to hide, dissemble, cheat, and evade. The amount of information available continues to grow, and it is increasingly susceptible to computer analysis by the computerized surveillance of authorities. While we generally have mixed feelings about the authorities' increasing ability to watch us and the possible bad uses that can sometimes be made of this ability, we have to recognize this for what it is and make the best possible use of the new abilities.

Taxation authorities around the world have already begun to use new information technology to improve their methods of apprehending tax evaders. In the future, evading taxes by paying in cash and keeping no records will be harder and harder. As various forms of electronic money become more common, anyone who does a business in cash will become increasingly suspect of evasion or criminal activity. In the future, paying in cash may become regarded as a shady or suspicious activity. While the ability to pay other individuals using electronic money is not yet commonplace, when it becomes commonplace, it will further speed the end of the underground economy.

Encryption technology, the technology of private communications using codes, is of course an aspect of new digital technology that makes it easier, in some ways, for people to evade and cheat, but in practice the technology may have just the opposite effect. In some cases, the

79

very use of encryption technology inappropriately will be grounds for suspicion. Encryption technology will actually help foster risk management when used appropriately to enforce privacy and prevent information from being inappropriately used. With encryption technology properly in place, people will more freely share information with others and more freely bind themselves to reveal information in the future, therefore enabling them to make better contracts.

The inability of citizens to evade and cheat offers opportunities for social planners. We will be able to achieve a more equitable income distribution because we will be observing it more accurately.

The underground economy as it exists today has its own culture, a culture of loyalty to one's close friends rather than to a larger society, a culture dominated by the sense that people can work things out together without interference from any government. A widespread conviction in this culture holds that our common humanity surpasses rules and regulations set by distant lawmakers. As the underground economy disappears, its denizens will drift toward other outlets for such anti-mainstream feelings and will have to find other venues for this expression of their individuality. But the passing of the underground economic culture will be of great benefit for society's ability to manage risks and secure a more equitable distribution of wealth.

Increased Complexity and Enforceability of Contracts

Computer searches of mortgage records today determine if a property submitted for a mortgage has already been mortgaged to someone else. We can do this search for other mortgages because the mortgage contract is common and standardized and an industry has developed procedures to ensure that there are relatively few frauds. We also have credit reports available on line that summarize an individual's loan contracts and past payment performance. But we do not yet have the ability to find out if someone has made other contracts, outside of the mortgage and credit arena, compromising his or her ability to fulfill the terms of new contracts.

In the future, however, such reports will be possible and might include information about a broader spectrum of commitments that people make, including rental agreements, employment contracts, and income risk management contracts. As more and more of new kinds of contracts become standardized and are integrated into an electronic reporting system, the extent to which information about the terms of the agreement can be communicated for systematic use will grow.

At the present time, an individual sometimes cannot effectively make a contract to do something in the distant future in exchange for a payment today because no one can ascertain whether the person has made the same contract with someone else. And difficulties enforcing a contract arise when people can move from one country to another and disappear from our radar screen.

A smart computer network system could keep track, in an intelligent way, of all contracts that individuals make so that the system ensures that the contracts do not conflict with one another. While some dangers are implicit in such a system, in terms of possible invasions of our privacy or misuse of the information about our contracts, and while any such system still has to recognize the limits of the humans who use it, a positive good can result from such a network: It will make possible more effective and more extensive contracts.

Technological Opportunities

The new information technology has provided us with so much more information about risk, and the resultant economic dislocations and inequality, that it puts economics today roughly where astronomy was when the telescope was invented or where biology was when the microscope was invented. We can see so much more about the circumstances that make some people successful and others unsuccessful that we no longer have to rely on blunt instruments to remedy the unfortunate situations that often appear.

And we can design responses to these situations with our computers. We can integrate our lives better with these computers, with our improved identification technology and our encryption technology. And we can make more reliable, and more complex, contracts with one another. Powerful steps can be taken to improve our lives with this technology in the future. It provides the raw materials for the innovations that will shape the new financial order.

SIX

The Science of Psychology
Applied to Risk Management

THE LAST FEW DECADES have seen great progress in research in the science of psychology. Financial innovators can make use of this research to help them better understand how the human mind assembles its view of the world and better devise new risk management technology that can manage society's biggest risks. These risks evolve over very long periods of time and thus any institutions developed to manage them require substantial long-run reliability and stability. Ultimately, these institutions must make sense to people—which means they must start from a firm psychological footing.

While the new information technology makes many things possible in principle, there are inherent *human* limits in its application. Ultimately, the computers that implement the new information technology must interact with real people. Designing risk management solutions to work well for real people is analogous to what engineers call "human factors engineering," the engineering that takes account of human foibles, such as designing an automobile dashboard so that human errors are minimized. What we need might be called human financial engineering.

Computers' management of information is infinitely variable; to change it, one needs only rewrite the computer program. Programmers can enter a computer program and rearrange it at will, and can allocate billions of bits of information from one storage location to another with no trouble at all. But the human mind is stuck in certain patterns of thought. Thus, the computer programs must be designed around existing parameters of the information processor that the computer must interface with—the human brain—which is why the study of human-computer interaction (HCI) is one of the most rapidly advancing fields of computer science today. In recognition of this fact, many computer-science departments offer degrees with an HCI specialty.

The first step, then, in designing a new risk management infrastructure is understanding of the frailties of human decision-making.

Cognitive psychology has revealed many kinds of errors that tend (not always, but often) to occur.

Psychological Framing

Notably, psychologists have shown that the human mind is vulnerable to errors of *framing;* that is, how we frame the picture, the categories into which we mentally place things, affect our decisions. Here, I am using the term *frame* as introduced by psychologists Daniel Kahneman and Amos Tversky in the 1970s and refined through much subsequent psychological research. Kahneman defines term "framing" as "the dependence of choices on the description and interpretation of decision problems."[1] This dependence is a sort of "bug" in the human program, creating fundamental inconsistencies and fallacies in human actions unless the subject is in an environment that helps protect from these errors.

Issues of framing have played a fundamental role in psychology, political science, and sociology. Psychologists have shown through experiments how fragile human judgments are, and how they are affected by context or reference points.[2] Political scientists study how ideological or political questions are influenced by deliberate reframing, or "spin," given by political leaders and amplified by the news media, and how public responses to political issues are subtly but powerfully altered by such framing.[3] Sociologists have studied how changes in media emphasis, or media assumptions about what is important, shaped social attitudes.[4] Financial innovators have to combine the insights from these other social sciences, along with economic theory, to make fundamental progress in risk management.

The names and symbols we attach to things comprise one important element of framing. The human mind easily accepts an array of assumptions and contexts about the names we give things, and the named object takes on these assumptions and attributes. For example, a number of psychological experiments indicate that calling a risk management contract "insurance" may make people more receptive to it.[5] The word *insurance* has the association, in our culture, of safety, good sense, integrity, and authority.

Leland O'Brien and Rubinstein (LOR), a California financial firm, launched a campaign in the early 1980s to sell a sophisticated "dynamic-hedging" product to protect institutional investors against losses in their investments. Hayne Leland, one of the firms' founders, had written an article in 1980 about the product, titled "Who Should Buy Port-folio Insurance."[6] But when LOR tried to market their product to in-stitutional investors, they were told that they could not call it insurance because it did not satisfy the legal definition of insurance. LOR offi-cially referred to their product with the abstract and technical name "dynamic asset allocation," and carefully explained to their clients that their product was not really insurance. But their clients, and the media, were stuck on the name "portfolio insurance" and would not accept the new name. LOR tried informally calling it "portfolio assurance," to avoid using the word "insurance," but that did not take either. The market became eager for portfolio insurance, and LOR did not stren-uously correct their customers when they used the term. LOR's de-mand swelled and they sold tens of billions of dollars worth of the product. Names matter.

Effective innovators have always been attentive to names and sym-bols, as must we be in any further innovation. The recent advances in in-formation technology also offer us an advantage in appropriately adopt-ing new names and symbols. User-friendly computer technology has recognized the importance of symbols, such as the Windows icons and the succession of names and symbols that are activated through mouse clicks. The new information technology represents a watershed for the creation of names and symbols. It also presents us with an opportunity to attach names and symbols to programs and formulas so that these are no longer complex and forbidding but natural and simple.

Efforts to frame risk management products in ways that will in-crease their acceptance by the public will be enhanced if they draw upon familiar concepts, known as "primitives." Primitives in human thought are words and categorizations that come naturally to people, that provide an intuitive frame of reference for all thinking, to which more advanced or more derivative concepts will naturally be mentally anchored.

Primitive concepts include *private property, government, law, family, parents and children, kindness, sharing, charity, gift exchange, social hierarchy, religious symbols, honor, obeisance, leaders, heroes,* and *fairness,* concepts that are recognized by three-year-old children, by every nor-mal person in the world. Their use in names of fundamental concepts, and in the forms that applications take, must be done judiciously to en-sure public acceptance and compliance.

Anchoring

Psychological experiments confirm that when people must make quantitative judgments their conclusions are easily influenced by any easily visible quantity—an anchor—even if this quantity is irrelevant. For example, on a questionnaire that asks respondents to indicate into which of a number of income brackets their income falls, their answers tend to be "anchored" by the brackets given. If the questionnaire suggests high incomes, people will give higher answers for their own income. Or if people are asked to estimate some physical quantity, after having recently seen another totally unrelated quantity, their answer is affected by the unrelated quantity.[7]

Anchoring can affect even serious and expert judgments. In one experiment, real estate brokers were asked to estimate the value of a house by inspecting the house for up to twenty minutes and reading a ten-page packet of information about it, which included characteristics of the house and the recent selling prices of comparable homes. The experimental design centered on manipulating one number that appeared in the packet: the seller's proposed asking price. Those brokers who saw a much higher asking price gave values that averaged over 10 percent higher. When asked later to name the top three facts that influenced their estimated appraisal, less then 10 percent of the brokers mentioned the asking price.[8]

The lesson is that when people do not have clear ideas how to value things, they are highly influenced by arbitrary anchors. We must therefore design the anchors afforded by our economic institutions to provide as sensible a guide as possible.

Many of the ideas for a new financial order that I will present in detail in part 3 of this book involve important changes in anchoring. Macro markets would change anchoring from local and current to global and long-term. Inequality insurance would change the anchors for our tax system from arbitrary tax brackets to a measure of income inequality. Intergenerational social security would change the anchor for our social security system from an absolute standard of living for retired persons to a standard of sharing between the generations Moreover, indexed units of account would change reference points from nominal to real. The literature on psychological framing supports the notion that these ideas can yield stable devices that will work as intended.

Framing of Gains versus Losses

People's preferences and judgments are fundamentally affected by their frame of reference, by their assumptions about the present, the comparison point, the natural starting point. People may behave in ways that appear erratic and inconsistent if changing circumstances alter their frame of reference.

The psychologists Kahneman and Tversky showed the importance of reference points in a number of experiments. For example, in one experiment they asked each of two groups of experimental subjects to choose between medical programs to treat an outbreak of a rare disease that was expected to kill six hundred people.[9] Both groups of subjects were given descriptions of the same two programs, but the wording, and suggested reference point, was different. One group was asked to choose in terms of gains, between Program A that would save two hundred lives for sure and Program B that had a one-third probability of saving six hundred lives and a two-thirds probability of saving none. Most said they would choose Program A. They were risk averse for gains, preferring the "safer" program that guaranteed that two hundred lives would be saved. The other group was asked to choose in terms of losses, between Program C that would result in four hundred people dying, and Program D that had a one-third probability that no one would die and a two-thirds probability that six hundred would die. Most people said that they would choose Program D. One could say that they were risk-seeking as regards losses in the sense that they were willing to risk two hundred more deaths with the hope of getting off with no lives lost at all, much as gamblers who have lost money often take bigger and bigger risks with the hope of regaining their losses.

It should be clear that in the Kahneman and Tversky experiment that the only difference between the descriptions of the programs was the reference point—whether lives are measured as lives or as lives saved, and so the experiment is revealing of fundamental human patterns of behavior. Many other experiments have confirmed the importance of framing of gains versus losses.

This human tendency to be risk seeking for losses, to follow the impulse to make a dangerous gamble, to get off scot-free without any losses, can impose a strong barrier to improving the amount of risk management in our society. This tendency has the potential to make people unwilling to pay insurance premiums to prevent losses, if they frame the insurance premium as itself a loss. The insurance premium must somehow be reframed as something other than a loss. We shall see later that the life insurance industry made great strides in the nineteenth century when it was able to reframe insurance premiums as investments. Implementation of other risk management devices, such as some of those described here, must be similarly attentive to framing of losses versus gains.

After losses are realized, they are felt differently from gains. A loss may generate feelings of regret, or other painful feelings. One knows in advance that experiencing a loss produces these feelings and thus one takes actions to avoid the prospect of such feelings.[10] In this sense, the reference point matters fundamentally, for with a different reference point one would experience no regret. If one has become accustomed to thinking that one has something, one may make efforts, endure hardships, take risks, or make enemies, to avoid losing it. But if one never thought of having it in the first place, one may view not having it with equanimity.

The dependence of decisions on framing of gains versus losses is central to the design of risk management devices. Some of the innovations described below have such dependence as fundamental parts. The inequality insurance innovation, for example, is fundamentally linked to reframing the standard of comparison. It is important, according to that idea, to decide on and enforce a standard for limits to economic inequality *before* the increased equality is realized so that the impact of the new economic institutions can be viewed as sharing gains rather than imposing losses.

Risk as Feelings

Psychologists have noted that individuals tend to focus irrationally high concern and worry on small risks, risks that hardly matter for their lifetime livelihoods, risks that should average out over long intervals of time and amount to nothing. At the same time, they pay little attention to some of their most significant risks. This poses a challenge for designers of risk management devices, for unless these are properly framed, people will not perceive their benefits.

The tendency to devote inordinate attention to small risks is a keystone of the psychological theory of individual reactions to risk developed by Kahneman and Tversky.[11] Thus, for example, many people routinely buy extended warranties on small appliances but neglect to buy disability insurance. As such large risks appear in our lives, we cannot bring ourselves to forget about the little day-to-day risks, but we seem to be able to easily forget about the big lifetime risks.

People are unstable in their viewing of risks, sometimes becoming emotionally involved, sometimes showing complete indifference. People tend to focus on risks for which there are vivid mental images—for example, catastrophic events that generate vivid television coverage invariably lead to immediate public recognition of risks.[12] One famous example of overreaction to vivid images is the public's interest in insurance against their death in a crash of an airplane they are about to board, even if the insurance is wildly overpriced given the minuscule probability of a crash.[13]

Risks that evolve gradually over long intervals, such as the risk of a decay in one's occupational income, tend to lack vivid images. And yet, in terms of frequency of serious damage, these risks are likely to be the far more important. That is why a central design element of risk management devices is to create a focus of attention on these bigger risks. Risks that relate to hypothetical events in the distant future are not normally capable of arousing emotions in people.

Psychologists have found a considerable amount of evidence for the "risk as feelings" theory, that is, that people's responses to risky situations depend directly on emotional influences such as worry, dread, or anxiety, responses of the primitive part of the brain rather than the cortex.[14] Purely intellectual recognition of risks does not lead to action against the risk but must be accompanied by emotional content. The frontal lobe of the cortex transforms images of absent events into experiences of pleasure or discomfort. Frontal lobotomy patients, for whom part of the brain in this area has been removed, seem always confined in their attentions to the present, blithely unconcerned about any distant risks. Normal people, unfortunately, can share this same lack of concern if their emotional responses are not triggered.

The risk as feelings theory has been anticipated in books on how to sell insurance, which, while sometimes advocating what seems to be cynically manipulative sales tactics, nonetheless provide confirmation from a different quarter about psychological barriers to human action against risk. One such book, *Why People Buy* by Guy E. Baker, emphasizes that the insurance salesperson should start with a fact-finding session that reveals the prospect's exposure to risk, vividly describing the potential bad outcome and highlighting the error the prospect has made in not yet buying insurance. The book then describes the moment when the sale becomes real.

> Once the prospect comes to grips with the reality of his circumstances, he becomes agitated and will want to remedy the problem. This agitation is the key to the sales process. It is here the negotiation begins. . . . I believe this is the process that everyone goes through when they are faced with tough decisions. The buyer takes action because he believes the action will relieve the pain and solve the problem.[15]

Because actions are not taken without emotion, the ability of any economic institution to generate actual human action against risks depends on the kinds of images and associations it embodies. The mechanism by which human emotions are triggered by abstract concepts such as risk is tied in to the vivid mental images that are mentally associated with the abstract concepts.

Some of the reframing described part 3 of this book can encourage people to see their risks more vividly. Creating markets for long-term claims on occupational incomes, or for prices of homes by city, will call attention to the risks that individuals face. Hearing on a television news show about large changes in a day in the value of one's occupation or the value of the homes in one's city will create a vividness and sense of reality. Creating livelihood insurance on occupational incomes or for home prices may then create a route of escape from these concerns.

Commitment and Prior Choice

Issues of framing go far beyond mere naming. We can change the way we frame some of our basic concepts. How we describe ourselves and divisions in our society can have profound impact on how risks are borne and how wealth is distributed. People ultimately have no natural way of fully knowing how much ought to be theirs and how much should belong to others. The world of business can force us into many very difficult situations in which who gets what has not been unambiguously established, with no easy way of deciding how much one should by rights demand and fight for and how much one should let others take as a matter of fair-dealing, honesty, and consistency with one's own image as a decent person. One's behavior in these ambiguous situations can be easily changed by reframing.

One psychological experiment shows the importance of the framing of *one's own expectations of oneself* in decisions of whether to share with others. In this experiment, a person who was identified as a psychology lab student telephoned random people, asking them to answer some survey questions for a research study to find out how people respond to various telephone requests. One of the questions on the survey was whether the subject would agree, if asked, to collect money for the American Cancer Society. Forty-eight percent of the respondents answered yes. This was cheap talk, of course, since they were only answering a hypothetical question. Three days later, apparently as an odd coincidence and with no apparent connection to the earlier survey, a representative of the American Cancer Society called the same subjects, asking for three hours of their time collecting money. Thirty-one percent of those who were questioned by the psychology lab student earlier agreed to do the work, compared with only 4 percent of a random sample of others who were contacted only by the representative. Apparently, those who were asked the first question (and answered yes) felt that they had committed themselves, in their own minds, as contributors to this cause and felt that consistency demanded that they should be true to their word, even though they had actually made no promise. The simple experience of being asked by a lab student a few days earlier appears to have reframed people's images of *themselves* as civic-minded people[16]

The same human tendency revealed by experiments such as this is at work in ensuring public acceptance of some of our most fundamental risk management devices, such as our progressive tax and welfare system. People may harbor selfish and unfeeling impulses at times, but their images of themselves and of their relations to society prevent them from acting on these impulses. Hence, they tend to accept government redistribution programs that may cost them personally, if the programs are framed right.

These experimental results have powerful implications for our hopes to produce a good society. If we can institutionalize changes in framing, we can then expect to achieve fundamental changes in our willingness to share with others, and to share risks with others. A number of the innovations presented here can help achieve that. That we have made private risk-sharing compacts can help us view ourselves as cooperative people; that we have elected a government that makes such compacts can help us view ourselves as a cohesive nation.

Consistency

People have a fundamental preference for consistency, a fundamental urge to be true to their principles and beliefs, and tend to experience negative emotion when they feel that they have been inconsistent. Psychologist Leon Festinger called this tendency "cognitive dissonance."[17] The preference for consistency, while sometimes creating rigidity in judgment, is a valuable human trait overall because it makes us reliable and systematic. This human tendency can be used in framing new risk management devices so that cognitive dissonance serves to enhance the stability of the devices. Successful innovators in the past have implicitly recognized this, at least at an intuitive level.

The theory of cognitive dissonance recognizes that a preference for consistency is not absolute and that people can and do change their beliefs, not only for good reasons but also for self-serving, duplicitous reasons. Festinger argued that such changes are usually social processes:

> If a cognitive element that is responsive to reality is to be changed without changing the corresponding reality, some means of ignoring or counteracting the real situation must be used. This is sometimes well-nigh impossible, except in extreme cases which might be called psychotic. . . . Usually, for this to occur, the person would have to be able to find others who would agree with and support his new opinion. In general, establishing a social reality by gaining agreement and support of other people is one of the major ways in which a cognition can be changed when the pressures to change it are present.[18]

The danger in the context of risk management is that after the outcome of the risks becomes known, the losing parties would disavow the risk management contract and even lobby the government to cancel the contract retroactively. The risk of such an outcome is reduced if it is made extremely clear at the outset of the contract that the contract was made with a good purpose, that the use of such contracts requires the good faith of all parties, and that there was social consensus for such a contract from the outset. This perception can be reinforced by social rituals and public ceremonies that reveal the general consensus for the risk management purpose. It will then be difficult for people to argue against this general consensus, to set in motion a process whereby such a public consensus is replaced with another. Framing the risk management contracts with the appropriate names and symbols can reinforce our commitment to the contracts with every use of these names and symbols.

Proper framing can make all the difference as regards risk management institutions that involve large payments of money, as do many of the ideas for a new financial order described in this book. Any such payments must be regarded as freely chosen by enlightened society, and as corresponding to an objective logic and good sense that was apparent to everyone when the contract to make the payments was made.

Reciprocity and Fairness

A basic human behavior pattern is a "preference for reciprocity."[19] People tend to want to do kind acts if they view themselves as treated kindly, and to do hostile acts if they view themselves as treated badly. A sense of reciprocity is important for many financial innovations for it can enhance their stability through time.

A preference for reciprocity is expressed through a common culture representing what is fair and what is unfair.[20] There are cultural differences in interpretations of fairness, but international comparisons show a basic similarity across cultures, suggesting that attitudes toward fairness reflect a fundamental human tendency.[21]

Experimental game theorists have demonstrated the preference for reciprocity using an experiment called the "ultimatum game." A pair of experimental subjects is asked to agree on the division of a fixed sum of money. One of the subjects is designated by the experimenter as the proposer, and this subject is asked to propose how the money should be divided between the two. The second subject is designated as the receiver, and this person is given the choice of accepting the proposer's division of the money, or rejecting it altogether, in which case both subjects receive nothing. If both subjects behaved in accordance with conventional economic theory, the proposer would always selfishly take all the money but a penny, the smallest unit of currency, and the receiver would accept the penny, since there is economic gain in doing so. In fact, the proposer tends to split the money fairly evenly. More significantly, when the proposer offers 20 percent or less of the money, the receiver tends to reject about half the time, even though that means turning down the share of the money. This experiment demonstrates that matters of reciprocity can overwhelm the principle of economic interest.[22]

Psychologists Lee Ross and Steven Samuels have shown that changing the name of a game can determine whether people behave selfishly or cooperatively.[23] Their experiment involved a game known as the prisoners' dilemma. The prisoners' dilemma is one of the most famous examples used in the field of game theory to reveal people's behavior in choosing whether to cooperate. In the original example, two prisoners suspected of committing a crime together are seated in separate cells, unable to communicate with each other. As a device to extract a confession, the police tell each prisoner that if he alone confesses, he will go free and the other will go to jail for a long time. If both confess, they will both be given medium-term sentences. If neither confesses, the police will give both of them very short sentences on other charges. Each prisoner is told that the other has been offered the same deal. Of course, the best thing for both to do is not to confess. But since the prisoners are not able to communicate, the dilemma that they face is profound, involving judgments not only of the others' trustworthiness, but also the others' perception of one's own trustworthiness, and of the other's perception of one's own perceptions of the others' trustworthiness. Even though the best cooperative strategy is not to confess, it has been shown in experiments simulating this dilemma with human subjects that many do.

Ross and Samuels devised an experiment in which two groups of players were given exactly the same criteria to play a game simulating the prisoner's dilemma. The only difference between the two groups was the name of the game: the "community game" and "Wall Street game." Those who played the "Wall Street game" played less cooperatively.

Thus, any change in framing that bears on whether others are "naturally" viewed as cooperative can have a basic influence on human generosity and compliance. It is vitally important to maintain a society in which a sense of reciprocity is generally assumed. Such a sense is especially necessary if our institutions of income risk management are to survive the years. The risk-sharing innovations in this book would establish a better sense of public reciprocity. When risk sharing is massive, people will see a symbol of reciprocity that is lacking today.

Examples of Psychological Framing
in the History of Finance

We can find examples of psychological framing having a profound impact on the outcome of financial contracts, for good or for ill. These are, in fact, examples of the utmost importance, which will help establish some (though not all) of the psychological principles discussed above. Examples illustrating other of these principles will appear later in this book.

The first example concerns the reparations payments required of Germany after its defeat in World War I. These debt instruments were framed in terms of vengeance, punishment, and dishonor, primitive concepts eliciting the most negative affect. The Allied and Associated Powers imposed these substantial reparation payments on Germany with the 1919 Versailles Treaty, and they were finalized by the Reparations Commission in 1921, when wartime resentments were still very high. The Germans protested that these reparations were excessively burdensome, pleaded for postponement of payments, and then failed to make payments. In response, the French and Belgian governments marched their troops into the Ruhr in 1923 to enforce payment by direct control of the Ruhr industries. Even this failed, because of passive resistance by German workers. Germany was then offered the Dawes Plan of 1924 that reduced the reparation payments to only about 2.5 percent of Germany's national income.[24]

German taxes in 1924 were about 25 percent of national income and lower than taxes in the United Kingdom at the time. It would seem Germany should have had little trouble paying the lower reparations specified by the Dawes Plan. But the German government chose not to raise taxes or cut expenditures sufficiently, but instead chose to run a government deficit, postponing dealing with the reparations by substituting another foreign debt.[25] In the end, Germany paid little of the reparations and the remaining debts were practically forgiven at the Lausanne Conference in 1932.

Germany's failure to make the payments was ultimately due to immense resentment. There should be little surprise that the reparations induced such resentment. Indeed, the Reparation Treaty included a guilt clause, whereby Germany was forced to accept all blame for the war, thereby unambiguously framing the reparations as punishment.[26] This left no sense at all among the Germans that the reparations were a freely made national choice or that honor dictated that the reparations had to be paid. The Germans had no sense at all that their pride in their consistency dictated that they should make the payments—it was not a matter of honor. Instead, they tended to frame the losses represented by the payments as the violation of their property rights. The Germans felt no sense of reciprocity. Instead, the occupying army vividly reinforced the sense of self versus others. By some accounts, the resentment that all these factors created was so great as to be a factor leading to World War II.

In contrast, the payment of national debts freely entered into by countries is routinely accepted by most citizens in advanced countries, with only some grumbling. Income tax burdens of 30 percent, 40 percent, or more of national incomes are common, and a good share of this can go to interest on the national debt. National debts that exceed a year's GDP are routinely serviced, with interest as a percent of GDP often well exceeding the reparations the Germans were supposed to make. Defaulting on the national debt would normally be considered a national disgrace, inconceivable to most citizens. The difference between these debts and the German reparations is entirely accounted for by psychological framing.

Let us consider now an example of the opposite extreme, of successful framing that led to payments being honored over generations— old age insurance as part of the U.S. social security system. The social security system takes money from young working people and immediately uses it to support the retired elderly. In return, these young working people are told that they will in turn, when they are old enough to retire, receive retirement benefits taken from the young working people of that future date. The system seems inherently unstable because the young working people of the future, many decades later, could vote to reduce or eliminate their obligation, and so the retired people—who would have already contributed substantial amounts of income—would not then get their benefits.

The stability of the U.S. Social Security System in the 1930s was assured by its creators by the creative uses of names, allusions to property rights, repetition of symbols, so that the concept would be reinforced that the System was a social compact in effect agreed to by the generations. All of these are principles of framing.

The U.S. Social Security Act of 1934 and its amendments have incorporated wordings that create some appearance of fundamental rights. The phrase "Old Age Insurance" brought into play the powerful word "insurance." The choice of the word "contribution" rather than "taxes" for amounts paid to social security suggests that the individual is contributing to a fund for his or her own benefit, and thus that he or she has property rights over the ultimate benefit. By introducing the system by a vote in Congress, thereby anointing it with clear evidence that U.S. citizens had freely chosen it, if only indirectly, and by paying no monthly benefits at first, requiring that the first beneficiaries earn their benefits through years of contributions, gave the system the framing of a commitment undertaken with free prior choice.[27]

The acronym FICA, which appears on individual's pay stubs in explanation of the payroll deduction, stands for Federal Insurance Contribution Act. While most people probably do not know what the letters in FICA stand for, the fact that this acronym appears on pay stubs could be used in the future to argue against removing individuals' rights to benefits from these contributions. All those pay stubs with FICA on them—embodying the concepts of "insurance" and "contribution"—are repetition of symbols that would seem to stand as extensive documentation of property rights.

In fact, President Franklin Delano Roosevelt, who made the creation of social security the cornerstone of his New Deal, argued along just such lines. Roosevelt responded to critics who claimed that, despite appearances, the contribution scheme defined by the social security acts was not insurance because there was no insurance contract. Roosevelt said,

> I guess you're right on the economics, but those taxes were never a problem of economics. They are politics all the way through. We put those payroll contributions there so as to give the contributors a legal, moral and political right to collect their pensions and their unemployment benefits. With those taxes in there, no damn politician can ever scrap my social security program.[28]

The question of the constitutionality of a social security that appears to promise to transfer money from young to old far in the future was brought to the U.S. Supreme Court in 1937, on the grounds that a U.S. Congress cannot contractually bind future U.S. Congresses. The Roosevelt administration filed a brief arguing that social security was not really insurance—that there was in fact no insurance contract and that Congress could change the provisions whenever it wanted—and so no such issue of constitutionality existed. Social security was insurance only in name. Accepting these arguments, the Court ruled the system constitutional.

Despite that decision, the language that the Social Security Administration used afterward to describe the system continued to state that it was insurance, an insurance contract between government and the participant, and that the participant had a "right" to the social security benefits. In 1953, U.S. Representative Carl T. Curtis, incensed by this, held hearings in which the Social Security Commissioner Arthur Altmeyer was taken to account. Altmeyer dodged questions about what was meant by this labeling. He insisted that social security benefits were a right of the participants, even though Congress could change the benefits whenever it wanted. When it was pointed out that Congress had in fact amended Social Security to reduce benefits, and so had canceled "rights" in the past, Altmeyer answered, "It was amended to give them a better right. . . . I am confident that the Congress of the United States will continue to improve and increase the rights of the workers."[29] The social security commissioner thereby asserted a principle of extra-constitutional obligation for Congress based on good faith. To this day the Social Security Administration continues to use similar language, showing that the original framing of the U.S. Social Security System has made it a stable system of risk sharing.

The inventive use of framing, as illustrated by the history of U.S. Social Security, is not one of manipulation. Rather, it consists of setting things up right for our society, putting things in the right boxes in terms of our underlying mental structures, to guarantee the long-term stability of our arrangements. In the case of social security, the proper psychological framing done in the 1930s created a substantive claim of right that survives to this day. These aspects of the framing of insurance and social insurance have worked in the past to encourage public acceptance of some important risk management institutions. Looking to the future, we must again be inventive with reframing.

Psychology in the Ideas That Follow

Such careful attention to psychology is fundamental to radical financial innovation. With proper psychological framing, financial contracts can be made highly stable, lasting from generation to generation and from government to government. It is fundamentally important that they be stable over long periods of time, since, as we have seen, our most important risks evolve over long periods of time.

This evidence is of particular relevance for any efforts to change our basic economic institutions for risk management. Just as we can change the visual impact of a painting by putting it into a different frame, so too we can reframe economic institutions and devices by changing the apparently inessential surroundings: their reference point, context, language, and accounts of origins and reasons, with attention to the psychological impact of these changes. We can also reframe by changing the units of measurement, the conventional or standardized contractual terms, or the institutional categorization of the institutions. And we can reframe by changing the kinds of information that we see everyday, that represent our economic ambience and the context and positioning of what is seen.

SEVEN

The Nature of Invention in Finance

THUS FAR, we have reviewed some of the largest economic risks that people face, as well as the information technology and science of psychology that can help us devise powerful new financial technologies that will improve our lives. In part 3, I will offer some ideas of the major directions that such innovations might take.

Before getting into the specific ideas, however, a few brief reflections on the nature of invention in finance are called for. For some readers who are already involved with financial innovation, these reflections may be unnecessary. But many readers may be unaccustomed to thinking of our world as capable of being substantial improved through invention in finance.

An Example of Invention in Finance

Achieving a new financial order requires invention, not just simply the application of basic principles of financial theory. We need to invent specific financial devices if we are to make these things happen. Inventing takes work and time.

We may not often think of financial risk management devices as inventions: They usually involve no unique physical equipment, the inventor is rarely well known, and financial innovations have not, until recently, been recognized as patentable.[1] But they are true inventions nonetheless—indeed, some of the most exciting of inventions because they help us deal with the more profound risks to our livelihoods.

A simple example of an already well-known financial invention is a standard insurance policy on a major risk, such as a homeowners insurance policy or a life insurance policy, an invention of profound importance to our lives. Modern insurance, while it has ancient precedents, first appeared in Italy in the fourteenth century and was gradually expanded in scope after the fire of London in 1666 impressed the need to manage major risks upon a public newly sophisticated in probability theory and statistics.[2] Over the succeeding centuries, the invention of insurance became much elaborated and improved.

As with inventions of physical hardware, insurance has a number of necessary elements that function together with a certain logic. Insurance is a beautiful thing if one considers how cleverly it overcomes obstacles to achieve its aims. Not only does it help people in all manner of troubles, but it also makes possible so many enterprises that would otherwise be too risky.

The elements of a modern insurance policy include a carefully defined contract between insured and insurer, a corporate or mutual form for the insurance company, and a set of government insurance regulations that make reasonably sure that the insurance company can live up to the terms of the contract and so that the insured might know this. The contract between insured and insurer must specify a loss and a way of quantifying the claim in the event of loss so that the loss is well defined, not manipulable by the insured, and represents to the insured a genuine and significant loss.

The insurance company must use a database of loss experience and a mathematical model to create reasonable assurance that the insurance company can make good on its contract with the insured. And, just as important, the insurance policy must also be framed in a way to overcome public psychological resistance. Note that a simple insurance policy contains many elements, all of which are essential to its functioning well as intended. The modern idea of insurance was not obvious a few hundred years ago because people then had trouble imagining how these elements might be developed to work together, but it is second nature to us today.

Contagion of Inventions

Once discovered, successful inventions, whatever their provenance, tend to be copied around the world. Inventions are contagious. We see similar looking cars and airplanes all over the world because people have seen them and have realized that these designs work well. For the same reason we see similar financial institutions everywhere.

We are not usually aware of the contagion of financial inventions. People may imagine that our financial and social insurance institutions appeared when they did because they were motivated by some moral or political force rather than any inventive idea. They may imagine that the invention was instigated through the personal authority of some visible local leader rather than copied from country to country by anonymous people who, in trying to produce solutions to problems, adopted inventions from elsewhere in the world. But the truth is, the real source of the ubiquity of these institutions is simple contagion of ideas from the vast sea of inventing humanity around the world.

Inventions for dealing with financial problems, such as managing the risks to our livelihoods, are less prominent in public memory than are such conventional inventions as airplanes or light bulbs. This has much to do with the large amount of time it takes to prove the worth of an invention in the arena of risk management. When Wilbur Wright launched his "Flyer" at Le Mans, France, in 1908 in front of an audience, flying in neat, controlled circles just over the racetrack, the dramatic success of the invention of the airplane was immediately obvious to everyone and the world learned of the success within days. Making such a spectacular and sudden demonstration of the value of a scheme to protect our lifetime incomes is impossible.

Examples of Socially Moderated Invention

A great many inventions tend to spread slowly at first because their adoption requires a broad social recognition of their usefulness, a recognition that may be very slow in coming. Consider a couple of familiar examples, nonfinancial inventions that illustrate the problems and ultimate success that innovations may find.

Nowadays, as one passes through airports or train or bus stations, one finds that most people have suitcases with little wheels on them so that they need not carry the suitcase but can pull it along after them. Suitcases with wheels on them make the traveler's burden much lighter. The idea of putting wheels on suitcases seems so elementary that it ought to have been invented with the suitcase itself. Yet, as recently as the 1970s, they were nowhere to be found. Why is that?

The first successful patent on wheeled suitcases was filed by Bernard David Sadow in 1972, in Fall River, Massachusetts.[3] Sadow recalled to my research assistant that the idea of his wheeled suitcase encountered much resistance at first, and buyers at all the major department stores rejected the idea as unsaleable. They did not argue that the wheeled suitcase was a bad idea, only that no one would buy it. Such is the fate of millions of inventions, rejected not because of any flaw in the concept, but because of a perception that the public is not interested.[4]

Sadow's suitcases were a big improvement over suitcases without wheels, but they tended to wobble and fall over when pulled. The next great advance did not come until nearly twenty years later when a Northwest Airlines pilot, Robert Plath, invented a suitcase with two wheels widely spaced, so that the suitcase rolls along sideways with a wide axle between the two wheels. This, combined with a rigid re-tractable pulling handle finally yielded a stable, easily pulled suitcase that can also be used as a platform for other articles. He called it the "Rollaboard."[5]

Looking at Plath's final design, one would think that it should have been obvious all along. With simple experimentation with a few obvious wheel configurations, one would think, the advantage of the final design should have been quickly discovered. But for decades, for centuries, it did not happen; simple ideas can take a very long time to develop. What could be more obvious than a wheeled suitcase? We may note in passing that the pre-Columbian Western hemisphere knew no wheeled devices of any kind, except some wheeled children's toys.[6] Sometimes the "obvious" is just not so obvious.

Subtitles on movies, another simple invention, offer another good example of an excellent idea that was slow to evolve but eventually caught on massively. Subtitles translate in writing what is being said when the actors speak in another language or are otherwise hard to understand. Today, people widely view foreign movies in the original language with subtitles in their own language. More-over, for greater realism, domestic movies may feature brief appear-ances of characters who speak a foreign language accompanied by subtitles.

One wonders, then, why such subtitles were not used in the silent movie era. Silent movies almost invariably used intertitles for the dia-logue, which interrupted the movie: The intertitle filled the entire screen when it was displayed. Because of the completely intrusive char-acter of intertitles, they were used only infrequently in the film and the dialogue was therefore very sparse. With dialogue so sparse, the actors were obliged to engage in much exaggerated pantomime, which, in the view of most of us today, often degrades the quality of the movie to a childlike level. Producers during the silent movie era could have shot an entire movie with normal dialogue and normal action by using subtitles like those we have today.

Failed initial experiments may have prejudiced movie-going audiences against movies with subtitles. The silent movie *The Chamber Mystery,* made in 1920 by Abraham S. Schomer, used words superimposed on the picture. They were placed in comic-strip style balloons coming from the mouths of actors, not along the bottom of the screen. The movie was not a success, and the text in balloons was apparently not used again.[7] Perhaps the balloons were an annoying disruption of the visual image, and perhaps *The Chamber Mystery* itself was not good. Initial failures to win public acceptance with an invention can harm the mood for more experimentation.

Most invention takes the shape of gradual improvement of existing forms, so initial conditions matter. Invention often has to see an economically viable path of little steps from old technology to new technology. As for subtitles, their true power could not be seen before the invention of the modern sound movie. Movie producers were not about to discover changes in their art that exploited the technology of subtitles if there was not an audience for it at the time.[8]

An important factor in the slowness of the public to adopt the wheeled suitcase or the movie subtitle is that consumers only infrequently experience these inventions. Decades may pass before one needs a new suitcase after the prior one wears out. Having bought the wrong design, one lives with it for years. If one goes to one movie where balloon-style subtitles seemed especially annoying, it may be many years before one is willing to try that again.

Inventions to manage risks to livelihoods face an analogous, and much worse, problem: one has only one lifetime, one opportunity to experience the success or failure of one's risk management system. If we fail to appreciate these sorts of obstacles to the contagion of inventive ideas, we may overestimate the extent of experimentation in the past and the chances such experimentation had to succeed. We may erroneously suppose that if no one is already using an idea, then it must be a bad one.

Thinking that all good ideas have already been developed is a most common human error. Of course, assuming that current technology is the best possible is a pretty good working hypothesis to maintain as one goes about everyday life. But we often stumble in rejecting new ideas just because they are simple—thinking them *too* simple to have been overlooked—when perhaps the real reason is that almost no one has tried to implement the idea, or if and when someone did, they did not implement the idea just right, the conditions were not just right, chance events conspired against success, or the public lacked a way to appreciate it.

Radical Financial Innovation

The kinds of innovations that can transform our society are of the kind that will be slow to be adopted, then will suddenly be contagious. They may be "obvious" ideas that no one wants to deal with because everyone assumes that there is a reason why they do not work. Everyone avoids them until they see that a lot of people are using them.

Financial inventions are harder to get established than wheeled suitcases or subtitled movies because they usually require government approval and the blessing of authorities before they can be implemented. Anyone can make a wheeled suitcase at home and start carrying it around in public; no law forbids it. The only barriers are individual limitations, inhibitions and doubts. The problems are much more serious for major financial inventions.

But modern society does have the ability to make grand and important changes. We do have authorities who will listen to a case for a major financial invention and agree to allow it. We do have large corporations who are often willing to spend millions on marketing campaigns for important new ideas.

The six new ideas that follow in part 3 of this book, one in each chapter, build on the legacy of institutional evolution, offering a way of bringing economic security up to speed with the accelerating pace of economic and financial upheaval. These ideas compose a coherent picture of greater economic security, presenting a challenge to the government, businesses, and researchers intent on building an effective and humane global capitalism.

Part Three

Six Ideas for a New Financial Order

EIGHT

Insurance for Livelihoods and Home Values

CONSIDER THE SITUATION of a young person who is considering seriously preparing for an ambitious and focused career, for example, a young man who is thinking of a pursuing an advanced degree in biochemistry with a specialty in recombinant DNA technology, writing his dissertation in a laboratory specializing in adenovirus vectors. Getting the degree would be an investment measured in years and would prepare him with highly specialized knowledge. As with the novice violinist in the introduction to this book, our potential biochemist is confronted with a personal dilemma that reflects a range of risks.

Who knows what incomes of biochemists specializing in DNA technology, will be in ten or twenty years? There is evidence that there are real risks. In recent years, the livelihoods of young biochemists have appeared threatened by a scarcity of well-paying research positions as universities increasingly substitute low-paid postdoctoral appointments for regular positions. In a 1998 study, the U.S. National Research Council issued a report finding a "growing `crisis in expectation' that grips young life scientists who face difficulty achieving their career objectives."[1]

Many talented researchers already find themselves confined to a sequence of low-paid short-term jobs as their lives pass by. If this trend continues, their economic situation could be very bad. Alarmed by the trend, U.S. postdoctoral researchers recently established the National Postdoc Association to protect their economic status, but whether such an association can really stem the decline in incomes is not clear. Even though biotechnology includes some of the most impressive examples of human achievement, biotechnicians themselves may be becoming commodities with quite low incomes. Universities and biotech firms seem increasingly able to hire them on the cheap, for instance, importing technicians trained in less developed countries, which are now producing biotechnicians in great numbers.

There are other issues. Biotechnology appears to be a field in which the "winner-take-all" effect is particularly strong. Individual careers can be dramatically harmed by being just marginally less productive, as by discovering a key scientific result a week later than others. As a result, senior biotechnicians tend to demand that their juniors work long hours in their labs, sacrificing family and life satisfaction for what is ultimately a risky endeavor.[2]

Recombinant DNA technology may be fundamental to our economy, or it may be a disappointment. To date, no gene therapy using any kind of vector has been approved for clinical use. Progress may even be severely limited if the technology raises ethical or public health issues, such as researchers' unwittingly creating and unleashing a new deadly disease, that could arouse legislators against the technology. The death of teenage volunteer Jesse Gelsinger in a clinical trial in which he was injected with a genetically modified adenovirus at the Hospital of the University of Pennsylvania in 1999 received international attention.

Recombinant biotechnology could go the way nuclear engineering did years ago after concern over safety halted the construction of nuclear reactors and sharply reduced the demand for nuclear engineers, or the way aircraft engineering did after the end of the Cold War reduced governments' demand for military aircraft. Less dramatically, the field could see a glut of people or a bust in biotechnology stocks that hampers employment opportunities, or a sudden technological breakthrough that redirects the field and renders such training obsolete. Specialized scientists' careers can be highly variable, depending on the research needs in the specialty. We do not know what the future will bring.

As it is today, our biochemist personally must bear these future risks if he chooses this career, and so may decide not to pursue an advanced degree in biochemistry at all. Even if he does pursue the degree, he may be overly cautious about the specialty within it. The adenovirus vector is a highly speculative therapy at this time and might turn out to be a dead end. Scientists are studying other viral vectors besides the adenovirus, and are now aiming their research at a variety of nonviral vectors. Fearing these uncertainties, he may shift his dissertation topic away from adenovirus vectors, even though this exciting field may provide cures for cancer and other diseases.

He knows that with such specialized knowledge he may be sorely needed and may have a lucrative career, but the problem is that he also knows that risk is involved. It would be a shame if he chose not to go into a narrow field for this reason, since the risks are not big when considered from the viewpoint of society as a whole, which may need experts in specific branches of biotechnology in the future.

Now imagine that livelihood insurance policies for various fields of biotechnology were available. The biochemist could buy one of these policies for recombinant DNA technology to insure him for many years against a decline in incomes in the field, and partly against his own individual economic misfortune. The policy would be designed to pay him a regular supplement to his income over the years in the event of a decline. He would pay for this policy by committing to pay as an insurance premium a fraction of his future income over the future years, or by committing to pay a fixed indexed sum per year over the years, or by committing to pay a combination of these two. Some policies might also be written for a fixed all-at-once premium up front, an amount that he might borrow from a bank or other lender against his future income (as described in chapter 10).

He could view his prospective career in biotechnology in an entirely better light, one with considerably less risk. With livelihood insurance, he would be much like the president of a biotechnology firm with a good incentive contract, in that a floor is guaranteed on his income and exciting prospects remain for him if he excelled in the field. The risks that he would otherwise bear personally would be largely borne by an insurance company, and investors in this insurance company could diversify their portfolios so that this risk is hardly noticeable to them. Thus, livelihood insurance would serve as a vital institution in a newly democratized financial order, making the same kind of risk management available to individuals planning their lives that is available today only to corporate managers planning their companies' strategies.

Our young biotechnologist's livelihood insurance policy would have to be designed correctly. It would have to insure him against the actual loss of income, properly measured, that young people who choose a career in biotechnology will incur years later. What are these costs? If this field of biotechnology turns out to be a bad choice, years later, the costs could be high. He might have to learn a different field, perhaps in a different branch of biology. In this event, he may lose the advantage of his youthful years; he may no longer be free of responsibilities to a family in setting him on a career trajectory. He may have to go back to school to learn something else, which might cause him to suffer years of lower income if he does so after losing years of his life in a declining field. He may decide not to go back to school and try to sell himself on the market for generic biochemists, but he thereby loses the special opportunities for good income that he has prepared for. He may retire from the field of biotechnology altogether, after wasting years of his life. Even then, he may continue to face risks that are tied to his earlier career decision or tied to his broader labor-market characteristics.

Livelihood insurance that protects this particular career might encourage him when he is young to go into his chosen field, knowing that a bad outcome for recombinant DNA technology means that he will receive compensation from the insurance company over the years. He is more likely to decide to specialize narrowly, acquiring great expertise in an emerging branch of the field and disregarding a more general education in biotechnology, taking even greater chances with his lifetime career than he would ever have considered wise, but with the possibility of even better outcomes.

We can compare such career insurance to another risk management device already in place at universities—academic tenure. By guaranteeing lifetime employment at a satisfactory income to professors who are high achievers when young, universities encourage them to take risks with their choice of specialization and research directions. The universities combine this with an extensive—and ultimately very expensive—monitoring system that reduces moral hazard risk. An important part of the reason for the success of our universities is the extraordinary diversity of the expertise among their faculty that this risk management system encourages; universities are wellsprings of highly specialized knowledge for society. We need to extend the advantages of this system of risk management (without guaranteeing employment) beyond university faculties to society at large, and our new information technology should make this possible. That is what livelihood insurance would do.

Constructing Livelihood Insurance

The above example of biotechnology career insurance is just one example of livelihood insurance. As far as I have been able to determine, no precedent for such insurance exists, but for good reason: The contracts would have to rely on reliable data on career incomes available over long periods of time, which do not exist today. But with modern sources of data about income and modern information technology, and especially with the GRIDs discussed in chapter 14, an institution could be designed so that such insurance could serve everyone. Such insurance could exist for every occupation or labor market, not just those requiring specialized preparation or advanced degrees. Employers could provide livelihood insurance as an employee benefit, or labor unions could sponsor it for their members. The principle of insuring livelihoods against risk is a broad and basic one.

Private insurance policies aimed at individuals and families should cover all major risks to their livelihoods. Livelihood insurance is basic to risk management; as insurance it falls within the domain of the private sector, not of the government. The government, however, can take important steps in the realm of regulation and infrastructure to institute and foster livelihood insurance.

Livelihood insurance policies would differ from existing insurance policies, such as disability insurance or life insurance, in that they would cover losses to livelihoods from *all* causes, not just a list of special disasters. A policyholder could collect on the policy based on evidence of decline in economic value; no evidence is required that the cause of the decline appears on a pre-agreed list.[3]

Insurance institutions that hedge livelihoods will be fundamentally different from insurance institutions for most conventional risks. Risks that are already covered—disability or illness—tend to occur suddenly and catastrophically. The insurance industry is accustomed to verifying the cause of the catastrophe when it occurs and paying for the loss. A slow erosion in one's earning power over years or decades are never covered. Livelihood insurance would cover such risks, thereby helping stabilize some of the most important assets held by virtually everyone.

This slow erosion of earning power can be measured continually through time by the construction of appropriate occupational income indexes. In my 1993 book *Macro Markets* I presented a mathematical theory how such indexes can be constructed, developing a method that infers changes in income only from changes in actual individuals' incomes.[4] In a 1998 paper, Ryan Schneider and I constructed, using this mathematical theory, such labor income indexes for seven different job clusters in the United States from 1968 to 1987.[5] These indexes were based on data following *individuals* through time, rather than just computing the average income of individuals in an occupation at each point of time. A person is classified as in an occupation whether or not that individual *stays* in that occupation; this is important since when the economic status of occupations falters, many will find a different occupation, leaving behind only those who are still doing well in the occupation. In this case, indexes of actual income in that occupation may fail to measure the decline in the occupation. Properly constructed indexes that represent the true fortunes of people who start out in an occupation would be much better for risk management purposes than the available average incomes of people in occupational categories, such as those published by the U.S. Bureau of Labor Statistics and by the International Labor Organization, which are affected by the change in mix of people within an industry or occupation.[6]

Conventional insurance policies typically provide for the policyholder to pay a fixed and regular premium through time, and give the policyholder the option of canceling at any time and stopping paying the premium. Such policies work well for risks of losses that are sudden and catastrophic, such as fires or deaths, when the probability of such catastrophes does not change much through time. But this kind of policy will not work for losses about which information gradually and cumulatively unfolds through time, such as the erosion of compensation accruing to a particular career. Policy holders who see that no loss has been developing will tend to cancel their policies over the years, eventually leaving the insurance company collecting premiums only from people who are experiencing large losses. The insurance company would then have trouble covering the losses from the premiums. Thus, livelihood insurance should be designed to take account of the risk of such cancellation, and to deal with it by restricting cancellation, as by issuing policies to people who are in such circumstances that they are unlikely to cancel, or by requiring an up-front payment.[7]

Traditional insurance policies tend to be written in terms of sudden catastrophic events partly because insurance companies have learned through experience how to limit losses due to moral hazard, that is, a policyholder's deliberate creation of loss with the intention of collecting on the insurance policy. When a catastrophic event occurs suddenly, the insurance company finds it relatively easy to collect information at that time about the circumstances of the loss and to verify that the policy holder did not deliberately cause the loss. With livelihood insurance, insurers must take another route to preventing any such moral hazard. As with all insurance policies, moral hazard is a central consideration.

The concern about moral hazard would require livelihood insurance policies to be designed to insure individuals heavily against an index of *aggregate* risks, over which there is no individual control and hence about which there is no individual moral hazard. Dealing with moral hazard in this way is one of the important lessons from finance.

These policies ideally should also insure individual-specific risks at a reduced level and make the policy contingent on certain observable activities of the person covered. For example, a policy for recombinant DNA technologists could pay to the covered person 50 percent of the decline in the income of the average person who has started working in the field (and who continues to work, though not necessarily still in the field, or has gone back to school for retraining) below a specified lower level for the income. It would also pay 50 percent of the decline in the covered person's income below the specified floor for the person, and the second 50 percent contingent on the person's remaining fully employed or going back to school for retraining. In this case, so long as the person covered earns the average income for recombinant DNA technologists and continues to work, the policy will put a guaranteed floor on the person's income, thus reducing risks. So long as the person's income does not fall much faster than recombinant DNA technologists as a group, the floor will still hold approximately, and if the income does fall much faster, still the individual will be partly compensated for the extra drop. Moreover, since the person is only reimbursed for half of his or her own income drop, he or she still has an incentive to work hard, reducing, if not eliminating, the moral hazard problem.

In many cases, such as when the policy is large and moral hazard appears substantial, or when basic monitoring for moral hazard is costly or impossible, payments may have to be tied exclusively to the index of aggregate incomes to avoid excessive risk of the moral hazard. The insurance industry will have to learn under what circumstances the moral hazard is likely to play a significant role. Learning this can only be a function of years of experience with the product, as it has been with now-standard insurance.

A Menu of Livelihood Insurance Policies

The information age, with declining costs of business administration, should spawn an enormous variety of different kinds of livelihood insurance policies. For example, an individual could buy an insurance policy against an erosion of income of people in his or her occupation, against erosion of income of people with his or her characteristics (in terms of job history or education), or against erosion of incomes of currently high-income, middle-income, or low-income people as a group. No moral hazard costs would be associated with such insurance contracts because the individual has virtually no control over indexes of incomes of aggregates of people.

Livelihood insurance policies should also offer a variety of provisions for the policyholder's family members. Close family members already implicitly share risk, so livelihood insurance policies should account for the number and age of the family members, their incomes and income vulnerabilities, and even the nature of their implicit risk-sharing assumptions. Families change unexpectedly through time, through marriage, divorce, birth, and death. Moreover, the creation of new risk management policies may change the stability of the family if it displaces too much of its economic rationale. Work remains to be done to define the policies to deal with such problems, and we will need to rely on a database designed to allow livelihood insurance contracts to be settled in rather complex terms.

Some question whether livelihood insurance policies should be differentiated on the basis of genetic information. The Human Genome Project has spurred a great deal of concern about privacy of genetic information, and many people fear that if they are discovered to have a genetic predisposition to disease they could be discriminated against by health and life insurance companies.[8] As a result of this concern, governments have been involving themselves in the insurance industry's use of genetic information. In the United States, the Health Insurance Portability and Accountability Act of 1996 forbade the use of genetic information in determining eligibility for group health plans. In the United Kingdom, under pressure from the government, the Association of British Insurers agreed in 2001 to a five-year moratorium on the use of genetic test results in underwriting life insurance policies.

There is a legitimate concern that if genetic information serves as the basis for insurance, many risks will no longer be insurable because their outcome will be substantially known in advance. On the other hand, if we take a longer view of the possibilities for insurance in the future, there is an offsetting advantage to allowing insurance companies to make use of genetic information: They can use such information to identify specific risks of individuals that should be specifically insured against (such as risks that an index of incomes of people of their genetic type will decline) and to define groupings of people who have advantageous opportunities to share risks with each other. Over coming years, with further genomic research, a great deal will be discovered about the genetic basis for human behavior, and while some of this research will probably help predict future incomes, some of it will probably help identify risk classes of people for whom a livelihood insurance policy could be tailored.

Public policy in the future will have to sort out the appropriate use of the growing amount of information about individuals' future incomes but public policy need not be blunt or simplistic in its regulation of the use of such information. Measures that allow appropriate use of such information for a risk management purpose can be encouraged, while at the same time misuse can be discouraged or compensated for by governmental insurance.

Combining Livelihood Insurance
with Disability Insurance

Currently, insurance companies are able to offer insurance against adverse income shocks that result from recognizable health causes—what we call disability insurance. The essential idea has been to insure against only a certain exogenous cause to loss of income—health problems—and not to cover losses of income from other causes, such as poor fortune in business. To the extent that disability can be objectively verified, there is no moral hazard that the insured will stop working merely to collect on the policy or that the insured will stop working hard to enjoy life more, expecting the policy to cover the lost income.

But even today's disability insurance does not work perfectly. Disability cannot be positively identified; to identify it at all, the insurance company incurs a substantial cost by occasionally sending agents to observe a claimant's home and interview neighbors in an attempt to find people who are falsely claiming to be disabled to collect on their insurance (for example, observing a claimant alleging a bad back playing tennis). Such efforts to catch fraudulent claims cost money and are ultimately of limited effectiveness.

In the future, less inquisitorial and more effective techniques are likely to be developed to identify people who are pretending to be unable to earn a good income so that they can collect on disability insurance. An increased ability to catch malingerers, so long as it is not too intrusive on privacy, actually serves the policyholders' interests since it makes possible insurance companies' offering policies at lower cost.

If people who buy the policies will accept certain kinds of contractually-defined electronic scrutiny of their purchases and sales, of their Internet activity, and of biometric identification systems that track their economic activities, these could be used with computerized detection programs to isolate people who could make an income but are not trying to. Policy holders may not want to accept such an intrusion on their privacy, and no one should be forced to, but probably many would to reduce the cost of their premiums. As the digital information base increases, it may be possible, with improved information, to broaden widely the kind of "disabilities" that are insured against, including certain hard-to-diagnose disabilities.

Technology to monitor disability insurance could be combined with livelihood insurance. The livelihood-disability insurance policies could insure especially heavily variations in income that are linked to causes with very little moral hazard, such as illnesses due to diseases that cannot easily be feigned, less against disabilities that can be feigned somewhat, and even less against individual income losses that are not associated with individual disability, as well as against declines in incomes associated with occupational index changes. Combining all of these elements in a way that takes account of our knowledge of the varieties of moral hazard can result in livelihood-disability insurance contracts that have great risk management power.

Employers who today purchase health and disability insurance for their employees could establish programs offering their employees livelihood-disability insurance policies that take detailed account of the individuals' own economic circumstances. Such programs could be part of employer-run training programs for their employees and might enhance the attractiveness of such programs for employees by protecting them not only against the risk of disability but also against the risk that the training will be for naught.

Combining Livelihood Insurance with Employee Ownership Plans

Employee ownership plans, plans that encourage employees to acquire shares in the company they work for, have desirable incentive properties, reducing employee moral hazard, but tend to put employee livelihoods at great risk. These employee ownership plans can be recast by combining them with appropriate risk management, a form of livelihood insurance, that offsets the risks that the plans create. A democratized finance can provide a focused approach to incentives without incurring excessive risks.

Employee ownership plans have been growing rapidly all over the world. In traditionally capitalist countries, they are becoming increasingly common as firms try to better incentivize their workers. Often, governments actively encourage such plans through tax breaks.[9] In formerly communist countries, notably Russia, they are an adaptation of capitalist principles to the countries' collectivist past.[10]

An important motivation to set up employee ownership plans is the psychological principle that people feel more committed to their work if they know that they have partial ownership of the fruits of the labor.[11] Any effect of the plans must be largely symbolic or psychological, since the actual incentives to work harder for any given employee must be negligible for all but the smallest companies because each employee has only a minuscule effect on the overall value of the company.[12] But we should not disregard the psychological impact of symbols, not only on the success of the company but also on the work satisfaction of the employees. A substantial body of research reveals some advantages to these plans in terms of workers' attitudes and productivity.[13] But offsetting these advantages are the risks that these plans focus on the employees.

These risks are not just hypothetical: We have observed some bad outcomes. The UAL Corporation, the parent of United Airlines, has the most widely watched employee stock ownership plan in the United States. Employees now own 55 percent of the company, a most unfortunate situation for the employees because UAL stock has declined over 95 percent since 1998. In this case, heavy investment by employees in the company stock has had disastrous consequences, sometimes wiping out their retirement savings. Enron Corporation also encouraged employees to invest their pensions in Enron stock. In this case, some in the top management of the company were corrupt and effectively preyed upon their own employee-investors, with disastrous consequences when the company went bankrupt.

Employees should be able to achieve a psychological sense of personal ownership in the firm without subjecting themselves, as the employees at United Airlines and Enron did, to the risks of the corporation. Employees should be given not only investments in their own firm but also short positions (negative stock ownership) in an index of the industry to which their firm belongs so that the overall impact of changes in the industry have no effect on them. They should also be given occupational livelihood insurance protecting them against the personal economic risks to their future incomes that they incur by developing their own skills in line with the corporation's needs. These less risky positions may create the good effects of employee sense of ownership and good employee incentives without subjecting the employee to unnecessary risks.[14]

Home Equity Insurance

Creating insurance on the *market values* of individual homes, home equity insurance, even if somewhat less important than insurance on individual or family income, is probably easier to achieve at the present time. In fact, there have already been important experiments with precedents for home equity insurance, although indexes of home prices did not play a role in the insurance design as proposed here.

In 1977, the city of Oak Park, a suburb of Chicago, Illinois, began a "home equity assurance" program to help stem the "white flight" afflicting their city during a time of racial change. Supporters argued that whites would sell their property as soon as they saw a hint of racial change, because they feared the decline of value of their house. Such sales are regrettable because they create a segregation of neighborhoods even though people wanted to live in harmony with their new neighbors. Dumping houses en masse on the market because of fear of loss of property value could have the effect of creating the very property value decline that prompted the selling—a self-fulfilling prophecy. Creating insurance against losses in the value of homes not only serves a risk management purpose, but it also may prevent, by breaking the self-fulfilling prophecy, the losses from ever occurring in the first place. A similar program, modeled after the Oak Park Experiment, the Southwest Home Equity Assurance Program in Chicago, was begun by voters' referendum in 1988.

No more than a few percent of homeowners actually enrolled in the Oak Park and Chicago programs. But anyone who was particularly worried could enroll, and in fact the neighborhoods have retained their property value as racial change has progressed. Thus, the programs appear to have been a success. These programs, however, have never really been fully tested. Prices of Chicago single-family homes have been relentlessly increasing ever since the Case Shiller Home Price Index for Chicago began in 1980.[15]

Even though home equity assurance has been around for decades, it remains controversial. The forms we see today may not have been designed as well as possible. One of the complaints about the Chicago programs is that an individual must sell his or her house to collect. The program thus could possibly generate strategic selling, which could have the effect of encouraging long-time residents to exit the city. Thus, the program could conceivably have the depressing effect on real estate prices that the program was designed to alleviate. But such an eventuality could only happen after the program had already failed to prevent a housing price decline, which has not occurred.

Allan Weiss and I have made a number of proposals to improve such insurance. The most important of these is to settle the insurance claims based on indexes of home prices. With the vast electronic data sets on home prices now available, it is possible to devise indexes for many small geographic areas, even for individual neighborhoods within a city, so that the index on which the policies settle represents the price of homes whose price experience will most likely match the policyholder's. By basing the policies on such indexes, we make the insurance policy cover as close as possible the risks that the home in question faces, without creating moral hazard problems.

We also had proposals on how home equity insurance policies can be defined to deal with such issues as strategic cancellation and strategic selling.[16] According to our models, if these retail insurance products were introduced after macro markets for real estate were created, then insurance companies could hedge themselves in the macro markets for the risks that they took on by writing home equity insurance policies for individuals. Moreover, the macro markets for individual cities would provide helpful risk management as well as guidance to insurance companies who write home equity insurance policies.

There continue to be efforts to develop home equity insurance products. The Yale / Neighborhood Reinvestment Corporation Home Equity Guarantee Project has developed home equity insurance products for initial use in the city of Syracuse, New York, to help deal with concerns about the possible effects of declines in property value on the city. The project is directed by economists William Goetzmann and Barry Nalebuff. This plan, in contrast to the Chicago plans, does not stipulate that the cause of the decline must be neighborhood change.

Plans are eventually to implement these products in many cities. Two products have been developed for Syracuse: a mortgage-based product that adjusts the outstanding principal balance as housing prices fluctuate, and a direct insurance product written on a measure of the value of the home, irrespective of financing. Both products are based entirely on housing price indexes and not at all on the value of the insured house because of moral hazard and cost considerations.[17] In 2001, the U.S. Congress appropriated five million dollars to subsidize this project. However, we still must do much more before home equity insurance becomes a reality on a substantial scale.[18]

The Future with Insurance for Livelihoods and Home Values

Compelling reasons exist for the development of the kinds of insurance described here because they deal with some of the most important economic risks that people face. These policies would help prevent some individuals from falling into economic hardship for the rest of their lives. And they could help prevent unnecessary disruptions of neighborhoods and collapse of cities.

If these insurance policies were implemented for most people, they would comprise an enormous institution in our economy, far more important than the life insurance and other kinds of insurance we already have. Creating these institutions on a significant scale would be a transforming event.

NINE

Macro Markets:
Trading the Biggest Risks

IMAGINE A MARKET for the entire U.S. economy made possible by a security that pays on each share a quarterly dividend equal to a specified fraction, say, one trillionth, of that quarter's U.S. GDP. Each holder of a share would be entitled to receive this dividend each quarter indefinitely. The U.S. government or private U.S. entities who contract to pay these dividends could issue these securities.

Based on the current U.S. economy, with a fraction of a trillionth of GDP, the dividend on one share would be about $2.50 quarterly, or ten dollars each year, and this dividend would subsequently go up or down with the U.S. economy. If the U.S. economy did well in the next five years, the annual dividends then could go up to, say, twelve dollars per share. If the U.S. economy slipped into a serious economic crisis in five years, the annual dividends could fall to, say, eight dollars a share.

Potential investors in this security would want to predict the likely dividends that it would pay in the future, so the valuation they place on the security, and hence its market price, will represent the value of a claim on U.S. GDP. If the investors expected the U.S. economy to grow roughly in line with the past, and if investors in this market behaved as stock market investors have in the past, then they might value this share at $200, so that the annual dividend yield is 5 percent. If this were the price, then the market would be placing a value on the entire U.S. economy (multiplying by the inverse of the fraction, that is, by a trillion) of two hundred trillion dollars, on the order of twenty times the value of the U.S. stock market. This figure is just for example. Of course, we would have to create the market before we know the valuation it would place on the U.S. economy.

These securities could be designed to value not only GDPs of countries but also incomes by educational category or other personal characteristic, by initial income level, or by occupation, and indexes of the price of single-family home prices by city or commercial real estate by type. These securities would pay regular dividends proportional to these income flows, or proportional to the prices of major assets. The prices that these securities would command in the market would represent the market's estimated long-term value of these incomes or real estate investments.

The creation of macro markets would allow trading of enormous risks that have never been traded before. The securities tied to the U.S. GDP would allow investors around the world to invest directly in the economy of the United States. They would thus be able to diversify their portfolios much more broadly than is possible now, to include the entire U.S. economy, not just the U.S. stock market. Moreover, those who represent the economic interests of Americans could use the macro markets by issuing the U.S. GDP securities to foreigners to reduce the economic risks that Americans share.

Americans must first recognize that the great economic prosperity of their country is not guaranteed, that the hidden economic risks discussed in chapter 2 are in fact real, and that the American economy may quite possibly suffer setbacks not shared by the rest of the world. Recognizing this, American businesses can use macro markets so that during hard financial times for America people in other countries can help macro securities issuers representing people who live in America. That may sound odd to some Americans who are accustomed to thinking that America is forever guaranteed to lead the world absolutely and that no one else would ever be in a position to help Americans, but in fact this is just sound risk management. The same kind of risk management would be possible for every country: Institutions representing people in each country can issue securities against their own country's GDP and invest in the portfolio of the GDPs of all other countries, thus replacing some of their own idiosyncratic risk with the most broadly diversified portfolio possible.

There is no market for claims on the aggregate output of a country, on the GDP of the country. There is no market for claims on components of GDP either, nor for claims on various occupational or personal incomes.[1] It is very important to allow trading of the biggest risks because this allows the most massive risk sharing, and such massive risk sharing can make possible all kinds of risk management products that help individuals. The creation of the macro markets thus contributes to the kind of risk management infrastructure that is needed for the effective democratization of finance, even if most individuals never buy or sell on the macro markets. Those who issue the risk management products to individuals can do the buying and selling on the macro markets.

For example, large insurance companies that issue the kinds of livelihood insurance discussed in chapter 8 can use the macro markets to manage the risks that they incur by writing these policies. U.S. insurance companies can issue macro securities on U.S. GDP and invest the proceeds in macro markets representing the national incomes of many different foreign countries. In doing this, they are in effect swapping the risk of the U.S. national income for the better-diversified portfolio of national incomes all over the rest of the world. They will be paying dividends to foreigners tied to U.S. GDP and receiving a more stable income from all the other GDPs, which is just what the insurance company needs to offset the risk they incurred by writing the policies protecting individual livelihoods in the United States. If livelihood insurers in countries all over the world do just this sort of risk management with macro markets, then the markets can function well, with both a steady supply of issuers of the securities representing every country and a steady demand for them. This kind of risk management for insurance companies may sound complicated and technical but is well known in financial circles. What is missing is the macro markets.

Comparison with Stock Markets

If these markets are one day established, then we would regularly hear on radio and television how much the United States (not just the Dow Jones Industrial Average) and the United Kingdom (and not just the FTSE 100) moved up or down today. We would hear for example that China closed down three points today and that Brazil closed up five, and these numbers would truly represent those countries and not just stock exchanges within them. And we might hear, for example, that the medical profession went up five points and the law profession went down six. Hearing such news may seem alarming at first, especially if the macro market prices turn out to be volatile, but in fact the markets would only be revealing risks that are already present in our economies, risks that would be managed all the better because they would now be so visible.

I stressed in the introduction to this book that stock markets are not really very important to the economy, relatively speaking. When one buys or sells stocks, one is trading claims on only the small component of national income called corporate profits. Still, many people are surprised to learn that the stock market in a country is not something like a market for that country. It isn't, and in fact there is no way at all to trade the risks of a whole country.

Not only are stock markets small relative to their corresponding economies, but changes in stock prices do not correlate very well with changes in measures of the aggregate economy.[2] But the news media, ever attracted by grand and simple stories, has created the impression that a country's stock market is like an index of the country's performance. Ever focused on whether we are entering a recession or coming out of one, the media create the impression that forecasting the stock market is like forecasting recessions.

Thus, we tend to imagine that the U.S. stock market is a proxy for the U.S. economy, the German stock market a proxy for the German economy, and so on. But getting past the story telling and looking at the data, one sees surprisingly little similarity between stock prices and the overall economy. Over extended periods of time when the stock market was doing very well, we have had numerous recessions, and over extended periods of time when the stock market was doing very poorly, we also have had numerous recessions. The recessions really do not matter so much for stock markets' overall performance. Ultimately, the stock market represents claims on only a small sector of the economy, corporate profits, that does not bear a close relationship to the economy as a whole. There is nothing like the macro markets for GDP today.

Creating Macro Markets

In a path breaking new development in 1994, Citibank N.A. arranged a loan (in the form of a bond) of US$1.865 billion to Bulgaria with an interest rate tied to the growth rate of its economy.[3] The higher the economic growth rate in Bulgaria, the more Bulgaria pays as interest. This bond has served its risk management function for Bulgaria well: the growth of the Bulgarian economy since 1994 has been disappointing and so Bulgaria has not had to pay much interest. The investors who lent this money to Bulgaria are of course not happy to have received less money as interest than they hoped, but these are presumably portfolio investors whose diversified holdings can manage this.

But note that Bulgaria has successfully transferred some of its national risks to diversified investors, an especially important step for this transition economy.

The New Singapore Shares (NSS) announced by Prime Minister Goh Chok Tong in 2001 and issued to Singaporeans later that year represent yet another example. The shares, in force until 2007 and amounting in value to US$2.7 billion, guarantee a 3 percent return plus dividends equal to the economic growth rate in Singapore. While they are an interesting parallel to the macro securities described here, they are not tradable and so do not reveal any price of a claim on national income. They do not help Singapore manage its aggregate risks because they cannot be sold to foreigners. If foreigners are not assuming risk of Singapore economic growth, then these risks still remain squarely with Singaporeans.

The New Singapore Shares were distributed disproportionately to lower-income people as a device to reduce income disparities, but the distribution was also designed to give them a feeling of participation in economic success, thereby encouraging them to feel more involved with and committed to their economy. While this will indeed help lower-income Singaporeans feel better connected to their economy, it would be much better, from a risk management standpoint, if the government let them sell most of these shares to foreigners, who would then hold Singapore's risk as part of a diversified portfolio. Their sense of participation in the Singaporean economy could be achieved more in symbolic ways that would not expose them to risks, just as with the combined livelihood insurance–employee ownership plans discussed in chapter 8.

The Economic Derivatives Market created in 2002 by Goldman Sachs in the United States and Deutsche Bank in Europe is a third example. This market creates synthetic options, using the parimutuel digital call auction technology of Longitude, Inc., for such macroeconomic variables as nonfarm payroll, retail sales, and confidence indexes. These short-term options are not directly tied to economic growth rates, but the macroeconomic variables they chose have some correlation with growth rates.

These recent developments resemble the macro markets that I proposed in 1992, but they are not quite what I wanted. They do have some impact on how national income risks are borne, but they do not achieve for national incomes the same thing that our stock markets achieve for claims on corporate incomes. We need macro markets that are available to everyone, and we need enough participation in them to ensure liquidity so that one can easily buy and sell large amounts at the market price. We need pure markets, markets for conceptually simple claims, not a hodgepodge of claims. We need really long-term markets that, like the stock market, represent claims into the distant as well as the near future. Then the markets will provide "price discovery" for the value of claims on national incomes so that we know from day to day what a claim on the income of a nation is worth, not just what some unusual bond with attached warrants is worth.

In the future, some more general ways of creating vehicles for macro markets ought to be developed, ways that do not depend on an individual country's government or a large company to issue the bonds or shares. The problem with relying on governments or major companies to issue these securities is that the supply of the securities becomes too focused on the decisions of the government or the few large entities. Macro markets should provide a way of hedging risks for everyone, so there should be a mechanism whereby anyone who wants to supply these securities can.

In *Macro Markets* I proposed one way of achieving this called *perpetual futures*. They are analogous to the kinds of contracts traded at the Chicago Board of Trade or other futures markets today, except that they have no expiration date.[4] The market price of these perpetual futures should be very much the same as the price of the kind of security proposed in this chapter. A problem with perpetual futures, however, is that they really are futures contracts rather than securities. Most people are unfamiliar with futures contracts and do not like to have to deal with margin requirements and margin calls.

My business colleague Allan Weiss, with whom I discussed these problems at some length, called me one morning in 1997 with an idea of how to create ordinary *securities* whose supply automatically expands and contracts with the natural demand for them. Starting from his essential idea, he and I worked it into a patentable invention. In 1999 we secured a U.S. (now international) patent on these *macro securities*.[5] In their simplest form, macro securities are automatically issued and redeemed on demand (by a stock exchange or other entity) but only in pairs, one an "up macro" that is designed so that its price moves up when the index moves up, and the other a "down macro" that is designed so that its price moves down when the index moves up. Though the macro securities are issued and redeemed only in pairs, after they are issued the two securities, the up and the down, can be sold separately, and each can find its own price in the market. Each member of a pair has a cash account that is adjusted according to a specified economic index (GDP, for example) by reallocating across accounts. Each macro security pays dividends equal to interest on its cash account.

Suppose a pair of securities is issued for $200 when the index is 100. The account of the up macro is initially credited with $100 and the account of the down macro is also credited with $100. If the index rises to 102, the custodian of the cash accounts takes $2 from the down macro account, reducing it to $98 and puts them in the up macro account, so that the balance in the up macro account again equals the index at $102. This action means that, subsequently, the dividends on the up macro security will be higher, and the dividends on the down macro security will be lower. In this way, through subsequent dividends, the holder of the up security will be rewarded by the rise in the index. Because investors can anticipate these higher dividends now that the account balance is higher, investors should bid up the price of the long security immediately, even before any of the new higher dividends are paid. Responding quickly to new information, the price of the security will likely be rather volatile, just as are prices in the stock market.

If the index falls to 97, the custodian takes funds from the down macro account, reducing its balance to $97, and transfers them to the up macro account, increasing its balance to $103. The dividends on each security are adjusted proportionately. Investors should then quickly bid down the price of the up macro and bid up the price of the down macro, anticipating the changed future dividends.

The custodian can always make these transfers, since it amounts only to reallocating funds across accounts. After interest is paid, the total amount in the two accounts always equals $200. Moreover, the custodian can always redeem pairs of the securities because after interest payment the combined balances always stay at $200.

The transfer and interest payout mechanism ensures that the up macro will always represent a long-term claim on the index, just as a stock represents a claim on earnings. Thus, the price of the up macro security should behave much like stock prices do, anticipating future increases in the index and anticipating future decreases in the index. The price of the security need not *track* the index but will rather *anticipate* the index. This is especially important to note as regards application of macro securities to some indexes that are substantially fore-castable, such as GDP. As long as markets for macro securities are open to a broad investing public at low cost, the prices of the macro securities cannot be very easily forecasted. The prices will represent in a sense the present value of the underlying index.

Since the dividends on the macro securities are tied to the index value, the up macro is really a claim on the flow of index values extending into the indefinite future and therefore resembles a stock, which is a claim on corporate earnings extending into the indefinite future. The price of the up macro should in equilibrium reflect market valuation of a claim on the cash flow represented by the index. The price of the down macro security will move opposite that of the up macro, since the value of the two together sums to the value in the combined accounts, in this case $200. People who want to invest in the index can buy the up macro security, while those who want to protect themselves a preexisting risk related to the index can buy the down macro security.

The macro securities have the advantage over perpetual futures in that they are securities, which can be traded on stock exchanges. Investors who are exposed to a risk can buy a down macro security to create a cash flow that offsets their own risk, which they can include in their portfolio indefinitely so that they can have the satisfaction of knowing that the security is helping protect them against this risk. They will not be subject to any margin calls and have no need to buy or sell securities through time. Thus, macro securities offer a simple and user-friendly way of managing large risks.

The macro securities are automatically created whenever both a long and a short place a buy order at the same price, and automatically liquidated when a long and a short place a sell order at the same price. This automaticity resembles that of the exchange traded funds (ETFs) first created in 1993 by the American Stock Exchange with its Standard & Poor's Depository Receipts (SPDRs, or "spiders"), and now duplicated with numerous "iShares." The macro securities also bear some partial resemblance in form, if not motivation, to the "Protection SuperShares" and "Income and Residual SuperShares" invented by the firm Leland O'Brien and Rubinstein, Inc., and traded briefly on the Chicago Board Options Exchange in collaboration with the American Stock Exchange starting in 1992.

With macro securities, just as with perpetual futures, for every economic entity (person, company, or government) that holds a share that is positively exposed to the index, there is another entity (person, company, or government) that holds a share that is negatively related to the income index. In other words, for every "long" there is a "short." Ideally, the shorts would be people (like the Bulgarians referred to above) who are exposed to the risk of an index (as a Bulgarian national income or GDP index), and the longs would be international investors. In this way, the macro markets would fulfill their basic risk management function. Macro securities can be applied beyond GDP: energy costs, health costs, education costs, and other costs that impinge on individual economic welfare. Individuals could then tilt their investment portfolios that help protect them from the economic changes that concern them. But the GDP application is arguably the most important because GDP is the broadest index of economic risk.

Morality and Macro Markets

In the introduction to this book I made reference to the Rawlsian concept that distributive justice could be cast as a risk management problem. Viewed from this perspective, macro markets are a financial step toward justice.

The Jubilee Debt Campaign of 2000, represented most visibly by the rock star Bono but also championed by economists such as Jeffrey Sachs and Lawrence Summers, ostensibly aimed toward economic justice. The campaign's goal was an international agreement to forgive the foreign debt of troubled less-developed countries. Bono pressed his campaign with visits to heads of state and religious leaders.

Certainly, humanitarian reasons prompt consideration of such forgiveness; some of these countries whose economies have collapsed are suffering enormously. But canceling their debts at this point, at the expense of lenders, raises questions about the future. What effect would such a policy have on willingness to lend to such countries, if they expect that such debts will be canceled by international agreements in the future?

In the future, it would be better to prevent such dilemmas from arising by including such policies in the initial debt contracts. Countries that experience difficulties would automatically find their debt substantially forgiven, but this would mean linking their debt payments to some measure of their own GDP, just as Bulgaria has already done for a small part of its national debt. This is one of the functions macro markets would secure.

Such a plan is not welfare—it is risk management. The market would put the risk of a bad outcome into the prices seen in the macro markets. Investors around the world are perfectly capable of handling the risks of Bulgaria, or of any other country, by putting it into a diversified portfolio. In effect, the macro markets would be creating the same kind of humanitarian relief that the Jubilee Debt Campaign called for. Moreover, it would have worked. In contrast, the Jubilee Debt Campaign, despite obtaining statements of good intentions from governments, was not much of a success.[6]

A Market for the Entire World

If a macro market for claims on GDP is created for each country in the world, then one could put all of these securities together into one gigantic investment portfolio that would represent a claim on everything of economic value in the entire world. Since GDP is supposed to measure the entire income of a country (after appropriate allowances for such things as depreciation), this portfolio would represent, really, everything that matters economically. It would be the ultimate diversified portfolio, vastly more diversified than any portfolio that one could possibly construct today—the financial theorists dream, representing the theoretical idea of the "market portfolio" or "world portfolio" that is only an abstraction in finance theory textbooks today.

My colleague Stefano Athanasoulis and I have argued that for such a market for the world we do not have to wait until a market has been created for each country in the world. In fact, we might instead want to create this world market first, a sort of *world share,* before any other macro markets are created.[7] We can do this merely by creating a macro market for long-term claims on the combined GDPs of all countries of the world today. Creating this market is entirely feasible today, for there is already a published GDP for every country and a world economic growth, from the International Monetary Fund.

The ups and downs of the price of the world share would reflect changes in the value of everything we have, subject to the limits of the accuracy of our measures of national incomes. If national incomes are reflective of all sorts of income, then the value of these flows capitalized in this world market would be a sum of all the risks that impinge on this planet.

One might think that we would have little use for a market for risk that impinges on all of us, that this risk is already effectively shared by the mere fact that we are all directly exposed to it. In reality, however, there is a use for such a world share because we are not all exposed equally to world risk and because we all experience the world risk differently.[8]

If this market for the combined incomes of everyone in the world existed, then its prices would go fluctuate through time in response to information about the outlook for everything. This price would reflect the total impact of all global events: of fundamental technological progress, of the availability of all forms of energy, of changing world population and its level of education and health, and of such environmental shocks as global warming. The price may be considered the most informative of all prices.

The value of this market (its "market capitalization") today would likely be on the order of a quadrillion U.S. dollars. The reader can be assured that no genuine value of this magnitude has ever been quoted in our financial markets.

Markets for Claims on Other Income Flows

The existing contracts for national income aggregates are constrained to use GDP or its variants because data representing GDP are widely available by country. The historical record and public familiarity with these is sufficient that the risk management contracts written on them may be widely accepted. GDP, however, is not a perfect measure of economic welfare. For example, GDP might rise dramatically because of a national disaster that necessitates much repair work or because the country becomes involved in a major war, which puts more people at work and for longer hours. We would not want risk management contracts to cause this country to have to pay more to foreigners as if they were experiencing unexpected good fortune.

The alternative Measure of Economic Welfare (MEW) proposed by William Nordhaus and James Tobin in 1972 is based on the same National Income and Product Accounts that contain GDP, but it incorporates various adjustments so that it is effectively a measure of sustainable consumption.[9] For example, in arriving at MEW Nordhaus and Tobin corrected GDP by subtracting defense expenditures, since they view these as a sort of input to production that does not contribute to welfare except indirectly. They also imputed income from consumer durables and made corrections for the increasing amount of leisure that people have been enjoying. They also made corrections for the disamenities of urbanization and for the depletion of natural resources.

Measures of economic welfare like the MEW have not attracted much interest partly because contracts have not been settled on such measures. Another reason for lack of interest is that the numbers Nordhaus and Tobin produced did not show markedly different growth rates from year to year in their sample than did GDP. But for the purposes of risk management, we must still consider the improvements offered by concepts like MEW because in the future their growth rates might differ substantially from GDP growth rates. More research on such measures would be needed, and any such measures should be based on clearly objective standards, making only unambiguous changes in GDP, so as to avoid the ambiguities of opinion.

Markets for Income by Occupation

In a classic 1971 study, labor economist Richard Freeman showed that incomes of occupations sometimes go through long cycles due to a feedback mechanism called the "cobweb" cycle (so called because of the appearance of the supply and demand diagram that introductory economics professors have long used to illustrate it). The cobweb cycle works as follows: When incomes earned by people in a given occupation are high for some years, this circumstance entices more young people to decide to prepare for that occupation. Years later, when these young people have finished their education and training period, the newly trained people seeking jobs overwhelm the labor market for this occupation, and hence incomes fall. At this point, the next batch of young people starting their training and contemplating what occupation to pursue are deterred from this profession because of the low incomes. Thus, fewer people prepare for this occupation, and, some years later, a relative shortage of people in this occupation appears, creating high incomes. The cycle repeats again and again. Of course, the record is not that precise, so there is no rigid cycle, but certain labor markets do seem to produce alternating boom and bust periods.[10]

Because of such problems, incomes by occupation are another important income aggregate for which long-term markets could be created. These markets would provide important risk management functions for individuals, and could be created today with existing occupational information measures, such as are now published by the U.S. Bureau of Labor Statistics. For example, imagine a market for incomes of medical doctors, a profession that has recently taken losses in the United States, at least relative to expectations of previous decades. If retail institutions, such as livelihood insurers, took the appropriate positions in these markets (issuing the securities rather than buying them) on behalf of doctors, they would have protected the doctors, at least in part, from these losses. Alternatively, medical schools could make investments in these markets and thereby be in a better position to offer livelihood insurance to their students. Or medical associations could offer protection, obtained through the macro markets, for doctors. In the last few years, medical school applications in the United States have been dropping at an alarming rate, and this no doubt reflects at least in part both the declining outlook for doctors' income as well as increased uncertainty about the incomes. The declining medical school applications portend a lower average quality of life for our doctors in the future. To the extent that this decline is due to increased uncertainty about medical careers, the ability to hedge could have an indirect impact improving the quality of our medical care.

Markets for occupational incomes could also provide some important information about the demand for occupations in the future, information that would help guide people who are choosing a career. Those who are considering a career in medicine, for example, might be able to view market rates for doctors' incomes twenty years hence, represented in today's market prices.

Such information from market prices, at least when the macro markets are behaving efficiently, may be more valuable than any information we now have. In the United States, the Department of Labor has on its Web site the *Occupational Outlook Handbook,* which offers individuals advice about prospects for various career choices.[11] The developers of the site have good intentions; they want to help direct the labor force into places where it is most needed and prevent errors of training for the wrong jobs. Unfortunately, the Web site appears to be only modestly helpful for people trying to choose careers.

The Web site faces a problem in that it offers as information projected average employment growth rates in broad occupational categories, created by extrapolating past growth rates. This does not appear very helpful for individuals who have specific job plans: trends in employment numbers in broad occupational categories are of little relevance for judging the long-term prospects for the earnings in the occupation. However well intentioned the people at the Department of Labor are, they can do little to predict the prospects of narrowly defined occupations in coming decades. Market prices for long-term claims on finely disaggregated incomes by narrowly defined occupation, as should be possible in the future, would give more important information for people choosing careers. To the extent that young people actually use these markets to hedge the risks of their anticipated future careers, the prices in these market will incorporate information about their actual intentions and plans to enter these careers, thus helping to break the cobweb cycle that Richard Freeman described.[12]

Markets for Income by Income Level and Personal Characteristics

Income by labor income level is another important aggregate for which macro markets can be created, since one of the most important risks that people face affects their wage and salary levels. Labor income levels may proxy for unobserved characteristics that have market value for individuals. People of similar characteristics, through the process of searching for the best possible job, may tend to arrive at the same income level, though in may different occupations, and hence the income level may possibly be the best available basis on which to measure these characteristics, though of course subject to errors.

Both low- and high-income people can use these markets to hedge the risk that their economic status will be eroded. By hedging their general income risks in these markets, people can make decisions about spending money today better than they otherwise could. The precautionary need to save will be reduced, and people will be freer to spend on investments for the future, such as educational or other self-improvement investments that are ultimately illiquid and cannot be sold in a time of economic adversity.

As we develop better databases of individual characteristics and their incomes, we can also develop markets for income flows by personal characteristics. Assuming that personal identification systems and databases about people's backgrounds and skills, and possibly even their genetic characteristics, become more and more sophisticated, people will increasingly see their risks defined in terms of these characteristics. As discussed in chapter 8, we most likely will choose to restrict the use of databases that contain such information, but to the extent that we do allow such use, macro markets for income flows associated with such characteristics would serve a real purpose.

Liquid Markets for Real Estate

Another important source of uncertainty in people's lives is the risk that their homes will lose value or fail to maintain value over long intervals of time with inflation. When people borrow to buy a house, they are putting themselves in a risky investment situation, where a drop in the home price of only 10 percent can often wipe out their down payment, destroying their home equity.

There is no liquid international market for a country's real estate. There is no international market for the houses, condominiums, and apartments of any nation, only the local market among homeowners. We do have large markets for mortgages, but this is a market for debt, not a market for the real estate itself. The lack of these markets results in a significant lack of risk sharing around the world today. But all these macro markets can be created.

Single-family home prices have, in the past, gone through both boom and bust cycles that strongly affect prices. The United States experienced major booms on both East and West coasts in the late 1980s, followed by a bust. After the bust, single-family home prices fell by over 25 percent in Los Angeles and over 15 percent in Boston. In real inflation-corrected terms, the fall was over 40 percent in Los Angeles and nearly 30 percent in Boston.[13]

Changes in single-family home prices are partly forecastable.[14] Because the costs of transacting in single-family homes is essentially prohibitive to speculators who would buy and sell homes to profit from forecastable price changes, the market does not display the kind of near-unpredictability that we see in the stock market. In fact, my firm,

Case Shiller Weiss, Inc., has been forecasting single-family home prices for major U.S. cities, and, according to the Scorecard on our forecasts published regularly in the *Wall Street Journal*, we have been successful in forecasting about half of the variation in single-family home prices one year ahead.

A futures market for single-family homes for a city could be created, based on a price index for homes.[15] Case Shiller Weiss, Inc., launched a campaign in 1990 to establish a futures market for single-family homes, getting the Chicago Board of Trade to put out a press release in 1993 saying that they had tentative plans to have futures markets in single-family homes by city.[16] But fearing that the markets might not succeed, they changed their mind and the markets were never even tried. In the meantime, in 1991 the London Futures and Options Exchange attempted—unsuccessfully—to create futures contracts on single-family homes and commercial real estate in the United Kingdom. Since then, again in London, both City Index and IG Index have started futures markets for single-family homes and commercial real estate. Before it went bankrupt in 2001, Enron Corporation had plans to create a futures market from commercial real estate in the United States. In 2002 Advanced e-Financial Technologies, Inc., in the United States announced plans for residential and commercial real estates futures. The efforts to start such futures markets have been uninspiring so far, but we continue in our efforts to encourage futures exchanges to list such contracts.

It may well be better to create longer-term markets for single-family homes than were envisioned by the Chicago Board of Trade when we were working with them in 1993, and longer than the City Index contracts, which are also limited to no more than a year's horizon. Short-horizon futures markets for real estate may not work as well as we might wish, since the price may be fairly forecastable out to the horizon. Given the illiquidity in the markets, creating perpetual futures or macro securities to allow trading of single-family home price risks are likely to be preferable.

Psychological Reframing Afforded by these Ideas

Today we have almost no established markets for long-term claims on broadly defined incomes, only on narrowly defined incomes such as corporate profits. As a result people do not see the prices of the long-term claims for these other aggregates and hence do not see the volatility of these claims. This volatility has no salience, no presence, if people do not see it reflected in market prices.

When people are actually able to see the price in macro markets for GDP, they will be able to see an indicator of the long-run situation, diverting the framing from the small short-run ups and downs of the economy that so captures our attention today. They will be seeing much more dramatic movements up and down in the long-run value of the economy, reflecting the future as well as the present, and it is this long-run value that really matters to economic welfare. This reframing will create important new reference points, important new focuses of attention, just as the creation of stock markets centuries ago did for our appreciation of the long-run value of corporate earnings. The presumably large change in value in GDP macro markets is likely to have the effect of impressing on people the substance of risks to their livelihoods that impact the nation as a whole.[17]

When people are finally able to see the market price in macro markets for the income of their occupation, or on the income of people with background and personal characteristics like theirs, it could utterly change the way that they view various professions. They will be cognizant of the long-term risks of various professions and cognizant of the opportunities seen in them by others.

When people are finally able to see the market price of claims on single-family homes as traded in a liquid market for home price indexes, and hence not subject to the inertia that we see in present-day markets for single-family homes. The asking prices for the homes themselves will probably be tied in future markets with the price in the liquid market.

This reframing does, of course, have a possible downside: The public, once it becomes focused on macro market values, could adopt an excessively speculative attitude toward macro market prices, and these markets could sometimes see speculative bubbles and bursts much as we have experienced from time to time in the stock market.[18]

The World with a Full Set of Macro Markets

The systematic accumulation, analysis, and organization of basic data that has increasingly been taking place over recent decades is making macro markets ever more likely. The macro markets would represent a most fundamental advance for our world economy. They would make tradable the largest sources of wealth that we have, would establish market prices for all of them, and would allow fundamental risk management on a global scale.

If we one day in the future have a full set of macro markets, then we will see a multitude of applications. There will not only be a few bonds with GDP warrants attached: Practically all international government debt will be replaced by debt indexed to the national incomes of the issuing countries. Macro markets will also facilitate livelihood insurance contracts by allowing insurance companies a new way to spread the risks they incur by writing such policies. People will make important international risk-sharing agreements, effectively swapping their own country risk or their own occupation risk for a diversified portfolio of risks. Homeowners or mortgage lenders will hedge their real estate risks in markets for individual cities, and home equity insurers will use the markets to enable them to offer policies to homeowners. The world might have the same risks in totality, but individual risks would be markedly reduced.

Income-Linked Loans: Reducing the Risks of Hardship and Bankruptcy

IT MAKES LITTLE SENSE, now that our information technology has improved so much, to subject borrowers to conventional fixed nominal interest rates on their debts. This old system deals with income uncertainty by letting financial problems build until they reach a breaking point, sometimes creating great distress, at which time borrowers can obtain some relief, at the expense of some humiliation, by bankruptcy proceedings. Far better would be the smooth adjustment of debts to new economic circumstances. Loans that are designed to do this could be the standard, the generic personal loan, to purchase houses, to upgrade houses, to provide education, or even to invest in livelihood insurance or other risk management devices. Corporate loans, even loans to governments that achieve this, can be implemented as well.

Just as modern finance makes possible a host of new macro markets for major risks, it also allows for new and better forms of loans. Lenders such as banks and mortgage originators would offer long-term loans whose repayment terms would be tied either to aggregate incomes or to individual-specific or firm-specific income or both. The higher the subsequent income, the more interest and principal have to be repaid. These loans would thus fulfil a risk management function for the borrower, the payments automatically offsetting fluctuations in the borrowers' income. If loans are long-term, extending over many years, then the risk management they afford could be substantial and could significantly reduce the problem of personal bankruptcy.

This idea goes back to Milton Friedman and his discussion of educational loans in his 1962 book *Capitalism and Freedom*. He contrasted our conventional educational loans financing with the stock market financing used by businesses. "The counterpart for education would be to 'buy' a share in an individual's earning prospects; to advance him the funds needed to finance his training on condition that he agree to pay the lender a specified fraction of future earnings."[1]

Friedman made no campaign for this proposed new kind of educational loans, and offered it only as an "amusing" speculation. He thought that this idea would likely meet "irrational public condemnation," and that, beyond this, it would be costly to administer.

> One reason why such contracts have not become common, despite their potential profitability to both lender and borrower, is presumably the high costs of administering them, given the freedom of individuals to move from one place to another, the need for getting accurate income statements, and the long period over which the contracts would run.[2]

Today there is no reason to expect irrational public condemnation, there is no reason to tie these loans exclusively to education, and there is no reason to restrict these loans to individuals—businesses and governments could receive them, too. And with the advent of new information technology, the administration-cost obstacle that Friedman lamented may be drastically reduced. With our improved information technology (and especially with the GRIDs, described in part 4) implementing such loans should be much easier. Electronic databases would make it possible to process accounts and payments easily, and identification systems would track people as they move. Such innovations would dramatically reduce obstacles. It is time to consider income-linked loans.

Tying Income-Linked Loans to Income Indexes

Along lines described in chapter 8 regarding livelihood insurance, it would be generally desirable to make a modification in Friedman's original idea so that the loan payments would not be defined exclusively in terms of an individual's (or family's or corporation's or government's) own income but rather in terms of a combination of that income and an index of the average of incomes of similar loan recipients. In the case of personal loans, defining payments in this way would reduce the moral hazard that people will work less hard or even take early retirement to reduce their obligations on the loan, and the selection bias problem that people who know they will choose a less-demanding, low-paying job are attracted to the program.

Income-linked personal loans would be defined differently than those loans we are familiar with. Lenders could compete not on interest rates but on what fraction of future income, by alternative measures, they would require for the loan. For example, to borrow $200,000 for thirty years, the Jones family might shop around and find that one lender offered an income-linked personal loan that would require that they pay 10 percent of their family income for thirty years, another lender that would require they pay 5 percent of their family income and 4 percent of the income of an index representing incomes of families like theirs for thirty years, and yet another lender that would require they pay 7 percent of the income of the index alone. They would have to decide among the loans, some charging a slightly higher rate but with better risk management for their family, others charging a lower interest rate but a less good fit for their own individual family income. The more tightly connected the loan is to the individual's own income, the more moral hazard risk will raise the cost of making the loans. Perhaps loans tied exclusively to individual income will be so beset by moral hazard risks as to be impracticable, though in some cases, depending on occupation and the associated ability to preclude shirking, they may well be possible without generating excessive moral hazard costs.

Loans might also differ in terms of the kind of income index used to define a loss. Supposing that the primary breadwinner in the Jones family is a dentist. One lender might offer a loan in terms of income of dentists in the entire country, while another might offer a loan in terms of income of medical people in the Jones's city. One of these is more focused in terms of occupation, the other more in terms of region. The family would have to decide which more accurately portrayed their interests, depending on how committed they are to standard dental practice and how likely they are to move. Thus, they will try to choose a loan based on an index that they feel is most likely to reflect any loss in family income due to a changing market for the breadwinner's services, as they themselves see that market.

They could use the loan to pay for an education or to buy a house. Borrowers guided by sound financial advice from their financial planner, their employer, or their labor union might even use the loan to buy a portfolio of macro securities that provided income that helps protect them against possible declines in their household income, and they could purchase some livelihood insurance that further protects them against declines in their income or against declines in the value of their house.

Instruments resembling income-linked loans already exist (as we shall see below), but they are very rare and those that do exist generally do not make use of indexes for defining claims. Making such loans more widely available would entail work from both the private sector and the government. These loans would require a standardized contract, a contract designed around existing information sources about individuals' or corporations' income, and a pricing theory for such loans. The arrangement would also require a firm legal principle that states that these contracts are applicable to all individuals, not just accredited investors, and that the government will regulate the contracts in the future so that there will be no doubt about their future enforcement, so that there will be no future obstacles to investors collecting on their investment in income-indexed loans, and so that the individuals who borrow with them cannot use bankruptcy law inappropriately to frustrate the purpose of the loans.

The government would be well advised to put into place protections for large income-linked personal loans much as it does for other consumer products. Individuals or families should be prevented from misusing a large loan, such as by consuming it at once or gambling it away. We already have such protections on other kinds of significant debt that individuals incur, such as student loans, which can be used only for educational purposes and which in the United States cannot be canceled by declaring personal bankruptcy.[3]

Precedents for Income-Linked Loans

There are precedents for income-linked loans both on the corporate and individual level. At both of these levels, however, such income-linked loans are extremely rare.

In the year 2000 Swiss Re New Markets and Société Générale created a GDP-linked loan for an individual company. The French tire maker Michelin was given a US$1 billion borrowing facility that was contingent on GDP growth in its main market falling short of a threshold. The form of this loan was a subordinated loan facility expiring in 2012 that can be drawn upon by Michelin only if GDP growth in Michelin's main markets declines to specified levels.[4] This has helped Michelin pursue business opportunities with less risk, since the GDP growth is a proxy for Michelin's own revenue growth. This loan sets an important precedent, although today such corporate loans are still of virtually no practical importance for corporate lending.

The Bulgarian GDP bonds described in chapter 9 might, even though they took the form of marketable bonds, be considered another precedent for income-linked loans, although in this case to governments rather than corporations. Here, as with the Michelin bonds, the loan terms reflect Bulgaria's subsequent ability to repay.

Economists at the international monetary fund have recently launched a program to study the possibility of encouraging other less-developed countries to issue debt linked to their own GDP.[5] Such a change could effectively be implemented at the time of a major default, when the need for a change is especially apparent, and defaulting countries might be especially receptive to new ideas.

The Tuition Postponement Option (TPO) sponsored by Yale University allowed students to pay tuition and at the same time manage income risks. The plan, developed under the direction of Professor James Tobin, enrolled financial need students from 1971 to 1978 in a system that would pay their tuition, with the provision that higher-income students would later pay back more than lower-income students.[6] All students who enrolled would pay 0.4 percent of their annual income for each one thousand dollars borrowed until the entire cohort, or class, had paid off their debt, or until thirty-five years had passed, whichever came sooner.[7] Because Yale is a university with a strong sense of community among alumni throughout life, it had an ability to make such a contract with its students and expect the contract to be honored. The program helped manage the risk that individual future income might below. Those Yale alumni who turned out to earn relatively lower income received a benefit, in effect, of lower debt.

The plan was an innovative attempt, originating from the Yale economics department, to use modern risk management against individual income risk. The scheme, however, generated great opposition in recent years from those enrolled, and Yale canceled the remaining 3,300 students' obligations in 2001.[8] The plan was a wonderful idea, but it was not integrated into other risk management systems, did not take proper account of individual information, and affronted then-current individual impressions of fairness.

The plan failed, in part, because it did not take account of predicted differences in incomes of students in different academic majors. The plan was not administered with any attention to likely future occupation, and so its design produced a severe selection bias. Its enrollment was thus biased toward students, like law school enrollee William Jefferson Clinton, later U.S. president, who expected to go into social service or other occupations that do not portend high incomes.

The tuition postponement option does live on, however, in similar programs at major law schools that automatically forgive part of the student loans for students who take low-paying jobs. The Yale Law School's Career Options Assistance Program (COAP), begun in 1988, the broadest of most effective of these programs, is widely viewed as contributing an important part of the law school's identity, allowing an unusually high percentage of its graduates to take low-paying but socially conscious jobs, such as clerkships or advocacies for the poor, avoiding the necessity of taking high-paying jobs just to pay off their student loans. But, of course, the program is more than a subsidy for idealism—it is clearly a risk management device as well.

But why are such plans in force today only in law schools? Confining the plans to law schools may help solve the selection bias problem, since law students are unlikely to choose careers that involve low income in exchange for purely personal gratification. Law Students do not usually become ski instructors or artists.

Another income-linked student loan plan was created in 2001 by two former New York University students, Vishal Garg and Raza Khan. Their plan can be found on their Web site, MyRichUncle.com. Their plan includes a significant improvement over the original Yale TPO plan: It has different rates for different academic majors. But it is too soon to know if their plan will succeed.

A rather different plan to allow people, in this case wealthy artists, to borrow against their future income was created in 1997 by the financier David Pullman. He arranged for the issuance of bonds backed by future record royalties of the rock singer David Bowie. Prudential Insurance Co. purchased a $55 million issue of the 10-year 7.9 percent bonds. Since then, bonds tied to future income have been issued for other artists, including James Brown, Ron Isley, Rod Stewart, and Dusty Springfield, and for song-writing team Nicholas Ashford and Valerie Simpson.

Bonds backed by an individual's income remain rarities. Those who issue such bonds complain about the great difficulty of arranging them.[9] But all these difficulties may be diminished by efforts to standardize and routinize the instruments, and to make use of our information technology to verify income efficiently so that many more people may make use of such a financial instrument. With modern technology available to everyone, we should all be David Bowies in our ability to hedge our risks.

Family Problems

A technical problem with personal income-linked loans is that the fundamental economic unit may not be the individual but the family. The family is not a stable unit, due to divorces, remarriages, and deaths, and children are born, grow up, and move away. The complexity of the family as an economic unit has been an important reason why institutions like the income-linked personal loans (or, for that matter, the livelihood insurance described in chapter 8) have not become a standard.

Part of the reason the Yale TPO failed has to do with issues of the family and the relatively primitive nature of the U.S. income tax system at the time. The Yale TPO payments were tied to adjusted gross income, a line on the federal income tax form. Not having the data on income available to define the contract in a precise way, the framers of the Yale TPO were forced to rely on something already reduced to paper and documentable: the tax return. Since most married couples file their taxes jointly, this form lumps both spouses incomes together. It would be too difficult to ask that a Yale alumnus recalculate his or her own income, separate from the spouses income, and in any event there would be no governmental oversight on such a calculation. Thus, the Yale TPO in effect taxed the income of both the former students and the former students' spouses. Since the future spouses had had no part in the contract with Yale, the plan had the potential to create surprise and resentment.

The issues related to family go beyond resentment. If one member of a family took out an income-linked personal loan based solely on his income, then there would be a moral hazard created by his ability to substitute income from family members; that is, the individual who took out the income-linked loan could reduce his own income and thereby pay less back, while receiving substitute income from family members. Thus, loans issued to persons in careers that are more often interrupted may have to charge higher rates, reflecting such a risk. Loans may need to have different provisions during the child-bearing years of the family than during other years. Income-linked personal loan contracts may ideally include complex provisions about marriage, divorce, and remarriage that weigh both practical and psychological factors.

Such family issues were presumably less relevant for the David Bowie bonds mentioned above. Bowie's own large income can be well defined and warrants efforts to be computed separately from any spouse he may have. These issues created by the complexity of the family have, in the past, limited income-linked personal loans to a few people who, like David Bowie, are in exceptional circumstances. In the digital age the contractual obligation defined for an income-linked personal loan may be made fairly complex and contingent on information about family structure so that the contract balances the issues of the shifting involved parties and at the same time creates some liquidity and opportunity for risk management.

Changes in Bankruptcy Law

How the government should deal with inability to repay debts has been a perennial issue. Much of this issue has been created by our failure to create income-linked loans in the past, which would have provided a cushion against bankruptcy.

Modifying bankruptcy law poses a complex problem. Such laws change the opportunity set that people face, creating incentives for some and frustration for others. Bankruptcy can have many causes, and the appropriate government policy should vary based on the reasons for a particular bankruptcy. But the law cannot be infinitely complex and has to establish simple rules for bankruptcy. Fortunately, in the digital age, when information can be processed much more efficiently, bankruptcy laws, like many other laws, can be safely made more complex.

The history of bankruptcy laws in the United States has been dominated since its very beginning by the need, from time to time, for the government to respond to occasional national financial crises that thrust hundreds of thousands of people into personal insolvency.[10] The conventional wisdom of the eighteenth century that those who could not pay their debts should sometimes be sent to debtors' prison began to be eroded by the national discussion of these crises, which focused national attention on some of the systemic causes of bankruptcies, those beyond individuals' control. The frequency with which people observed friends or neighbors in financial trouble made plain the point that personal financial difficulty is not necessarily proof of indigence or bad character. The outcome of this discussion was bankruptcy laws, which, in the early nineteenth century, were intended as only temporary measures to alleviate the crisis but which became permanent. These laws eventually allowed individuals to wipe out their debts and start life anew with a clean slate. This was an important risk management innovation for the information technology of the time, preventing some individual bad outcomes in a practical and feasible way. But the appropriateness of that innovation has changed with our new information technology.

The creation of income-linked personal loans would mark a time to change the bankruptcy law. To facilitate the operation of the income-linked personal loans, the law should prevent, or partially prevent, the loans from being canceled as part of a personal bankruptcy just as it exempts student loans from such bankruptcy cancellation today. Otherwise, the investor would have to factor the risk of this cancellation into the pricing of the loan, which would partially frustrate the risk management purpose of the loan. Protecting the loans from cancellation at bankruptcy would mean that a person could indeed effectively pledge income for the remaining years of his or her life, thereby opening up the possibility of more effective risk management.

While we may take the existing bankruptcy laws for granted, they are not the only way for society to help individuals cope with adverse economic fortunes. Today's bankruptcy law is not part of natural law; it is not inevitable. Indeed, some countries do not have personal bankruptcy provisions at all, and people there can never escape their debts. In these countries, other adjustments are made to deal with the risk of insolvency. When we have other risk management devices in place, such as the very index-linked personal loans under discussion here, then the reason to have these bankruptcy laws in their present form is diminished.

The Importance and Feasibility of Income-Linked Loans

The relative scarcity today of income-linked loans, whether to individuals, to corporations, or to governments, reflects the only limited application to date of our emerging information technology. We should not infer any long-term problems with the concept of income-linked loans from their scarcity today. Emerging information technology will rapidly expand the potential scope of such loans.

Efforts to date to market income-linked loans (to students) have not carefully confronted the problems of moral hazard and selection bias. These problems could be reduced if we had finely detailed income indexes by personal and career characteristics. The contracts could then be settled substantially on the index rather than just on the individual's actual income. Other serious issues that need attention are those that arise from family interactions and personal bankruptcy. If all of these obstacles to income-linked personal loans can be solved, then people will be able to put themselves in a far better risk management situation than is possible today.

Existing income-linked loans are usually relatively small, such as student loans contracted by students for just part of their tuition, and they seem to be regarded as little souvenirs from our student days. But the income-linked loans need not be small. If we can implement the right standards and institutional structure, they can be dominant.

Individuals, corporations and governments could, and from a risk management perspective, should, commit a substantial share of the future lifetime income to such loans. Thus, these proposed income-linked personal loans are not just curiosities, they could ultimately be life savers. If, for example, the kind of technology-induced loss of income described in part one of this book strikes many people, then having borrowed money in the form of an income-linked personal loan could be one of the most momentous decisions that these people had made in their lives.

ELEVEN

Inequality Insurance: Protecting the Distribution of Income

IF THE WORLD IS TO MANAGE its political and economic affairs effectively, society must prevent any substantial worsening of economic inequality among its citizens. We will want to arrest any possible tendency for the fruits of our economy to be distributed much more unequally between rich and poor in the future.

The idea for inequality insurance presented here is that the government should set by legislation the level of income inequality, in most cases probably initially roughly equal to the level of inequality today, and create a tax system that prevents inequality from getting worse. The idea is that if income inequality begins to get worse, then taxes automatically become more progressive as a correction. The tax changes would be automatic because the tax system would be framed as enforcing a measure of inequality rather than specifying tax rates.

I am calling the program *insurance* here, quite loosely, to frame the program in the public mind as the risk management vehicle that it is, and to highlight that it will not wrest money from anyone from the standpoint of today. Inequality insurance not a Robin Hood plot to take money from the rich and give it to the poor. Like other risk management devices, it focuses only on protecting all of us from future risks.

How Inequality Insurance Payments Would Be Calculated

Let me first explain just how inequality insurance would work. This discussion gets a little technical, but we must understand the proposal to appreciate it. Today, governments around the world legislate and publish income tax *schedules*, which assign to each income level that a household may fall into an income tax for that amount of income. In its simplest form, inequality insurance would replace the income tax schedules with a different standard. The governments would legislate not the tax schedule but the total amount of taxes raised and a target level of after-tax income inequality using an economic measure of inequality called the *after-tax Lorenz curve.*

What is the after-tax Lorenz curve? It is a curve or plot showing, on the vertical axis, the percent of national income after taxes earned by all households up to a certain percentile by income, against the percentile (on the horizontal axis). For example, one might see from the Lorenz curve that the bottom 30 percent of the population receives only 10 percent of the after-tax income, while the bottom 50 percent receive only 30 percent of the after-tax income. The Lorenz curve must by construction be 0 at the zeroth percentile (the zeroth person receives none of the income), and 100 at the hundredth percentile (100 percent of the people receive 100 percent of the income), but between those two extremes the curve measures inequality. If all households were equal in terms of after-tax incomes, the curve would be a straight line between 0 percent and 100 percent: the bottom 30 percent of households would receive 30 percent of the income and the bottom 50 percent of households would receive 50 percent of the income, and so on. But if households are unequal, the curve connecting zero and 100 would sag below this straight line. The more unequal are after-tax incomes, the more drastically the after-tax Lorenz curve sags below the straight line.

The Gini coefficient, a measure of inequality, describes how much the Lorenz curve sags.[1] Estimated Gini coefficients for the countries of the world may be found on the Internet via the United Nations Development Program World Income Inequality Database or the World Bank's World Development Indicators.

Under a system of inequality insurance, the tax authorities every year would have the responsibility to calculate the taxes necessary to make the actual after-tax Lorenz curve equal the legislated one, thereby fixing the Gini coefficient. Each year the government would automatically restate the tax schedules, and we would pay taxes just as we do today. The only difference is in what is legislated, what is debated publicly at the time the legislation is introduced, and what is likely to stay fixed over time if the government makes no changes. Inequality insurance would change the psychological and institutional framing or anchoring of the tax system.

To make this clearer, let us go through the steps that the tax authority would use in computing their taxes once given the task of translating the legislated after-tax Lorenz curve into a tax schedule for tax-payers. Ideally, the tax authority would start with a spreadsheet—a gigantic spreadsheet, with millions of rows—in which column A would display this year's pre-tax income of everyone in the country, one cell per each household. In practice, since tax rates have to be announced in advance, the spreadsheet would have to be created in advance using forecasts of this year's incomes based on last year's incomes.

The first step would be to sort this column in ascending order, with the households with the lowest pre-tax incomes at the top and those with the highest incomes at the bottom. From the total of these incomes—the national income—would be subtracted the total amount the government has decided to raise as taxes to pay for government operations, to arrive at after-tax national income. Column B, listed adjacent to the pre-tax incomes column, would allocate this after-tax national income among everyone in such a way that the legislated after-tax Lorenz curve is realized and no household's position in the income ranking is changed. To arrive at a household's income after tax, one need only multiply the after-tax national income by the change in the legislated after-tax Lorenz curve between the percentile of this household and the percentile of the household above it in ranking. Finally, column C, equal to column A minus column B, gives the tax that each household owes. Column C, perhaps after some smoothing, becomes the tax schedule for this year. The same procedure would be repeated every year, causing the tax schedule to respond automatically to changes in inequality even if the tax code remains constant. The yearly adjustments to tax rates may in some cases be rather large, but in no case would the procedure ever push marginal tax rates up above 100 percent.

This is the basic idea behind inequality insurance, although it may not seem like much of a change from our tax system today, since it only changes our framing and anchoring of the tax system. After the system is instituted, most people would probably not at first notice any difference when they actually pay their taxes. If the legislated after-tax Lorenz curve is close to what we already had before inequality insurance, then we would not immediately experience much change in the tax rates. But a system that prevents any further worsening of income inequality would make a world of difference.

Inequality insurance is by its construction concerned with the inequality of income at all levels and does not focus exclusively on antipoverty as has much of the discussion of inequality. Many discussions of inequality seem unconcerned about the possibility that a significant share of the population could see their incomes fall to just above the poverty level. And yet such a possibility is disturbing. From a risk management perspective, avoiding a high incidence of abject poverty is important, but preventing gratuitous increases in inequality at higher levels of income is also important.

Some exercises on a spreadsheet showing how the tax rates might change as the result of worsening of inequality over the decades shows that inequality insurance can eventually automatically make some rather radical changes in tax rates, at all income levels, changes that are far more radical than governments are likely to legislate if they see their job as setting tax rates directly. Establishing inequality insurance now, thereby fixing the current level of inequality, will make it far more likely that such radical changes in the tax system actually happen. This is not, however, a radical proposal in terms of our lives today because it leaves the extent of inequality at its present levels.

Why Inequality Insurance Is Desirable

Most of us in most advanced countries appear accepting of the inequality that we now observe, but would likely have real doubts that we would like to see it get much worse. Most of us are accepting that Bill Gates can be as rich as he is, but likely would have great trouble if the nature of our economy changed so that Bill Gates were one thousand times as rich or if there were one thousand times as many Bill Gates at the expense of the rest of us living in relative poverty.

Once we understand, as we saw in chapter 3, that technological change or other factors can indeed drastically change the income distribution, for reasons that are beyond anyone's control, we likely will want to prevent this possibility. Incomes that people earn in a free market depend ultimately on what they can individually contribute to an economy constantly buffeted by changing technology. Viewed from Rawls's original position, the buffeting that people take from such shocks is not good for either individuals or society. There is no natural justice in it. And people often do experience shocks to their incomes that have nothing to do with their level of effort, their talent, or their responsibility. These shocks can create shattered dreams and suffering.

Rapid advances in information technology and robotics, or any of the other "forty thieves" that I discussed in chapter 4, have the potential to cause great inequality in the future. Should inequality get substantially and chronically worse, it would create classes of resentful people and fundamentally change the nature of our society. These shocks can wreak havoc on our lives.

But these economic factors could also improve the income distribution in the future. The essential fact is not that we know that inequality will get worse, but that we are uncertain about the future. We can deal with such uncertainty using financial methods, and this is the point here.

Some degree of inequality is inevitable in a free economic society. As I stressed earlier, certain people have a taste for working hard and earning more income and some jobs are unpleasant and have higher wages as compensation for their unpleasantness. Moreover, striving for a higher income and using our talents to the fullest and accepting some risks for higher income are part of the adventure of life. But a sharp deterioration in the equality of income distribution that is unrelated to changes in any of these factors is a serious risk. We would be wise to deal proactively with this risk—and before the worst happens. Instituting inequality insurance would not be costly, and would not create any loss if inequality does not worsen through time. But it promises enormous benefits if inequality does worsen.

Variations on the Basic Idea

The basic idea for inequality insurance contains the kernel for some important variations. One of them is to take account of government transfers, as well as taxes, so that the benefits people receive from the government are included in the analysis. Another is to take account of demographic changes. For example, we generally do not want the transfers to respond to changes in inequality that are due only to changes in the age distribution of the population, or we may want to make adjustments for changing trends in household size. Another is to make the transfers respond to objective changes in the needs of different elements of the population; the plan may allow deductions for medical expenses, for example. Another is to legislate that the income distribution is allowed to become more equal than it is today if it does so naturally, that inequality insurance will not try to return inequality to its former level if it naturally improves. Another is to put an upper limit on the marginal tax rate, to avoid marginal tax rates getting too close to 100 percent, which might create excessive disincentive to work, an issue we will return to below.

Inequality insurance is not best defined exclusively in terms of *annual* income, as in income tax systems today, because doing so would penalize people who earned high income in isolated years, thereby subjecting them to high inequality insurance payments in those years even though their lifetime income is not high. Income averaging could be used to reduce this problem. Another way of preventing timing of income from having a distortionary impact on lifetime taxes is to alter the tax into some form of consumption tax. The government would apply the method only to the portion of income that is spent on current enjoyment and not invested.[2] On the assumption that an individual smoothes consumption over his or her lifetime, consumption would be a better indicator of lifetime income, and thus may be a better basis of taxation than is income.[3]

Given all these potential considerations in the design of inequality insurance, it is important that substantial research be done to design the system right, and in accordance with basic standards of fairness and incentives.

The Urgency

Because we do not know whether inequality will become worse in the future, our lack of knowledge represents an opportunity. Just as we must obtain fire insurance for our houses before they burn down, so we must set up inequality insurance against worsening of inequality before we know it will happen.

Although social insurance provided by the government is different from private insurance, in that unexpected benefits could possibly be given after the fact, even after the risk is realized, it is far more likely that such social insurance will be effective if the insurance becomes law *before* the risk is realized. Our tax system may need massive overhaul if it is to alleviate a significant change in the income distribution, and overhaul is more likely to come to fruition if the nature of the changes is agreed upon in advance. And if the redistributions are part of an earlier insurance contract, then they will be framed in the public mind as just and honorable public policy, not as charity.

As we saw in chapter 6, psychological experiments have shown that when people freely and actively make a decision to volunteer, then their later sense of commitment and obligation can be strong. It seems that people have no clear idea how much they ought to contribute to others but believe on principle that they should live up to existing promises, whether explicit or only implicit. Inequality insurance makes good use of this human tendency. If people believe that they, or their representatives, freely and actively created a risk management contract before the risks were realized, then they are likely to accept the resulting obligations more than if they are told after the inequality had substantially worsened that they had new obligations that involved new payments. The framing change proposed here uses this aspect of human nature to redefine property rights so that inequality cannot get worse.

If we wait until later, and if inequality is much worse, then it will be harder to get public acceptance for reversing a level of inequality to which they may have become accustomed. Economically successful people tend to take their success as a measure of their worth, and to imagine that their economic success is the same as their intrinsic superiority. Even the losers, the unsuccessful, often seem to internalize their failures and blame themselves for their own relative low status. People arrive at such views even if the cause of their success or lack of success is obviously purely random, as has been shown by a number of psychological studies, for example, a study comparing people who got high numbers in the Vietnam draft lottery with those who drew low numbers.[4] Once an unacceptably extreme level of income inequality is experienced by people and incorporated into their mechanisms of self-esteem and concepts of social status, it will be harder to achieve consensus for reversing it.[5]

The notion that we should set up a system now to constrain our future tax rates has a number of precedents. Inequality insurance falls into the category sometimes referred to as *fiscal mechanisms* or *fiscal constitutions*. But I believe my particular formulation, as well as its basis in concepts of human psychology rather than in pure economic or political theory, is new.[6]

Risk management can be secured in public approval by reframing of our thinking, renaming of standards of comparison, and renaming of basic institutions. The time to do such reframing is now, when changes in our information technology and our associated institutions involve some reframing anyway. The government could label inequality insurance payments beyond the original tax rates as insurance premiums and benefits rather than as tax increases and welfare benefits, comparable to their labeling of social security contributions and benefits. That labeling will be most convincing if we act before the inequality worsens, not after.[7]

The Role of Government

Inequality insurance is a function of the government, not private markets, although it would interact with private market institutions. A fundamental problem with exclusively private—that is, free market—solutions to the major risks outlined in the preceding chapters is that they rely on individuals' making provision for the risks before knowing the outcome. There are some obvious limitations on people's ability to take risk management action before the risks are realized, and these limitations necessitate a role for the government. Though these limitations are well known, listing them is valuable because it is important to be clear why government is needed to perform such a function.

First, minors and the unborn cannot possibly undertake risk management. We are facing risks that evolve over many decades, so risk management designed to deal with them must be contracted for decades before. For example, the risk that new technology will marginalize common labor is a very long-term risk, and the consequences may even last over many subsequent generations.

Second, many people are incapable of understanding the hedging implicit in these markets. In an extreme case, the mentally retarded or the mentally ill may be incapable of making good decisions. More commonly, people of normal intelligence may have trouble summoning the energy and self-discipline to make the optimal decisions to hedge or insure their future incomes.

Third, existing government institutions and laws may prevent people from taking actions in their own self-interest. Notably, legal principles such as bankruptcy law are themselves government risk management institutions designed on the assumption that other private risk management institutions did not exist. Such government institutions may conflict with private risk management initiatives unless redesigned to avoid this conflict. The government can reframe laws for these other institutions to the extent that they come into conflict with inequality insurance.

Psychological Framing and the Setting of Tax Rates

Because inequality insurance is fundamentally tied to psychological framing, we should first consider how psychological framing has affected income tax rates in the past. How have governments actually set income tax rates and what principles does their practice embody?

Legal scholar Edward McCaffery has listed a number of psychological framing principles that, he argues, can explain much of the historical changes in U.S. tax rates.[8] He argues that lawmakers often instinctively use basic principles of psychological framing to raise taxes without upsetting taxpayers. Lawmakers, says McCaffery, are aware that the highest income tax rate— the marginal rate for the highest tax bracket—is the most salient of the tax rates because public discussion tends to focus on it. Therefore, to raise taxes lawmakers can first raise the top bracket to a high level, but keep the tax bracket definition such that few people pay this rate. The highest tax rate initially applies only to the highest incomes, so high that almost no one pays at this rate, but it establishes a standard of comparison, a reference point.

The lawmakers can then raise tax revenue while lowering rates by lowering the income cutoffs for the tax brackets or allowing inflation to erode them. Cutoffs for tax brackets are not so salient in public attention as are the rates themselves. In a growing economy, effectively these cutoffs can be lowered even if the brackets are indexed to inflation, provided they are not indexed to the real growth of the economy. This so-called bracket creep has been a powerful device to raise taxes.

This strategy is most effective if the top tax bracket is first raised to a high level at a time of war, when it seems only fair that the rich should pay more. After the war, the lawmakers may cut tax rates slowly, and the declining rates are framed by the public as gains, even though the actual tax cuts are small. The public senses that the rates are coming down, and protests only ineffectively that the rates are not being cut faster. That is, people focus their attention on the advances they are making with lower tax rates, but not on the still-high level of the rate itself.

High marginal income tax rates were imposed for the first time in the United States during World War I, when protests against the higher taxes were quashed by public perceptions of soldiers' supreme sacrifice. This was no time for the people who were staying home to get rich. Thus, the war was used to reframe the public's concern for property rights. Indeed, reacting to the unfairness of the distribution of the burden of the war, some people called for a "conscription of wealth" to match the conscription of soldiers. On annual incomes of over one million dollars, marginal tax rates reached 77 percent in the United States by 1918. Few breathed the rarified air of an income of a million dollars a year, so the tax was not really very progressive on most incomes, but the principle of high marginal tax rates was established at that time, setting a new psychological anchor even though the rate was gradually cut after the war.

World War II led to more effectively progressive income tax rates, and represented another step up in psychological anchoring. In the United States, the top income tax bracket rose to 94 percent during World War II. The top tax bracket was only gradually cut after the war, in irregular downward steps, and taxation at the higher brackets began to include some not-quite-so-enormous incomes. The framing established by the world wars enabled the imposition of a highly progressive tax system during subsequent periods of peace.

We need depart from such absurd determinants of our progressive tax rates and move toward a sensible principle for the setting of tax rates. Inequality insurance would do just that by defining a simple public standard for tax rates in terms of a limit on inequality. Citizens should easily be able to understand the system, and hence it could be consistently maintained over time.

The Problem of Immigration and Emigration

Today, many young people can expect to spend their lives in countries other than the one in which they were born.[9] As a result, inequality insurance needs to take account of immigration and emigration to function well. With the advance of technology, moving to other countries to work is becoming easier and easier. With the proliferation of multinational corporations, the increasing prevalence of education abroad, the decline in costs of air travel relative to incomes, the emergence of English as a world language, and the Internet's allowing people to connect with one another across national borders, more and more people will want to relocate themselves around the globe in their economic connections. If immigration and emigration are free enough, this could conceivably frustrate the efforts any of one country to manage the distribution of income within its borders.

As regards progressive taxes, this problem is largely manageable. High income people do not generally want to move to the third world to avoid high taxes, and the countries they would realistically move to do not have sufficiently lower taxes to motivate them to move. Rich Frenchmen do like to set up domiciles in Belgium to escape wealth taxes, but mostly people stay in their own country even at the expense of higher taxes. And people from developing countries typically cannot move to developed countries because of prohibitive immigration laws.

These existing barriers to immigration are enough to allow substantial income redistribution through progressive income taxes to proceed within countries today. But these barriers have their costs. It is a tragedy that hard-working and well-meaning people from developing countries are denied entry into developed countries where they could lead better lives. We can do relatively little to change this since their free entry would in many cases harm the interests of the indigenous population, who do have rights of citizenship that must be honored.[10]

The system that developed countries currently use to keep people from less-developed countries out is inefficient. The United States has strict immigration policies but lax enforcement, so many people manage to slip illegally over the border. Once here, the illegal immigrants pay dearly in terms of quality of life. Then, periodically, the United States considers granting amnesty to illegal immigrants.[11] This is a crazy system, and we could imagine a better one that could someday handle immigration.

A number of economists, including Julian Simon in 1986, have proposed auctioning off immigration rights to the highest bidder.[12] That would seem to be a logical and orderly way to handle immigration. Auctioning off a quota of immigration permits would allocate the rights to those who can best use them, or most want them. The payments could be structured so that immigrants would not have to pay the fixed up-front cash fee that some countries charge for immigration.[13] Instead, the immigrants could make payment out of a tax on future income so that the winners of the auction are not necessarily confined to wealthier, and more likely older, people. This proposal has not gotten very far. Implementation of Simon's proposal might be workable today, more so than it was in 1986, because we have more modern identification systems, and a better ability to keep track of people, to tax them later, and to apprehend illegal immigrants. A market for immigration rights may also be more in accord with current attitudes toward markets than in 1986, though it may require some modification since citizenship is an obligation not to be taken lightly.

The market for immigration rights would best be a heavily regulated one, with special taxes for persons who have benefited more from a country's educational system, waiting times before trade is made, and rules against frequent trade. Moreover, when people can be identified through time as immigrants, inequality insurance might apply differently to them. These conditions might not seem unfair if the immigrants were informed of them on entry.

Disincentive Effects of High Tax Rates

Inequality insurance might have additional problems in application because of the disincentives to work that may be caused by the high tax rates. Public finance economists have been debating for decades the extent to which high tax rates placed on high-income people create disincentives to work effectively. Clearly, if the government taxes 100 percent of incomes above a certain level, most people would stop working when they reached that level. But what if the government taxed 70 percent of income? Would people put in substantially fewer hours at work? Would people try less hard to be effective? Would spouses more often decide to stay at home?

Until the last couple decades, little evidence implied that people respond negatively to relatively high marginal tax rates by working fewer hours or working less hard. But some recent studies that rely on the changing incomes of high income people at times of tax changes have been interpreted as implying a strong response to tax rate changes.

Lawrence Lindsey, who was appointed chief economic advisor by U.S. President George W. Bush when he took office in 2001, wrote one of the most influential papers on this subject. Lindsey studied how taxpayers responded to the initial tax cuts under President Ronald Reagan, and found a striking increase in incomes, representing, he thought, an increase in work effort in response to the lower tax rates.[14] Studies such as Lindsey's, however, are inconclusive since they looked at a single short time in history when tax changes might have been viewed as temporary and when other changes were taking place that could plausibly account for the changes in incomes.[15]

Standard public finance theory of tax distortions, as presented initially by economist William Vickrey and developed further by James Mirrlees, assumes that individuals view the labor-leisure choice by weighing the displeasure of work against the pleasure of spending the income.[16] People are assumed to decide how hard to work by thinking of how much they will enjoy what they could buy with the extra income against the displeasure of working more to get it. Undoubtedly, people do often frame their labor-leisure decisions in these terms, at least in part. But psychological research on regret and mental categories, which bears on how people react to lost opportunities, suggests a modification of this analysis.

Largely, people make labor-leisure choices using naturally suggested frames. The fraction one "gives" to the government may be viewed as a central mental construct. People may react with anger and a sense of injustice if forced to give most of the income they earn above a certain level to the government. In that case, a decision to work less may be mentally framed as a principled decision to get revenge against the government. This kind of decision may be independent of any calculations of the pleasure obtained from leisure relative to the pleasure obtained from consumption.

This sense of anger or regret may be only a temporary response to increases in tax rates. Moreover, when tax legislation is defined in terms of the level of inequality rather than the level of tax rates (the rates themselves being variable from year to year as the amount of income inequality changes) then tax rates themselves will be less salient and less likely to be the object of anger. People would not view the higher tax rates generate by higher inequality as payments to the government, but rather as payments to other less fortunate people. To further alleviate this problem, we could make the inequality insurance payments a tax paid by the employer, in effect framing the employee's income on an after-tax basis.

People may not always compare their after-tax pay with their before-tax pay. They may be inclined to compare their after-tax pay with the after-tax pay of others (as revealed by their living standards). Psychologist Leon Festinger has shown the fundamental importance of social comparison process to human behavior, and a tendency of people to continually reassess themselves in comparison with others close to them.[17] Economist Robert Frank has pointed out that at very high incomes, much of the utility obtained from incomes operates through comparisons with others, not from the direct consumption benefits.[18] High-achieving people enjoy the process of working for an ambitious goal, and certainly as long as the goal allows them to achieve high social status, they will probably want to work hard.

Yet another comparison is to one's own former take-home pay—the after-tax pay that one had before rates were increased. One may be so distressed that one is able to consume much less than one used to from an hour's pay, that one might choose not to put in that extra hour. To the extent that people make this comparison, short-run changes in taxes are likely to have substantial short run effects. Eventually, if the higher tax rates are part of the background assumption of our lives for many years, then such a comparison will be forgotten. With inequality insurance that merely fixes the level of inequality at present levels, there will never be any sudden changes to get used to.

People who view themselves as in lifelong careers that mean something to them personally, rather than as merely hiring themselves out for disagreeable work by the hour, are unlikely to respond much to income tax rates. A young businessman who is starting a business is not likely to be much affected today by whether a dreamed-for highly successful outcome years down the road is going to make him only ten million dollars, and not a hundred million dollars.

These considerations suggest that the negative incentive effects of tax rate increases may be rather small, even if the increases are to high levels. We still have reason to worry, however, about the work-discouragement effect of an inequality insurance program, and such concerns may limit its application.

Distributive Justice without Large Collateral Effects

Some countries have set high standards for public action against inequality. Canada and Sweden, for example, have become very egalitarian since the middle of the twentieth century.[19] The tax and welfare systems in both these countries have been substantially more progressive than those in the United States. What these countries have not done is adopt inequality insurance, which would finally quantify an acceptable level for inequality and correct it automatically if inequality increased beyond this acceptable level. Instead, the tax system in these countries still leaves the determination of tax rates in a politically determined nexus. People in these countries abhor inequality but have no standard for the amount of inequality that can be tolerated and maintain a sense that any remaining inequality is evidence of injustice.

Critics of the egalitarianism in these countries have argued that this public attitude toward inequality has had the unfortunate consequence that economic success itself is viewed with some negativity, as if it is nothing other than evidence of a failure of our their democratic system and a mockery of their values. Canadian observers of the downside of the egalitarian values are outspoken. In a memorandum to Prime Minister Jean Chrétien, the Canadian Business Council on National Issues wrote,

> Success at both the personal and corporate level should be an aspiration to be nurtured, a goal to be encouraged and an achievement to be celebrated. Instead it seems to be a vaguely embarrassing anomaly that should be taxed until it goes away. The future of our economy and the quality social programs that it supports depend on changing that attitude.[20]

Similar complaints about the Swedish tax have also been aired. One Swedish author, Nils-Eric Sandberg, wrote in 1997,

> The equality concept in Sweden has not only become a reaction to unjustified income differences or "injustices" but has developed into a general intolerance of differences. "Serious" journalism is to a great extent concerned with tracking down differences between groups and criticizing them as manifestations of "inequality."[21]

Swedish economist Assar Lindbeck has expressed similar views about the egalitarian policies in Sweden:

> [S]uch policies necessarily result in *politicization* of the distribution of income. Many individuals are then likely to start regarding the distribution of income as "arbitrarily" determined by the political process, rather than fulfilling important functions for the allocation of resources and economic efficiency. As a result, distributional conflicts may in fact, after a point, be accentuated by reduced income differentials.[22]

This intolerance to differences is itself a barrier to achievement incentives, quite apart from the high marginal tax rates in these countries.

When countries have tied their national identity to a sense of equality, and take piecemeal action against any signs of positive economic achievement, and people start to see something morally wrong with achievement itself, then achievement incentives will drop, no matter what happens to tax rates.

This problem can be remedied by adopting inequality insurance, thereby creating a different standard for our sense of justice in society, a symbol that does not require that we see complete equality everywhere and in every aspect of life.

With inequality insurance in place, people will know that the system itself is society's answer to problems of economic inequality. With inequality insurance in place, it should be possible to prevent inequality from ever expanding so far that it causes the kind of resentment and social conflict seen in the most unequal countries of the world. The inequality insurance system itself should stand as a symbol that citizens care for one another within a nation, even though it leaves some with better economic fortunes than others.

TWELVE

Intergenerational Social Security: Sharing Risks between Young and Old

IN AN INFLUENTIAL 1994 REPORT, *Averting the Old Age Crisis,* the World Bank sounded an alarm for most of the world.[1] The report asserted that certain of our hopes for social progress, the reduction of the once-rapid world population growth and the improvement of life expectancy, have succeeded so well that they will create an unprecedented new problem: a rising number of elderly people as a fraction of the world's population.

According to the report, in 1990 there were five hundred million people in the world over the age of sixty. By 2030, there will be 1.4 billion. Either the relatively small number of the younger people who are still of working age will take on a large burden of caring for these elderly, or many of these elderly people will be facing a miserable existence.

This old age crisis was unknown a generation ago, when the world was instead concerned with overpopulation—too many babies, too many mouths to feed for the world to support. It is remarkable how our concerns change through time. This new crisis is another example of the kind of surprises history produces for us.

Ultimately, this new crisis was at least in part generated by technological progress, by such things as the introduction of the birth control pill in the mid 1960s, which lowered the birth rate, and improved medical care, which raised life expectancy. Indeed, it was technological change that made social security imperative in most countries in the twentieth century: technological progress raised the life expectancy in developed countries from around forty-five years in 1900 to around seventy years by mid century, creating a vast class of retired elderly and causing us to have to invent institutions to deal with their problems.[2] The risk of similarly important changes precipitated by our technology should be a central focus of any current debate. The effects of new technology have surprised us, and they will surprise us again.

It is important to note that the financial problem that this old age crisis highlights is one of *intergenerational* risk, risk that affects different generations alive at the same time. The fundamental principle for risk management then is sharing this risk between the generations.

Finance can do nothing about demographic changes, but it can ensure that the risks of unexpected changes in demographics, or in other factors affecting the relative welfare of the generations, are shared between the generations. We need to replace the old age insurance of social security with one designed to protect both young and old against risks by sharing risks between them rather than to protect the old exclusively. The immediate problem is how to divide up the burden if either the elderly or the younger people unexpectedly encounter a bad situation.

Reframing social security means all that reframing has meant to earlier ideas in this book; it means changing our frames of reference, our sense of institutions, our assumptions about the motivation for our institutions, and our formulas and standards of measurement.[3]

Today's Social Security Benefits and Contribution Formulas

Let us first consider where social security stands today. Most countries' government old age pension systems are earnings-related contributory systems defined by fixed contributions and benefits formulas. Workers are obligated by law to make contributions from their paychecks according to a formula, and these contributions are used to pay the benefits of the currently retired. The amount that retired persons receive in the form of benefits is defined by a formula related to their own prior contributions. A 1999 study of social security systems of 173 countries found that 136 countries (79 percent) had such contributory systems in which benefits are related to prior earnings.[4]

The statutory social security contribution formula in the United States is an example of such a system. Employed workers must contribute 6.2 percent of their earnings, up to maximum earnings, $84,900 in 2002, and their employer contributes another 6.2 percent of their earnings up to this maximum, for a total of 12.4 percent. Self-employed workers must contribute 12.4 percent of their earnings, up to the maximum earnings. The 12.4 percent is fixed from year to year, and will not be changed, unless Congress passes legislation to change it.

The statutory social security benefits formula in the United States specifies retirement benefits by first calculating the worker's "average indexed monthly earnings," the average of the thirty-five years over the worker's lifetime with the highest earnings (indexed for wage inflation and truncated at the maximum earnings for each year). One's benefit upon retiring is determined according to a fixed formula with no other inputs but age at retirement and average indexed monthly earnings.[5] In the years following retirement, one's benefit is automatically increased in proportion to inflation as measured by the Consumer Price Index for Urban Wage Earners and Clerical Workers (CPI-W) so that the buying power, the real value of one's benefit, never changes. There is no risk at all to retired people's benefits.

Similar benefits and contributions and indexation formulas are used in many other countries. For example, in France, workers contribute 6.55 percent of pensionable earnings and their employers contribute 8.2 percent of covered payroll and 1.6 percent of total payroll. Benefits range (depending on age or duration of insurance) from 25 percent to 50 percent of average salary for the best twenty-five years. In Brazil, workers contribute 8 percent, 9 percent, or 11 percent of earnings according to three wage levels, and employers contribute 20 percent of payroll. Benefits equal 70 percent of last thirty-six months' earnings plus 1 percent of average earnings for each year of contribution, up to 100 percent.

The contribution formulas are designed so that the contributions received roughly equal the benefits paid, that is, these are typically well described as "pay-as-you-go" systems. Since contributions and benefits do not match exactly, a trust fund is designed to take up the slack. In the United States, the Social Security Trust Fund had approximately $1.2 trillion in 2001, a small amount compared to the roughly $10 trillion that would be needed if we were to pay the expected future benefits entirely from the trust fund. If the trust fund runs out of cash and the statutory benefits continue to exceed the contributions, then the system becomes "insolvent," that is, it becomes impossible for the Social Security Administration to continue paying according to the formulas. Ultimately, then, over the years the payment of benefits must come overwhelmingly from new contributions.

Because of declining birth rates since the mid-1960s in most developed countries, and the longer life expectancies—the "old age crisis" that we have stressed here—the public has paid sustained attention to the potential insolvency of social security. Analyses often stress that if current formulas are unchanged, the contributions collected will eventually fall short of the benefits paid.

Often, the public discussion of this problem is excessively formulaic because participants forget that the contributions and benefits formulas are essentially arbitrary. Often, the discussion is framed in terms of making good on our promises to the elderly, as if these were solemn promises that were entered into with a vow. In fact, the benefits and contributions formulas were merely invented by some lawmakers, and hardly anyone remembers why they set them as they did.

The lack of a clear standard of risk sharing between generations has meant that public discourse on social security taxes and benefits have often been appallingly empty. When the U.S. Congress first imposed in 1983 the federal income tax on up to one half of social security benefits received by people with incomes over $25,000, the public discussion relied only on such abstract principles as "the principle of equality" or "progressive taxes." There was outcry against "double taxation," since the social security benefits formula was already progressive. But no standard existed for setting tax rates based on these general principles. The real center of the discussion was that the government "needed" the money to control a ballooning deficit and could not raise tax rates since President Ronald Reagan had "pledged" not to. The debate over taxing social security benefits was highly unsatisfactory then, and nonexistent now. Now that the tax is part of the background of institutions, taxation of half of social security benefits continues without any public attention or discussion. And there is no discussion because there is no theory or standard about how retirees' benefits should be defined.

A Simple Example of an Intergenerational Social Security Scheme

Consider how social security's old age insurance benefits and contributions formulas might be easily conceived of as intergenerational social security, at least in a somewhat simpler world than the one we live in.[6] Suppose, to simplify the story, that all nonretired adults work full time, that retirement occurs at a fixed age, that no retired people work part time, and that there is no difference in the economic needs between young and old. Moreover, assume that the only income that people receive is income from their labor: this means that social security will be absolutely essential, since the retired not only cannot work but also have no savings at all to support them.

Under these assumptions, social security amounts to dividing up the available labor income, provided by the young, between young and old. The natural thing to do would be to divide it equally, subject to the restriction that benefits and contributions must be proportional to incomes so that those who contribute proportionally more receive proportionally more.

In this case, an attractive simple intergenerational social security scheme would merely specify contributions as a percentage of every working person's income (after taxes and after the inequality insurance described in chapter 11) equal to the percentage of people who are retired. Currently, about 11 percent of the U. S. population is retired,[7] so the contributions would be 11 percent of every working household's after-tax income, leaving the remainder (89 percent) for the household, including children. Here, the contribution formula is not determined by political factors or arbitrary formulas but rather by demographics, and changes automatically as demographics change.

Fairness dictates that the benefits that retired people receive bear a relation to their incomes when they were young and working and hence to the amount they contributed then. A simple benefits formula would then be that each retired person receives benefits proportional to his or her average indexed earnings (income the retired person earned while working computed in much the same was as U.S. social security system does today, but without any limit on social security income), where the factor of proportionality in each year equals the total contributions paid by working people this year divided by the total average indexed earnings (over the years when they were working and contributing) of all retired people. This way of allocating benefits adds up, in the sense that the total contributions of the young equal the total benefits received by the retired. But it adds up in such a way that those who contributed more to the system receive proportionately more in benefits.

Note the fundamental difference between this system and the system currently in place in the United States and other countries. The fixed schedules in the current systems mean that the retired people are promised a fixed income *whatever happens* to the fraction of the population that is retired or the income of the working people relative to the income that retired people once had. These systems do not share risks between generations. From a generational standpoint, they transfer the income risks of retired people to the working people and their dependents who thereby bear a magnified risk, the risks of both generations. The proposed system instead divides up the available income among people alive at the time so that they all share properly in the state of the economy.

The actual implementation of an intergenerational social security system would have to account for other factors not included in this simplified example: savings, incentives for saving, risks to savings, retirement income, the relative needs of young versus old, and the relative moral hazard impact on the young versus the old. But the basic risk management principle, sharing risks between the generations, would remain the central principle of design.

Risk Sharing within the Family

Intergenerational social security is a formalization of roles undertaken by the family, which, in the past, has been the primary mechanism for sharing intergenerational risks. Because individuals have had no ability to make intergenerational contracts on financial markets, and because one cannot make deals with children—who will become the ones who will care for us when we are old—we have instead relied on family traditions for intergenerational risk sharing. Traditionally, only the family has had good information about individuals' relative needs and abilities to contribute, and only the family has had the kind of informal intergenerational understandings that allow the management of such risks. In the information age, however, the situation is quite different, because the proliferation and availability of relevant information can allow a transferring of much of this risk management from the family to broader social institutions. If social security systems were redesigned to resemble the family as a risk managing institution, they would be better able to take account of relevant information.

For virtually all of human history, care of the elderly has been pay-as-you-go: in each generation young adults help their children; when these same individuals are middle aged, they help their elderly parents. Thus, when one is young, one "saves" in the form of creating indebtedness from one's children rather than by buying stocks, bonds, or physical capital. The pay-as-you-go social security systems around the world today may be regarded as improved versions of this ancient system, with the improvements coming from the formalizations and larger pool in which risk is shared.

The family is a fundamental institution that we do not want to replace. But relying *exclusively* on the family for sustenance in old age is intrinsically risky.

Formalizing the system of parental care into the social security system has certain advantages over the older family-based system because it eliminates random elements. Some people have no children or have children who die young; when they retire, they will have no one to care for them. Some parents have children who do not care about them and who will neglect them. In older days, the extended family might exert pressure on neglectful children to take up the burden of caring for their parents, and other relatives or caring friends might step in their place, but such a mechanism is not secure. Having the government manage a pay-as-you-go social security system eliminates such uncertainties.

But we do not want the government system to ignore the flexibility inherent in traditional family ways of sharing incomes. In traditional families, the obligations between generations are naturally somewhat flexible and responsive to the incomes and needs of all generations alive at a time: the elderly and their grown children who are now working, and their grandchildren who are still very young. Flexibility means give-and-take depending on needs and abilities to contribute. If elderly parents have done very well economically, for example if they had successful business dealings while still employed or if they invested in a stock market that soars, then, when they are old, their middle-aged children will probably be expected to bear less of a burden of caring for them. If parents do very poorly in their investments, on the other hand, then they will expect their children to help them out more. Within the family, the same responsiveness generally applies with regard to children's incomes. If the grown children become very wealthy as middle-aged adults, because of a successful career, or because of successful investments, then they will tend to be expected to help to a greater degree with the financial needs of their elderly parents. If, on the other hand, the children are thrust into poverty in their middle-aged years, then their parents will tend to expect less of them.

Social security systems do not now incorporate such flexibility. The fixed real benefits after retirement, if they are indeed interpreted as promised to the elderly and not changed, mean that retired persons bear no economic risk; all the risk is transferred to younger people.

It appears that no social security system in the world today fully embodies the basic aspects of intergenerational risk sharing. But the Swedish social security system adopted between 1998 and 2001 is one example that incorporates some degree of risk sharing. In the new Swedish social security system, each individual's contribution (including employer contribution) is 18.5 percent of pensionable income, of which 16 percent of pensionable income goes to a pay-as-you-go system, and 2.5 percent to individual financial accounts. The pay-as-you-go contribution, the 16 percent, is used immediately to pay benefits to retired persons (some of this will be put into a "buffer fund"); this part of the contribution will also be recorded as going into a "notional account" that pays "interest" and which then determines the individual's benefit when he or she retires. Since the "interest rate" in this notional account is defined in terms of the rate of growth of average income, according to a complicated formula that ensures that total benefits and total contributions approximately balance, the amount that participants will eventually receive as pensions when they retire will be related to the then-working people's ability to pay. Thus, this system has part but not all of the features outlined in this chapter. While contributions do not depend on demographics or the needs or incomes of the retired persons, benefits received by the retired do depend on the ability of working people to pay.[8]

Intergenerational Social Security versus Individual Accounts

The most prominent recent proposals to reform social security are those that would allow participants to invest part of their contributions in individual accounts, in the stock market or in other investments of their choice. That is, social security would be converted in part into a sort of mandatory savings and investment plan. These proposals, which have been under discussion in many countries and already implemented in some, are described by their promoters as connecting with our modern appreciation of the importance of financial markets. Their proposal falls short on exactly that score. Those who appreciate modern financial theory well will reflect that the essence of finance is reducing the impact of risks by spreading them around to many people, and not just by diversifying an investment portfolio. With social security, we must share the risks of the generations in a constructive way. Making the generations depend on the success of their investments for their own retirement is not risk management.

Those who advocate these individual accounts appear to have drawn the wrong lessons from modern finance. Many seem to think that the deep wisdom coming from our collective experience with financial markets is that the stock market always returns 12 percent a year in the long run, so forcing social security participants to invest in the stock market will dramatically cure the budget problems of the social security system. This is not financial wisdom. It is simply betting that we will have as good luck with stocks in the future as we have had in the past.[9]

Many who advocate individual accounts also seem to think that another lesson from modern finance is that people differ from one another most importantly in their attitudes toward risk and preferences for investments, so the paramount consideration must be to allow them to choose, in allocating their social security contributions, between stocks and bonds, or between risky stocks and not-so-risky stocks, to accord with their own individual preferences. In fact, however, consistent and large differences across people in attitudes toward risk are hard to find; rather, people seem to differ from one another more significantly and consistently in such personal circumstances as their age and generation than in terms of their risk preferences.[10]

Security for Society as a Whole

We must redesign social security to effectively share risks widely across generations. When these risks unfold within a closely-knit family, their importance is obvious. When families are strong and caring, family members will remember the contributions a relative has made in the past and will make sure that he or she will be taken care of. Society as a whole cannot and should not replace the caring family, but it must recognize that caring, closely-knit families are not universally ensured. Even when families are very closely knit, they are still small units and cannot fully diversify the risks that the individuals within them face. Society cannot provide the love that occurs within a good family, but it can provide much of their risk sharing, and it can even carry risk sharing farther than any family can.

THIRTEEN

International Agreements for Risk Control

BETWEEN 1965 AND 1990, the economic fortunes of two countries on opposite sides of the globe—Argentina and South Korea—experienced a sharp reversals. In 1965 the per capita real GDP in South Korea was $1,754. That same year, the per capita real GDP in Argentina was $8,371, nearly five times as high. At that time, South Korea looked like a country that might humbly ask Argentina for foreign aid. But by 1990, twenty-five years later, South Korea's per capita real GDP had risen to $10,087, while Argentina's per capita real GDP had *fallen* to $7,158.[1] Now South Korea was the rich country and Argentina the relatively poor one. No one had expected this severe reversal of fortunes.

Things could have been different if South Korea had been able in 1965, presumably with the help of an international agency, to make financial arrangements with other countries, including Argentina, to share their development risks. With such arrangements, South Korea would pay the other countries if its GDP did better than expected relative to the other countries' performance during the contract period, and they would pay South Korea if its economy did less well than the others. The international agency that arranged the deal might well make such arrangements among countries that are far away from each other since distant countries are more likely to have differing economic experiences. Perhaps such a deal might be best arranged not directly between the two countries, here Argentina and Korea, but as a pair of contracts, one between Argentina and the international agency, the other between Korea and the international agency. Such a pair of contracts would amount to the same thing as a contract among the countries themselves, differing only in political ramifications.

We now know that the outcome of any such contract would have had South Korea paying Argentina a large sum of money, substantially mitigating the economic disaster in Argentina. South Korea could easily afford to pay large sums to support Argentina, given her great fortune. This is an odd outcome—the developing country helping the developed country—and not our expectation, but that is what would have happened.

On the other hand, South Korea's fortunes *could* have gone the other way, with her GDP per capita not rising substantially from the $1,754 dollars she started out with, and Argentina could have had had the economic success. In that case, South Korea may have been saved by Argentina from decades of hardship.

In 1965, no one knew which eventuality would prevail. Either way, if such a deal were made, we can reasonably suppose that really substantial help could have been sent between the two countries, depending on relative economic performance. On an ex ante basis, viewed from 1965, the contract clearly benefits both countries.

Moreover, if such a deal were made in 1965, higher standards of living might have prevailed in both countries on an ex post basis. This is possible because the risk management created by the agreement would have encouraged both countries to take calculated risks, to seize opportunities that would have been impossible for either country to make alone.

How International Agreements
for Risk Sharing Would Work

This chapter explores substantial international economic risk sharing among countries arranged by their governments, presumably with help from international agencies. Governmental risk sharing, which augments the economic risk sharing done by individual citizens through devices such as livelihood insurance, macro markets, and income-linked loans, would take the form of contracts between nations.

Governmental action for risk management, rather than just private action, is necessary because even though individuals could arrange international risk management for themselves, individuals cannot commit to contracts that extend beyond their own lives. Further, they cannot commit their children or grandchildren to such contracts except through government action. Finally, dealing with the moral hazard that people in a country might work less hard when their incomes are substantially shared abroad, may be best handled by governments.[2]

I am proposing very long term (perhaps fifty-year or even longer) risk management contracts among countries on behalf of all citizens of the participating countries. These risk-sharing contracts would be directed at sharing the total effect of all risks to the countries as measured by economic impact gauges such as per capita GDP or its analogues. The contracts would specify a formula according to which countries whose per capita GDP grew more than expected would pay countries whose per capita GDP grew less than expected. The contract could also impose limits on the fraction of GDP paid by any country, to make ultimate compliance more likely under extreme circumstances.[3]

This implementation of international risk-sharing agreements would involve a number of elements. First, the contract representing the international agreement would have to specify the expected growth rates of the economies, based on information available when the contract is initiated, so that we will know later whether any realized growth rate is a surprise. Second, the contract would specify a schedule of annual payments, with the countries whose GDP growth relative to expectations turned out to be relatively higher paying those whose GDP relative to expectations turned out to be relatively lower. Third, the contract would specify the weights given to the various countries in the contract, depending on the relative magnitudes of their risks, the relative per capita GDPs, and the relative populations of the countries. Principles drawn from financial economics can be used to optimally make these decisions about contract terms.[4]

Of course, there likely would be international disagreements about these contract terms. But there would also be mutual self-interest among all countries in arriving at a decision, since the optimal contract would be designed to make all countries better off.

Such contracts would thus create protections for nations that go far beyond protections against specific and narrowly defined risks, just as the macro markets described in chapter 9 would do this for individuals or corporations. Any risks whose outcome can be measured in terms of effects on GDP would be covered.

An Example: A Risk Management Agreement between India and Other Large Countries

Suppose that a ten-year contract were made between a poor country on one side—in this example, India—and such wealthier countries as Canada, Mexico, the United States, Brazil, Japan, France, Germany,

Italy, and the United Kingdom on the other, to swap unexpected future changes in Indian GDP for unexpected future changes in the combined GDPs of the other countries. This contract would be designed to protect India against the risk that her economy will falter in the future, a scenario that would represent enormous human hardship because so many in India already are so poor and cannot easily bear even slightly lower incomes or the loss of social services of a faltering economy. It is by no means a welfare program for India. The contract is designed so that it is beneficial to all parties, not just India.

Stefano Athanasoulis and I described and analyzed a hypothetical contract that could be signed among these countries.[5] The contract would have the form of a swap, a well-known kind of financial contract today. The first step in creating such a contract would be to agree on future expected growth rates for per capita GDP in all these countries. This would be difficult to do, of course, since there is so much uncertainty about the future, but there is incentive for all parties to come to such an agreement about expectations.

It would seem reasonable to suppose that India will catch up eventually with these other countries in terms of per capita GDP. With annual per capita GDP growth in India of almost 5 percent a year between 1995 and 1999, it is closing the gap. But since these other countries are expected to grow, too, it will probably be at least many decades before India catches up.

This then is the expectation, but expectations could prove to be incorrect. India could become even worse off: The economy could suffer some significant reversals, related to war or to political instability or to misguided government policies or to purely economic reasons like exclusion from economies of scale (profit opportunities that only very large, already established industries can enjoy simply because of their size) or some combination of all these reversals. On the other hand, India might enjoy a spectacular economic miracle that puts her on par with the other countries much earlier than expected. Thus, relative to this expected scenario, India might equally do better or do worse.

If there are macro markets for countries' GDPs, as defined in the chapter 9, then the difficulty of defining expectations may be reduced. Market prices for the macro market contracts would indicate expected future values. We need not wait for such macro markets, however, to implement these international agreements; the definition of expectations can be part of contract definition.

According to the proposed contract, if over the ten years the Indian GDP turned out lower than expected relative to the other countries' combined GDPs then the other countries would be contractually obligated to shift economic resources to India, thereby reducing the impact of the bad news for India. On the other hand, if over the ten years the Indian GDP were higher than expected relative to the other countries' combined GDPs, then India would be contractually obligated to shift resources to the other, richer, countries.

The swap between India and the other countries might take the form of a parallel (or back-to-back) loan agreement—much as foreign exchange swaps or interest rate swaps were often arranged between companies in the 1970s.[6] India would owe a debt to each of the other countries that is specified as a fraction of the increase of Indian GDP beyond the expectations for the increase specified in the agreement. Each of the other countries would owe a debt to India that is specified as a fraction of the increase in their GDP beyond the expected increase specified in the agreement. The effect of the agreement is an exchange of unexpected GDPs. When the swap is arranged as a parallel loan agreement, it is more likely to be honored than if it were an outright promise to swap unexpected GDPs, since each component of the agreement could be framed psychologically by all participants as simple debt for which there is a long tradition that obligations should be met.

The agreement would also entail a fixed annual fee that is paid between countries, in addition to the payments that are contingent on GDPs. In the case of the contract between India and the other countries, Athanasoulis and I concluded that in the optimal agreement the fixed annual fee that India would pay for achieving the risk reduction in this swap would actually be negative. That is, despite the fact that India benefits most strikingly from this contract, the other countries benefit sufficiently that in a free market for such swaps they should be willing to pay India to participate in this agreement.

It should be clear that the contract would be designed to cushion India against the risk of failing to do as well as expected, in exchange for a little help from India to the other countries if the other countries do less well then expected. With this contract, India is able to buy a lot of "insurance" from the other countries for nothing more than the promise that India would help these other countries a little bit if events turned against *them*.

It may seem callous to write a contract that would require India (whose per capita GDP is less than 10 percent that of the United States) to pay on balance a significant fraction of its GDP to the wealthier countries under any circumstances, but it is precisely the possibility of such circumstances that gives the wealthier countries a real incentive to make such a contract with India. India would pay the richer countries only if her unexpected growth in GDP, relative to theirs, turned out to be more successful than expected, and in this circumstance India would not need the money as much as it would have had it been unsuccessful in increasing GDP. The value of the contract to India comes because of the benefits it provides if India's GDP did much more poorly than the others', when money might be needed desperately there.

It may seem unreasonable to some to expect that India would ever pay on such contracts, should her economy improve more than expected. Some may think, Why would a poor country ever live up to its promises and actually pay a much richer country? In fact, however, India pays her debts today, and such extra debts would come due only when her economy did better than expected. There would be no moral high ground to take to justify reneging on the obligations at such a time. Note, too, that after the collapse of the Soviet Union in 1991, some questioned whether India was obliged to repay to the former Soviet republics money India had borrowed from the Soviet Union, but it paid anyway. One might think that India could have claimed that the reality of the much lower per capita income in India should have resolved the ambiguity of the debt situation in favor of her repudiating the debt then. Still, India did not repudiate this debt.[7] From this and other examples, there is no reason to expect that India would repudiate a risk management contract after its economy had done well.

Athanasoulis and I calculated that under our assumptions, the ex ante economic value of our proposed risk management contracts for India would be over 10 percent of a year's GDP in India.[8] That is, just creating such a contract, and doing nothing else, would create an increase in expected economic welfare roughly equal to a tenth of a year's income. And the economic value would be substantially higher if the contract ran for more than ten years. The value is so high because the cost to India of suffering a drop in GDP is significant, in terms of the poverty it would create for a country that already has so many people living marginal economic lives. The ex ante economic value of participating in the contract to the United States, on the other hand, is only

0.2 percent of a year's GDP. That number is much smaller since the agreement is not focused on the United States, lumping it in with many other countries on the other side of a contract with India. Still, getting 0.2 percent of a year's GDP in economic welfare just for signing this contract is worthwhile for the United States.

Even these calculations of the economic value of the contracts may be underestimates because they did not take into account the effect of the risk management contracts on the country's risk-taking behavior. As it stands now, with no such contract in place for India, the Indian business community feels constrained from major initiatives that might generate risks for the whole country, and the Indian government can not well afford to provide incentives for major risk taking at a national level for fear that a bad outcome of such risk taking would have devastating consequences for millions of people there. With the contracts in place, India might see major new industries, major new national specializations, that are not even seriously considered now because of unnecessary sensitivity to risk.

The same kind of risk management contract described above between India and a group of other countries could be extended to help all countries of the world. There could be risk management agreements between the United States and the European Union, between the European Union and Japan, between Latin America and Asia, and so on.

Magnitude of the Proposed International Agreements

These international risk management contracts would have to be large to be effective, potentially transferring significant fractions of national incomes across countries. Compare such transfers with those implicit in conventional foreign aid as it is offered to developing countries by developed countries. Foreign aid ranges from about 0.1 percent of U.S. GDP to 1 percent of some Scandinavian countries' GDP. To be really significant, the potential transfers of income might have to be ten times as large, or even greater.

Moreover, the foreign aid we observe today tends to be directed toward a given country's former colonies or to countries that serve the political interests of the developed country. Under no system at work in the world today is aid substantially given to the countries that have suffered the most in their economic progress.[9]

For foreign aid to be expanded to substantial levels and toward the countries that most need it—those that turn out to have substantial misfortunes—it is important that it be conceptualized in ways that are potentially advantageous to all involved countries, which is exactly what the international agreements I am proposing would achieve. While we might hope, alternatively, that efforts to develop an international sense of altruism could increase conventional foreign aid, this end is unlikely and is not the subject of this chapter. Countries would not enter into international risk management contracts from a sense of altruism; such contracts are advantageous to all parties from the perspective of pure self-interest.

International risk sharing certainly does not mean world government or the ceding of national rights to foreign bodies. It means only that governments undertake the same kind of financial risk sharing that I described earlier for individuals. It means that countries would adopt a genuine risk management perspective in their international relations.

These contracts differ from the minimal international risk-sharing pacts in force today in their magnitude and their more formal structure. Most potentially valuable are agreements to exchange unexpected national income between blocks of countries that are very different from one another in their economic activities and thus that have independent risks that can be swapped and thus reduced in their impacts.[10]

Risk Sharing among Countries Today

The risk sharing we actually observe among sovereign countries today is mostly inadequate and is informal rather than contractual. There has apparently never been the sort of contract of substantial and effective scale as Athanasoulis and I proposed among countries. Such contracts have not been made because governments lacked the theory and vocabulary of modern risk management that would have enabled them to define such a contract. The contracts between countries proposed here are rather like financial contracts between individuals and companies that we see today, but the language of finance has never entered fundamental international agreements to allow such sophistication in risk management.

Today, aid to countries in distress from other countries is offered as a form of charity after economic hardships have developed, and is not generally based on any contractual risk management arrangements. As such, the only advantage to the richer countries is political advantage. Moreover, the aid tends only to be given in response to sudden crises that grab headlines and that have political impact. Even under such circumstances, aid packages typically are small.

That said, we should still recognize that some groups of countries do engage in some form of international risk sharing.

The Commonwealth of Nations has a sort of mutual-aid spirit to it that does result in some risk sharing among its member nations. The Commonwealth of Nations, formerly called the British Commonwealth, is a loose alliance of fifty-four independent nations that were once part of the British Empire or associated with it. Established by the Statute of Westminster in 1931, when it consisted of only the United Kingdom, Australia, Canada, and New Zealand, the Commonwealth has grown so that its 1.7 billion inhabitants now comprise roughly 30 percent of the population of the world. It has in its very name—common wealth—a suggestion of common welfare and risk sharing. And yet there is no substantial contractual risk management function, no arrangement among countries that the more economically successful countries, whichever those turn out to be, will help those who become less successful.

Richer members of the Commonwealth of Nations appear to favor other Commonwealth members, as opposed to non-Commonwealth countries, as beneficiaries for foreign aid. To the extent that this foreign aid reflects changing circumstances in their economies, it functions as a risk management institution. But the aid is in effect small.

The European Union, a union of nations of Europe created from the European Economic Community that comprises roughly 6 percent of the population of the world, has some explicit provisions for effective risk sharing among member nations. The European Union collects a share of the Value Added Tax assessed by its member countries and has other revenues bringing its total budget to about 1 percent of the Union's GDP. About a third of this revenue is used for Structural Funds to help poorer regions in Europe, and there is also a smaller Cohesion Fund for the same purpose. These funds provide risk sharing, but the amounts involved are a tiny fraction of GDP.

The Commonwealth of Independent States was formed when the Soviet Union collapsed in 1991, from eleven of its former constituent republics, and comprises about 5 percent of the world's population. Its bylaws state its purpose and aims in terms of collective military security, prevention of conflicts and resolution of disputes, coordinated actions in economic, social, and legal fronts, and strengthening of sovereign equality among its members. But the bylaws do not mention the sharing of economic risks. Indeed, the Commonwealth of Independent States has been criticized for abandoning interregional risk sharing that once was somewhat effective within the Soviet Union.

Major international agreements, such as trade agreements and formations of trade unions among nations, do not contain significant provisions for risk sharing among nations.[11]

Even the risk-sharing agreements that we do see, such as the Structural Funds within the EU, tend to occur among similar countries that are geographically and politically close. It would be much better if the contracts were made between dissimilar countries that are geographically distant from each other because their fortunes are more likely to diverge, creating greater potential for risk sharing.

Risk Sharing as Integral to International Agreements

The basic problem of economic risks and their possible solution by international risk-sharing agreements has not been part of the vocabulary and tool kit of those diplomats who make international agreements. There is virtually no recognition of the kind of slowly evolving risks to standards of living of countries that add up over many years to substantial changes. There is virtually no recognition that we have measures, in our GDP accounts, of the combined effects of numerous and heterogeneous risks on the well being of countries, measures that could be the basis of risk management contracts. And there is no recognition that contractual arrangements could help offset such risks.

Of course, a mutually advantageous agreement between countries would have to acknowledge the current economic superiority of the richer country as well as the fact that the superiority is likely to persist for many decades, if not indefinitely. A richer country will not find the contract advantageous if the contract taxes away their current advantage with certainty. The contract has to be about future changes relative to expectations, so defined that they really could go either way for either country.

It is generally advantageous for wealthy countries to make risk management contracts with poorer countries, rather than just rich countries making contracts with other rich countries, since the former circumstance are more likely to see more differences in economic outcomes and hence more idiosyncratic risk to share. Risk sharing is generally more potent among dissimilar parties than among similar parties. And yet it is just such risk-sharing contracts that appear difficult to make since they look only at the future risks and not at the inequality already in place today, which is likely already to be a source of resentment.

Making an agreement among nations that involves future payment of large sums of money contingent on economic outcomes may be difficult. If these agreements are framed right, however, in the language of insurance and finance, and if they are framed as mutually advantageous risk-management contracts, it would appear that most people would accept them and live up to their terms just as they accept and live up to our existing risk-management contracts.

Part Four

Deploying the New Financial Order

FOURTEEN

Global Risk Information Databases

PRESENT-DAY INSURANCE and financial systems, so vital to individual well-being and social welfare, would be impossible without data—from actuarial tables to corporation balance sheets, drivers' records, employment information, credit and housing histories, tax records, and more. Data sources of all kinds allow for the effective estimation and pricing of risk and facilitate the smooth and continuous negotiation of contracts, claims, adjustments, and payments. If we as a society are to expand these risk management institutions to incorporate more kinds of risks, all of us—citizens, insurers, investment managers, bankers and government agencies—will need better, more encompassing databases and data management technologies to cover these risks.

The ideas presented in part 3 of this book suggest the kind of fundamental new risk management institutions that could improve the lives of individuals, families, communities, and societies. Mere mention of such new institutions, however, reveals some basic information-related problems that must be solved if we are to deploy the radical financial innovations needed to reduce these heretofore unhedged risks. After all, the idea of sharing risks depends on the willingness of one person or entity to exchange large personal risks with another, to the mutual benefit of both. But to do this, we will need a free exchange of relevant information so that we can specify and quantify these risks. For that, we will need bigger and better databases to help buyers and sellers create these insurance contracts. Hence, these databases would constitute the very foundation of a newly democratized financial order wherein society can make extensive use of digital information to reduce and manage a whole range of previously uninsured risks. This chapter contains the core of a proposal to develop a set of global risk information databases (GRIDs) for the creation of economically sound, legally enforceable, easily transacted risk management contracts of all kinds.

The proposed GRIDs would provide finely detailed, continuously updated, widely available data on incomes and asset prices as well as aggregated data on these and other values relevant to the risks faced by individuals, organizations, corporations, and governments. Properly used, this new universe of information would allow better management of an ever wider spectrum of risks that would help not only to secure people's lives but also to reduce economic randomness and inequality throughout society.

Here are some snapshot examples of how the GRIDs would work. First, the GRIDs would help risk management contracts respond to data on *individual* people or organizations. Our biochemist (from chapter 8), wishing to purchase a livelihood insurance policy on a career in recombinant DNA technology, would provide a password that would allow the insurer access to data on a certain portion of his detailed personal information so that the insurance contract can pay claims in part in terms of his own actual career outcome. The insurance contract would not be confined to the information provided in a line on his tax form; it could define benefits in terms of a wide variety of determinants of his economic status, so that it could protect his ultimate career risks. Our violinist in Chicago (from the introduction), wishing to borrow money with an income-linked loan tied partly to her own individual success as a violinist, could similarly give access to her records on a GRID in a way that links to relevant personal information about her career and excludes irrelevant information. It could to allow the risk management contract to test various aspects of her career success so that it rewards her only if her career turns out badly, thus avoiding bad incentives that would lead to moral hazard.

The GRID would also provide a research function that would make it possible to devise new risk management contracts. An insurance executive in Manila interested in proposing a new form of insurance for covering, say, risks to professional education would use the detailed information in a GRID on individual professional career incomes to structure the proposed policies. The head of a public service labor union in Rome, seeking to negotiate a new contract for his membership, could consult a GRID showing municipal employees' income information to define a contract to hedge his union's salary gains or losses. The president of a community association in Bristol, seeking to offset the losses in housing values associated with the departure of a major local employer, would access the relevant data in a GRID on other communities housing prices and their relations to homeowners' incomes. The executive director of an international employee stock ownership plan in Ottawa, seeking to provide her member organizations with a means to hedge their holdings in their parent company, would use a GRID to make an array of hedging instruments specifically designed for the members' risks.

Despite seeming futuristic and sprawling, this undertaking is really not too far a reach, especially for a generation raised on computers. Nowadays, people pay their taxes, manage their bank accounts, trade stocks and bonds, play games, find mates, and conduct virtually every conceivable kind of business over computer networks, often with anonymous parties halfway around the world. The proposed databases would enable people to use their present computer skills to greater effect for their own security and would also provide new incentives to the existing information and financial technology industries to find new and rewarding applications for computer-related services.

We already have the beginnings of a network of economic data available on the Internet. But there are various aspects of the proposed GRIDs that would allow new forms of effective risk management. I will outline the proposed GRIDs in general terms; the details of any such database would of course be discovered and designed through time.

Groundwork for the GRIDs:
Public Information and Privacy

The essential first step for creation of the proposed GRIDs is governmental: setting standards and legal underpinnings. There must be rules about what is acceptable information to include on the GRIDs, rules about what kinds of information people are required to have on the GRIDs, rules about the kinds of information publicly available on the GRIDs, and a governmental commitment that certain kinds of contracts written in terms of the GRIDs will be honored even in the distant future. Since the GRIDs will make certain kinds of information public goods, government subsidization of information gathering may also be necessary. There must also be rules to insure privacy. Governments would have to define and enforce fair information practices. Laws regarding privacy, such as the U.S. Federal Privacy Act of 1974, would have to be updated.

GRIDs could be designed so that researchers or contract designers have free access to a wide variety of data on incomes that masks individual identities, and on an immediate and up-to-date basis. This would allow them to construct thousands or millions of indexes of incomes that are relevant to economic risks and that could be used for risk management contracts.

Privacy of individual or firm records can be ensured even while allowing researchers access to their data without the restrictive implications of the old-fashioned cell-suppression system that made the data hard to interpret. Technology can mask individual identities in such a way that researchers can still use the data, and even link multiple data sources, for most legitimate purposes. One method of ensuring privacy is dynamic assessment of risk of breach of confidentiality in the course of repeated data queries and refusal of additional queries.[1] Another method is matrix masking and the addition of noise.[2] Another, more sophisticated method masks microdata using the predictive distribution of confidential data, so that statistical inferences from the masked data should be unaffected by the masking.[3] These systems are now in active development and would allow researchers to access individual data for just about any legitimate research purpose, and this then will enhance the risk-management possibilities provided by the GRIDs.[4]

Operation of the GRIDs

The computer technology that would make a GRID work effectively would probably be best developed through private initiative, after governments complete the necessary groundwork, providing standard ways of entering and accessing information. This would allow people to avoid arduous searches for information, instead accessing the processed and filtered information for easy use. Ideally, private companies would develop competing systems, and users of GRIDs would ideally have some choice as to which system to use.

Because new forms of risk management covering livelihoods are intended to protect incomes, the most essential data on a GRID would concern the incomes of individuals, corporations, and governments. The databases should be global because risk management opportunities tend to exist with people who are far away and whose economic fortunes are subject to different risks. There should ideally be sufficient information so that users understand the meaning of the definition of income and can even change the definition.

A GRID should be designed with a common data socket, that is, a protocol for accessing the data in a standardized form, so that it can be automatically used by computer programs.[5] Then, for example, people wishing to create risk management contracts can access standardized programs that allow them to define aggregates that represent their risks and to make contracts in terms of these new aggregates so that all parties can use their own software to understand the contracts.

To further facilitate the creation of appropriate long-term risk management contracts, the databases should include an identification system that tracks people and organizations over time. Contracts could be signed based on future outcomes as revealed by a GRID, and the GRID will keep track of such contracts. The databases should be designed so that actions can be taken on them, so that the databases become a vehicle for individual choice and economic action.

Facilitating Contracts Based on Individuals' Income

Ideally, data on the entire income history of each individual, along with other information about the individual and the individual's family, would be available on a GRID, including built-in privacy protections. Despite the privacy filters, the individual would be able to permit access to the relevant income information to others to allow the GRID to fulfill its risk management function. Further, individuals would be able to access the GRIDs to review information about their own income, and would also be able to choose to reveal, for risk management purposes, their own income status relative to others. But they could choose to reveal their income incompletely, for example, by specifying a range for their income. The intended receiver of the information, however, would know what such data mean and could trust the information for what it is.

A GRID would contain not only current incomes but also an historical record of incomes, their components, and their correlates, because risk management functions cannot be fulfilled without information about how these incomes have behaved. The risks that we have observed in the past, and the correlates of these risks, while not a perfect guide to the future, are indispensable aids to our judging the future risks.

Associated with the individual income data are data on characteristics of the individual—date of birth, sex, family structure, and educational and occupational history, possibly even genetic information, assuming that regulations are in place to prevent misuse of such information. If these are available on a GRID, risk management can take account of some individual characteristics because these characteristics may signal risks unique to that individual.

The GRIDs could also include components of income and costs to earning income to allow computation of alternative definitions of income, such as the Measure of Economic Welfare (MEW) that William Nordhaus and James Tobin first constructed from national income accounts data in 1972.[6] Even other variations more remote from our concept of income such as consumption or consumption adjusted for certain life events may be useful for risk management. Measurement of individual consumption might be made far more sophisticated than is possible today by linking the GRID to data on individuals' electronic purchases.

A GRID could provide increased information for calculation of broad indexes, such as national incomes or GDP. The more information widely available on a GRID, the more people will be able to calculate national income or verify government figures. The more detailed information available on a GRID, the harder it would be for governments to falsify their national incomes to manipulate the payments they owe on income-linked debt, international agreements, or macro markets. Their fraud would have to take altogether higher proportions, concerning the components of national income as well as its overall level, and substantial fraud might well be impossible.

Currently, governments keep records about individuals' incomes in connection with income tax collections. In this sense, the invention of the GRIDs is really not so radical; much of the information already exists. But tax authorities do not have systems in place to allow these data to be used constructively for risk management purposes. Moreover, the public cannot access these tax returns, for the information collected is for the sole purpose of guaranteeing that taxes are paid correctly.

Projects are already underway to collect data about people's incomes to give us some understanding of the broader picture of their incomes and their family structure and other characteristics. For example, in the United States the Panel Study of Income Dynamics (PSID) has followed a sample of families since 1968, recording their income, wealth, and characteristics as they change through time. The PSID now has data on 62,000 individuals, a seemingly large number, but only 0.02 percent of the U.S. population. A GRID should include at least a simpler version of the PSID for the entire U.S. population.

Many developed countries have data-collection efforts similar to the PSID.[7] The proliferation of these panel studies attests to their perceived importance and to their feasibility. But these databases are still not very useful for risk management. When Ryan Schneider and I attempted to devise improved indexes of income by occupation and educational level for use in risk management devices such as livelihood insurance, we ran headlong into the limitations of existing data sources.[8] We wished to base our indexes on repeated measures of individual incomes, but our data were limited to the households surveyed by the PSID, which allows repeated observations of the same households. While this was the best source of income data available, still our information about individuals' occupations and characteristics was sketchy. Moreover, the PSID results are always years out of date, since their methods require years to process survey data and make it available. Use of our indexes for risk management contracts at the present time would be impossible.

My proposal here is to move these databases out of the realm of research by extending their coverage to all people, to make sure the data are kept up-to-date, to make the results available instantly while at the same time assuring privacy, and most importantly to give the data a legal foundation so that risk management contracts, such as livelihood insurance policies, can be written in terms of the data with the expectation that they will be enforced.

Supplying Information about Corporations' Incomes

GRIDs can make available similar kinds of data for corporations' incomes. This information should be available in great detail because of the complexities of evaluating companies' incomes. Data on the incomes of companies could then be used, separately or as part of indexes, to determine gains or losses to settle insurance or financial claims. These functions could be pursued between companies, by allowing them to share some newly defined risks between them, or by individuals, by allowing people to enter into risk management contracts to hedge their personal risks for working in a certain industry.

Moreover, this corporate incomes GRID would help us fulfil the longstanding principle of public disclosure. Louis Brandeis (later a U.S. Supreme Court justice), in his 1914 classic *Other People's Money*, wrote that public disclosure is the best protection against corporate abuses that were seen in his day: "Sunlight is said to be the best of disinfectants; electric light the most efficient policeman."[9]

Brandeis proposed that public corporations should be forced to disclose fundamental information and to take steps to make sure that the information will be widely disseminated. "But," he argued,

> the disclosure must be real. And it must be a disclosure to an investor. It will not suffice to require merely the filing of a statement of facts with the Commissioner of Corporations or with a score of other officials. That would be almost as ineffective as if the Pure Food Law required a manufacturer merely to deposit with the Department a statement of ingredients, instead of requiring the label to tell the story.[10]

His thinking was one of the factors that led to the establishment of the U.S. Securities and Exchange Commission (SEC) in 1934. The SEC, through data dissemination and the public trust that this practice has created, substantially accounts for the strength of U.S. stock market.

The SEC has made disclosure real, much as Brandeis called for, and it has made impressive steps to integrate our new information technology in its operations. Today, one can learn many things about the income history of any public U.S. corporation appears on the Web site of the Securities and Exchange Commission (www.sec.gov), in their Electronic Data Gathering, Analysis and Retrieval (EDGAR) unit. This unit, planned for in the late 1980s, was made available in the United States from the very beginning of the widespread public use of the Internet in the 1990s.

The availability of company information online is increasingly becoming a reality around the world.[11] Moreover, recent moves toward global standardization of accounting rules, such as the European Council's adoption in 2002 of International Accounting Standards as part of the Financial Services Action Plan for Europe, will make it easier to represent such data on electronic databases.

Maximizing the usefulness of any such systems means establishing accompanying laws for rapid financial disclosure of important information. As the technology for rapid disclosure has advanced in recent years, so have the requirements for such disclosure. In the United States, the SEC forced rapid electronic public disclosure of company information with its Regulation FD, implemented in the year 2000. Regulation FD required that companies, when they reveal material information to anyone outside the company, must also make that information known immediately to the general public. While the regulation did not specify how they should make this information known to the general public, clearly the regulation was made with the expectation that modern electronic technology would make such dissemination feasible and economical. Now such disclosures are routinely are made accessible on companies' Web sites or made available through live Internet broadcasts of analysts' meetings, which hundreds of thousands of people can listen to; only a few years ago such meetings were private.

Regulation FD has already had some repercussions around the world. Shortly after Regulation FD was established, the Australian Securities and Investment Commission released a similar set of guidelines, and regulators at Italy's Commissione Nazionale per la Società e la Borsa have been working on similar regulations. In the United Kingdom, the Financial Services Authority (FSA) has issued new guidelines that set out a more comprehensive communications policy involving such things as webcasts and chatrooms.

Even in the United States, however, the data on EDGAR and the dissemination of information in accordance with Regulation FD are not always adequate. For instance, until the last minute, the public did not have knowledge of events leading to the recent Enron bankruptcy. Further steps must be taken to improve public information about public corporations. If we have better information about our corporations, our society will benefit in many ways—not the least, by preventing fraud and reducing the likelihood of speculative bubbles.

Efforts to improve corporate accounting are best done in coordination with an ongoing expansion of our electronic dissemination capabilities. Those who improve our accounting rules must constantly think about how the information in corporate accounts will be distributed electronically, and how this expanded information set can actually be used. Most of this can be done by private sources such as Edgar Online, which today provides online analysis and regularization of the government-supplied information on EDGAR. But government regulators and those who set accounting standards have a role in the development of standards and specification of the nature of required disclosure, and in policing proper disclosure.

Integration of the GRIDs with the System of Taxation

The more integrated the GRIDs are with the internal revenue system, the easier it will be for individuals and corporations to pay taxes. Complexity of tax laws and the resulting difficulty of complying with them will no longer be as much of an issue. If the system has comprehensive information about individuals' and corporations' incomes, tax authorities could automatically calculate taxes owed. Moreover, taxes might even be collected automatically. The option to leave tax computation and payment to the government is important for some individuals for whom any computations are very burdensome.

We already have a system whereby people can pay taxes online, and we already have government computers with partial information about individuals' sources of income. But at present in the United States no system exists, in most cases, for the government to compute people's taxes. But by integrating GRIDs with the tax system, we could guarantee some accuracy to the data in the GRID, since when paying taxes people must make an oath of honesty and are subject to audits and possible penalties for dishonest reporting. Thus, the data in the GRIDs could be relied upon for settling risk management contracts, such as the livelihood insurance contracts described in chapter 8.

With a sophisticated tax interface on the GRIDs, we could make tax rates dependent on more things, so the tax system could become a more effective tool for risk management. The tax system could become more effectively intertemporal (depending on taxes paid in earlier years and the circumstances of these earlier years) and interpersonal (depending on the amounts of taxes being paid by others, such as family members, and the circumstances of these others).[12] As long as this complexity is incorporated into automatic tax computation programs, it imposes no extra compliance burden on taxpayers.

If income averaging is to be resurrected, it should really be based on lifetime income history or accumulated taxes paid rather than just the past few years.[13] The GRIDs can help with this.

Incorporating Information about Risk Management

Once the tax system is incorporated into the GRIDs, the quantitative nature of the system's effects on risk management in various risk scenarios could be made available on the GRIDs. One ought to be able to compute not only one's actual taxes paid on past incomes, but also the effects of the taxes on current and future incomes. Projected future tax laws could be made available on the GRIDs for planning of the effects of long-term risk management devices on after-tax income.

Every insurance policy that an individual has purchased could be programmed to appear on a GRID so that the effects of the policies can be accounted for in interaction with taxes as well as other insurance policies and other risk management devices. Individuals could ideally enter data on other risk management contracts they have undertaken, for instance, options they have purchased or employee incentive options, or even their judgments about approximate determinants of employment bonuses they might receive. While some of these parameters are ultimately judgmental and difficult to measure, the GRIDs could be designed to take account automatically of as much information as possible and to make it as easy as possible for people to refine this information. The data sockets on the GRIDs that would make the information available could be designed so that proprietary personal risk management software could, in a comprehensive way, make use of the information about these contracts and about additional contracts that individuals might yet make.

An Interface for Charitable Contributions

Charitable contributions—the lucky giving to the not so lucky—can be considered an important part of societal risk management. The GRIDs can be adapted to facilitate such contributions. We could create a system, as part of a GRID, in which people could obtain information about charitable causes and distribute information about their own charitable activities. This would be an information-dissemination and retrieval system, easy and pleasant to use in which people could learn and connect to charitable and related activities in whatever community they follow and, if they choose, gain public recognition for their own charitable donations.

A GRID could also make it possible for people to be sure that their donations reach the really needy, and not just those posing as needy. Ideally, the GRIDs would contain a facility for making charitable donations to truly low-income people with various characteristics (geographical, age related, even church related). At present, no broad technology for doing so exists. If there were such, and if especially if it also allowed people to restrict the gifts according to their individual affiliations and values, there might be more charitable giving.

Before the invention of insurance, charity dealt with all manner of risks. The use of charity to manage such risks was necessitated by the poor information technology and the lack of development of financial thinking. Even in ancient times, some noted that the outcomes of such a risk management system were highly uneven, with sometimes excessive compensation bestowed upon the already rich and no compensation for the poor.[14] Our modern institutions of insurance, using our better technology, deal with some of these problems but can do better. Charity will still have a role to play, since charitable giving can respond to information about need and worthiness of support that no formal institutions can manage. Charitable giving can fulfil this role even better if it is done in connection with an integrated database that supplies much more relevant information.[15]

An Interface for Wills

A GRID could also be designed to provide an infrastructure to facilitate the handling of last wills and testaments. The system that we have is expensive, relying on lawyers and trustees. Only the wealthy can easily make complicated plans for the use of their life savings. Moreover people have no effective way to publicize the charitable parts of their wills if they want to. For these reasons, perhaps, most people leave nothing to charity in their estates. According to estate tax data from the U.S. Internal Revenue Service, as reported in *Giving USA,* only 13.4 percent of male decedents and 24.3 percent of female decedents left anything to charity in 1995. In recent years in the United States the amount given to charity in bequests is only about a tenth of that given by the living.[16] A pleasant, user-friendly interface on the GRID to design one's will, allocate some of the estate to genuinely low-income people or to other causes, and publicize that one has done so, might increase the amount of such giving and make it more effective.

If bequests were handled as part of a GRID, then people could direct that part of their bequests be used to help the really needy. Or, alternatively, they could direct that part of their bequest be held in trust to help whichever of their children or grandchildren, or members of their church or people in their own town, is ultimately the neediest in coming decades. With an effective GRID making such gifts feasible, in-

dividuals can make the kind of complicated bequests that today are re-
served only for the wealthy.

Databases for Managing Our Economic Lives

The proposed global risk information databases are designed to provide detailed information about individual and corporate incomes in
such a way that people can manage their risks more effectively, monitor their risks, and direct their income in ways that are more meaningful to them. The most central purpose of the GRIDs is to supply up-
to-date, accurate, and plentiful financial information so that effective
contracts can then be signed that hedge our biggest risks. But, as we
have seen, there are many uses of the GRIDs.

The examples for using the GRIDs alluded to here, including livelihood insurance, long-term contracts, taxes, bequests, and charitable
contributions, are only part of its potential uses. While GRIDs are not
necessary for the beginning of some of the ideas presented here, they
are necessary for their full development.

FIFTEEN

New Units of Measurement and Electronic Money

THE FAILURE OF MONEY to serve as a stable and sensible unit of measurement for financial transactions has caused innumerable financial dislocations. The dislocations caused by inflation or deflation are so well known that the public in virtually every country of the world has become fixated on the uncertainties of the value of money.

A computer search of English language newspapers in the late twentieth century shows that the word "inflation" was the most commonly used economic term of all; in fact, newspapers use "inflation" more than "sex." All this public attention to inflation is not because of some inherent fascination with that abstract economic topic. Instead, people pay attention because, with the value of the currency unit changing in unpredictable ways, they have become wary of its impact on their lives.[1]

One wonders, then, why we do not have units of measurement, for our financial and other contracts, that remain stable and meaningful through time. Our scientific units of measurement—liters, meters and grams—do not change. Why do we not have stable fundamental economic units of measurement too? Achieving such stable units of measurement, which may through time begin to replace the unit-of-account function of money, is the subject of this chapter.

A look at history reveals some extreme examples of the problems caused by an unstable monetary standard. In 1923, Germany experienced a rise of prices, called the "hyperinflation," that was so great that the value of the currency, the mark, fell to a billionth of its value of a few years earlier. Prices rose so high that the Germany government had to print one hundred million mark notes to serve as hand-to-hand currency, and three million mark postage stamps. Today one can buy these old notes at coin and stamp collectors' stores, now practically worthless.

The consequences of the enormous German inflation were absurd redistributions of wealth. Those German citizens who put their life savings in government bonds before the hyperinflation (bonds whose value would stay fixed in terms of marks, staying at just hundreds or thousands of marks without any zeros added later, even after a postage stamp cost millions of marks) lost essentially everything. Those German citizens who had gone deeply into debt benefited greatly: They saw the real value of the debt magically reduced to virtually zero. The decline in the value of the German government's post–World War I borrowing from foreigners more than compensated for all the war reparations Germany had paid to that date. The anger that these redistributions created, both at home and abroad, was a significant factor that may have helped the rise of fascism in Germany, and, ultimately, possibly even helped cause World War II. Indeed, Adolf Hitler, sensing the public mood, chose November 1923, the very peak of the German inflation, for his Munich Putsch, his first attempt to grab power in Germany.

The German hyperinflation case is an extreme example from history, but lesser examples are found everywhere. Every major country of the world has seen significant changes of the value of its currency since 1950, and, in consequence, major redistributions of personal wealth. And yet people still today write their financial contracts and set prices in terms of currency units whose real value is at least a little unstable, and potentially very unstable. It does not have to be this way.

People must recognize that the problem of inflation is really fundamentally a problem of changing units of measurement, of a yardstick whose length changes randomly and unpredictably through time. It is not primarily the problem that money itself loses value. It will surprise many people to learn that the value of U.S. dollars in notes and coins held by the public and in bank vaults amounted to less than 3 percent of U.S. household financial wealth in 2002. Moreover, much of this currency is probably held in criminals' stashes. Most of us, in every country of the world, hold very little of our wealth in the form of money: just a few bills in our wallets, some change in our pockets, and perhaps a few more coins and bills in a jar on the dresser. The impact of inflation or deflation on the value of these hardly matters to us.

Most of our accounts denominated in currency are really held in something other than money: savings accounts, for example, are really invested in assets that produce a return, and stocks are really shares in businesses, though we may mistakenly think of them as money because the account value is measured in currency units. Our paychecks are denominated in currency, and sometimes transacted in currency, but the real source of our pay is our ability to contribute to a business activity, which has nothing to do with the value of the currency. With currency itself a rather unstable and insignificant quantity, it makes little sense that the bulk of our accounts and transactions should be denominated in currency.

We ought to be able to change the unit of measurement so that the dollar or other currency is no longer the preferred unit for financial or other significant transactions. We should instead substitute other units—indexed units of account—which can replace money for many purposes. If before 1923 German borrowing and lending were done in terms of such units, and if the German government debt were defined in such units, then the hyperinflation would hardly have mattered, and perhaps it could have been avoided altogether. The same improvement would have been afforded in any other historical period of inflation. If contracts are made in terms of such units, then most of the important problems caused by inflation or deflation will disappear.

The Invention of the Chilean Unidad de Fomento

Chile's *unidad de fomento* (UF, or unit of development) is the world's first indexed unit of account. Created in 1967, when inflation there was much higher than it is now, it has been in use ever since. In Chile to-day, people buy and sell, and sign long-term contracts not only in terms of their currency (the peso) but also in terms of UFs. The UFs would seem like money, since some trade is done in these terms, but in fact there are no UF coins or notes. The UF is just a unit of measurement, like the meter or gram, but one with stable value in terms of purchasing power. Because the UF is stable and the peso unstable, the exchange rate between the UF and the peso is constantly changing. The UF is actually defined in terms of this exchange rate, calculated by government statisticians using their consumer price index so that the UF has stable value.

Today, the peso value of the UF is published in Chilean newspapers each day and appears on a government Web site. The UF is upheld by the government and by the legal system as a unit of account for trans-actions.[2] If one defines a future payment in UFs, one must later, on the date the payment is made, calculate the payment in pesos by multiply-ing the UF amount by the number of pesos per UF shown in the news-paper on that day. People in Chile today will quote the price of houses for sale and of apartments for rent in UFs, and they specify mortgage payments, tax payments, and even child support and alimony payments in UFs. Wages and prices of everyday items, however, are still defined in pesos.

It is important to be clear about the advantages that the UFs have and that account for the success of the UF in Chile. Let us take a very simple example. Imagine that you were living in Santiago and had a small apartment in your house that you wanted to rent out. In this case, would it not have been convenient for you to quote the rent to your tenant in UFs rather than pesos?

Before deciding on how much to charge for rent, you would go to a local newspaper and look up the exchange rate between pesos and UFs—16,326.94 pesos to one UF on June 1, 2002.[3] On that same day, there were 690.85 Chilean pesos to one U.S. dollar, and hence one UF was worth US$23.63. Suppose on that day you decided to charge ten UFs a month rent on the apartment, or 163,269.40 pesos a month (US$236.30). But you did not quote the rent to your tenant in pesos; you specified the rent in UFs; pesos were not even mentioned in your rental agreement. A month later, since there was inflation in Chile, the peso value of the UF was higher. The newspaper quoted the rate of 16,355.74 pesos per UF. Then the rent, staying constant at ten UFs, was automatically adjusted in terms of pesos, to 163,557.40 pesos a month. Ten years later, in 2012, the same rental contract could still be in force, and all the while the rent measured in pesos would be going up (or down if there is deflation) to preserve the real value of the pesos transferred.

Using the UF in this way is analogous to a similar practice, which is sometimes used in countries where inflation is a serious problem, of defining the rent in terms of dollars, euros, or some other more stable foreign currency, and asking the tenant to consult the newspaper for the exchange rate between the local currency and the foreign currency and to pay the appropriate amount in the local currency. If the foreign currency maintains its value, so will the rent. Defining the rent in in-dexed units of account is much better because no foreign currency can be trusted to have a stable purchasing power in local terms. The va-garies of international trade (to say nothing of the vagaries of the U.S. economy) mean that the purchasing power of the U.S. dollar in Chile or in practically any other country can fluctuate wildly from year to year. Argentina, who attempted to fix her economy to the U.S. dollar, learned this through bitter experience.

A Simpler Name: Baskets

The unit should be given a simpler name that stands for the real value it represents.[4] Moreover, an electronic payment system would make the units easy to use, and so the ultimate means of payment, money or something else, would be of no concern to individuals.

I have stressed in this book that naming matters. The name *unidad de fomento,* translated as "development unit," is too abstract. I propose renaming the UFs, when they are created in other countries, "baskets," which refers directly to the market basket concept used by those who construct consumer price indexes. The consumer price index reflects the price of a representative market basket of items most people buy, so that the index effectively represents the "cost of living." The units, the baskets, then refer to these market baskets, so buying and selling in terms of the baskets amounts, in essence if not form, to handing over or receiving these market baskets in exchange for other goods. This simple name change better reveals the substance of the idea of indexed units of account.

With the correct institutions, you could pay for just about anything electronically, using electronic checks, credit cards, smart cards, or the like for the payment in terms of baskets, and the payment would automatically be translated into currency or other units by the computers through which the payment is processed. You would never really have to talk in terms of currency or look in the newspaper or at a web site to find the exchange rate with the currency. Whether the electronic payment system made actual payment in terms of domestic money, foreign money, precious metals, or anything else would be a matter of indifference to most people. You would probably start to think in baskets rather than in currency. Effectively, the baskets would be a new kind of electronic money for which inflation would never be a problem.

Money Illusion

An important motivation for indexed units of account comes from the great difficulty that people have in understanding the changes in the purchasing power of money through time. The general public appears to have sufficient difficulty with indexation, with tying payments to indexes such as the consumer price index, that they will do so only in rare or extreme situations. Even in times of moderate to high inflation, most people will not purchase inflation-indexed debt, will not borrow with an indexed mortgage, will not agree to indexed alimony or child support payments, and will not ask for indexed rent or wage contracts. Prices of many items and wages tend to stay fixed in money terms for months or even years, and this stickiness can cause unfortunate wealth redistributions in times of economic change. The stickiness is also, by many accounts, a factor that tends to increase the amplitude of business fluctuations.

Simon Newcomb, the astronomer who became internationally known for standardizing a system of measures for astronomers, and who discovered the widely acclaimed "first digit phenomenon,"[5] turned his attention to the measure of value that we use, and wrote in 1879:

> All men in this and other countries are accustomed from youth to measure the increase or diminution of wealth by dollars or other denominations supposed to be units of value. . . . Even when the facts are understood, the idea that the change is in the value of the commodities measured, and not in that of the dollar itself, is so natural that a long and severe course of mental discipline is necessary to get rid of it. Indeed, we question whether the most profound economist can be entirely successful in this respect.[6]

In the 1920s Yale economist Irving Fisher called public attention to values defined in money, rather than real inflation-corrected values, "money illusion."[7]

The problem of money illusion could *in principle* be cured by indexation, by expecting people to devise formulas for adjustment of all prices and wages to indexes of inflation. For example, a rental contract would specify a formula, involving the consumer price index, to be used to adjust the rent each month for inflation. To mathematically confident people, that sounds easy enough. But, in terms of framing, it is not at all the same. It is fundamentally different to promise to pay so many baskets each month than to calculate with a mathematical formula each month. Baskets have a universality that no formula can ever have. Redefining in baskets ought to cure money illusion.

The advantage to quoting the rent in baskets is not always that you have committed yourself any differently. Unless you chose to sign a contract fixing the rent in baskets through time, you could still change it later. In this case, the advantage is instead that, by quoting the rent in baskets rather than currency, you would have achieved a different conventional or psychological framing of the contract, and the new framing has the advantage that you would not have to take any action to adjust your tenant's rent for inflation; it happens automatically. You might be able to leave the monthly rent in UFs where it is for years.

In contrast, under present arrangements and in practice in virtually every country outside of Chile, the real inflation-corrected rent (that is, the buying power of the rent) that tenants are charged has a strange saw-tooth pattern through time. Because it is administratively and emotionally difficult, both for renter and tenant, to change the rent, the rent tends to stay fixed in terms of currency for long periods of time, often more than a year, and then to suddenly jump when the renter finally decides to do something about the real rent lost to inflation. Through time, as inflation progresses more or less steadily and the rent is adjusted only periodically, the real value of the rent traces out a saw-toothed pattern through time, falling gradually between rent adjustments and then suddenly jumping up, only to fall again. The system generates such periodic conflicts between tenants and renters, and generates such an irregular pattern of real rents.

The system we have allows indexation, and it is sometimes done. Still, the public has trouble with the idea of indexation. The reasons for public resistance to indexation are varied. Most people are not fully attentive to the potential uncertainty in future inflation and are not attentive to the income redistributions caused by unexpected inflation. The vast majority of people are afraid of mathematical formulas (indexation rules) in contracts, and at some level the public habitually thinks in terms of units of money, as if these were the final measure of value.[8]

I recently saw a brushed metal sign with enameled red and black lettering on a commuter train in Boston that said "No Smoking— General Laws Chapter 272 Sec. 43A—Punishable by imprisonment for not more than 10 days or by a fine of not more than $50 or both." I wondered how these two penalties could be displayed together, since by anyone's standards ten days in prison is so much more severe a penalty than a fine of just $50. I thought that if the two are meant to be comparable, then the implied valuation of a day is $5, while in fact the minimum wage is $5.15 an *hour*. I realized that a reason for the discrepancy is that these penalties were established long ago, when $50 was more in line with ten days' income. I learned later that these punishments were legislated in 1968, when wages and prices were less than a fifth of their present levels. Legislators did not index the fine to inflation then—of course not. Railroads were not going to install signs on their trains stating that the fine was $50 times the Consumer Price Index in the current year divided by the Consumer Price Index in 1968. No one would even consider such a plan, nor would they consider such indexation in a million other applications.[9]

The consequences of our failure to index have been most notable with regard to savings instruments denominated in units of currency. Bonds have long been recommended as the "safe" investments that more risk-averse individuals should turn to as a haven from the stock market. But, as Jeremy Siegel has amply documented, over long intervals of time, twenty years or more, stocks have actually been the safer investment in *real* terms in the United States between 1802 and 2001.[10] And yet still, to this day, money illusion inclines many people to think of ordinary bonds as riskless if held to maturity.

Some unfortunate consequences of money illusion became apparent in the late 1970s and early 1980s when inflation reached well into the double-digit ranges in many advanced countries, briefly over 15 percent a year in the United States. Reflecting this high inflation, mortgage interest rates became very high, reaching 20 percent a year for some mortgages in the United States in 1981. One consequence was that the real, inflation-corrected, payment schedule of fixed rate mortgages became very high at the beginning of the mortgage. Conventional fixed-rate mortgages have a constant payment through time, measured in currency, for the life of the mortgage. But if prices are expected to continue to rise at 15 percent or so a year, this compounds to a 4-fold increase in a decade, and a 66-fold increase over the life of a thirty-year mortgage, which means an extremely high real mortgage payment at first, dwindling dramatically through the life of the mortgage.

It was thus very difficult to buy a house in 1981, since the initial annual mortgage payments would be enormous, on the order of 20 percent of the price of the house. It was little consolation that the real payments would be much lower in the future if one cannot make the payments today. There were simple solutions to this problem, either through indexing mortgages to inflation or by merely having the homeowner's mortgage payment schedule, measured in currency, increasing through time so that the real schedule is constant through time. But these alternative mortgage forms never got a strong foothold,[11] partly because some financial experts, for example, those reporting in the most prestigious consumer advisory magazine in the

United States, *Consumer Reports,* advised people, as a matter of principle, not to enter a mortgage contract that entailed their automatically going deeper into debt for a while, deeper in terms of currency, even if their real inflation-corrected debt steadily declined.[12]

Money illusion apparently affected even these experts. Home prices were relatively quite low in many cities in 1981 because of this problem with mortgages. The subsequent rapid home price increases in many cities around the world in the 1980s was the result of the sharp decline in worldwide inflation after 1981, which solved this mortgage financing problem.

When the U.S. government first issued indexed government bonds in 1997 it faced an uphill a battle with the public, which found it very difficult to comprehend indexation. Again, even the experts at *Consumer Reports* advised people against buying the U.S. indexed bonds.[13] Today inflation-indexed debt accounts for only 2 percent of the U.S. total interest-bearing public debt, and there is virtually no U.S. private indexed debt.

The U.S. government in 1997 decided to index the principal only on the plus side: Inflation would increase the indexed principal but deflation would not decrease the principal. Probably, this decision reflected the government's understanding of money illusion: people would likely not be receptive to financial arrangements that could in some circumstances cause them to "lose money" even if the real value of their returns were fixed. As a result, the U.S. indexed bonds were not a good model for the private sector to copy, since they did not protect the issuer from deflation. Further, the tax system is not indexed to inflation, and so if inflation increased, bondholders would owe big tax payments due on the inflation part of the return, and so bondholders would really not be fully protected from inflation by the indexation.

All of these problems would be solved by the reframing of our thinking into real terms that the creation of indexed units of account would have accomplished.

Evidence from the Success of Indexed Units of Account

Chileans seem to view the UF as a kind of money, even though there are no UF coins or notes. Newspaper advertisements of condominiums for sale or apartments for rent prominently feature UF-denominated prices, without translating them into pesos.

As further evidence that the UF is treated as if it were a kind of money, one may note also that prices denominated in UFs tend to end in the numeral 9 more often than the numeral 1[14]—just what we see with prices set in units of currency. For example, a price of \$1.99 tends to be used much more often than a price of \$2.01, merchants choose the former price because it seems much lower to customers and makes them more willing to buy. That UFs share this tendency suggests those who set prices in UFs know that their customers are thinking in terms of UFs, and that consumers do not automatically translate UF prices into pesos.

Although the Chilean UF was invented in 1967, its use did not become really widespread in Chile until after the tax system was clearly specified in UFs in the early 1980s. Today, The UF is used widely in Chile. In 2000, the World Bank issued the first Chilean *unidad de fomento* bond to international investors. The 5-year 55 billion peso (\$105 million) Euronote pays in Chilean pesos as dictated by the UF conversion. According to a World Bank news release, 75 percent of the issue was purchased by Chilean investors, the remainder by European and American investors.

Five countries (Brazil, Colombia, Ecuador, Mexico, and Uruguay) have followed Chile's lead in establishing indexed units of account. In the Uruguayan case, the index is of wages, not consumer prices. In Brazil, the *unidade real de valor* (URV) was a sort of indexed unit of account, now discontinued. In response to the Chilean innovation, Colombia has created the *unidad de poder adquisitivo constante* (UPAC), Ecuador the *unidad de valor constante* (UVC), Mexico the *unidad de inversion* (UDI), and Uruguay the *unidad reajustable* (UR). In Venezuela, apartment rents are often expressed in units of "*salarios mínimos*," the minimum wage. But in none of these countries is the use of the indexed units of account as widespread as it has been in Chile.

Curiously, the spread of the concept of index units of account has been geographic, apparently not spreading beyond Latin America. The "conventional unit" (*uslovnaya yedinitsa*) of Ukraine is really only a disguised U.S. dollar.

The European currency unit (ECU), created in 1979, might be described as a sort of indexed unit of account analogue; it does not appear to have been inspired by the UF. The ECU was defined as a basket of European currencies, and hence one might say as a sort of index, and here again we had a unit of account that was divorced from any one currency. It did not guarantee purchasing power, but it did fulfil an important inflation risk management purpose. A market for ECU-denominated bonds developed, and part of the motivation for buying such bonds was diversification, to manage the risk of instability in the buying power of any one currency. Ultimately, after the Maastricht treaty fixed the exchange rates among European currencies, the ECU lost its economic rationale as a diversifier of risk. It evolved into, and was replaced by, a conventional currency, the euro. The transition was completed in 2002.

Confronting Risks of Inflation

I am proposing here that the indexed units of account be adopted in countries far beyond Latin America. This need not entail any coercion, only the governments' defining the units, affirming that they are legal tender and that contracts defined in them will be upheld and ensuring that the conversion rate between the units and the currency will be maintained. These are easy steps for governments to take, which can have the effect of preventing enormous effects of inflation on individual lives.

When I have presented the indexed unit of account idea at seminars, I often hear back that, rather than create indexed units of account, it would be better if the governments could just guarantee that the real purchasing power of the currency will remain constant, obviating the need for the indexed units of account. But no government has any way to guarantee that purchasing power of its money will remain constant over long periods of time.

It is common today to say that the problem of inflation has been cured. In his book, *The Death of Inflation,* Roger Bootle described a world in which inflation will never again get out of control, but in fact he offers no persuasive argument for such a claim.[15] Nor does anyone else offer a persuasive argument.

Even at their very best, central banks allow some variation in inflation rates. And even only small variations in the rate of annual inflation can add up to substantial changes in values over many years. We are generally accustomed to thinking that annual inflation in the 1 to 3 percent range is inflation completely under control, so such inflation has few political repercussions. But 1 percent inflation per year for thirty years (a time interval over which a typical retiree might hope to spend savings) means a 26 percent decline in real in value of a unit of currency over thirty years, while 3 percent inflation per year for thirty years means a 59 percent decline in the real value of currency over thirty years. That difference would cause substantially different outcomes for people whose income or wealth is not properly indexed to inflation.

Moreover, there is no guarantee that our central banks will succeed in containing inflation within such a range, and they may once again spur major inflation in the future. Recent moves in many countries to secure the independence of their central banks from short-term political pressure is widely cited as a reason to expect that inflation will be kept under control in the future,[16] but in fact independent central banks are still operated by real people who, as members of our society, are still under indirect political pressure. Independent central banks are no guarantee against high inflation; indeed, the United States in the late 1970s and early 1980s had double digit inflation, despite having an independent central bank and Fed chairmen, such as Arthur Burns, who widely proclaimed their commitment to price stability. High inflation has occurred so many times in history under so many different circumstances that it must be wishful thinking to suppose that it cannot recur in the future.[17] A sequence of past failures ought to discourage any such optimism. In today's economy, politically appointed people who run independent central banks have the ability to make, by creating inflation, major redistributions of wealth across people, between debtors and creditors. The can do this gradually and almost imperceptibly through time, and those who lose in real terms as a result will have no recourse, no legal claim that their wealth has been usurped by inflation. This is a sort of power that creates many temptations, and hence is ultimately difficult to control.

It is far better to define our contracts and set our prices in sensible units, rather than trust a political process to protect the stability of our currency. Making this change to baskets might even reduce the probability that inflation will get out of hand, because it depoliticizes the price level and reduces the ability of monetary authorities to redistribute wealth across segments of society.

Indexed Units of Account and the New Financial Order

The habitual use of currencies as units of account, which are not indexed to inflation, is especially frustrating when our purpose is to move to more sophisticated financial institutions. If we must define quantities for the general public in currency units, then we will forever be fighting the inconstancy that these units introduce. In the absence of the indexed units of account, we may well decide not to try to move to fundamentally different institutions. We may try to make little patches here and there in our economic institutions, fearful that any fundamental change runs the risk of new problems because of the changing units of measurement.

A convenient unit of measurement for real values encourages all manner of contracts to be written in real terms, rather than in terms of a unit whose value is politically determined in the future. It puts the legal status of such contracts in more sensible terms, the contract specifying outcomes in terms of the welfare of the contractors, rather than in terms of arbitrary units.

People can of course devise any units of measurements that they want for the purpose of writing contracts. But there are advantages to having generally accepted units of measurement that are carefully constructed and that have currency, just as money does. Engineers recognize the importance of the metric system used by engineers all over the world. Physics textbooks put definitions of basic units of measurements in the inside cover. Biologists recognize the importance of the Linnaean system of nomenclature for species, and are modifying that system to account for the massive improvement in our genetic relationships. All of these reflect the importance of measurement and naming.

Adoption of indexed units of account is important even in low-inflation countries like the United States, in part because there is no guarantee that we will remain in the present low-inflation regime. Risk management must be put in place before the risks are realized, not after, so it makes no sense to wait until after inflation becomes serious again to adopt the units of account. Moreover, indexed units of account can also be designed to allow prices to adjust conveniently to factors other than inflation.

We must make the adoption of a system of indexed units of account as a *permanent* feature of our economy, sanctioned by legal and regulatory authorities and integrated fundamentally and displayed prominently on the GRIDs.

Overcoming the Barrier of Mistrust

A barrier to the use of indexed units of account may be mistrust of the government to produce the indexes reliably. In 1996, I confirmed this mistrust of government-produced indexes through a questionnaire survey that I distributed to random samples of people in the United States (a low inflation country) and in Turkey (a high inflation country). One item asked respondents how much they agreed with the following:[18]

"An important reason not to trust contracts indexed to inflation is that someone in the government might deliberately falsify the inflation numbers to take advantage of people like me."

Strongly agree (21 percent U.S., 18 percent Turkey)
Agree somewhat (24 percent U.S., 43 percent Turkey)
Neutral or no opinion (16 percent U.S., 4 percent Turkey)
Disagree somewhat (27 percent U.S., 21 percent Turkey)
Strongly disagree (13 percent U.S., 13 percent Turkey)

That so many people in both countries think those in the government might deliberately falsify the indexes seems surprising, but not entirely without reason. There are examples, if not in the United States or Turkey, of just such manipulation of inflation numbers.

In 1983 in Australia a technical debasement of the consumer price index was made as part of a deal, called The Accord Mark I, between the Australian government and the labor unions. The labor unions, which had advocated Medicare, got their wishes granted on that issue in exchange for acquiescence in a tax change that lowered the consumer price index, allowing the government to lower the impact of cost of living clauses on wages. Apparently, the labor unions accepted this decline in real wages since the decline would be disguised, and hence not clearly the labor union's fault. As long as political deals are being made, and since the accuracy of the consumer price index is a technical matter that many people ignore, such a risk is clear.

In Brazil, after the Fernando Collor administration took control in 1990, the government arbitrarily changed the price index that it said should be applied to contracts that were indexed to inflation: The new price index made a large part of the inflation disappear.[19] The public learned from this experience, and after that indexed contracts were careful to clearly indicate which price index should be used. Brazil has many alternative consumer price indexes available, computed by different groups. The consumer price index is computed not only by the National Statistics Institute but also by the Economic Research Department of São Paolo University and by the Getulio Vargas Foundation. These multiple sources give greater legitimacy to price index construction in Brazilian society.

There is more authority when various elements of society share in the computation of statistics. Private competitors to government statistics could help boost public trust in their indexed units of account. The more contracts are settled on economic indexes, the more incentive there is for such private alternatives. The more electronic our economies become, the more databases we have, the easier it will be for private research groups to compute alternative indexes.

Predecessors of Indexed Units of Account

In 1911 Irving Fisher (rediscovering an idea first proposed by Simon Newcomb in 1879) proposed that a new hand-to-hand currency, the compensated dollar, be created whose gold content was constantly adjusted so that its real buying power was constant.[20] His invention would maintain the indexed units of account as the medium of exchange as well as unit of account.

Fisher's invention received a great deal of public attention for some years, but was eventually mostly forgotten. His invention suffered from a potential problem, for if the change in the gold content of the dollar became even partly predictable, speculators in gold and dollars could exploit and ultimately bankrupt the system. By the 1920s it became clear that the chances that it would be implemented in any country at all were slim. Governments are less likely to accept his idea than the indexed units of account, because the first step to implement it, the step of changing the currency itself, seems more radical than the first step of merely announcing an optional new unit of measurement, and, today, since there are still no examples of actual use in any country of the compensated dollar.

The use of indexed units of account for at least some prices is not such a radical idea, as is proven by the proliferation of these units in Latin America already, and the creation of the indexed units of account for some uses might eventually lead to their general use for most prices. Moreover, as regards Fisher's plan, we must realize that today, in the age of computers and electronic communications, there is little or no need for his indexed hand-to-hand currency. Hand-to-hand currency is rapidly being displaced by electronic money of various sorts, all of which can take account of variations in indexed units of account.[21]

Expanding the Concept of the Unidad de Fomento

Ideally, there should be an array of indexed units of account, reflecting different concepts of real values. Such an array will give people much more flexibility in defining payments. We should not limit ourselves to indexed units of account whose real purchasing power is constant through time. Imagine now that you are a business manager and are hiring an employee whom you expect to have for many years and that we have an indexed unit of account called "common hours," which reflects the typical wage rate for employees in your area, not a statutory minimum wage but an index (perhaps with a deliberate downward bias, as we will discuss below) of actual market wages as measured by a published wage index. Suppose you decided to pay your employee 3 common hours per hour worked. If the wage index is $5.25 an hour today, then a common hour is $5.25, and you would pay your employee $15.75 an hour. If the wage index later rises to $5.50 an hour, you would pay your employee $16.50 an hour. You could always change your wage measured in common hours, but the point is that you would not have to take any action to keep your employee's wage in line with the wages of others. Defining wages in common hours rather than dollars would make it unnecessary to reevaluate the wage rate every year or so for inflation or other changes in the economy. It would prevent mistakes in adjusting pay and would make for easier employee relations.

Today, individual wages follow the same kind of saw-tooth pattern that we see in rents, falling gradually behind wage changes, jumping up suddenly, then falling again. We repeat this same irregular pattern throughout our lives, but it makes no sense to set up our institutions so that this happens. The use of common hours would prevent this.

We could also have other units of account. Senior baskets, for instance, would be similar to baskets, except that they would use a market basket of items consumed by the elderly. While common hours would be hours of common labor, professional hours would stand for hours of professional labor. These units have simple names, reflecting their simple conceptualization, so that people can readily learn to use them.

We might also have, as alternatives to common hours or professional hours, indexes of labor productivity or of the "marginal product." Some employers might want to set their wages in terms of these rather than in terms of common hours or professional hours. Wages would then be increased when the workers are becoming more productive in the economy, not just when the labor market has already recognized their productivity.

There could also be units proportional to GDP, or even to world GDP.[22] Such units would allow us to define payments in proportion to total world resources, corresponding to the ultimate "market portfolio" of theoretical finance.[23]

When designing indexed units of account initially, it may be advantageous to define a *set* of alternative units. Public acceptance of more than one indexed unit of account might not be significantly harder to achieve than public acceptance of only one, if all are defined initially and if the nature of their definition and publication suggests that they are equal possibilities for use in setting prices, wages, or payments. By analogy to the metric system, we should, in defining the units, define a system of measurements that serve a variety of purposes.

There is not yet any example of the public's adoption of more than one indexed unit of account at a time, but there are examples (in the countries today using indexed units of accounts) of people using two units of account simultaneously, the currency and the indexed units. We could very much reduce the role of the currency as a unit of account and substitute some other unit, so that at least two indexed units would be actively used simultaneously.

Biasing Common Hours Down

The common hours units of account that I have described (as well as the productivity units of account) might serve best if they are biased downward, both in level and rate of change. The reason is psychological, having to do with envy and comparisons, and with saving face. The level of the index of common hours might best be something like that of the statutory minimum wage that we have today, that is, at a level so low that practically everyone except teenagers in their first job is paid more than one common hour per hour worked. Even though the index itself might best reflect wages earned by a broad class of workers, to turn this average into an index it should be multiplied by a number less than one so that the index itself would be lower than almost all wages. This would eliminate the need ever to humiliate some by paying them less than one common hour per hour's work. Such matters of tact are important.

The rate of increase of common hours might best also be biased downward relative to the rate of increase in actual average wages. The increase in the index of average wage could be pushed down by, say, 3 percent a year relative to the actual average wage. This would allow employers to make regular perfunctory monthly wage increases, at a 3 percent annual rate, in wages measured in common hours, without changing the relation of the employee's wage relative to the labor market. This will give people some sense of nominal, if not real, progress in their wage, measured in common hours.

If the common hour were defined this way, it might be described as an index of the most common labor and of people who are not improving their skills and job qualifications as much as most people do. Defining wages as a multiple of common hours suggests an unambitious comparison group, which will help maintain workers' self-esteem; they will mostly be doing better than the common wage, both in levels and rates of change, even if the common hour wage increases to keep them at the average level of wages. This framing of wages represents humane behavior for employers, allowing their less successful workers to save face.

The downward bias in the rate of change in common hours can also deal with a real problem of downward wage rigidity that we observe today. People rarely if ever tolerate wage decreases within the same job, even though they frequently experience real wage decreases caused by inflation's eroding the real value of their wage.[24] Apparently because of an irrational fixation on income as measured in dollars, people feel that a wage decrease measured in dollars is a terrible affront, an insult, and so employers are reluctant to cut anyone's wages, even if they are not producing as much as they used to. Such wage decreases are thus largely confined to disciplinary situations, situations in which the manager wishes to make a strong, aggressive, or angry point to some workers, or to situations in which the company is in serious risk of bankruptcy and can ask the workers' understanding. Workers are not so sensitive to inflation-induced real wage when their wage in currency units does not fall.[25]

If people cannot be given pay cuts within a job, then employers' natural alternative, when employees are no longer sufficiently productive to justify paying them the same wage they used to get, is to terminate them. A possibly important reason why retirement age cutoffs have been imposed has been that it is difficult to cut the pay of older, less productive, workers. In this time of lower inflation in most countries of the world, when money illusion offers less help in disguising decreases in the buying power of wages, the problem that has caused earlier forced retirement may be more severe.

Will the people whose incomes do not increase in terms of common hours eventually conclude that the disguising of the real income decline is in a sense a deliberate illusion, and thus lose the psychological benefit of the less ambitious standard of comparison of the common hour units? I think probably not, at least not fully. Surely, if both baskets and common hours are in use, these people will note that their incomes translated into the baskets are declining. But noticing this is hardly different from noticing that incomes may not be keeping up with inflation today, and people do not appear to react to the implied declines in the buying power of incomes as much as they do to income cuts measured in terms of money. Even those workers who fully understand that the buying power of their wage is declining may appreciate not seeing "in-your-face" documentation of the decline on their pay stubs.

Transforming the Economy by Changing the Units of Account

I have argued here that adopting some form of indexed units of account could have profound effects on the economy. It would tend to reduce random interpersonal real shocks currently caused by unanticipated inflation. If the use of the units were carried farther than they have been in Chile, so that wages as well as major prices are set in terms of appropriate indexed units, then this might reduce the need for layoffs or early retirements due to sticky wages, reduce the amplitude of unemployment rate changes during business fluctuations, and allow better sharing of income risks. The adoption of indexed units of account has been a successful movement in Latin America, reason enough to suggest the adoption of such units in other countries. Perhaps this should be done with some of the changes discussed here: the adoption of multiple units and the biasing downward of the growth of the income units.

The national government can take an important and simple toward creating indexed units of account by redefining its tax system, and tax payments, in terms of indexed units of account. Chile did this with the UF, which finally made the unit take hold in public use. This step will do more than just promote public familiarity with and acceptance of the new units. If the entire tax system is restated in terms of baskets, then we will have gotten past the current piecemeal approach to indexation, where little problems are plugged one at a time, here and there, by little indexation fixes to the tax code. Such a piecemeal approach introduces tremendous unnecessary complexity to the tax system and is ultimately unsuccessful in really achieving uniform indexation.

We can and should go far beyond Chile, though, by integrating the units of account into the electronic payment system, allowing credit cards to charge to various units, so that a number of different such units have the appearance of electronic money. These various units can ultimately be established as permanent features of our economic system and everyday language.

After all these things have happened, the indexed units of account will foster much more innovations in risk management. No longer forced by practicality to define payments in terms of currency, and having a wide array of units of measurement to use, designers of innovative risk management products will be free to do so much more than is done today.

SIXTEEN

Making the Ideas Work: Research and Advocacy

TO MAKE THE IDEAS for risk management work, we need more than has already been outlined. We need further research on risks, research that can be done in conjunction with information on the GRIDs, research to identify the opportunities for risk sharing. And we need broad advocacy by public groups and authorities who represent the interests of various segments of society.

Research for Risk Identification

Risk identification means the discovery and measurement of opportunities for risk sharing. Learning where the large uncertainties lie is vital, as is identifying where different people have very different kinds of risks. Only when we deal with these large risks, and only when people face different varieties of risks, can effective risk sharing take place.

The first step in the identification of risks is improving our measurement of them through devising better indexes. Most developers of indexes operate on limited resources and with relatively little public attention. Since the indexes are usually not yet used in financial contracts, no great incentive exists to dispute them, with the notable exception of the consumer price indexes, which are used in cost of living allowance contracts and which have been subjected to the scrutiny of study commissions and public debate. We need to apply the same kind of scrutiny to many other indicators of economic welfare.

I personally saw the importance of economic indexes when my colleagues and I tried to get futures exchanges to start futures contracts on single family home prices around the time of the recession of 1990–91. One problem we faced was that while our indexes began around that time to show clear price declines in major cities, the indexes of the most widely cited source on single family home prices, those of the National Association of Realtors (NAR), were in some cases quite erratic. The economists at the futures exchanges wondered to us if anyone really accurately knew what home prices were doing now.

The NAR data were simply median prices of single-family homes and were not constructed from changing prices of individual homes as were our indexes. It was impossible for us at that time to dislodge the appearance of authority that the NAR median prices have because the news media had adopted their indexes uncritically, preferring the simpler concept of the median and (circularly) noting the prestige the NAR indexes had attained in the media. The problem was that since no one was settling contracts on the NAR median, no one really cared to look hard at their methods. So we were stuck with a double burden in our advocacy of futures markets for single family homes, not only having to advocate the markets themselves but also having to advocate the index used to measure the risks.

This situation can be expected to improve as data become more available and as more and more economic indexes are used to settle contracts. Providing indexes of economic risks will itself become a business opportunity once it becomes clear that such indexes will be used extensively for contracts; suppliers of copyrighted indexes will be able to charge fees for the use of their indexes, royalties when their indexes are used to settle contracts, and even someday tiny fees every time their index is accessed, assuming the development of micro-price billing on the Internet. The private market will produce many competing indexes to choose from, and public attention will focus more on these indexes once money is at stake on them. Moreover, more government support for measurement of economic risks could be very helpful.

Research on measures of economic welfare, generalizing the national income concept of Nordhaus and Tobin to subindexes such as income by income level or income by occupation, would be desirable so that we do not ignore the major components of national welfare or occupational rewards. Doing this, however, is a potentially tricky business. Today, popular publications offer indexes of job quality, such as the *National Business Employment Weekly's Jobs Rated Almanac*, which rates jobs not only on income and benefits but also on working environment, job security, stress, physical demands, and travel opportunity. But because these ratings involve so many factors, many people think them so subjective as to be meaningless. These job ratings were not designed for contract settlement purposes but instead to sell a magazine. With sufficient public discourse we likely can derive indexes of the economic welfare of occupations so that people will want to sign risk management contracts based on them. Ultimately, consumers would be able to choose which index to believe in, as many competing groups use the GRIDs to produce their own indexes.

Part of the problem we face in designing risks is deciding the categories by which risks are measured. Risks by country or risks by job category are natural, but if we accept conventional geographic or occupational definitions, we may be missing something very important. We have to look through the data for clusters of risks and not merely accept conventional categories.

In my work with Ryan Schneider using data on individuals and their incomes, we used a statistical procedure called "cluster analysis" to find groupings of jobs that are similar to one another in terms of shared risks.[1] This created labor income indexes that were more descriptive of people's risks than conventional occupational indexes, in which the membership in the occupation follows traditional boundaries. Much more work on this could be done in the future with the GRIDs.

Risks that are shared by everyone and experienced the same by everyone, such as the risk that global warming destroys all economies equally, cannot be reduced through financial risk sharing.[2] When risks are already equally shared and equally experienced, no further sharing or diversification is possible. Only risks that different people experience differently—such as global warming to the extent that it harms the economies of tropical zones and helps the economies of temperate zones—make risk sharing beneficial. For instance, people of tropical zones can sign a contract with people of temperate zones, the people in temperate zones to compensate those in tropical zones if the global warming is relatively worse for the latter than expected. By the same token, people of tropical zones would compensate those in temperate zones if the effects of global warming go the other way relative to expectations.

Stefano Athanasoulis and I have developed a mathematical and econometric model that indicates a method for discovering the most important risk-sharing agreements around the world, adapting a statistical procedure called "principal components analysis."[3] Our procedure starts with historical data on individual incomes to discover the patterns of correlation and variance across individuals in various parts of the world. These results are then inserted into a mathematical model that reveals large groupings of people whose economic risks are as different as possible from other large groupings, thereby identifying who should share risks with whom.[4]

Our work, while establishing some theoretical foundations on how the work should be done, was only the barest beginning. When GRIDs become available, a much more sophisticated analysis could proceed. A great deal of scientific expertise, beyond that of econometrics, ought to be used to contribute to the effort, given the importance of the problem. When trying to identify large groups of people for risk sharing, researchers must not be conventional in decoding who belongs to the various groups. This means finding strange bedfellows in risk management contracts. It means reaching beyond the kindred spirits, beyond the geographical neighbors, beyond one's own socioeconomic group, beyond one's generation.

Our financial institutions today are already adept at finding risk-sharing opportunities. Investment banks match those with unusual risks with others who have the opposite risks. We need to develop this system further to assure that their efforts are broadened in scope—to democratize and extend their efforts.

Risk identification also means devising objective measures of risks that are not excessively subject to moral hazard, so that our management of risks will properly create the incentives for people to do good work and to avoid losses. Highly developed GRIDs could make possible detailed attention to moral hazard issues in risk management contracts. The proposal for GRIDs puts us on a path towards risk identification in a systematic way. The more information we have on the GRIDs, not only about individual incomes but also on other individual circumstances that could someday be related to terms of risk management contracts, the closer we come to the goal of risk identification.

We should take the first steps today toward risk identification: the expanded collection of data on economic risks that might someday appear on a GRID and the sponsoring of research on these risks by universities and foundations. If we do not take these first steps now, with the passage of time much of the information will be lost. Researchers must have a history of the risks if we are to understand them. Private corporations with data files could take it as a public duty to preserve old data on individuals' income and behavior in a form that can someday be used in massive databases like the GRIDs.

Broad Advocacy for Massive Risk Sharing

To ensure that risk sharing proceeds on a truly massive scale, public advocacy will be needed. Society cannot just create exchanges to trade new risks and hope that people start trading. There has to be a human force behind the actual use of new risk management instruments. The benefits of such risk sharing are not so obvious to most people. Opinion leaders will have to take steps to make these ideas compelling.

Advocacy of risk management devices has always been difficult. This advocacy has to begin to substantial degree at an abstract level, like the advocacy for consumer product safety. Unsafe products, like cars that do not adequately protect passengers in accidents, often cannot be identified except by statistics of accident records, and so the risks are not really directly visible to the public. Even people who suffer excessively after accidents will usually not know that the product was really at fault, without the statistical evidence. Moreover, after the safety problem is corrected, one will generally not meet people who are thankful to know that they were spared serious injury because of the correction of the safety problem. The same is true with major economic risk management devices. People do not generally perceive risk management problems that might be solved through risk sharing. After the risk problem is corrected through financial innovation, years later, the financial arrangements will be so commonplace that most people will take for granted the innovation that helps them.

A major role of advocacy must fall on our governmental leaders. They can enunciate a new vision for a society spared from the random shocks that attend economic change. Their vision can lead to public support for the kind of information infrastructure essential to such change. History shows that much of financial innovation, even that which appears in the private sector, occurred only after some government initiative to improve financial markets.

Advocacy should come also from leaders from outside the government. Business leaders have their role to play. Those who are in the business of financial risk management should see democratizing finance as a major goal for them, a way for them to use their particular skills to benefit all of human society as well as to broaden their customer base. International economic development organizations, such as the World Bank, the International Monetary Fund, the World Trade Organization, and the United Nations Conference on Trade and Development, are particularly well suited to advocate major risk-managing arrangements because they deal with many countries and are familiar with their various economic weaknesses. These organizations are in an excellent position to encourage direct international risk-sharing agreements as well as national risk management securities issuance and investment.

Labor unions should have an important leadership role in democratizing finance. Sponsoring new risk management policies and procedures could be a life saver for their members, protecting them against a harsh outcome in the event of great income inequality, protecting them perhaps far better than any ongoing collective bargaining alone ever could. Unions are in a particularly good position to understand the risk management needs of their members, needs that are connected to their occupational niche and their personal circumstances. These unions could help design occupational insurance for their members and select labor income indexes that are particularly relevant to them. They could advocate home equity insurance policies for their members, with attention to special needs of members—attention, for instance, to the risk that a plant closing in an isolated community could harm the home values there. They could advocate pension plans that invest in macro securities that serve to offset risks to occupational income fluctuations. They could also provide information about the specific needs of their members.

Professional organizations—of doctors, lawyers, accountants, and the like—could arrange for similar risk management devices for their members. Their advocacy might take the form of recommending specific forms of risk management contracts, arranging for the creation of proper income indexes for settlement of contracts, and sponsoring livelihood insurance, macro securities, and other devices specifically designed for their members.

Charitable and benevolent and religious organizations, which are often the only advocates of the least advantaged elements of our society, could also play a fundamental role. Their support of risk management institutions would be a major source of stability besides the support afforded by the government. Some of their traditional causes have a risk management element to them, and their making this element more explicit and allying with others' risk management efforts can be of great help.

An extensive program of advocacy for fundamental risk management by all these parties may ultimately overcome the resistance to change in our institutions and lead to a safer economic environment for everyone.

Part Five

The New Financial Order as a
Continuation of a Historical Process

SEVENTEEN

Lessons from Major Financial Inventions

MOST FINANCIAL INNOVATION is accretive, that is, it builds in small ways upon past innovation. The steady improvement in financial technology that such accretion affords is important. Most of us, observing in our lives only the succession of small changes, are unfamiliar with the potential of radical financial innovation. Our unfamiliarity may lead us to underestimate the possibility of fundamental change, and to despair excessively that it will ever happen in the future.

The history of some of the financial devices that we already have can shed light on the possibilities for the new technology that we are developing today, and on the nature of possibilities for inventive activity in minimizing economic risks. It will help us to see the complex reasoning behind the institutions that we take for granted today—including reasons related to human psychology—and how this reasoning is vulnerable to change with new technology. It will thus help us to see how it is that ideas like the technologies developed in this book will one day be adopted.

In this part of the book, therefore, I will cap the arguments that such radical financial innovation in the future is possible, by comparing it with radical financial innovation of the past. In this chapter, I address private financial inventions; in chapter 18, with governments' public financial inventions. In this chapter, I will consider the invention of money, the modern stock market, the futures market, and life insurance. These financial institutions represent significant innovations that were not obvious until a lengthy process of innovations revealed them to the public. The process related to other technological advances of the times. The inventions were subject of much attention when first developed. There was initially uncertainty as to their success. After they were found to be successful, they were copied around the world.

The Invention of Money

Money itself is an important invention for us to consider, since coins have been around for thousands of years and paper money for hundreds. At a time when both familiar forms are being replaced by electronic money, it is helpful to consider what technology produced money in the first place and why new technology is changing it.

The invention of coinage, traditionally attributed to Lydia in the seventh century B.C. but possibly earlier, was not so obvious an idea.[1] At that time, precious metals were already used by merchants as a medium of exchange, but they had to be carefully weighed out and balanced against standardized weights. Divers still find elaborate sets of balance-pan weights in bronze-age shipwrecks. The invention of coinage corresponds to the discovery of methods to make the weights cheaply out of precious metals, and thus to use the weights themselves as money.

This invention would be practical only if the cost of making the coins was low. The advent of coinage appears to coincide with a technological advance in ancient times, a process using dies onto which a flan (or blank) of precious metal can be placed and then struck with a hammer, thereby making a sharp image on the flan from the die to identify the coin. Since each is marked with only a single blow from a hammer, coins can be manufactured cheaply.[2]

Since carrying about scales and weights was impractical for most people, the invention of coins substantially democratized the use of precious metals as a medium of exchange. This ancient invention vastly increased the scope of transactions that could be undertaken and increased the number of people who used the medium of exchange. The result, as noted by ancient historians,[3] was an enormous expansion of the scope of commerce, helping transform human society from a largely household economy to an exchange economy, with much further specialization of production and greater variety of goods available.

Paper money first appeared in the ninth century in China, but it disappeared there by the fifteenth century. Widespread use of paper money did not appear until it spread through Europe and around the world in the late eighteenth and early nineteenth centuries. While paper money too was propelled by a technological innovation, engraving methods that prevented counterfeiting, it did not have the same impact as did the invention of coins.[4] With coins, the world already had an effective money.[5]

The very recent inventions of electronic money and electronic means of payment offer the prospect of further democratizing the use of money in much the same way that the invention of coins did, and represent a far more important invention than paper money. Electronic money makes it feasible to use money for much smaller, even microscopic, transactions in which the price is varied in response to complex formulas depending on information. Because of their lower cost, all these transactions can happen with much greater frequency. This can have much the same effect in the twenty-first century that the invention of coins once had, creating an even sharper specialization of production and even wider variety of goods and services available. Among other opportunities that electronic money creates, it can help promote the ideas for risk management presented here by encouraging the providing of micro information and by allowing much more specialized products and services for risk management.

Considering the history of coins also brings insights into the proposed indexed units of account. A separation of the two functions of money—medium of exchange and unit of account—was a familiar fact of life in medieval times, given the technology of the day and its imperfections. Medieval Europe's many small kingdoms minted many different kinds of coins, at least one for each kingdom. Ultimately, these coins found their way all over Europe, and so a pocketful of medieval change would have in it a bewildering assortment of coins from different kingdoms. As a result, the unity of the medium of exchange and the unit of account that seems natural to us today broke down, and it became customary in the late middle ages and Renaissance to quote prices in terms of a coin that was increasingly scarce, practically nonexistent as the centuries wore on—the silver denarius issued by Charlemagne in 794. Payment would be made not in Charlemagne's denarius but in an assortment of the available coins, each at its own exchange rate with the denarius. The denarius itself became a sort of "ghost money" that almost no one ever saw.[6]

There is nothing natural or inevitable about combining the medium of exchange with the unit of account, as we do with our money today. In the future, as information technology advances, the two functions of money may better be handled with separate devices, just as they were long ago: an electronic medium of exchange and a system of indexed units of account for defining important prices.

The Invention of Modern Stock Markets

The development of modern stock markets in the nineteenth century was a cardinal development in the management of business risks. Before the nineteenth century, stock markets were so small as to be inconsequential for society at large. The creation of modern stock markets allowed a fundamental separation between the owners of enterprises and their founders and managers, so that the latter could pursue highly risky ventures without exposing themselves to the risks. With large international stock markets, the risks can be spread over investors all over the world so that by great diversification, the impact of the risks is much reduced.

But how to create these markets on a large scale was by no means obvious. Practical and psychological problems were important obstacles only gradually overcome. In fact, the stock markets that we know today represent a nonobvious invention for which human financial engineering was the vital element.

An essential factor that has promoted the development of modern stock markets is the guarantee, in law, of limited liability for investors in stock. The definition of a corporate stock as we know it today is a claim on the profits of a company, but no obligations on the part of a stockholder beyond paying for the stock. The stockholder has limited liability, meaning that he or she can lose no more than the purchase price of the stock.

This essential limited liability concept was not clearly defined for the market as a whole until the nineteenth century, although some individual stocks did have limited liability provisions in their charters before then. A breakthrough of worldwide significance occurred in the United States with an 1811 general act of incorporation in New York State. Not only did this act set the precedent of allowing any business that satisfied minimum requirements to incorporate, but it also initiated the radically new step of specifying that all investors in New York corporations have strictly limited liability.[7] Before this act corporations were usually creatures of government, enjoying a government-sanctioned monopoly, and incorporation was not available to business at large. Moreover, creditors of failing companies could in principle seize all the personal assets of each stockholder, even those holding few shares, until the debt was repaid.

Clearly, the limited liability required by this New York law was of historic importance. Before the passage of this law, investors could in principle lose their homes, life savings, and everything else, and even conceivably end up in debtors' prison, simply by owning a few shares in a company that later fails. Thus, investing in stocks could possibly have disastrous consequences for the investor. With such a frightening possibility, one would naturally be wary of investing in stocks.

Despite the obvious problem with unlimited liability stocks, limited liability was not obviously a good idea to lawmakers at the time. Historian David Moss has chronicled an extensive argument against limited liability around the time of the 1811 New York law.[8] In considering proposals for limited liability stocks, many legislators thought that protecting stockholders from the full consequences of the company's losses might spur the company to pursue excessively risky strategies. With limited liability, the stockholders would never have to pay the full extent of the losses they incurred if things turned out very badly, but they would stand to gain all of the profits they earned if things turned out very well. We would say today that these legislators were concerned about the moral hazard associated with limited liability, though the term moral hazard had not yet been invented.

Moreover, the U.S. Constitution, in Article 1, Section 10, specifies that the states shall make no law "impairing the obligation of contracts." Corporations were free before 1811 to sign contracts with their creditors preventing creditors from attaching the debts of shareholders, if such terms were mutually agreeable. The essential character of the limited liability laws that first appeared in New England in 1811 is that they *required* such contracts, thus diminishing freedom to make contracts. It was certainly not obvious that a law forbidding certain kinds of contracts, those implying unlimited liability, is a good thing. Should not free citizens be allowed to sign any kind of contract that they want? Moreover, unlimited liability hardly ever caused serious problems in practice since there were hardly any actual examples before 1811 of innocent shareholders being pursued for the debts of corporations.

But the New York experiment was obviously successful judging from the number of successful incorporations there, and eventually all states copied the New York law. California was the last to do so, in 1931. The New York law, which gave New York a head start as a financial leader in the world, was also the inspiration for incorporation and limited liability laws in the United Kingdom, Germany, France, and ultimately virtually every other country of the world today.[9]

Limited liability also fostered public acceptance of corporate stocks because investors tended to overestimate the minuscule probability of loss beyond initial investment. Psychologists have documented such a human tendency to sometimes overestimate small probabilities.[10] With unlimited liability, investors' imaginations could run wild with the fear that investing just a small amount in a stock would spell disaster.

With limited liability, stockholders have no fear of disaster. They can lose no more than the amount they put in to buy the stock. And yet they can imagine the possibility of a bonanza many times larger than the amount that they put in, a probability that they are likely also, given what we know about human psychology, to exaggerate in their imagination. Thus, as David Moss has argued, limited liability stocks succeeded so well because the human tendency toward exaggeration of small probabilities can make stocks a matter of pure pleasure: often only the potential upside is on investors' minds. Stock investing becomes like buying lottery tickets, which many people describe as pleasurable: the investor can savor the possibility of making a lot of money without worrying about any big troubles. Framing stock investments this way enhances the demand for stocks, encourages a great many investors to buy small numbers of shares in many companies, and thereby dramatically increases the supply of capital for corporations.

Limited liability also allowed investors to hold a highly diversified portfolio. Without limited liability, broad portfolio diversification was potentially a very bad idea because failure of any one investment could result in the seizure of all of one's assets. With the many investments of a highly diversified portfolio, the probability that one of them would spell serious trouble was perhaps not so small. While we today think of portfolio diversification as an obvious fundamental principle for investors, the principle was not valid and not even generally conceived of until the advent of limited liability laws. Framers of corporate law were not even thinking about portfolio diversification, but one invention led to another, from limited liability to a fundamental investing principle of diversification.

The demonstration of the value of the limited liability stock markets in New York State in the early nineteenth century revealed an important fact about moral hazard—that concerns that limited liability stocks would encourage excessive risk taking were not valid. It is true that in the early years of limited liability in New York there were a great number of failures of limited liability firms who took big risks, but the world was ultimately more impressed by the list of the highly successful survivors, whose importance outweighed all the failures.

As this history of stock markets illustrates, no abstract theory can accurately predict how moral hazard will play out, nor predict how extensively we will use new risk management tools. The inventors of limited liability stocks could not clearly see their full advantages. The experimentation with the invention revealed the possibilities of the modern corporation and the modern diversified investment portfolio.

Experimentation with any of the new ideas for risk management can be expected to generate similar concerns about moral hazard, but we will eventually learn how to deal with such problems. It can be expected to generate new business forms that could not exist without the risk management possibilities, and new methods of managing investment risks that are hard to fathom today.

The Invention of Futures Markets

Today we have futures markets for a variety of commodities, agricultural products, raw materials, and financial assets. In these markets, one can buy or sell promises of future delivery of standardized commodities or financial assets. The ability to do so fulfills an important risk management function for people who deal in these commodities.

Futures contracts and the markets where they are traded are quite an invention: Many elements of their operation work together to produce a nonobvious risk management outcome. These markets have no ancient antecedent, as do insurance and option markets. The first futures market did not appear until the 1600s, in Japan near Osaka. But now every developed country has futures exchanges. The United States has the Chicago Board Options Exchange, the Chicago Mercantile Exchange, the New York Mercantile Exchange, and many others; London, the London International Financial Futures Exchange; Paris, the Marché à Terme International de France (MATIF). These are now increasingly sophisticated electronic markets where fundamental risks are traded.

The basic function of a futures market is "hedging," creating a risk that offsets an existing risk. To illustrate, consider the example of risk management in the business of running a warehouse for a grain such as rice. Grains of a specific variety are usually harvested but once a year and must be stored for use throughout the year. Storing grains is thus an essential business for every economy.

The essential risk management problem faced by a storer of grains is that the price of grains fluctuates throughout the year, often widely. Even with an efficient and well-controlled warehouse, the manager who has bought grain and is storing it for later sale can easily lose money if the price of grain turns down. Obviously, if one is running a warehouse and trying to compete in that business by storing grains very effectively, one does not also want to take on the risky speculation in the price of grain. One's profit margins for storing grain may be small and easily swamped out by the uncertain price movement in grain. One wants to hedge, to take offsetting bets.

A warehouser of grains, fearing that the value of the contents of the warehouse will decline if the grain price drops, would like to place some kind of bet that the price of grain will decline. Then, if the price of grain does decline, the winnings from the bet will offset the losses on the warehouse full of grain. Alternatively, a prospective purchaser of grains, such as a baker, may fear that the price of grain may increase before the grains are purchased, and would like to place a bet now that the price of grain will rise. If the price of grain does rise, then the winnings from the bet will serve to offset the cost of having to buy grain at a higher price in the future. Placing such risk-offsetting bets is not gambling because the bets offset a risky position that was already in place due to the nature of the business.

The idea of hedging, of making risk-offsetting bets, is simple enough. But there are fundamental practical difficulties that make it difficult, in the absence of the appropriately designed markets, for a hedger such as a warehouser to place such a bet, difficulties that are sufficiently serious that such hedging bets will generally not be made without a futures market.

The most basic problem is that in the absence of a futures market, there is no well-observed price of grain on which to make a bet. If one placed a bet on the price of sale of grain at a local market at a specified future date, one would not know in advance the quality of the grain sold there, or the conditions of sale. One would run the risk that some unusual kind of grain was sold there on that day, or that an unusual deal was struck about transportation costs or insurance or other terms of sale, so that the price was unrepresentative of grain prices. Even worse, one would run the risk that no grain at all will be sold that day or that grain was deliberately sold at an artificial price to influence the outcome of the bet.

Grain futures markets solve this problem by carefully defining a certain kind of grain and the delivery date, delivery terms, and delivery place, so that there is no ambiguity. Futures exchanges announce these definitions and hire experts to verify that deliveries satisfy them. Thus, the day-to-day changes in the futures price has nothing to do with change in any of these characteristics of the grain, terms of sale or delivery.

The futures market essentially allows the placing of risk-offsetting bets, but the actual form that the hedging takes is the buying and selling of these contracts to deliver the grain in the future. The warehouser, who expects to sell grains in the future, sells a contract (signs a contract promising to deliver grain in the future) and buys it back later at its new market price. The baker who expects to buy grains in the future buys a contract, and sells it later at its new market price. The market price of these contracts is the essential price on which risk management is based, and the change in the price of these contracts is the random element that allows hedging.

The beauty of futures markets is that with this standardization of definition, people can hedge their risks even if they do not hold, or wish to buy, the exact kind of grain specified in the futures market and even if they do not wish to deliver or receive at the time and place specified in the market. One can hedge one variety of rice with a futures market for another variety, and one may have no intention of ever shipping to the delivery point. In modern futures markets, only a small number of contracts are ever held to delivery. Almost no one delivers or receives according to the contracts, and yet the option to deliver, or accept delivery insures, that the prices in the futures market bear a close relation to the price of the underlying grain.

The idea of a futures market is hardly obvious. The idea sounds unlikely unless we have experience with actual futures markets. How does one know that the price of the futures contract will provide a good hedge? How does one know that if the exchange provides too narrow a definition of the grain to be delivered, the price of that variety of grain will not become too erratic by the very fact that it is the basis of trade for risk management? To get the definition of the contract just right, the exchange must do a delicate balancing act and even then cannot know in advance, without experimenting, that it has done it correctly. Experimentation by the futures exchange is an essential element of futures contract design, and those contracts that work are the lucky survivors.

The exchange also has to ensure that the contracts are honored. Without this function, then even if the grain is standardized, the contracts may not be completely standardized, since the creditworthiness of the parties to the contract may not be uniform, which might affect price. Futures exchanges achieve absolute standardization of contracts by requiring margin from the contracting parties, regularly resettling the contracts, and closing out people whose margins are close to depletion.

The exchange must somehow define a settlement price and establish a time at which the settlement price is observed. The exchange has then to worry whether the price at such a time may be anomalous, and there must be institutions to watch for manipulative or dishonest trades at these times.

With complete standardization of contracts, each party can trade directly with the exchange, and not with particular other people. To allow such trade, the exchange must have a clearinghouse that settles trades. But then there are risks that the clearinghouse will fail, and the clearinghouses must have enough capital to make this unlikely.

All of the essential features of the invention were present at the first futures market on the island of Dojima at Osaka by 1730, and elements of a futures market were there in the 1600s. This first futures market had precise contract definitions of quality, of date and place of delivery, experts who evaluated the rice, and clearinghouses for the contracts. The grain traded was rice, and the exchange defined several varieties with different varieties deliverable at different seasonal times. The exchange maintained a trading floor where the contracts were traded, and a mechanism for deciding on a settlement price. The mechanism was the burning of a fuse within view of all traders at the exchange, the last price when it burned out being the settle price, at which time "watermen" would splash water over any who remained trading to stop them for the day.

While the watermen have not been copied, the essential details of the Dojima futures market were, in Frankfurt by 1867, Chicago by 1871, and London by 1877, and many other countries since. The early Japanese futures markets differed in some minor details from most modern futures markets but were essentially the same.[11] The hand signals that

Western traders use today are similar to those Japanese traders used to specify numbers of contracts, as testimony to their Japanese origin.

It may seem improbable that such a basic invention would come from the Tokugawa period in Japan, a time of Japan's isolation from most of the rest of the world. But in many ways, seventeenth and eighteenth-century Japan was very advanced. It also had the advantage that the one foreign country with which it had relations was Holland, which by the seventeenth century was the most financially advanced country in the world (even though Holland did not then have futures markets). But perhaps equally importantly, Japan had a large market for a single commodity, rice, that was substantially centralized in one city.

There is inspiration in this example for further radical financial innovation. The invention of futures markets was quite complex and was overlooked by the most sophisticated financial communities of its day. It benefited from an unusual environment in which a large community of inventive people were unconstrained by financial conventions that reigned in other parts of the world. The advent of modern information technology, and the rapid development of the world economy today, once again provides such unusual environments.

The Invention of Life Insurance

In chapter 7 I used an example of a useful economic invention, insurance. We can focus on the invention of one important kind of insurance, life insurance, to gain a greater appreciation of the importance of psychological framing and human financial engineering for economic inventions.

Although life insurance can be traced back to seventeenth-century England, in some forms even earlier, it did not achieve much importance until its design was improved in the nineteenth century. There were many obstacles obtaining public acceptance of this product. Despite the obvious practical importance of life insurance, the industry still does not depend to a large degree on consumers pursuing policies of their own initiative. Most people do not conceive of a need for life insurance in the same way they do for a new car.

Led by such people as Morris Robinson of the Mutual Life of New York in the 1840s, the industry has learned that this insurance must be actively sold to the public using professional insurance salespeople who are paid very large commissions on completed sales, commissions that motivate them to be persistent in their efforts to make sales.[12] After his success, large commissions for insurance salespeople were widely adopted in the insurance industry. As a consequence of these incentives, many books have been written on how to sell life insurance to the public, books that emphasize proper psychological framing.

Framing aspects of the design of the insurance policies themselves have also been crucial. In the late nineteenth century Henry B. Hyde propelled his Equitable Life Assurance Society into a highly successful model for the entire life insurance industry by inventing an insurance policy with a large cash value that would be paid out to policyholders who kept their policy for the stated period of ten, fifteen, or twenty years. This design enabled the insured public to mentally reframe their policy premiums as creating a large growing endowment, something to have satisfaction in, to offset the feeling of regret that people would otherwise have for paying premiums when no loss was in fact incurred. So successful was the Equitable that it extended its operations to England, France, and Germany by the 1870s, where insurance was not then sold so aggressively and the emerging American marketing methods were not then known. The whole-life, universal life and variable life insurance policies that dominate the insurance industry today are successors of Hyde's invention.[13]

A 1922 book *Selling Life Insurance* contains scripts for salesmen to use to close a sale. One of these scripts conveys how to connect the insurance product to an investment motive. The salesman is instructed to say to his prospective client:

> Life insurance has many good features. The investment feature, while good, does not tell the whole story. It gives you peace of mind, because it has enabled you to create an estate immediately that would have taken you years to accumulate—it makes possible the realization of your life's objectives if you happen to be taken away prematurely. Considering the question from all sides, can you invest your money to better advantage?[14]

This quote conveys the idea of putting two pictures—insurance policies and savings plans—in the same frame. The idea makes little sense from a rational economic standpoint but did make sense in overcoming emotional objections to buying insurance and thwarting a human tendency to miss payments on insurance and cancel the policies, which policy holders otherwise would be likely to do in times when they are feeling short of money.

Reframing was also a factor in the very choice of a name for the product of life insurance. Calling it "life" insurance rather than "death" insurance (which it really is), just as by referring to homeowners insurance rather than fire insurance, suggested a positive image for the product, and that its purchase is a normal, upbeat thing to do.

In *Morals and Markets*, her book about the slowness of the public to accept life insurance in the nineteenth century, Viviana Zelizer concludes that ultimate success in getting a large part of the population to buy life insurance was not possible until images for the insurance products were devised that accorded with the religious and mystic feelings of the time. By studying life insurance books and pamphlets of the time, she was able to infer the nature of the intense nineteenth century resistance to life insurance, resistance that was especially strong from women even though they were its main beneficiaries. Women apparently thought that purchasing the insurance challenged God and might even precipitate her husband's early death. Thus, insurance companies eventually learned to rephrase their rhetoric as if life insurance might convey a sort of immortality to her husband, whereby he might protect her even after death. Life insurance marketing, despairing of truly convincing people of the essentially random character of time of death and of their statistical models to deal with the randomness, instead concentrated mostly on imagery of comforting ritual for facing death, emphasized the "value and moral grandeur" of insurance, and presented the insurance salesman as a sort of missionary.[15]

The ultimate framing change for life insurance in the United States came when the federal government began to provide it for all working citizens, and gave it a different name. In 1939, amendments to the U.S. Social Security Act created survivors insurance, a form of life insurance whose beneficiaries are the children and spouse of a worker. Survivors insurance is important. For most people in the United States, the value of these survivors insurance policies is greater than the value of their life insurance policies.[16]

By labeling it survivors insurance rather than life insurance, the U.S. government achieved a major change in framing without which it might have been politically impossible for the government to start providing life insurance, since it would collide head on in competition with the already large life insurance industry. By calling this program "survivors insurance" and by not advertising it, the U.S. government guaranteed that few families fully understand that they have government-provided life insurance, even to this day. Thus, commercial life insurance salespeople can proceed without mentioning the government program because most people will never fully realize that they already have some life insurance. Offering the insurance salespeople this advantage is probably a good thing for society as a whole, since most people would benefit from buying life insurance beyond the government levels.[17]

The same kind of experimentation and framing has to proceed with the newer kinds of risk management devices described in this book. A path has to be found around consumer reluctance to consider long-term risks. But, with suitable experimentation, a path can be found, and once it has been, the fundamental risk management that these provide will make the public acceptance of these tools endure.

Concluding from These Examples

A remarkable string of radical inventions in finance peppers human history, a string of inventions that has improved our lives in fundamental ways. Observing how those inventions overcame barriers in the past offers hope for the future.

Experimentation with new institutions that seem to imply moral hazard risks have taught us in the past when it is that the risks are not so important as once thought, or are outweighed by other benefits of the institutions. Experiments have shown that financial innovations that seemed fraught with complexities and problems can become standard tools for widespread risk management once professionals learn how to use them properly.

Complex and hardly obvious financial institutions have arisen through experimentation and out of the diversity of our cultures and experiences. This gives great hope that the current speed of change in will give rise to unimagined new financial inventions that we will soon be copying around the world. Psychological reframing of risk management institutions have on occasion suddenly propelled these institutions into massively important pillars of our economy. This gives great hope that one day the great unmanaged risks in our lives will yield to new human-engineered inventions in finance.

EIGHTEEN

Lessons from Major Social Insurance Inventions

LET US NOW CONSIDER some of our most important social insurance inventions (risk management created for every member of a nation by its national leaders, usually members of the government), and their relevance to the future. Consideration of social welfare systems for risk management is especially important if one considers the risk posed by new technology, new information technology, automation, and the like, possibly in combination with other changed economic factors such as the "forty thieves" discussed in chapter 4—risks that could cause a major worsening of income inequality that lasts for decades or even centuries. This sharp increase in inequality may or may not happen, but if *any* risk threatens that most people may be marginalized by our economic system, then this is a fundamental issue for us to confront today. Studying how society has handled social insurance in the past allows us to inject some realism into what otherwise might be an abstract discussion.

As with the history of the purely financial inventions, considered in chapter 17, this chapter should help us to understand the origins of important public risk management devices, the role that invention played in their original construction, the reasons for their success related to other technology, and their relation to patterns of human psychology. And, as with chapter 17, the insights we gain by such a study will help us to look to the future, where, with new information technology and better understanding of human psychology, we can hope to achieve major improvements in these devices.

I will discuss the tithe and zakat, income taxes, negative income taxes, the earned income tax credit, health and accident insurance, social security, and unemployment insurance.

The Invention of the Tithe and the Zakat

The earliest inventions for society's risk management had to operate with little more information available than the observations people make going about their everyday life. And yet risk management tools were invented, and preserved and disseminated in respect of their obvious success.

The book of Deuteronomy (26:12), written in the sixth century B.C., commands that the Israelites set aside a tenth of all their produce and "give it to the Levite, the alien, the fatherless and the widow, so that they may eat in your towns and be satisfied." This plan, with its stress on then-disadvantaged minorities, includes aspects of social insurance, and with its mention also of orphans and widows, it also sounds rather like life insurance. The 10 percent one pays is like an insurance premium, and the tithes one receives if impoverished like an insurance benefit.

In the middle ages, the Catholic Church decreed that a tithe should be paid to the Church, which would use part of it for alms for the poor, though another part of it would be used to support the clergy and to build cathedrals. The church, however, still did not make the tithe a tax that could be enforced with auditing of incomes. Enforcement, in the Church's scheme, was left up to God.

One of Islam's Five Pillars is the practice of zakat, which is nearly the same as the tithe. The zakat was embraced by Mohammed in the sixth century and incorporated into the Qur'an. One must give 10 percent of one's produce and 2.5 percent of one's wealth each year to poor people of one's choosing. Like the tithe, no authority exists to verify that each individual complies. As with the tithe, although others in one's community may have some impression of the magnitude of giving, adherence to the 10 percent and 2.5 percent rules is purely a matter of conscience.

The tithe and the zakat demonstrate good human engineering of a risk management device. That is, they take into account how people might think, and how they feel observed by others. They do not rely on any government institutions, which at the time of their creation were generally incapable of dealing reliably with individuals' incomes and obligations. The fraction of income given away is only 10 percent, a level low enough, and far below the 50 percent level that income taxes often reach today, that compliance based on purely moral obligation, even without legal enforcement, has a chance of being effective. The 10 percent figure is probably higher than most people would give if they were merely urged to give to others, without a specified percent; by stating the 10 percent figure, tokenism is eliminated.

Lacking any modern precision of our income tax and social welfare systems, the tithe and the zakat are pretty blunt risk management instruments. They allow risk sharing only within a small community, a village, but no risk sharing between villages or between nations. But we may assume that they were very important inventions in their day: They often helped prevent the worst and most easily avoidable consequences of sudden poverty.[1]

The Invention of Income Taxes

Taxing people on their income is one of the most important forms of risk management that we have, since it collects more from more successful people, and less from less successful people. Moreover, the tax revenue is used to provide services for everyone. The concept is very simple, but the implementation required a great deal of invention, particularly in the realm of information technology.

Because of primitive information technology, property taxes were a predominant mode of taxation until the income tax found a secure footing in the twentieth century. Adam Smith, in his *Wealth of Nations,* written in 1776, and twenty-three years before Parliament established the first true income tax, explained why income taxes suffer from the government's inability to obtain accurate information about incomes:

> The state of a man's fortune varies from day to day, and without an inquisition more intolerable than any tax, and renewed at least once every year, can only be guessed at. His assessment, therefore, must in most cases depend upon the good or bad humor of his assessors, and must therefore be altogether arbitrary and uncertain.[2]

In speaking of the inquisitorial nature of the tax, Smith was basing his conclusions about the income tax on an information technology problem. He was anticipating the major complaint about the first income tax when it was actually enacted. Income could not be verified then from a paper trail alone since there was usually no paper trail, so each taxpayer would have to be put through public exposure and observation to ascertain income.

Smith offered as a substitute to the income tax a tax on houses, which are certainly easily visible at all times just by walking down the street and looking: "In general, there is not, perhaps, any one article of expense or consumption by which the liberality or narrowness of a man's whole expense can be better judged of, than by his house rent."[3]

John Stuart Mill expressed a similar view in 1848, after the British income tax had already been established:

> A house tax is a nearer approach to a fair income tax than a direct assessment on income can easily be, having the great advantage, that it makes spontaneously all the allowances which it is so difficult to make, and so impracticable to make exactly. For, if what a person pays in his house rent is a test of anything, it is a test not of what he possesses, but of what he thinks he can afford to spend.[4]

For this informational reason, taxes on homes have long been a major source of government revenue, and continue to be. Unfortunately, there is an obvious problem with a tax on houses alone, as Adam Smith recognized in 1776. "If the tax indeed was very high, the greater part of people would endeavour to evade it, as much as they could, by contenting themselves with smaller houses, and by turning the greater part of their expenses to some other channel."[5] Experimentation with income taxes over the years reflected society's struggle with this shortcoming of the property tax, as well as other narrow taxes, as against the information cost of taxing based on a broad measure of income.

The landmark income tax in world history was created in 1799 in Britain by an act of Parliament, a progressive tax with various deductions with a top tax bracket of 10 percent.[6] But it was rescinded in 1816 amid complaints of the "obnoxious, oppressive and inquisitorial machinery by which that tax has been distinguished."[7]

The year 1799 and succeeding decades were a time of primitive—and costly—information technology. While paper and printing were available then, they were expensive, and with inadequacies of paper trail, as well as problems with filing and retrieval, the British government was obliged to rely more on direct observation and reports by neighbors, which contributed to make the tax appear so inquisitorial. The U.K. income tax was reinstated in 1842 but at a much lower rate of 3 percent.

The United States enacted its first income tax in 1862, and since the tax was progressive, it may be regarded as the first attempt in the United States of a sort of national social insurance. The tax revealed some of the same problems that afflicted the U.K. system. For the United States, the problems were fatal. The United States was not possessed of the requisite information technology to enforce an income tax with any accuracy, and its income tax was rescinded in 1872 amidst complaints that the Bureau of Internal Revenue was unable to enforce the tax and that the great majority of people who should have paid taxes evaded the tax altogether. This first U.S. income tax appeared before the advent of the typewriter, before the proliferation of printed forms, and before the extensive paper trail of business forms and documents that today enable the government to catch tax evaders.

Lacking evidence on people's income, the U.S. tax collectors resorted to publishing the taxes paid by taxpayers in local newspapers, thereby encouraging those who noticed the absence of names of some high-income persons to report them. Although taxes paid, and not incomes, were reported, and although individual tax statements were kept private, people could easily determine taxpayers' incomes since the tax rate schedule was published. This method of enforcement unfortunately created great public resentment because of its invasion of privacy, and neither did it work well at exposing evaders anyway. At that time, the government simply did not have a way of collecting information about incomes, with or without exposing the information to the general public.

Another problem for the collection of income taxes was the incompetence and poor motivation of the personnel of the internal revenue system. E. A. Rollins, the commissioner of internal revenue, commenting in 1867 on the difficulties his bureau faced, wished that he could have a bureaucracy like that of Germany.

> The civil service of Germany is superior to that of England or France. Throughout the entire confederation special education is added to the requirements made of moral fitness, and a certain measure of attainments tested by competitive examination. As with us there are normal schools for the preparation of teachers, and academies for those who are to officer our army and navy, so there are, in Germany at public charge, schools and universities for the special and appropriate education of those who are to become connected with the public administration of the laws. The higher the standard of requirements has been raised the larger has been the number of aspirants for employment, because the elevation of the character of the service itself has persuaded men of the highest position and attainments to offer themselves as rivals for its honors and its emoluments.[8]

249

The commissioner went on to say that he felt he could not expect the same in the United States.

I am aware that the peculiarity of our institutions, and the fact that all political parties have learned to expect much actual service from their office-holders, may prejudice and for a time prevent, in this country, the adoption of a system as universal and valuable as that of Germany.[9]

Indeed, the U.S. Civil Service Commission, which began the professionalization of U.S. government employees and their service, was not established until 1883, and its job was not done for decades more.

Because of these problems—loss of privacy, and corruption and incompetence in the Bureau of Internal Revenue—the income tax became highly unpopular. In 1871, Alfred Pleasanton, the commissioner of internal revenue reflected in his report to Congress on the failure and imminent demise of the income tax.

The tax was one of the most obnoxious to the people, being inquisitorial in its nature, and dragging into public view an exposition of the most private pecuniary matters. Such an unwilling exposition can only be compulsorily effected through the maintenance of the most expensive machinery, and both the nature of the tax and the means necessarily employed for its enforcement appear to be regarded with more disfavor from year to year by the better class of citizens.[10]

In that same year, Henry George made a proposal that all taxes be replaced with a single tax on land. His proposal received great public interest and spawned a political movement. The reason so many people were attracted to his idea must be in part the recent failure of the progressive income tax to offer any hope of reducing the sharp contrast of the time between wealth and poverty that was so evident during the depression of the 1870s. George explained in his 1879 book *Progress and Poverty* why he opposed any effort to reinstate the income tax.

The object at which it [a graduated tax on incomes] aims, the reduction or prevention of immense concentrations of wealth, is good; but this means involves the employment of a large number of officials clothed with inquisitorial powers; temptations to bribery, and perjury, and all other means of evasion, which beget a demoralization of opinion, and put a premium upon unscrupulousness and a tax upon conscience.[11]

His tax on land was appealing then because, according to his arguments, it offered reduction of economic inequality but did not require, for effective and discrete administration, the kind of information technology that was lacking.

If we fast-forward to the twenty-first century, we can see a repeat of the same abandonment of progressive taxes in Russia, and for the same reason. Because of an inability to collect high income taxes on high incomes the progressive income tax in Russia was abandoned in 2001 in favor of a flat 13 percent tax on incomes. This is a negative development in a country that already has very high income inequality, but one that may have been necessary given the size of the underground economy there. We may hope that the development of information technology will eventually make it more possible to collect income taxes on an orderly basis there, too, and that a progressive tax will someday be restored in Russia, just as it eventually was in the United States after failure in the nineteenth century.

The important impact of income taxes on our risks is something that grew gradually over the years. Income tax rates were very low in the nineteenth century, when our abilities to measure income accurately and to enforce collection were low, and so they were of limited effect as risk management devices. But in the twentieth century, information technology progressed to allow a better tax collection effort, and income taxes became an important, if often maligned, pillar of our good society. In the twenty-first century and beyond, the success of the tax will continue to grow as better information technology continues to reduce its inequities and irritations. Its "inquisitorial nature" will continue to become less important because modern electronic technology will collect both information and taxes in almost unseen ways, thus ensuring the greatest individual privacy.

The Invention of Negative Income Taxes

If one views taxes as a risk management device, one naturally wonders whether taxes should not only be low but actually negative for people with the lowest incomes, though not so negative as to incur too serious a moral hazard problem. In this case, income taxes might be an even more effective risk management device, more sharply reducing income inequality. This question is of special relevance here, for the inequality insurance discussed here may well under some circumstances imply negative income taxes in certain income ranges.

The negative income tax for low incomes is a striking invention for risk management. Although it has not been fully adopted anywhere, it has been and continues to be an important political cause. Moreover, we should consider it here because it is a clever invention that has inspired changes in the tax systems in many countries.

The negative income tax has been offered as a substitute for existing welfare systems, a substitute that is designed to reduce poverty in a more systematic and continuous way than welfare systems have. The most important argument for the negative income tax is that it can be designed so that they actually *reduce* the extent of moral hazard already in the welfare system that the negative income tax would replace. Lady Juliet Rhys-Williams first proposed the negative income tax as a plan to alleviate poverty without generating ill incentives to avoid work in 1942.[12] She was troubled by the fundamental dilemma that welfare destroys the incentive to work.

> The lion in the path of curing want by means of insurance is the fact that if the standard of unemployment pay is raised to the level at which real want is banished, and if all classes of workers and their families are included in the scheme, besides all other persons likely to benefit from it, then the advantages of working for wages very largely disappear.[13]

In attempting to minimize the resulting shirking problem as best they could at the time, the government looked out for people who were working only little or at very low pay. Thinking that their work implied that these people were *able* to work, the government enforced a "means test," that would cut off all their welfare if they had any means, any income at all. But Lady Rhys-Williams found that the means test was itself totally destructive of any work effort. "As things are, if a man bestirs himself to earn small sums when he is unemployed, or if his wife attempts to work, or his children are able to bring in a few pennies, they are immediately penalized for doing so by the loss of their allowance."[14]

She confronted this fundamental conflict between curing poverty and destroying incentives to work with a striking proposal.

The old "Lady Bountiful" basis for the relationship between a man and his government is out of date and must be swept away. *The prevention of want must be regarded as being the duty of the State to all of its citizens, and not merely a favoured few. In short, we must abolish the Means Test, and provide benefits equal to those paid out of unemployment assistance to every individual man, woman, and child in the whole country.*[15]

She means then that *everyone* receives the allowance, with no questions asked. Since she would leave the nature of the progressive income tax system unchanged, the implication of her proposal is that people with very low incomes are taxed only at very low rates on extra income that they earn beyond the basic allowance. Rhys-Williams did not use the term "negative income tax," but her proposal was, if one considers the benefits and the tax system together, for an income tax schedule such that every person with no income receives a substantial negative tax from the state, and that taxes rise smoothly as income rises above zero, from a very negative sum to a moderately negative sum as income increases from zero to a very low amount. There is a crossover income (between zero income and the average income) at which total taxes paid are zero; for all incomes above that total, taxes paid are positive. With such a tax schedule, each additional penny of income that someone earns, no matter at what income level, is taxed at a rate much less than 100 percent, so that there is always an incentive to earn it, in contrast to the then-current welfare systems in every country in which the means test tended to deprive the people on welfare from any advantage to working.

Rhys-Williams called her invention "the proposal for merging the income tax and social security systems." Milton Friedman renamed it the negative income tax in his book *Capitalism and Freedom* in 1962, and his name stuck. A benefit for people with no income has also been referred to variously as the "basic income," the "citizen's income," or the "social dividend."

The proposal has a certain incontrovertible logic to it, but it faces an obvious problem: Giving an allowance to people who do not work at all, even if it does not penalize them from working a little, still permits total laziness and irresponsibility. This is the fundamental moral hazard dilemma; we seem to be left only with unattractive choices. If we means-test—that is, deny all benefits to poor people who have some income—then we destroy incentives for the poor to work even a little, while if we do not means-test, we end up distributing large sums of money to those lazy people who just do not want to work at all no matter what the incentives.

Political support for the Rhys-Williams invention did not come until it was reframed into something we could be passionate about, first achieved by Robert Theobold in his 1963 book *Free Man and Free Markets*.[16] Theobald's book came out at a time when many people were discussing a theory that proposed that all of our economic problems had been solved and, therefore, we had no inspiring problems left to tackle.[17] John Kenneth Galbraith's 1958 bestseller *The Affluent Society* had created the impression that the problem of the times was excessive affluence. The assumption behind Theobald's "Basic Economic Security" plan was that because of the technological progress, people had more consumer goods than they knew what to do with, so those with money had embarked on wasteful extravagances, building ever bigger houses and buying ever fancier cars for no more purpose than to impress others. At the same time, Theobald argued that it appeared that someday soon computers would be replacing many people, and questioned our "concept of the value and virtue of labor" when the labor can only be "merely repetitive toil, easily performed by a machine."[18]

Thus, Theobald argued that, given all this affluence, the popular presumption that everyone must work was ridiculous, and it made no sense for the government to try to compel unemployed people to find a job and thereby to force them into "conformity to the prevailing views of society."[19] Theobald argued that it was better to give everyone a due income by taxing the high income people and giving to the poor; it was better to let all people use their own moral judgments and sense of purpose to find good uses of their time than to make them jump onto the treadmill of our economy, which produced ever more useless and wasteful products.

Theobald's book generated real and impassioned support for the negative income tax or basic income from some quarters. Support was apparently especially strong among people who were not impressed with the seemingly extravagant lifestyle of many high-earning people, or who felt unsympathetic to the values of the business community.

Milton Friedman, like Theobald, argued that to receive the negative income tax, there should be no need to look for a job, no need to prove inability to earn income, no visits from a social worker, and, most important, no stigma to unemployment. An essential element of a negative income tax is really psychological reframing—renaming what used to be called "welfare" as a negative tax, therefore changing the stigma attached to it and the institutional assumptions about it.

For Friedman, the negative income tax was an economist's rational invention to deal with income inequality in an incentive-compatible way and in reaction against government officials' (in this case, verifiers of job search) meddling in our lives. Friedman's emphasis was totally different from Theobald's, as different as right wing from left wing, even though the inventions work out to be basically the same.

Friedman's reframing of the Rhys-Williams invention received much attention in the 1960s, and helped breed many negative income tax experiments, culminating in the Seattle–Denver Income Maintenance Experiments, which involved 4800 families and cost $70 million. President Richard Nixon proposed a negative income tax ("Family Assistance Plan") in 1969, and the U.S. House of Representatives passed a Family Assistance Plan bill in 1970; the bill never passed the U.S. Senate. Similar bills were introduced in other countries, and each died. According to U.S. Senator Daniel Patrick Moynihan, who wrote a book on the failure of these plans, the proposal "had become politically charged, came to stand for the proposition that people ought not to have to work for a living."[20]

But the negative income tax movement was really not a failure in that it led to a whole array of changes, both incremental and substantial, in many countries around the world. In 1992, for instance, the Council of the European Communities issued a recommendation that every worker of the European Community should have a guaranteed minimum income provided by the government with no expiration date. In the European Union today most countries now have some form of guaranteed minimum income.[21] These programs have various names—*Sozialhilfe* (Germany and Austria), *Revenue Minimum d'Insertion* or RMI (France), Income Support and Income-Based Job Seekers Allowance (United Kingdom), and *Socialbidrag* (Sweden).

Since the guaranteed minimum income is not based on prior contributions, and never expires, it may appear to resemble a basic income or negative income tax. Every European Community country with such a program but France, however, has a requirement that citizens be available for work to receive the minimum income. Thus, the guaranteed minimum income carries with it the stigma of welfare. Moreover, in most European countries one cannot, except in some cases during a transitional period, collect both the minimum income and earn money, even from part-time employment.[22] Hence, the guaranteed minimum income, in contrast to the true negative income tax, provides a strong disincentive to start working. The effective tax rate on the first dollar of extra income may be 100 percent.

The basic income (negative income tax) movement has been especially strong in Europe. The Basic Income European Network has been holding regular congresses in Europe since 1986. However, the basic income movement in Europe today, which advocates modifying the guaranteed minimum income by eliminating the work requirement and eliminating the incentives built into the guaranteed minimum income to avoid work, has not been successful yet. It will face a difficult battle to establish a basic income, since it offends a fundamental presumption that everyone should be required to contribute to society.

No country yet appears close to adopting the negative income tax. The obstacle seems to be widespread public opposition to abandoning means-testing in the guaranteed minimum income, thereby transforming the guaranteed minimum income into, so it would seem to many, a gift to lazy people. It is ironic that popular concern with promoting laziness causes the European countries to adopt a system that does just that (by penalizing working while on a guaranteed minimum income) in preference to a system that would encourage some work. This problem with public acceptance might be overcome through the reframing of the basic income proposals, as for example by renaming the basic income "participation income" as proposed by Anthony Atkinson, and requiring some kind of community work for it.[23]

The Invention of the Earned Income Tax Credit

In the United States, objections to the negative income tax proposal led to a different formulation, one that did not require that recipients look for work but instead required them to have some income. The earned income tax credit (EITC) was proposed by Democratic Senator Russell Long in 1975 as an improvement on the negative income tax. It was a negative tax rate, not a negative tax intercept; one must have income (as well as a child, to further demonstrate that one deserves a tax break) to pay a negative tax. Thus, the invention avoided framing the tax relief as a free gift for doing nothing. One could not escape work altogether and have the benefit of a negative tax; the benefit instead took the form of allowing low income people to keep, in effect, more than 100 percent of their income. Initially, the maximum one could receive from the government under the EITC was only $400 per year. But under the administration of Bill Clinton, the EITC was raised substantially—in 2000 a family with earned income of $10,000 paid a federal income tax of a negative $3888.

Analogous tax credits have been adopted also by other countries. New Zealand reformed their social programs along similar lines in 1990. In 1993 Canada adopted a more radical version of the EITC, which benefits the nonworking poor families with children as well as those who are earning income. In April 2000, the United Kingdom adopted a Working Families Tax Credit (WFTC) modeled on the EITC, repackaging the former family credit as a tax credit, rather than welfare. The WFTC, in turn, is being copied in Belgium. The CESifo Council of Economic Experts recommended in 2001 that the European Union adopt a form of the EITC modified to accord with the 1992 EU recommendation of a guaranteed minimum income for all Europeans; the proposal was for a European EITC with a small guaranteed income attached for nonworkers.[24]

The EITC is a significant invention in that it reduces poverty without generating an incentive to shirk work. If people are told that they can receive an income by doing nothing at all, then the moral hazard is likely to be strong. The option of receiving an income for doing absolutely nothing is so striking an opportunity that even the most inattentive people are likely to notice the option and also to spread information about it to others. In contrast, the EITC forces them to cross the threshold of working. Even though the present earned income tax credit has a fairly abrupt phaseout, implying high marginal taxes for some people just at the phaseout threshold, effects on these people's willingness to work is probably less strong. Once people are working, the moral hazard effect of the tax rates on modest incomes is likely to be less compelling, and most of these low-income people are probably not so conscious of the phaseout.

The earned income tax credit has been an interesting experiment in risk management. It has done a great deal to alleviate poverty among the working poor. Moreover, it suggests other analogous systems, such as the inequality insurance proposed here.

The Invention of Health and Accident Insurance

The initial implementation of health and accident insurance was a triumph of economic logic. The case for these plans was exceptionally clear and was made well. We still have these plans today, in one form or another, in virtually every country.

The first national program of workers' health and accident insurance began in Germany under the government of Otto von Bismarck, with a national health insurance program appearing in 1883, and the first national accident insurance in 1884. These programs were true insurance in the sense that workers and employers paid a regular premium, and a benefit would then be provided at times of specified illnesses or accidents.

The success of the German experiment led to a transformation around the world, spreading the basic structure of worker and employer contributions to government health insurance and accident insurance. Within a decade, the German program was copied by Austria, Italy, Sweden, and The Netherlands, and ultimately by almost all advanced countries.

Mandatory participation in these plans solved the problem of selection bias: Without it only those with high risks would freely sign up with optional plans, thus making the plans prohibitively expensive for others. While participation was made mandatory by the German government, the actual insurance plans were run by numerous funds controlled by the insured and their employers. The funds' standing on their own created an incentive was thereby created for someone to watch that the workplace became healthier and better protected from accident risks, since these affected the regular premiums paid.

It is critical to observe an essential element of the original accident insurance scheme of Germany in 1884: the separate mutual association to insure the risks of each industry. Trades that were thought to have a similar degree of worker risk were combined into the same associations. Firms in industries that pose high risks to their workers must therefore pay higher insurance premiums to their mutual associations than do other firms, and thus these firms must pass these higher costs along to the consumers of their products in terms of higher prices. The result is that consumers of the products will ultimately pay the full cost of producing, including the health costs imposed on employees, leading to greater economic efficiency. If most consumers do not want to pay the higher cost, then there will be a tendency for the industry to contract in size, a desirable turn of events from an economic standpoint.

When the German accident insurance was copied in the United States, it was called "workman's compensation" (now worker's compensation). John R. Commons, professor of economics at the University of Wisconsin and campaigner for worker's compensation in the United States, argued for it on the basis of what he called "the internalization principle," the principle that society should impose whenever possible all costs that firms cause for society onto the firms themselves, so that firms will have an incentive to contain these costs, thereby "internalizing" costs that were formerly borne externally to the firm. Commons noted that many turn-of-the-century workplaces were needlessly dangerous, and hence workers would occasionally incur a disabling injury at work. With worker's compensation, firms began to have an incentive to make the workplace really safer, and not just to create an appearance of safety so that lawsuits against them could not prove that negligence of the firm caused the particular accident.

Common's own state, Wisconsin, along with New York State, led the way by adopting worker's compensation in 1911. By 1920, all but six states had adopted it, the last of whom followed by 1948. Commons was successful in selling the state governments on worker's compensation because his internalization principle was so lucid and simple. Adopting the worker's compensation would improve economic efficiency in an essential way, by encouraging employers to make workplaces safer from accidents, and would have tangible benefits in reducing the number of people who lived out their lives as cripples and the number of families who faced extreme economic hardship with the injury of a breadwinner. Commons could not argue with the same force to compel firms to purchase life insurance or health insurance for their employees, since the employer has less control over these losses from more general causes, and even today they are not required to do so in the United States.

The Invention of Social Security Old Age Insurance

The world's first national old age insurance plan, supported as with health and accident insurance by employer and employee contributions and again compulsory, was installed by the Bismarck government in Germany in 1889. By relating benefits to contributions made, this pension plan clearly had elements of an insurance plan and was not just a pure redistribution scheme. People were placed in income groups; those who had higher incomes paid higher contributions (premiums) and received back higher benefits. Clearly, this was not a poor law or charity.

The old age insurance system adopted in Germany in 1889 was remarkably similar in form to the system in developed countries today, such as the U.S. Social Security System. The similarity provides a striking illustration of the international copying of inventions.[25] Hardly anyone in the United States today knows that their social security system was copied so slavishly from a German system of the 1880s.

According to the original 1889 German program, half of the payment was to come from the employee's pay, the other half from the employer. (The same thing is done in the United States today.) The amount of the contribution for each employee was determined by which of four classes the worker's income fell. Workers in Class I, with annual income up to 350 marks, paid 12 pfennigs a week; Class II, with an annual income up to 550 marks, 18 pfennigs a week; Class III, with an annual income up to 850 marks, 24 pfennigs a week; and Class IV, with an annual income above 850 marks, 30 pfennigs a week. (In the United States today, the contribution is a constant percentage of income up to a cutoff income, and is thus a sort of interpolated version of this German scheme.) If the worker had made contributions for exactly thirty years, the annual pension upon retirement at age 70 would be 50 marks plus 4 pfennigs for each Class I week, plus 6 pfennigs for each Class II week, plus 8 pfennigs for each Class III week, and plus 10 pfennigs for each Class IV week. If the worker contributed for more than thirty years, the annual pension would be determined by the thirty-year period for which the most favorable result could be obtained. (The same thing is done in the United States today, except the retirement age is earlier, progressivity is established according to a continuous formula, and the period is the most favorable thirty-five years rather than the most favorable thirty years.)

While the form of the 1889 system was very similar to plans seen today, the method of administering it was different, reflecting the information technology of the day. The 1889 German plan was administered by requiring that employers and employees make weekly contributions by purchasing stamps at the local post office, which would be pasted onto a card, one card for each employee. At the end of the year, the worker's completed card was taken to an appointed place where it was recorded and stored, and a new card was issued, marked to indicate where the preceding card was stored. These records of completed cards were stored until the worker retired, usually decades later, when they would be used to compute the worker's pension.

Such a complicated information system could never have been implemented without prohibitive cost and chance of major errors until basic late nineteenth-century information technology (discussed in chapter 5), had developed quite significantly, including an efficient bureaucracy, filing systems, postal service, and backup and storage of records for long intervals. Even in 1889, substantial skepticism abounded that such a program could be feasible. *The Times* of London expressed doubts in 1889 about the feasibility and cost of administering the German plan:

> The second important question of finance concerns the costs of administration. These are set at an annual mark per head—a moderate sum, if we consider the stamps, the cards, the clerk's work, the ordering, the sorting, the storing, the calculating, the supervision, the arbitrating, the judging, the appealing that are thrown in for this modest shilling. Yet those modest shillings amount to rather more than half a million sterling yearly, and do not include the extra work put upon the post and the ordinary administrative authorities. Still less do they include the vast amount of labour done for love. The mere sticking in of 11,000,000 stamps every Saturday evening is an appalling item. Add the service of unpaid members on their district boards, on tribunals of arbitration, as local officers to certify local cases, on committees and on councils of supervision, and the total of machinery set in work by this single Act mocks all conception.
>
> It is when we come to this section of the subject that we see how exceptionally Germany is fitted to be the scene of this great philanthropic experiment. Nowhere is the ponderous, conscientious, plodding, incorruptible bureaucracy so effective and so cheap.[26]

But, despite these doubts, the German old age insurance plan worked well. Social insurance was copied, as are other successful inventions, because it was observed to function well. There is ample testimony that others had their eyes on Germany when they adopted similar plans. In 1908 David Lloyd George, then chancellor of the exchequer in the United Kingdom, remarked as he introduced a plan for a social security system after visiting Germany: "I never realized before on what a gigantic scale the German pension system is conducted. Nor had I any idea how successfully it works."[27] In the United States in 1911, Louis Brandeis said that his observations indicated that following the "same path" as Germany, France, and England would lead to "social efficiency."

Evidence does point to some more fundamental reasons than simple political expedience for Germany's invention of social insurance in the 1880s, for instance, an inventive spirit and public discussion. The origins of social insurance in Germany came ultimately from the social thinkers outside of the German government. The "social question" became a popular subject of conferences and community meetings, no doubt encouraged by the broadening communist threat. The more moderate citizens naturally wondered how to address the same complaints that the communists took as their rallying point. The Society for Social Politics was founded in Germany in 1872 to consider innovations in social policy.

All these discussions impressed upon government policy makers the possibilities of extending the concept of insurance beyond its traditional limits. Gustav Schmoller, a leading professor of economics at Strassburg and then Berlin, and dominant force behind the Society for Social Politics wrote later of the nineteenth-century advances,

> The triumph of insurance in every imaginable area was one of the century's great advances in social progress. It was an entirely logical development that insurance should spread from the upper classes to the lower classes; that it had to attempt, as far as possible, to eliminate poverty; and that the older charitable relief funds for the workers were more and more constructed on the sound principle of insurance.[28]

The invention of social security old age insurance was the outcome of a process of experimentation in a land with much enlightened dialogue about the risk problems, where a recognition emerged of the basic problems of human psychology that had prevented effective and comprehensive risk management in the past. The invention in Germany was the result of increased sophistication with insurance concepts and the real beginnings of the field of behavioral economics. The social security experiment was daring at first and doubted by many, but then, when found to be successful, widely copied and retained in its essential elements to this day.

The Invention of Unemployment Insurance

Britain created the first national program of unemployment insurance in 1911 as part of a grand social insurance initiative shepherded by David Lloyd George. Except for its unemployment insurance initiative, the initiative was basically an imitation of social insurance programs in other countries. But the British unemployment insurance program was a completely new concept and its success spawned imitators. Unemployment insurance programs were instituted in Austria and Belgium in 1920, in Switzerland in 1924, and in Germany in 1927. The United States did not implement unemployment insurance until the catastrophically high unemployment rates of the Great Depression; the Social Security Act of 1935 created the first U.S. unemployment insurance by providing Federal backing for state unemployment compensation schemes.

Until the early twentieth century, most individual income risk had been viewed as uninsurable because of moral hazard problems. If a worker knew that his income were insured, then the worker would be less inclined to work, so insuring individuals' own incomes appears impracticable both for private firms and for governments. Unemployment insurance, however, is a clever invention that succeeds nonetheless in allowing the insurance of certain kinds of income fluctuations by defining certain categories of income fluctuations not very subject to moral hazard and insuring only these.

The idea behind unemployment insurance relies on the nature of the employment contract between modern corporations and their employees, partly defined by the practice of laying off workers from time to time and by the kind of record keeping that is routine at these corporations.

Modern corporations routinely lay off some of their workers in times of slack demand rather than cut the wages and reduce the hours of all their workers. Why do they not take the latter course, so as to share the burden of the slack demand more equitably among their employees? The reasons, explored in a comprehensive book by the economist Truman Bewley, are varied.[29]

For instance, if firms did cut wages across the board, they would create in the minds of their workers a sense that their employment situation is not complete or full, and a concern that they should perhaps be looking for other employment. Such attitudes would be detrimental to the good working and long-run commitment of the workers.

Another reason that firms lay off employees rather than reduce hours of all employees is that employees are found to have a profound psychological negative reaction to cuts in income, and that such reductions may therefore have a negative effect on employee morale. The employers that Bewley interviewed said that they thought that employee morale was important to the functioning of the firm because the firm finds it difficult to monitor and motivate the employees to perform well and reliably at work. Better, they told Bewley, to concentrate the pain of the work contraction on a few people and get them out of the firm altogether, where they are not likely to grumble to other employees and poison the work atmosphere.

Yet another reason for laying off some workers rather than reducing the hours of all is that there are fixed costs of coming to work at all, which entails transportation costs and disrupts the day; a modern corporation usually operates at a location that draws workers from some distance, and it becomes less worthwhile for all employees to come in if they are working fewer hours.

Employers, in a time of slack demand, will try to find some apparently equitable means of deciding among existing employees who should be let go, so that the remaining employees will feel that the actions were fair. Employees whose jobs are clearly less needed in times of slack demand may justifiably be let go instead of employees whose jobs are essential to the minimal functioning of the firm. Less senior employees are also generally let go first, in deference to some common notions of fairness and rights. The employers may also have some latitude to use the opportunity to lay off employees who are not performing very well in their jobs, without ever admitting to this reason.

Even though some of those laid off may be among the poorer performers in a corporation, overall the risk of true layoff in a modern corporation appears sufficiently random to be relatively free of the moral hazard concern that the layoff is a disguised quit, and to be sufficiently important to be the subject of attention by social insurers.

But the actual implementation of unemployment insurance is fraught with difficulties. One must design the unemployment compensation system so that it is not subject to fraud, not excessively exposed to the important issue of moral hazard, and not subject to difficulties of definition.

A problem with the implementation of unemployment insurance is that all sorts of employer-employee contracts litter the market, not just the classical ones of full-time employment subject to layoff. Therefore, the unemployment insurance system must be designed to clearly apply to the kinds of employment that randomly visit layoffs on certain employees.

Many people move into or out of the labor force for reason of their own ambiguous attachment to the work world. They may wish to take repeated vacations or be home to take care of their family and household duties. In family-run occupations, there may be only a vague distinction between working and not working. One must find some way of defining unemployment so that employees cannot too easily ask their employers to redefine these spells as layoff.

Unemployment insurance systems therefore have systems of rules and conventions that define both employment and unemployment. Seasonal workers may routinely work only part of the year. It would be costly to the functioning of unemployment insurance if these people could collect unemployment compensation during the off-season of every year. So unemployment insurance systems have decided on ways of defining abnormal variations in seasonal unemployment, and allowing unemployment benefits only for the abnormal spells out of employment.

Because ways of surmounting such difficulties had not yet been worked out, unemployment insurance was not among the original German social insurance initiatives of the 1880s, although the thinkers behind social insurance were certainly cognizant of the importance of unemployment insurance. In his 1879 treatise on social insurance, German economics professor Lujo Brentano referred to unemployment insurance as "the first and foremost requirement" of a system of social insurance.[30] But technical difficulties stood in the way of any broad national unemployment insurance program, until, in 1911, Britain set an example of how it could be done.

The British unemployment insurance plan was devised in respect of knowledge about difficulties with various local efforts to create unemployment insurance. The British had learned from the completely voluntary unemployment insurance scheme of the cities of Berne, Basle, and Cologne that the insurance must be either compulsory or limited in scope. Having learned from these experiments, the British unemployment system was made compulsory, the premiums were deducted from paychecks and paid by the employer, not the individual, and those who collected on the insurance were required to cooperate regularly to find a job at one of the new government labor exchanges (unemployment offices). The unemployed would have to sign for their unemployment benefits at one of these exchanges during working hours, thereby discouraging the fraudulent application for benefits.

Despite these innovations, however, many doubted the plan's chances. One source of doubt was the idea that unemployment is in truth *always* a voluntary status in the sense that the person could get *some* job very quickly. A person who is unemployed could take a very undesirable or low-paying job by showing up, for example, at rural areas where manual labor is hired at the lowest rates—but they would then be employed.

Designers of unemployment insurance systems see no good purpose in encouraging people to take jobs for which they are ill-suited. Thus, unemployment insurance is inherently a subsidy for people's waiting for a good job or searching for such a job.[31] The original British unemployment insurance bill showed great insight in combining the enforcement of unemployment insurance rules with the labor exchanges that were also in the business of helping the unemployed find good jobs; ultimately, their judgment as to the reasonableness of decisions to turn down low-wage jobs allowed the system to function well.

Unemployment insurance had a difficult beginning, through a period of radical experimentation and discovery. But like the other social insurance inventions covered in this chapter, the details of its functioning and the travails of its invention have faded into the background, and today we mostly take it for granted.

Concluding from These Examples

Substantially over the past two centuries, civilization has made significant progress in managing the risks that individuals face. Progress has been halting and intermittent because the state of emergent information technology has made it difficult to see the risks and to appreciate the outcomes of managing them. Despite these problems, advanced countries are now able to provide protection against individuals' falling catastrophically through the cracks of our economic system, and against extreme risks of bad health and old age. The benefits that such systematic risk management has already offered are enormous, and untold numbers of personal catastrophes have been prevented.

And yet the examples in this chapter suggest even greater opportunities for the future. The examples trace a trajectory of ever-improving risk management so that we might expect in the twenty-first century to see a real transformation of our lives from further financial progress.

Medical science, after centuries of slow progress, achieved such a transformation in the twentieth century, extending life expectancies in advanced countries from forty-five years to seventy-five years or even more. Democratized finance has the potential to achieve a similarly important transformation in terms of the *quality* of our lives, reducing the risks to livelihoods that has stymied so many lives and prevented so many people from achieving their potential.

The lack of information technology in ancient times was the motivation for the very primitive risk management devices of the tithe and zakat. The information technology that permitted the first social security system in Germany in the 1880s took the form of pasting stamps on cards, primitive but effective enough for the time. Today's information technology should make much more possible, and if the information is organized into the GRIDs described here, and if a proper system of units of measurement called indexed units of account are implemented, risk management will move dramatically forward. Our social security old age insurance should not continue to be so closely modeled after a system invented in the 1880s, and should be redesigned as an intergenerational risk sharing system that effectively pools our major intergenerational risks in light of all available information about them.

The advantages already offered by our progressive taxes and earned income tax credit can now naturally be made more systematic, reliable, and pervasive. Our improved information technology makes it very easy to restate tax payments in terms of indexed units of account, eliminating all sorts of tax anomalies that persist today. But, more important, the rate structure can now be recast as inequality insurance. Indeed, the inequality insurance proposal resembles the earned income tax credit in that it taxes people in terms of how much they earn, and the more people earn, the more they keep. But the inequality insurance reframes it in terms of the outcome in terms of inequality, which means that the advantages we now see with the earned income tax credit become pervasive and systematic, affecting not just the people of the lowest incomes.

The advantages offered by unemployment insurance could be extended dramatically, and our ability to deal with moral hazard focused more precisely, with modern information technology. The various kinds of livelihood insurance, tailored to individuals' own needs as revealed by information on the GRIDs, could take a great burden off of the relatively primitive unemployment insurance systems of today.

None of the social insurance systems described in this chapter has an international dimension. In fact, international risk sharing today is very minimal. Risk sharing cannot be really effective until it takes advantage of big differences across people in their risk situations, and that requires something like both the macro markets and the international risk-sharing agreements described here. The enormous intercountry differences in standards of living that persist today could be reduced in the future if we us financial techniques to manage the biggest international risks.

A Model of Radical Financial Innovation

IT REMAINS NOW to pull various ideas together into a model of really significant financial innovation, not just incremental innovation that has no larger direction or strategy, but innovation that can be transforming to our lives. We have already seen most of the basic elements of a model of radical financial innovation, with the various ideas for risk management institutions, the GRIDs and indexed units of account, the directions for research on risks and of advocacy for change. And we have seen some concrete illustrations of these principles in examples from history. But we need to distill from the analysis in this book several additional principles of innovation in economic risk management that have driven our success in the past.

Risk Manifestation

Perhaps the biggest obstacle to effective risk management is psychological. The public does not see its biggest risks and tends to focus more often on inconsequential risks that seem to them more salient. It is not enough for researchers and analysts to identify major risks statistically. If people at large do not appreciate their risks, they will neither take steps to deal with them nor give full support to institutions that deal with them.

This was the problem that hampered the advocates of life insurance, social security, and unemployment insurance: The public was not interested in managing these risks. But, eventually, the public was persuaded to take some important risk management steps. The process by which the first national disability insurance, health insurance, and social security were invented in Germany in the 1880s was one of intense public discussion. This led to a public understanding of the risks and helped people understand that purely random outcomes affect our economic well-being in important ways. The period of the Great Depression, a time of great public discussion of risk issues in the United States, also led to many personal risk management innovations. The Depression was so dramatic and sudden an event that it made the economic risks we face obvious to everyone. Today's leaders need to start talking about these risks, to make them apparent before another such economic disaster occurs.

Persuading the public of the other, bigger, long-term economic risks that remain unmanaged today will take some work. There seems to be hardly any public recognition of the risk of a major change in the economic status of nations, or of the possibility that the economic inequality within a nation could get much worse. There seems to be an almost exclusive focus among business commentators on predicting whether the business situation will improve in the next six months to a year, as if this were our only concern. Public leaders must be willing to talk about longer-term risks that we all face. This does not mean that they should be negative and pessimistic, only that they should address the long-term uncertainties that really matter, and do so within the context of risk management devices that can be realistically implemented—thus helping to alleviate such risk.

Creating the macro markets, markets for long-term claims on income flows or on illiquid assets such as our homes, would serve to make risks more palpable because they would allow us to see the day-to-day, even minute-by-minute, changes in fundamental economic values that are invisible today. When people see the price of a claim on the GDP of their nation or of a claim on their occupational income fluctuate substantially, they will see the risks much more vividly.

Proper design of the GRIDs, so that they are used well by individuals for detailed information risks, can also help with risk manifestation. The presence of detailed public data on individual livelihoods, finely disaggregated, will undoubtedly bring to the fore much more public discussion of risks than are seen today.

Finally, risk manifestation can be the subject of marketing campaigns by individual businesses once they have major new risk management products to sell. Life insurance companies have made hugely successful businesses doing this, reminding people of the uncertainty of the time of their own deaths. The time will be ripe for an industry of even bigger proportions that reminds people of their biggest economic risks and offers at the same time the means to deal with those risks.

Robust Psychological Framing

The importance of psychological framing is an essential lesson of this book. The names we use, the categories we delineate, the institutional arrangements we assign to these categories, all matter greatly for the success of our risk management institutions. Sound frames must be built from the beginning so that they make sense as long-term risk management vehicles.

Financial innovators, to be really effective, need to think about what kind of reframing of our basic standards and institutions they should encourage, so that their innovations can have their full potential. Innovators need to get past the mindset of incremental thinking, creating only small improvements in products that will immediately succeed in the current environment. They must try to think of major changes that are currently outside consumers' habitual frame of reference, planning a new psychological framing, and having the patience to promote the new ideas for a long time, until they take hold in public thinking.

Planning for society's risks must take account of the fact that, as we have seen, it is possible to foster an enduring personal sense of commitment and obligation to others. If an individual perceives a commitment as having been freely chosen, the fulfillment of this personal commitment becomes tied to that individual's sense of identity and self-esteem. Long-term public acceptance of risk management contracts can be enhanced if they are properly framed as enlightened actions that individuals undertake, acting freely and reflecting a common consensus, a consensus arrived at *before* the risk's outcomes are known. This aspect of framing would play a fundamental role in creating inequality insurance as well as establishing intergenerational social security, and would enhance the viability of other risk management ideas discussed here. These institutions require a sense of public commitment to a standard of risk sharing that must remain unchanged through time.

This kind of robust psychological framing has been achieved successfully in the past. Calling the original disability, health, and social security systems *insurance* in the 1880s in Germany created a sense of legitimacy to the institution. Calling the amounts paid in to the U.S. social security system *contributions* rather than *taxes* ensured the legitimacy of claims of eventual return on these payments. Renaming the negative income tax the earned income tax credit helped ensure public acceptance.

But robust psychological framing means not only choosing the right names for our institutions. It also means creating *sensible* designs for these institutions that can stand the test of time so that the original framing is reinforced by good sense that survives long-term changes in society. This is why intergenerational social security must be designed as a device that effectively balances the real and fundamental risks of generations. This is why international risk management contracts must be arranged between nations that really do face different risks, and with a sensible schedule of contingent payments that makes long-term good sense.

This design imperative requires, for instance, that in inequality insurance we replace our arbitrary standards for progressive income taxation with a method of defining progressive income tax rates that controls the distribution of income. By attaching this fundamental concept to the name inequality insurance, which makes its risk management function manifest, by making it part of a solemn social compact, society can control the risk that our income distribution may widen sharply in the future.

If a new financial order is to be truly effective, it has to employ proper psychological framing to ensure that it addresses the fundamental economic risks that we want to avoid, encoded comprehensively enough that it affects the bottom line of people's welfare, and defined sensibly enough that it cannot later be frustrated on the grounds that it was never based on solid principles.

Fundamental Experimentation

Despite all of our research, we will never know for sure how to design risk management devices on abstract principles alone. No one has a theoretical model of risks and of moral hazard that is so well defined that we can know how to build devices to work perfectly the first time we try. Over the years, businesses have conducted experiments, and their observations of the outcome have led to their business models. The same process must take place with radical financial innovations that transform our economy. We must begin with various small experiments.

People do not generally anticipate the full consequences of economic inventions. They do not and cannot know all the ramifications. But many countries, many local governments, many stock exchanges, many banks, and many insurance companies can all try somewhat different experiments. We must make a priority experimentation with new financial ideas that might well result in *fundamental* changes that may eventually be copied all around the world. This means making experiments whose stated and explicit goal is to discover such fundamental changes. These must include many experiments whose probability of success is low.

Government is fundamental in the area of experimentation with financial invention. Governments, for instance, can sponsor experimentation by offering research grants. For example, the negative income tax experiments in the 1970s led to fundamental changes in our tax code. Unfortunately, such experiments are not so common today, but government could spur experimentation by businesses by, for example, providing better resources for awarding financial patents so that the patent office can better evaluate the outcomes of experiments.

Private initiative, too, spurs many of financial inventions, turning businesses into major laboratories for the kind of experimentation needed to create a new financial order. The finance community has been extraordinarily inventive and willing to experiment in the past; we have good reason to hope they can be so in the future.

We must then continue studying examples of financial experimentation. We must even look for inspiration to developing countries, for inventions there can be extended for application elsewhere and many developing countries have more impetus to experiment. We learned of financial futures from Japan in the Tokugawa period. The Chinese special economic zones such as Shenzhen and the Russian free economic zones such as Kaliningrad might well provide experiments the likes of which the world may find valuable. We can also learn from countries that are in economic trouble since they are the most likely to experiment with new solutions to problems from high inflation to unstable exchange rates. We learned of indexation from countries undergoing uncontrolled high inflation and of indexed units of account from Chile during a difficult time in its history.

Most financial experiments that offer the hope of producing radical innovation need to be long-run experiments, lasting not months but years. The Chilean UF took fifteen years to firmly establish itself among the public as a unit of account. When social security was invented in Germany, it took decades before the world was convinced of its importance. Changing public modes of thought is necessarily a slow process. An initial financial invention may require both supporting inventions for its full implementation and new ideas on how to market the invention to the public. These will not come along until many minds have had the opportunity to reflect at length on the potential of the invention by observing it in action.

Activities and Opportunities

Six fundamental risk management ideas along with related ideas for an economic infrastructure are offered in this book that would extend the realm of financial management from the financial capitals of the world to all of us, wherever we live and whatever our wealth and the nature of our risk. Each of these represents quite fundamental changes. It may seem quite remarkable that *all* of these ideas would be implemented. But we must start somewhere. If we can achieve but one of them, in some form, it would be a major improvement. And the ideas feed upon and support one another, so that implementing one makes it easier to implement another.

In closing, we might reflect on the possible magnitude of the work needed to achieve the changes proposed here, if something like many of these proposals are really to be implemented. Democratizing finance means drastically expanding the financial sector so that it plays a deep role in our lives. Such an enterprise would generate whole new industries and major tasks for people to complete.

The advent of insurance for livelihoods and home values would require a fundamental transformation of the insurance industry, a transformation to make it far more important to our lives than it is now. We would write policies on risks far greater than the risks, such as the risk of early death, that our insurance industry covers today.

The advent of macro markets would require a fundamental transformation of our financial markets. Macro markets for single-family homes will mean liquid new international markets for assets that may be worth more than the world's stock markets. Macro markets for GDPs will mean markets that trade claims on income that may be worth over ten or twenty times the value of the world's stock markets. The presence of such markets, with their fundamental importance for the world economy, would represent a revolutionary expansion of the securities industry.

The advent of income-linked loans would require a major change in the lending industry, which would become involved in fundamental risk management, allowing it to contribute to people's lives by reducing their risks of bankruptcy and hardship. The institutions for making loans to businesses and to governments would be fundamentally transformed as well.

The advent of inequality insurance, intergenerational social security, and international agreements for risk control would bring finance principles into government policy in a way never seen before. This is not growth of the government sector, with the attendant moral hazard problems that it would entail, but the extension of governmental infrastructure so that some of our most important uncertainties can be managed. The implementation of ideas like these may help prevent some kinds of disastrous economic consequences that our rapidly expanding technology might otherwise bring to certain economic groups or to certain countries in coming decades.

Creating and managing the GRIDs is a task that would involve private companies as well as the government. We need to develop a broader industry of data supply, an industry of many firms supplying the GRIDs, an industry that covers the world, and that makes use of the best techniques to ensure individual privacy as well as the extensive public use of data pertaining to risks.

Creating the new units of measurements, the indexed units of account, is also a task both for private companies and for the government. The government would likely take the first steps, for instance by restating the tax system in terms of indexed units of account and establishing the legal status of such units. But, once established, it would be expected that there would be many privately offered alternative units that would offer focused alternatives to the government units and that would allow the system to diversify through competition and thereby better represent actual human needs.

The jobs that so many of us will have in making such a new financial order a reality are multitude, and yet well worth it. Changes as fundamental and transforming as the new financial order will have to occupy a good deal of our time and energies in transition.

Our methods of controlling our economic risks cannot remain where they are. The same breathtaking technology that generates new risks must be adapted to the purpose of managing these risks. Let us not take prosperity for granted. We must remember our economic vulnerabilities in this time of technological change, and we must take advantage of our new information capabilities to control these risks. We should be proactive in responding to the business opportunities that this new financial order produces. We should be willing to try risk management ideas that seem—at first—unnatural, possibly even unworkable. We should be ready to make risk management arrangements on a very large scale, aggressively pursuing the risks that have the potential for great damage.

Notes

INTRODUCTION
THE PROMISE OF ECONOMIC SECURITY

1. Robert J. Shiller and Allan N. Weiss, "Home Equity Insurance." NBER Working Paper 4860, 1994; published in *Journal of Real Estate Finance and Economics* 19(1) (1999):21–47.

2. Robert J. Shiller, *Macro Markets: Creating Institutions for Managing Society's Largest Economic Risks* (New York: Oxford University Press, 1993).

3. Stefano Athanasoulis and I have written three major mathematical analyses of global risk sharing: "The Significance of the Market Portfolio," *Review of Financial Studies* 13(2) (2000):301–29; "World Income Components: Measuring and Exploiting Risk Sharing Opportunities," *American Economic Review*, 91(4) (2001): 1031–54; and "Defining Residual Risk-Sharing Opportunities: Pooling World Income Components," *Research in Economics* 56 (1) (March 2002):61–84.

4. A substantial econometric literature tests and strongly rejects the hypothesis that people share their risks effectively. See for example Stephen P. Zeldes, "Consumption and Liquidity Constraints: An Empirical Investigation," *Journal of Political Economy* 97 (1989):305–46; John Cochrane, "A Simple Test of Consumption Insurance," *Journal of Political Economy* 99 (1991):957–96; Fumio Hayashi, Joseph Altonji, and Laurence Kotlikoff, "Risk Sharing between and within Families," *Econometrica* 64(2) (1996):261–94; Stefano Athanasoulis and Eric van Wincoop, "Growth, Uncertainty, and Risk Sharing," *Journal of Monetary Economics* 45(3) (2000):477–505; Eric van Wincoop, "How Big are Potential Welfare Gains from International Risksharing?" *Journal of International Economics* 47 (1999):109–35; Laura Bottazzi, Paolo Pesenti, and Eric van Wincoop, "Wages, Profits, and the International Portfolio Puzzle," *European Economic Review* 40 (1996):219–54; and Steven J. Davis, Jeremy Nalewaik, and Paul Willen, "On the Gains to International Trade in Risky Financial Assets," NBER Working Paper w7796, July 2000.

   Theoretical articles that explore some possible noninstitutional reasons for this lack of risk-sharing include Fernando Alvarez and Urban J. Jermann, "Efficiency, Equilibrium, and Asset Pricing with Risk of Default," *Econometrica* 68(4) (2000):775–97, and Narayana R. Kocherlakota, "Implications of Efficient Risk Sharing without Commitment," *Review of Economic Studies* 63 (1996):595–609.

5. These chain real GDP numbers, in 1996 U.S. dollars, are from the Penn World Table, Mark 6.0, preliminary version, available at www.nber.org. The Penn World Table is designed for accurate international comparisons, better than

the usual published GDP numbers converted by exchange rates, which sometimes overstate international differences.

6. See Karl E. Case, Robert J. Shiller, and Allan N. Weiss, "Index-Based Futures and Options Trading in Real Estate," *Journal of Portfolio Management* (Winter 1993):83–92. Case Shiller Weiss, Inc., in Cambridge, Massachusetts, now has twenty-three employees and 2002 revenues exceeding $10 million. The firm supports the Case Shiller Home Price Indexes for most of the United States, which were the first commercial repeat-sales home price indexes in the world. Our indexes now have many imitators. Billions of dollars of mortgages and home equity loans have been issued based on our online automated valuation model, Characteristics and Sales Analysis (CASA). Allan Weiss has been president of the company since its inception, and his creativity has been the prime reason for the success of our efforts. Other employees who are key to the success of this company include Howard Brick, Jay Coomes, David Costa, Linda Ladner, and Terry Loebs. In 2002, we sold the company to Fiserv, Inc., a Wisconsin financial services company, but Case Shiller Weiss, Inc., continues to function as a wholly owned subsidiary of Fiserv.

7. For example, these theoretical implications have been splendidly laid out in a new book. See John Y. Campbell and Luis M. Viceira, *Strategic Asset Allocation: Portfolio Choice for Long-Term Investors* (Oxford: Oxford University Press, 2002).

8. Most securities innovation has been achieved by commercial or investment banks, or by organized securities exchanges, rather than by firms issuing new securities, because the benefits of creating a new standardized security are likely to be larger for the former. See Douglas Gale "Standard Securities," *Review of Economic Studies* 59 (1992):731–55.

9. These innovations of the past are still in process, and much more will be done to extend their impact in the future. Catastrophe insurance, for example, is still of limited availability. See Kenneth A. Froot, ed., *The Financing of Catastrophe Risk* (Chicago: National Bureau of Economic Research and University of Chicago Press, 1999). An important idea that I will present in this book is that we should move to cover aggregate risks, covering measures such as GDP appropriately redefined, which would include risks of weather catastrophes as well as all other risks to standards of living.

10. Richard Thaler and I have been organizing conferences on behavioral finance at the National Bureau of Economic Research for a dozen years now. The complete list of our Behavioral Finance conferences, with links to the authors' Web sites, is on my Web site, www.econ.yale.edu/~shiller.

11. In my book *Market Volatility* (Cambridge: MIT Press, 1989), I concluded that substantial evidence exists for excess volatility for the United States stock market, but not for excess volatility in the relative prices of the subindexes, transportation, utilities, and industrials. Jeeman Jung and I have analyzed data from all U.S. firms that have uninterrupted dividend records since 1926, and concluded that Samuelson's dictum applies: the U.S. stock market has shown evidence of micro efficiency but macro inefficiency over this period. See Jee-

man Jung and Robert J. Shiller, "One Simple Test of Samuelson's Dictum for the Stock Market," Cowles Foundation Discussion Paper No. 1386, Yale University, 2002. Tuomo Vuolteenaho has analyzed individual firm data from 1956 to 1996 and concluded that most of their price movements are due to information about future firm cash flows. See Tuomo Vuolteenaho,"What Drives Firm-Level Stock Returns?" *Journal of Finance* 67 (2002):233–64.

12. Enron, an energy trading firm and financial innovator that collapsed in 2001, is an interesting special case. *Fortune* magazine ranked it as number one for innovativeness six years in a row, ending in 2001. Unfortunately, Enron's high level of innovation was not matched by high professional ethical standards at the top level of the firm.

13. Confiscation of private enemy property is expressly prohibited by Article 46 of the Hague Regulations. These regulations impose a principle of humanity, respect for individual rights. See Netsuke Ando, *Surrender, Occupation, and Private Property in International Law* (Oxford: The Clarendon Press, 1991).

14. The antagonism attending the end of World War I, and the heavy reparations imposed on Germany, might suggest that securities that German nationals held in other countries would have been confiscated. Moreover, if one reads John Maynard Keynes's *The Economic Consequences of the Peace*, written in 1919, one may well conclude that such confiscation was imminent. When the Reparations Commission met in 1920, however, it turned out otherwise. American legal opinion held that the securities should not be confiscated, and since the Reparations Treaty required unanimity among the Reparations Commission members, the Commission did not demand these securities. See Etienne Mantoux, *The Carthaginian Peace, or the Economic Consequences of Mr. Keynes* (Pittsburgh: University of Pittsburgh Press, 1952), p. 136.

Regarding the German social security system that was founded in the 1880s, Peter Köhler writes,

The development of social insurance in Germany in particular illustrates the astonishing inertia of institutions once they have been established. In organizational respects, the branches of German social insurance survived unharmed the effects of being bled dry financially during the First World War and by the galloping inflation of the twenties. Despite the massive restrictions on benefits and services during the global economic crisis, and despite the political instability of the Weimar Republic, the fundamental decision in favour of a subdivided social insurance system survived. The other side of the coin when an administrative organization has been perfected to such an extent that it cannot even be shaken by national disasters became apparent, however, during the national socialist regime and the Second World War: the national socialists quickly decided to refrain from imposing any fundamental changes on the system, but instead of that, it was 'forced to toe the party line.' Even when the objectives laid down had been changed to accommodate political and racist principles, the social insurance system continued to function until the bitter end, and, according to the astonished report by the British military government of May 1945, the German social insurance system was "continuing almost normally."

Peter A. Köhler, "Historical Context and Origins of Social Security," in B. von Maydell and E. M. Hohnerlein, eds., *The Transformation of Social Security Systems in Central and Eastern Europe* (Leuven: Peters Press, 1994), p. 28.

15. In Iran, those who were not convicted of corruption by revolutionary courts kept their pensions, and even saw their government pensions increased. Relatively little of value remained in formal financial markets in 1979 in Iran; what capital there was had already lost value or left the country. Most financial arrangements in Iran operated informally in the bazaar, and these arrangements were left intact by the revolution. I am indebted to Professor Sohrab Behdad of Denison University and Nader Habibi of DRI-WEFA for a discussion of these points.

16. John Rawls, *A Theory of Justice* (Cambridge: Harvard University Press, 1971). The core idea of Rawlsian theory had been stated earlier, first by economist William Vickrey, "Measuring Marginal Utility by Reactions to Risk," *Econometrica* 13(4) (1945):319–33, and then independently by economist John C. Harsanyi, "Cardinal Utility in Welfare Economics and in the Theory of Risk-Taking," *Journal of Political Economy* 61 (1953):434–35. I attribute the theory to Rawls here because Rawls gave the theory its most convincing exposition, tied it in with the history of philosophy and to our concerns about justice, and has remained influential to this day.

17. See John Harsanyi, *Rational Behavior and Bargaining Equilibrium in Games and Social Situations* (Cambridge: Cambridge University Press, 1977).

18. As regards probabilities, I am adopting the framework of Harsanyi; see his "Can the Maximin Principle Serve as a Basis for Morality? A Critique of John Rawl's Theory," *American Political Science Review* 69 (1975):594–606. Amartya Sen refers to this Harsanyi framework as "probabilistic egalitarianism"; see his *On Economic Inequality* (Oxford: The Clarendon Press, 1997). Ian Shapiro further articulates doubts about the maximin solution in his book *The Evolution of Rights in Liberal Theory* (Cambridge: Cambridge University Press, 1986). Rawls's own rebuttal of critics of his difference principle seems rather unconvincing. See John Rawls, "Some Reasons for the Maximin Criterion," *American Economic Review Papers and Proceedings* 64 (1974):141–66.

CHAPTER ONE
WHAT THE WORLD MIGHT HAVE LOOKED LIKE SINCE 1950

1. Oxford historian Niall Ferguson argues persuasively for the discipline of alternate history (also called counterfactual history or conjectural history). Such a discipline helps offset a human tendency to think of history as deterministic and to suppose that past events were somehow inevitable. See his book *Virtual History: Alternatives and Counterfactuals* (New York: Basic Books, 2000).

2. Senator Arthur H. Vandenberg, chairman of the Senate Foreign Relations Committee said in 1947 that he was finally influenced by the U.S. ambassador to Great Britain, Lewis W. Douglas, whom Vandenberg quoted as follows:

> It is almost a certainty that if we do nothing, such chaos, disorder and confusion will exist that men's minds will take hold of queer ideas hostile to their own traditions and inimical to ours. In a western world the consequences to us can be profound. The costs to us may be expressed in an incalculable number of billions of dollars. It may be expressed in impairments of our own historic free institutions. So it seems to me that our vital national interests are deeply concerned.

The text of Vandenberg's speech can be found in the *New York Times*, November 25, 1947, p. 14.

3. The completion theme regarding the Marshall Plan was explicit in a speech by Thomas E. Dewey, the governor of New York and Republican presidential candidate in the 1944 and 1948 elections: "It is unthinkable that, after a successful war at staggering cost in blood and resources, we should now stop and surrender the fruits of victory. We will be doing just that if we permit the free nations to fall into economic chaos and then under Soviet control." *New York Times*, November 6, 1947, p. 12.

    Psychological research on completion-of-goal tensions is extensive. Beginning decades ago, psychologists have studied the inner psychological tension generated by unfinished tasks. See D. L. Adler and J. S. Kounin, "Some Factors Operating at the Moment of Resumption of Interrupted Tasks," *Journal of Psychology* 7 (1939):355–67. A recent study shows that perception of unfinished tasks is a director of human attention, even at a preconscious level. See Gordon B. Moskowitz, "Preconscious Effects of Temporary Goals on Attention, "*Journal of Experimental Social Psychology*, 38(4) (July 2002):397–404. The extensive psychological literature on task motivation is surveyed in Edwin A. Locke and Gary P. Latham, "Building a Practically Useful Theory of Goal Setting and Task Motivation: A 35–Year Odyssey, *American Psychologist* 57(9) (September 2002):705–17.

4. Jonathan B. Bingham, *Shirt-Sleeve Diplomacy: Point 4 in Action* (New York: John Day, 1954), p. 245.

5. Although Japanese real per capita GDP doubled from a low base in the 1950s, the fastest growth was in the 1960s.

6. These chain real GDP numbers, in 1996 US dollars, are from the Penn World Table, Mark 6.0, preliminary version, available at www.nber.org.

CHAPTER TWO
THE HIDDEN PROBLEM OF ECONOMIC RISK

1. Economic theory does offer a number of reasons why wages may not equal marginal product. Labor unions may exert monopoly power, and insiders

(union members) may force the wage up so that it is not profitable for firms to hire outsiders even if the wage exceeds the marginal product. See Assar Lindbeck, *Unemployment and Macroeconomics* (Cambridge: Cambridge University Press, 1993). Employers may exert monopsony power, and thereby push the wage down below the marginal product. See Francis Green, Stephen Machin, and Alan Manning, "The Employer Size-Wage Effect: Can Dynamic Monopsony Provide an Explanation?" *Oxford Economic Papers* 48(3) (July 1996):433–55. The efficiency wage theory asserts that firms will take into account not only the direct marginal product of employees but also the effects of the wage rate itself on employee morale and productivity, and this again suggests deviations of the wage rate from marginal product related to social norms and expectations. See Janet Yellen, "Efficiency Wage Models of Unemployment," *American Economic Review* 74 (May 1984):200–5. Employee issues of status and fairness may create externalities within firms that disrupt the relation between wage and marginal product. See Robert H. Frank, "Are Workers Paid their Marginal Products?" *American Economic Review* 74(4) (September 1984):549–71. Models of income differences that do not rely on intrinsic differences in labor marginal product are reviewed in D. G. Champernowne and F. A. Cowell, *Economic Inequality and Income Distribution* (Cambridge, Cambridge University Press, 1998). It is also possible that compensation for certain kinds of work can be vulnerable to speculative bubbles, just as the stock market is. Much talk these days about the high executive salaries in the United States has suggested that at least part of the cause is in a temporary overestimation of the value that these superstars can achieve; see Rakesh Khurana, *Searching for a Corporate Savior* (Princeton: Princeton University Press, 2002). These reasons for deviations of wages from marginal product do not, however, inspire any more confidence that incomes are not risky.

2. Barbara Ehrenreich, *Nickel and Dimed: On (Not) Getting by in America* (New York: Metropolitan Books, 2001).

3. Data are from the Current Population Survey, Annual Demographic Survey, http://ferret.bls.census.gov/macro/032001/perinc/new01_001.htm.

4. Ehrenreich, *Nickel and Dimed*, p. 219.

5. Katherine S. Newman, *Falling from Grace: The Experience of Downward Mobility in the American Middle Class* (New York: The Free Press, 1988), p. 98

6. George Katona, *Psychology of Economics* (New York: Elsevier, 1975).

7. See Melvin J. Lerner, *Belief in a Just World: A Fundamental Delusion* (New York: Plenum Books, 1980).

8. Analysis of data on the consumption expenditures of individual households within families shows that there is only limited risk-sharing within families. See Fumio Hayashi, Joseph Altonji, and Lawrence Kotlikoff, "Risk Sharing between and within Families," *Econometrica* 64(2) (1996):261–94.

9. U.S. Congress, Congressional Budget Office, "Estimates of Federal Tax Liabilities for Individuals and Families by Income Category and Family Type for

1995 and 1999" (Washington D.C.: Government Printing Office, May 1998), table 6.

10. The public finance literature shows that if we want to discuss tax incidence, rather than tax rates, then the progressivity of the tax system is somewhat ambiguous. For example, there is a question of who really bears the burden of the corporate profits tax in the United States. The question is difficult to answer because part of the burden of the corporate profits tax can be shifted to consumers in the form of higher prices, and the extent of shifting is difficult to estimate. See Laurence J. Kotlikoff and Lawrence H. Summers, "Tax Incidence," in Alan Auerbach and Martin J. Feldstein, eds., *Handbook of Public Economics* (Amsterdam: North Holland, 1987), pp. 1043–94, and Joseph Stiglitz, *Economics of the Public Sector,* 2d ed. (New York, W. W. Norton, 1988).

11. Sven Steinmo has made the provocative claim that the Swedish income tax system is less progressive than that of the United States, though he acknowledges that the combined tax and expenditure system is much more progressive in Sweden. See his *Taxation and Democracy* (New Haven: Yale University Press, 1993). Eduardo Engel and his colleagues have argued that the "scope for direct income redistribution through progressivity of the tax system by itself is rather limited. By contrast, for parameter values observed in Chile, and possibly in most developing countries, the targeting of expenditures and the level of the average tax rate are far more important determinants of the income distribution after government transfers." Eduardo Engel, Alexander Galetovic, and Claudio E. Raddatz, "Tax and Income Distribution in Chile: Some Unpleasant Redistributive Arithmetic," *Journal of Development Economics* 59 (June 1999):155–92.

12. Daniel Patrick Moynihan, Commencement Address, Harvard University, June 6, 2002.

13. Peter H. Raven, "Science, Sustainability and the Human Prospect," *Science* 297(5583) (9 August 2002):954–58, p. 955.

14. The words in the epigraph to this book, the King James translation of the Hebrew text *Qohelet,* are ascribed to King Solomon, who lived in the tenth century B.C., though some scholars believe it was actually written as late as the third century B.C. The words are found in the Dead Sea Scrolls of the first century A.D. I am indebted to Professors Shlomo Carmy and Aaron Levine of Yeshiva University for an enlightening discussion of this ancient text. There is a question about the translation of the Hebrew word *Pega'* as chance. Perhaps it should be translated instead as accident. The modern concept of chance may not have been fully developed at the time this ancient text was written. On the other hand, the broader context of this work and its philosophical emphasis on repetition and exogeneity of the determinants of our lives' courses suggests that the translation is not far off the mark.

For an amusing and therapeutic, if somewhat irreverent, development of our human tendency to neglect the role of chance and to attribute our good luck to our own genius, see Nassim Nicholas Taleb, *Fooled by Randomness: The Hidden Role of Chance in Markets and Life* (New York: Texere, 2001).

CHAPTER THREE
WHY NEW TECHNOLOGY CREATES RISKS

1.   See for example, Malcolm I. Thomas, *The Luddites: Machine Breaking in Regency England* (Newton Abbot, Devon, U.K.: David & Charles Archon Books, 1970), and Kirkpatrick Sale, *Rebels Against the Future: The Luddites and their War on the Industrial Revolution* (Reading, Mass.: Addison Wesley, 1995).

2.   Another factor causing economic distress at the time was the French and American Wars, which disrupted overseas markets. The term *Luddite* has entered our language to refer to someone who opposes progress, but in fact the Luddites were not so different from any other labor agitators. According to one historian, "The Luddites had nothing against machines *per se;* they just didn't want to lose their jobs!" David Linton, "The Luddites: How Did They Get That Bad Reputation?" *Labor History* 33(4) (1992):529–37, p. 535.

3.   See Amy Sue Bix, *Inventing Ourselves Out of Jobs? America's Debate over Technological Unemployment 1929–1981* (Baltimore: The Johns Hopkins University Press, 2000).

4.   Inequality in the world income distribution has apparently been getting more severe through time since the Industrial Revolution, though the worsening of inequality has apparently slowed down since World War II. See François Bourguignon and Christian Morrison, "Inequality among World Citizens: 1820–1992," World Bank and Delta, Paris, 2001. According to one study, over the last two centuries almost all of the widening inequality has occurred between countries, rather than within countries. See Peter H. Lindert and Jeffrey G. Williamson, "Does Globalization Make the World More Unequal?" National Bureau of Economic Research Working paper w8228, April 2001.

     More recently, there has been a worsening of the income distribution within developed countries. A 1998 study from the Organization for Economic Cooperation and Development looked at twenty developed countries over the time interval between the mid-1980s and the mid-1990s, a time interval unaffected by a global recession or boom at either end. During this period, income inequality worsened in nineteen countries: Austria, Belgium, the Czech Republic, Denmark, Finland, France, Germany, Hungary, Italy, Japan, Korea, The Netherlands, New Zealand, Norway, Poland, Sweden, Switzerland, the United Kingdom, and the United States. Inequality remained unchanged in only one country, Canada, and became less severe in none. The study also notes that Australia showed a worsening of inequality over the 1980s. The note to the table states, "The results are based on several income inequality indicators and reflect general trends reported in national and comparative studies." See Organization for Economic Cooperation and Development, *Income Distribution and Poverty in Selected OECD Countries: Economics Department Working Papers No. 189,* March 1998, table 2.2, p. 36. Some further perspectives on the worsening income distribution can be found in Ray Marshall, ed., *Back to Shared Prosperity: The Growing Inequality of Wealth and Income in America,* Armonk (New York and London: Sharpe, 2000).

5. A prominent introductory economics textbook gave the following account of the "lump-of-labor" fallacy. "Whenever unemployment is high, people often think that the solution lies in spreading the existing work more evenly among the labor force. For example, Europe in the 1990s suffered extremely high unemployment, and many labor leaders and politicians suggested that the solution was to reduce the workweek so that the same number of hours would be worked by all workers. This view—that the amount of work to be done is fixed—is called the lump-of-labor fallacy." But the same textbook goes on to say "...a decrease in the demand for a particular kind of labor because of technological shifts in an industry can be adapted to—lower relative wages and migration of labor and capital will eventually provide new jobs for the displaced workers." In other words, the lump-of-labor fallacy is only a fallacy in its assumption that the results of a decline in the demand for labor must be seen in declining employment, and not in a declining wage as well as other disruptions of life. See Paul A. Samuelson and William D. Nordhaus, *Economics,* 16th ed. (New York: Irwin/McGraw-Hill, 1998), p. 239.

6. In the last half-century world, economic growth has been so strong as to mitigate the effects of growing inequality on the poor. In fact, economist Richard Cooper has pointed out that the world 20th percentile real income has grown 2.0 percent a year between 1950 and 1992, a growth rate that, over the decades, has resulted in a substantial improvement in living conditions for these people. See Richard N. Cooper, "Growth and Inequality: The Role of Foreign Trade and Investment," unpublished paper presented at William Brainard Festschrift Conference, Yale University, October 27, 2001. David Dollar and Aart Kraay have shown that higher growth rate countries have higher growth rates of their low-income populations too. See David Dollar and Aart Kraay, "Growth Is Good for the Poor," World Bank, Washington, D.C., 2000. There is also some evidence that, if one corrects for certain conditions (education, health, rule of law) incomes of poorer countries have tended to converge to those of richer countries. See Robert J. Barro, *Determinants of Economic Growth* (Cambridge: MIT Press, 1997), and Robert J. Barro and Xavier Sala-i-Martin, *Economic Growth* (New York: McGraw Hill, 1995). But this statistical literature hardly establishes a principle of growth for low incomes that can be relied upon for the future.

7. Norbert Wiener, *Cybernetics, Or Control and Communication in the Animal and the Machine* (New York: The Technology Press, John Wiley, 1948), pp. 36–38.

8. According to *Technology Review,* "The machine consists of a mobile platform on which are mounted an image-processing system, air blowers, and a mechanical arm with a gripper attached. As a tractor slowly pulls the platform through the field, cameras take pictures that the system analyzes. (The air blowers ruffle foliage to expose the fruit.) When the harvester sights a melon bigger than a certain size—and therefore presumed to be ripe—it extends the gripper to grab the fruit and lift it off the ground. Knives attached to the gripper slash the stalk, and the gripper places the melon on a conveyor belt." See

"Prototype: Straight from the Lab, Technology's First Draft," *Technology Review*, 104(8) (2001):16–17.

9. See Gregory D. Abowd and Elizabeth Mynatt, "Charting Past, Present and Future in Ubiquitous Computing," *ACM Transactions on Computer-Human Interaction*, 7(1) (March 2000):29–58.

10. This possibility is stressed in a theoretical paper by Philippe Aghion, "Schumpeterian Growth Theory and the Dynamics of Income Inequality," *Econometrica* 70(3) (May 2002):855–82.

11. The two most influential works on the winner-take-all effects are Sherwin Rosen, "The Economics of Superstars," *American Economic Review* 71 (December 1981):845–68, and Robert H. Frank and Philip J. Cook, *The Winner-Take-All Society: How More and More Americans Compete for Ever Fewer and Bigger Prizes, Encouraging Economic Waste, Income Inequality, and an Impoverished Cultural Life* (New York: Martin Kessler Books, 1995). Neither of these works presents a lot of data to back up their claims that incomes are becoming more concentrated in a few superstars, the argument being mainly abstract. Rosen apologizes by saying, "Confidentiality laws and other difficulties make it virtually impossible to obtain systematic data in this field" (p. 845). It might be that there are more singers today as a fraction of society than there were a hundred years ago, but that does not mean that there are more well-paid singers. Our generally higher standard of living may encourage people to spend more money on such things as modestly priced live music at weddings and parties. But it is also clear that a few professional singers make enormous incomes.

12. Another sign of our times is a 2002 film entitled "Simone," for Sim(ulation) One, by Andrew Niccoli, which tells a story about a director who tries to maintain the fiction that a simulated actress is real.

13. Lisa Guerney, "Software Is Called Capable of Copying Any Human Voice," *New York Times,* July 31, 2001, p. 1, col. 1.

14. Risks caused by globalization have been the subject of attention by various futurists, notably John Naisbitt, *The Global Paradox: The Bigger the World Economy, the More Powerful its Smallest Players* (New York: Morrow, 1994); Kenichi Ohmae, *The End of the Nation State: The Rise of Regional Economies* (New York: Free Press, 1996); and Alvin Toffler, *The Third Wave* (New York: Morrow, 1980).

15. "Back Office to the World," *Economist,* May 3, 2001.

16. Such possibilities are described in Michael Dertouzos, *What Will Be: How the New World of Information Will Change Our Lives* (San Francisco: Harper Edge, 1998).

17. The development of telephones during the twentieth century did not result in a decline in business travel, either. The rise of e-mail at the end of the twentieth century saw no declines in business travel or the use of ordinary mail. It is possible that traditional means of interaction that rely on physical proximity are complements, rather than substitutes, with the new electronic methods. See Jess Gaspar and Edward L. Glaeser, "Information Technology

and the Future of Cities," *Journal of Urban Economics* 43 (January 1998): 136–56. Industries where research and development, skilled labor, and university research are important tend to be more geographically concentrated, and this suggests that there could be more, rather than less, concentration geographically in the future. See David B. Audretsch and Maryann P. Feldman. "R&D Spillovers and the Geography of Innovation and Production," *American Economic Review* 86(3) (June 1995):630–40.

18. See John Seabrook, "Why Did the World Trade Center Buildings Fall Down When They Did?" *New Yorker,* November 19, 2001, p. 64.

19. See Martin Shubik, "Terrorism, Technology, and the Socioeconomics of Death," *Comparative Strategy* 16 (1997):399–414.

CHAPTER FOUR
FORTY THIEVES: THE MANY KINDS OF ECONOMIC RISKS

1. Elementary probability theory can be used to measure the amount of uncertainty in this example. If the thieves are all independent of one another, then the number of robberies follows the binomial distribution, and it follows that the standard deviation of the loss in this case is about 20 percent of wealth. If the thieves are not independent of one another, then the standard deviation of loss can be much higher, depending on the degree of association across the robbery events.

2. According to a recent survey of the literature, such variables account for between a fifth and a third of the variation across individuals in annual incomes within the United States. See Samuel Bowles, Herbert Gintis, and Melissa Osborne, "The Determinants of Earnings: A Behavioral Approach." *Journal of Economic Literature* 39(4) (December 2001):1137–76. If we considered the entire world, we would expect the amount explained by such factors (excluding parents' income) to be much lower.

3. See Lee Ross, "The Problem of Construal in Social Inference and Social Psychology," in N. Grunberg, R. E. Nisbett, and J. Singer, eds., *A Distinctive Approach to Psychological Research: The Influence of Stanley Schachter* (Hillsdale, N.J.: Erlbaum, 1987). A broadly based argument that our risks are larger than we easily imagine may be found in Michael Mandel, *The High Risk Society: Peril and Promise in the New Economy* (New York: Times Business, 1996).

4. For an account of the difficulties we face in understanding the aggregate economy, see Christopher A. Sims, "Macroeconomics and Reality," *Econometrica* 48(1) (January 1980):1–48. For an account of the complexity of the causes of macroeconomic fluctuations in the context of the Fair Model, a large scale econometric model of the U.S. economy, see Ray C. Fair, "Sources of Output and Price Variability in a Macroeconometric Model," Cowles Foundation Working Paper No. 815, Yale University, 1987.

5. A prominent macroeconomic literature on "real business cycles" starts from the hypothesis that all fluctuations are ultimately due to technological inno-

vation. See, for example, Finn Kydland and Edward C. Prescott, "Time to Build and Aggregate Fluctuations," *Econometrica* 50 (1982):1345–70. See also Kevin D. Hoover, James E. Hartley, and Kevy Salyer, *Real Business Cycles: A Reader* (New York: Routledge, 1998).

6. See Milton Friedman and Anna J. Schwartz, *A Monetary History of the United States, 1867–1960* (Princeton: Princeton University Press, 1963). Economist Robert Barro once tried to argue that 78 percent of the variation in the U.S. unemployment rate, 1946–77, was due to unexpected changes in the money stock, military employment, and the minimum wage. Robert J. Barro, "Unanticipated Money Growth and Unemployment in the United States," *American Economic Review* 67 (1977):101–15.

7. See Robert E. Hall, "The Role of Consumption in Economic Fluctuations," in Robert J. Gordon, ed., *The American Business Cycle: Continuity and Change* (Chicago: National Bureau of Economic Research and the University of Chicago Press, 1986).

8. David Lilien argued that a substantial source of economic fluctuations in the United States were "unusual structural shifts" such as a change in demand for produced goods relative to services. See David M. Lilien, "Sectoral Shifts and Cyclical Unemployment," *Journal of Political Economy* 60 (1982):777–93.

9. James Hamilton pointed out in 1983 that dramatic oil price shocks preceded all but one of the recessions in the United States since World War II. See James D. Hamilton, "Oil and the Macroeconomy since World War II," *Journal of Poliltical Economy* 91 (April 1983):228–48. There was also a sharp oil price increase at the time of the 1990–91 recession, and a threat of an oil shock in the 2001–2 recession. In the latter case, the failure of an oil shock to materialize was given as a reason for the mildness of the recession.

10. See N. Gregory Mankiw, David Romer, and David N. Weil, "A Contribution to the Empirics of Economic Growth," *Quarterly Journal of Economics,* 107 (May 1992):407–37.

11. See Ben S. Bernanke, "Bankruptcy, Liquidity, and Recession," *American Economic Review* 71 (May 1981):155–59.

12. See Julio J. Rotemberg and Garth Saloner, "A Supergame-Theoretic Model of Price Wars during Booms," *American Economic Review* 76 (June 1986): 390–407.

13. There is evidence that the persistence and severity of the Great Depression in the United States in the 1930s was related to government support of labor unions and toleration of cartels. See Harold L. Cole and Lee Ohanian, "New Deal Policies and the Persistence of the Great Depression," unpublished paper, UCLA, 2001.

14. See Gabriel Almond and Sidney Verba, *The Civic Culture: Political Attitudes and Democracy in Five Nations* (Princeton: Princeton University Press, 1963); James S. Coleman, "Social Capital in the Creation of Human Capital," *American Journal of Sociology,* Supplement, 94 (1988): S95–S120; Francis Fukuyama, *Trust* (New York: Free Press, 1995); Robert D. Putnam, *Bowling Alone: The*

Collapse and Revival of American Community (New York: Simon & Schuster, 2000); and Peter J. Dougherty, *Who's Afraid of Adam Smith? How the Market Got Its Soul* (Hoboken, N.J.: John Wiley & Sons, 2002).

15. See Hernando De Soto, *The Mystery of Capital: Why Capitalism Triumphs in the West and Fails Everywhere Else* (New York: Basic Books, 2000).

16. See Edward F. Denison, *Why Growth Rates Differ* (Washington D.C.: The Brookings Institution, 1967); and N. Gregory Mankiw, David Romer, and David N. Weil, "A Contribution to the Empirics of Economic Growth," *Quarterly Journal of Economics* 107 (May 1992):407–37.

17. See Paul Krugman, *Rethinking International Trade* (Cambridge: MIT Press, 1994); and Robert E. Lucas, "On the Mechanics of Economic Development," *Journal of Monetary Economics* 22 (July 1988):30–42.

18. See Kenneth J. Arrow, "The Economic Foundations of Learning by Doing," *Review of Economic Studies* 29 (June 1962):153–73.

19. See Michael Woodford, "Self-Fulfilling Expectations and Business Cycles," *American Economic Review Papers and Proceedings* 77 (May 1987):93–98; Christina Romer, "The Great Crash and the Onset of the Great Depression," *Quarterly Journal of Economics,* 105(3) (1990):597–624; and Roger E. A. Farmer, *Macroeconomics of Self-Fulfilling Prophecies* (Cambridge: MIT Press, 1999).

20. See Joshua D. Angrist, "Lifetime Earnings and the Vietnam-Era Draft Lottery: Evidence from Social Security Administration Records," *American Economic Review* 80 (June 1990):313–35.

21. Earnings data are from Alfred Cowles, who extended the Standard & Poor's Composite Index back to 1871. See Alfred Cowles, *Common Stock Indexes,* 2d ed. (Bloomington, Ind.: Principia Press, 1939). The earnings series, linked to the later S&P Earnings series to provide a continuous series from 1871 to the present, are available on my Web site, www.econ.yale.edu/~shiller.

22. Frederick Lewis Allen, "Who's Getting the Money?" *Harper's Magazine* 189(1129) (June 1944), pp. 1–10.

23. T. A. Bisson, *Zaibatsu Dissolution in Japan* (Berkeley: University of California, 1954), pp. 93–96.

Chapter Five
New Information Technology Applied to Risk Management

1. The London newspapers the *Times,* the *Observer,* and the *Oracle and The Daily Advertizer* all comprised four pages and all cost sixpence in 1799.

2. While the letter press saw only limited use at first, after some improvements were made, it became a business standard in the second half of the nineteenth century. Letters, written with a quill or, later, a steel pen using a special ink, were placed before the ink was fully dry between the tissue-paper pages of a blank book, and the book closed and placed in a letter press, which pressed

the pages tightly together. The special ink used to write the letter left a mark on the blank page, thereby generating a copy, which, although backward on the tissue paper, could be read normally from the other side. Carbon paper did not work well with quill or even steel pens, which could not apply enough pressure to the paper without spilling the ink, so the letter press was the premier copying technology of its day. Its limitations were that only one legible copy could be made and, moreover, the copies were bound in a pressbook in chronological order, and could not be filed separately. Tracking down a sequence of communications meant going through many pressbooks.

3. See Jo Anne Yates, *Control through Communication* (Baltimore: The Johns Hopkins University Press, 1989), pp. 54–56.

4. While formulary documents, such as printed standard stock option forms in Holland in the early 1700s, were occasionally seen much earlier, no well-developed industry existed for producing forms until the nineteenth century; the *Oxford English Dictionary* gives 1855 for the first use of the word "form" in this sense. By the 1880s carbon forms were available. These bound stacks of several identical paper forms with carbon paper between them became ubiquitous by the late nineteenth century. These, along with typewriters which applied great pressure to the paper, allowed accurate and systematic back up of information at multiple sites, an essential to reliable record-keeping and reliable record use.

5. The vertical file with the associated cardboard file folders appeared at the 1893 world's fair, The Columbian Exposition in Chicago, where it won a gold medal. The vertical file is a significant invention, copied around the world and found in nearly every office today. Before the vertical file, the dominant storage facilities were pigeon holes in desks, wooden drawers where documents would be lain on top of each other, and letter boxes kept on shelves. Large documents were typically folded over quarto or octavo, and a description of the content was written on the outside of the folded document. Groups of documents were sometimes tied together with ribbons or strings. One could look in a pigeonhole or drawer or shelf for the document that one needed by sorting through the octavos and reading the descriptions. This method of storage, however, was not efficient, and the need to remove documents from a stack to read the descriptions subjected the documents to risk of loss or damage. The vertical file eliminated the letter boxes and expensive separate wooden slots for files, which could not be flexibly expanded or contracted; it also replaced cheap cardboard file folders with projecting tabs on which a title can be read without displacing the file. Modern file drawers themselves involve a significant innovation, a wheel and rail support system for the drawer that allowed a deep file drawer to be pulled out all the way, to access the backmost file folder, without the drawer falling out of the file cabinet. The system has a double wheel, riding in a track, with a two-for-one ratio, so that when the file drawer is fully extended, the supporting rail is half extended, allowing support of the drawer when extended from the cabinet. With such solid and

reliable drawers, the files could be four or five drawers high and thirty inches deep, making effective use of limited wall space.

6. The late nineteenth and early twentieth centuries saw much progress in filing systems. The Dewey Decimal System was adopted by libraries in 1876, and the succeeding decades brought many alternative inventions of filing systems for printed material. Around the time of the introduction of the vertical file, businesses began to adopt a filing system in which all documents relating to a particular customer or client, including both incoming and copies of outgoing mail, were kept together and filed by name so that one could quickly find all the material relating to a given name. Copies were now kept on separate sheets that could be filed separately by name, eliminating the need to consult many press books for one name. A thoughtful discussion of these and related advances in office technology can be found in Yates, *Control through Communication*.

7. Document sizes were also becoming standardized so that they could be stored without folding, and could be read without unfolding, a significant advance for long-term storage where brittleness of paper was a serious cause of record loss, especially before the discovery in the nineteenth century of the role of acid in paper brittling.

8. Mechanical calculators that were developed in the 1870s and 1880s included the Odhner machines and the Felt Comptometer; these sped the operation of addition of numbers by a factor of about six. The punch-card electrical tabulating system of Hollerith was also developed in the 1880s, and used in the U.S. 1890 census. These devices are described in William D. Nordhaus, "The Progress of Computing," Cowles Foundation Discussion Paper No. 1324, Yale University, September 2001. Nordhaus estimates that since 1900, performance of computers, measured in the units of labor it saves, has increased by a factor between one trillion and five trillion.

9. Hans-Eberhard Mueller, *Bureaucracy, Education, and Monopoly: Civil Service Reforms in Prussia and England* (Berkeley: University of California Press, 1984), p. 80.

10. In Prussia in 1874 the birth and death records formerly kept by the churches were now made part of the national government, with a civil registry (*Standesamt*). This efficient bureaucracy was already keeping the kind of records that would be essential to social insurance, just before the creation of that insurance.

   According to historian Jürgen Kocka, in *Industrial Culture and Bourgeois Society: Business, Labor, and Bureaucracy in Modern Germany* (New York: Berghan Books, 1999),

   > In international comparisons with England and the United States, east-central Europe, and the south, one basic state of affairs repeatedly appears as something that can hardly be underestimated: For Prussia, Austria, and other major German States, and then later for Imperial

Germany, the construction of an efficient, influential, well-respected public bureaucracy happened early on—long before industrialization, before parliamentization, and especially before democratization. The civil-service state in Germany is a product of the eighteenth century; and despite all the expansion and change it experienced, it fundamentally survived the profound ruptures of German society all the way through to the twentieth century. (199)

11. The U.S. government first regularly published the Consumer Price Index during World War I to permit cost-of-living adjustments of wages, and began regular publication of national income statistics in 1942. Some estimates of these were available earlier. Annual publication of national income statistics in Japan began in 1953. Many other countries began publishing national income statistics around the middle of the twentieth century.

12. For example, there is the so-called substitution bias in many kinds of consumer price indexes. The bias occurs if the indexes neglect to consider that people substitute other goods for the goods whose prices increase most, thereby minimizing the impact of those price changes. Until the substitution bias problem was solved, any use of the consumer price indexes for risk management contracts (such as escalation clauses in labor contracts) was hampered.

13. Progress in methods of constructing prices of illiquid assets such as housing are surveyed in my book *Macro Markets*.

14. See Evan I. Schwartz, "Digital Cash Payoff," *Technology Review* 361(8247) (2001):62–68.

15. Innovative new electronic financial exchanges now under development, such as Opt4 and Hedgestreet, may help broaden the scope of tradable assets.

16. See Paul Milgrom, *Auction Theory for Privatization* (Cambridge: Cambridge University Press, 2001). Laboratory creation of artificial markets has allowed experimenters to test alternative market structures. See for example Alvin E. Roth, "The Economist as Engineer: Game Theory, Experimental Economics and Computation as Tools of Design Economics," Fischer Schultz Lecture, *Econometrica* 70 (July 2001):1341–78, or Stephen Rassenti, Vernon L. Smith, and Bart J. Wilson, "Controlling Market Power and Price Spikes in Electricity Networks: Demand-Side Bidding," unpublished paper, Interdisciplinary Center for Economic Science, George Mason University, 2001.

17. Right after the breakup of the Soviet Union, the Russian government wanted to sell the capital stock of the Russian Republic to its own citizens, who of course had no money to buy it. In one of the grandest innovations in world financial history, the Russian government made "privatization vouchers" freely available to all 147 million Russians in 1992 and 1993. The vouchers could be used by them to purchase shares in state enterprises. Of the 147 million vouchers, 144 million, or 98 percent of the total, were picked up, making Russia the country with the highest proportion of shareholders in the world at the time. The auction fundamentally transformed the Russian economy: After the

auction, most workers were employed by companies with private stockholders. See Maxim Boycko, Andrei Shleifer, and Robert Vishny. *Privatizing Russia* (Cambridge: MIT Press, 1995); and Alfred Kokh, *The Selling of the Soviet Empire: Politics and Economics of Russia's Privatization—Revelations of the Principal Insider* (New York: SPI Books, 1998). There is unfortunately a widespread perception that the Russian reformers who designed the auction were deeply corrupt, and that this accounts for most of the economic inequality in Russia today. But the inequality in Russia today did not result primarily from this auction. See Anders Aslund, "Inequalities in Wealth Should Not Be Blamed on Russia's Economic Reformers," *Financial Times,* May 31, 1996, p. 16. A balanced view of the workings, and shortcomings, of this auction can be found in Chrystia Freeland, *Sale of the Century: Russia's Wild Ride from Communism to Capitalism* (New York: Crown Business, 2000).

18. See Maureen O'Hara, *Market Microstructure Theory* (London: Basil Blackwell, 1997).

19. The parimutuel system of betting at racetracks, invented in France in 1872 by Pierre Oller, is an interesting precursor to, and stimulus for the development of, modern electronic financial markets, and the system was even a stimulus for the development of computers. Oller's parimutuel system eliminated the need for bookies, and relied on an automatic system to connect odds to amounts bet. But it was difficult for racetracks to achieve the necessary computations to display the odds (counterparts of financial prices) in a timely way. Starting in the 1880s, a series of primitive computer inventions progressively lessened this problem. By 1928, U.S. engineer Harry Straus, using electronic telephone switching technology, developed a "totalisator" that automatically totaled amounts bet in a central place as the tickets were printed from dozens of issuing machines, and automatically displayed the odds for crowds by lighting lightbulbs on a large tote board, each digit created by lighting the appropriate bulbs among a nest of twenty-four bulbs, a precursor to our modern digital displays. This totalisator replaced hoards of bookies, increased public trust, and strongly boosted the racing industry. See Fred S. Buck, *Horse Race Betting: A Comprehensive Account of Pari-Mutuel, Off-Track Betting and Bookmaking Operations,* 4th ed. (New York: ARCO, 1978); and John C. Schmidt, *Win-Place-Show: A Biography of Harry Straus, the Man Who Gave America the Tote* (Baltimore: The Johns Hopkins University, published with the assistance of the G.W.C. Whiting School of Engineering, 1989). Longitude, Inc., developed an advanced new trading system for financial risks that facilitates trade in a wide variety of economic indexes. See Jeffrey Lange and Nick Economides, "A Parimutuel Market Microstructure for Contingent Claims Trading," unpublished paper, Longitude, Inc., New York, 2001. See also Lloyd S. Shapley and Martin Shubik, "Trade Using One Commodity as a Means of Payment," *Journal of Political Economy* 85(5) (1977):937–68. The parimutuel digital call option system was inspired by an earlier idea, that of Nils Hakansson, called *supershares*. See Nils H. Hakansson, "Welfare Aspects of Options and Supershares," *Journal of Finance* 33 (June 1978):754–76.

20. According to research of Elizabeth Tibbetts of Cornell University, the wasp *Polistes fuscatus* can go far beyond merely recognizing whether another wasp is a nestmate. They can visually distinguish individual colony members within their nest by the stripes on their faces and abdomens, and the insect colony uses this ability in the maintenance of their system of social rank. See S. Milius, "Wasp Painting," *Science* 161(26) (June 29, 2002):405.

21. Congress passed annual prohibitions against issuance of the cards due to public concern about privacy of their health records. The 1996 Illegal Immigration and Responsibility Act funded another identification system, and was passed by Congress and signed into law by President Clinton, though the identification system was repealed by Congress in 1999. The plan was to issue a smart card to everyone who works in the United States; employers would have had to swipe the card into a special machine at the time of hire, which would have then accessed a federal database identifying whether the employee was an illegal immigrant. Congress repealed the bill because of a popular outcry by people fearing that the government could abuse the system and that the system might entail loss of privacy. Australia in the late 1980s and the United Kingdom in the 1990s considered plans for national identification cards but abandoned the idea because of strong public concern with privacy. In Canada in 1999, a task force composed of five federal agencies issued a report that described a national identification system for all Canadians. The Canadian provinces have discussed plans to merge the drivers license with a provincial health insurance card into a single provincial card, which could become a Canadian national system.

22. In Germany every adult is given a machine-readable national identification card. France uses a national identification card that is technically voluntary but is in effect compulsory, since it is increasingly difficult to live without it. Neither card is linked to a national database, and Germany has constitutional limits against a national database.

23. Larry Ellison, "Digital IDs Can Help Prevent Terrorism," *Wall Street Journal*, October 8, 2001, p. A26.

24. A number of governments in developing countries have expressed ambitious plans for developing their digital technology and integrating it into their society through identification systems. Other projects to harness digital technology are "Singapore One" in Singapore, "Internet City" in Dubai, and the "Smart Villages" in Egypt, as well as numerous attempts at creating new Silicon Valleys.

CHAPTER SIX
THE SCIENCE OF PSYCHOLOGY APPLIED TO RISK MANAGEMENT

1. Daniel Kahneman, "Preface," in Daniel Kahneman and Amos Tversky, *Choices, Values, and Frames* (Cambridge: Cambridge University Press and Russell Sage Foundation, 2000), p. xiii. Kahneman goes on to describe an ambiguity in the concept: "A significant and perhaps unfortunate early decision concerned the

naming of the new concept. For reasons of conceptual terminological economy we chose to apply the name 'frame' to descriptions of decision problems at two levels: the formulation to which decision makers are exposed is called a frame and so is the interpretation that they construct for themselves" (xiv). In this book, I am generally referring to the first level.

2. See, for example, Kahneman and Tversky, *Choices, Values, and Frames*.

3. In a survey about attitudes towards welfare, questions were given wording either from the "recipient frame" or the "economy frame." Answers were affected by frame. See Thomas E. Nelson, Zoe M. Oxley, and Rosalee Clawson, "Toward a Psychology of Framing Effects," *Political Behavior* 19(3) (1997):221–46.

4. For example, sociologists trace changes in the media's framing of affirmative action. See William A. Gamson and André Modigliani, "The Changing Culture of Affirmative Action," *Research in Political Sociology* 2 (1987):137–77.

5. See Colin Camerer and Howard Kunreuther, "Experimental Markets for Insurance," *Journal of Risk and Uncertainty* 2 (1989):265–300.

6. Hayne E. Leland, "Who Should Buy Portfolio Insurance," *Journal of Finance* 75(2) (May 1980):581–94.

7. Amos Tversky and Daniel Kahneman, "Judgment under Uncertainty: Heuristics and Biases," *Science* 185(4157) (1974): 1124–31.

8. See G. B. Northcraft. and M.A. Neale, "Experts, Amateurs, and Real Estate: An Anchoring-and-Adjustment Perspective on Property Pricing Decisions," *Organizational Behavior and Human Decision Processes* 39 (1987):84–97.

9. Amos Tversky and Daniel Kahneman, "The Framing of Decisions and the Psychology of Choice," *Science* 211(4481) (January 30, 1981):453–58.

10. Graham Loomes and Robert Sugden have presented a modification of expected utility theory that takes account of the avoidance of the pain of regret and has different implications for human behavior. A similar theory was presented by David E. Bell. See Graham Loomis and Robert Sugden, "Regret Theory: An Alternative Theory of Choice under Uncertainty," *Economic Journal*, 92 (1982): 805–24; and David E. Bell "Regret in Decision Making under Uncertainty," *Operations Research*, 30 (1982):961–81. Actions based on the pleasure of anticipation of future reward are also sometimes inconsistent with traditional expected utility theory, see John Leahy and Andrew Caplin, "Anticipation, Uncertainty, and Time Inconsistency," unpublished paper, Boston University, 1998.

11. In their terms, there is a kink in the "value function" at the "reference point." See Daniel Kahneman and Amos Tversky, "Prospect Theory: An Analysis of Decision under Risk," *Econometrica* 47(2) (1979):263–91. See also Matthew Rabin and Richard Thaler, "Anomalies: Risk Aversion," *Journal of Economic Perspectives* 15(1) (2001): 219–22.

12. See B. Combs and P. Slovic, "Causes of Death: Biased Newspaper Coverage and Biased Judgments," *Journalism Quarterly* 56 (1979):837–43.

13. See Robert Eisner and Robert H. Strotz, "Flight Insurance and the Theory of Choice," *Journal of Political Economy* 69 (1961):355–68.

14. See George F. Loewenstein, Christopher K. Hsee, Elke U. Weber, and Ned Welch, "Risk as Feelings," *Psychological Bulletin* 127(2) (2001):267–86. The neurological basis of this tendency is explored in Antonio R. Damasio, *Descartes' Error: Emotion, Reason and the Human Brain* (New York: G. P. Putnam, 1994).

15. Guy E. Baker, *Why People Buy,* 4th ed. (Newport Beach, Cal.: Standel Publishing, 2000), pp. 101–2.

16. See Steven J. Sherman, "On the Self-Erasing Nature of Errors of Prediction," *Journal of Personality and Social Psychology* 39(2) (1980):211–21. There have been a number of experiments revealing that individuals' commitment to others can be affected by their own sense of freely chosen past commitment. See also Jonathan L. Freedman and Scott C. Fraser, "Compliance without Pressure: The Foot in the Door Technique," *Journal of Personality and Social Psychology* 4(2) (1966):201. See D. Cioffi and R. Garner, "On Doing the Decision: The Effects of Active versus Passive Choice on Commitment and Self Perception," *Personality and Social Psychology Bulletin* 22 (1996): 133–47. A useful survey of research on framing and consistency is in Robert B. Cialdini, *Influence: Science and Practice* (Needham Heights, Mass.: Allyn & Bacon, 2001).

17. See Leon Festinger, *A Theory of Cognitive Dissonance* (Stanford: Stanford University Press, 1957).

18. Ibid., p. 21.

19. See Ernst Fehr and Urs Fischbaher, "Why Social Preferences Matter—The Impact of Non-Selfish Motives on Competition, Cooperation and Incentives," paper presented at Nobel Symposium on Behavioral and Experimental Economics, 2001.

20. Daniel Kahneman, Jack L. Knetsch, and Richard Thaler, "Fairness as a Constraint on Profit Seeking," *American Economic Review* 76(4) (1986):728–41.

21. My survey work with Maxim Boycko and Vladimir Korobov reveals a basic underlying similarity in many countries of the world in opinions of how fairness is seen as related to economic actions and policies. We compared answers to hypothetical questions about attitudes towards economic actions and institutions in the United States, Russia, Ukraine, East Germany, West Germany, and Japan. Robert J. Shiller, Maxim Boycko, and Vladimir Korobov, "Popular Attitudes Toward Free Markets: The Soviet Union and the United States Compared," *American Economic Review* 81(3) (1991):385–400; and Robert J. Shiller, Maxim Boycko, and Vladimir Korobov, "Hunting for Homo Sovieticus: Situational versus Attitudinal Factors in Economic Behavior," *Brookings Papers on Economic Activity* 1 (1992): 127–94. The same analysis was extended to yet other countries. See Fathollah M.Bagheri, Nader Habibi, and Aygul Ozbafly, "Attitudes Towards Free Markets in Iran, Turkey, and the Former Soviet Union: A Survey Analysis," unpublished paper, University of North Dakota, 1997.

22. The ultimatum game was invented by Werner Güth, Rolf Schmittberger, and Bernd Schwarze. See "An Experimental Analysis of Ultimatum Bargaining," *Journal of Economic Behavior and Organization* 3 (1982):367–88.

23. The original paper is still unpublished. See Lee Ross and Steven M. Samuels, "The Predictive Power of Personal Reputation vs. Labels and Construal in the Prisoner's Dilemma Game," unpublished manuscript, Stanford University, 1993. A description of the study may be found in Lee Ross and Andrew Ward, "Naive Realism in Everyday Life: Implications for Social Conflict and Misunderstanding," in Edward S. Reed, Elliot Turiel, and Terrance Brown, eds., *Values and Knowledge* (Mahwah, N.J.: Lawrence Erlbaum, 1996).

24. The estimate of the reparations as a fraction of GDP is that of Etienne Mantoux, *The Carthaginian Peace: The Economic Consequences of Mr. Keynes* (Pittsburgh: University of Pittsburgh Press, 1952), p. 116.

25. See Derek H. Aldcroft, *From Versailles to Wall Street 1919–1929* (Berkeley: University of California Press, 1977). John Maynard Keynes argued in 1919 that the German reparations were excessively burdensome, and that a "transfer problem" increased the difficulties. See John Maynard Keynes, *The Economic Consequences of the Peace. The Collected Writings of John Maynard Keynes Volume II* (London: Macmillan, [1919] 1971).

26. The Reparation Treaty (ß 231) stated, "The Allied and Associated Governments affirm and Germany accepts the responsibility of Germany and her allies for causing all the loss and damage to which the Allied and Associated Governments and their nationals have been subjected as a consequence of the war imposed upon them by the aggression of Germany and her allies."

27. Starting in 1937, participants who retired could get a small lump sum benefit, but only as a refund of contributions already made. Monthly benefits began in 1940.

28. Quoted in William E. Leuchtenberg, *Franklin Roosevelt and the New Deal, 1932–1940* (New York: Harper & Row, 1963).

29. *Analysis of the Social Security System: Hearings before a Subcommittee of the Committee on Ways and Means House of Representatives, Eighty-Third Congress on Legal Status of OASI Benefits, Part 6* (Washington, D.C.: United States Government Printing Office, 1953), p. 980.

Chapter Seven
The Nature of Invention in Finance

1. U.S. courts have long upheld the principle that business methods cannot be patented. A turning point came in 1982 when Merrill Lynch was awarded a patent on its cash management account. Though the patent was challenged by Merrill's rivals, the courts upheld it, and by the 1990s the principle of financial patents was firmly established. See Robert M. Hunt, "Can You Patent That? Are Patents on Computer Programs and Business Methods Good for the New Economy?" *Business Review,* Federal Reserve Bank of Philadelphia, Q1 2001, pp. 5–14. In the future, innovation could be further enhanced if the government would offer to buy out financial patents that might better be pursued in the public domain, as the government of France did for photography in the

nineteenth century. See Michael Kremer, "Patent Buyouts: A Mechanism for Encouraging Invention," *Quarterly Journal of Economics* 113(4) (1998):1137–68.

2. In ancient times, insurance-like provisions were attached to marine loans, and burial societies offered something analogous to life insurance, but the earliest known true insurance policy dates to 1343, see Humbert O. Nelli, "The Earliest Insurance Contract: A New Discovery," *Journal of Risk and Insurance* 39 (September 1972):215–20. According to the historian Johann Beckmann, the earliest known statement of the *concept* of insurance, in vaguely probabilistic terms, dates from the 1600s. According to Beckmann, "some ingenious person," in an anonymous 1609 correspondence to Count Anthony Gunther von Oldenburg, explained how individuals who, having put a value on their houses, could pay a yearly fee of 1 percent of that value, in return for which they would receive, if there is ever a fire, enough money to rebuild. This unknown person said that he "had no doubt that it would be fully proved, if a calculation were made of the number of houses consumed by fire, within a certain space, in the course of thirty years, that the loss would not amount, by a good deal, to the sum that would be collected in that time." See Johann Beckmann, *A History of Inventions, Discoveries and Origins,* vol. 1 (London: Henry G. Bohn, 1846), p. 241.

   According to Ian Hacking, a careful scholar of the origin of the concept of probability, the seventeenth century saw the first statements of probability as a concept. Even by the time of the Renaissance, there was no modern concept of probability. Hacking notes that Galileo often used the word *probabilità*, but with an entirely different meaning. When Galileo wrote "not improbable" he meant "not implausible, though incorrect." Science was viewed as concerned with fact, not opinion, and any intuitive notions of modern probability were grouped in the latter category.

   The first known attempt at constructing scientific mortality tables for insurance purposes was made by John de Witt, a mathematician who had a reputation for research in mathematics and who was well acquainted with the new probability theory, for presentation to the Estates General of Holland and West Friesland in 1671. See Ian Hacking, *The Emergence of Probability: A Philosophical Study of Early Ideas about Probability, Induction, and Statistical Inference* (London: Cambridge University Press, 1975).

3. U. S. Patent No. 3,653,474, "Rolling Luggage," inventor Bernard Sadow, filed April 1972.

4. Sadow managed to talk to a vice president at Macy's, who agreed in the early 1970s to start selling the luggage. The suitcases did indeed sell, and set off a major trend, even though Sadow's initial model, with four tiny wheels, was unstable. If one walked fast while pulling it, the suitcase wobbled from side to side and sometimes developed a rocking cycle with increasing amplitude until the suitcase fell over sideways. Since the suitcase in its normal upright resting position tended to be low relative to one's hand, the handstrap had to be fairly long, and because it was flexible, did not allow any control of side-to-side wobble. One tried walking in a bent-over position to keep one's hand closer

to the suitcase for better control, which was uncomfortable and still mostly unsuccessful in controlling the wobble.

5. U.S. Patent No. 4,995,487, "Wheeled Suitcase and Luggage Support," inventor Robert V. Plath, filed August 1989.

6. Pre-Columbian wheeled toys can be seen in museums. For example, the Museum of Anthropology in Xalapa, Mexico, contains toy dogs and jaguars on wheels from Veracruz, which date to the Late Classic Period, between A.D. 650 and 950.

7. See James Card, *Seductive Cinema: The Art of Silent Film* (New York: Alfred A. Knopf, 1994), pp. 57–58, which includes a plate showing a frame from the movie with a dialogue balloon.

8. Even after Schomer's experiment demonstrated continuous titling with normal dialogue, it must have been easier to splice in intertitles rather than superimpose subtitles, especially when making versions of the movie in various languages. The impetus to develop an efficient and easy-to-use subtitling machine did not come until the advent of the sound movie era created a large demand to make these movies accessible to foreign audiences.

   There are many simple ways of putting subtitles in movies; the only challenge is to make it economical to do so. The role of sound movies in propelling the first inventions of modern subtitling machines is described by Nina Kagansky, *Titra Film: Une Chronique cinématographique et familiale* (N. Kagansky, 21–Quétigny, Impr. Darantière, 1995).

CHAPTER EIGHT
INSURANCE FOR LIVELIHOODS AND HOME VALUES

1. National Research Council, *Trends in the Early Careers of Life Scientists* (Washington, D.C.: National Academy Press, 1998), available at http://www.nap.edu/html/trends/.

2. See Richard Freeman, Eric Weinstein, Elizabeth Marincola, Janet Rosenbaum, and Frank Solomon, "Competition and Careers in Biosciences," *Science* 294 (December 14, 2001):2293–4.

3. I am taking it for granted that government-sponsored health insurance should also be provided. Virtually every developed country has it for all their citizens, with the conspicuous and lamentable exception of the United States. In the United States, over forty million people are without health insurance.

4. Shiller, *Macro Markets*. I also described the method I called the hedonic repeated measure index in "Measuring Asset Value for Cash Settlement in Derivative Markets: Hedonic Repeated Measures Indices and Perpetual Futures," *Journal of Finance* 68 (July 1993):911–31. The methods are related to earlier work that Karl Case and I did on repeat-sales price indexes. See Karl E. Case and Robert J. Shiller, "The Efficiency of the Market for Single Family Homes," *American Economic Review* 79(1) (1989):125–37.

5. Robert J. Shiller and Ryan Schneider, "Labor Income Indices Designed for Use in Contracts Promoting Income Risk Management," *Review of Income and Wealth* 44(2) (June 1998):1–20.

6. Some problems with the International Labor Organization data are discussed (and partially corrected in the new Occupational Wages around the World data file) in Richard B. Freeman and Remco H. Oostendorp, "Wages around the World: Pay Across Occupations and Countries," NBER Working Paper 8058, December 2000.

7. The economist John Cochrane has provided a design for an optimal health insurance policy that can be canceled at any time by either insured or insurer. With conventional health insurance policies, the insured has an incentive to cancel if health is better than expected, the insurer has an incentive to cancel if health is worse than expected. In Cochrane's plan, whoever cancels must pay the relevant change in the expected present value of the insured's subsequent health costs into a "health account" that is maintained for the insured. Cochrane shows that, ideally, so long as people sign up for the insurance when they are young and in perfect health, the health account balance will never become negative. His proposal is somewhat academic because we have no objective measure of expected present value of future health costs. Moreover, his nonnegativity result depends on his assumption of a one-sided nature to health costs. Still, something that draws on these ideas might someday be developed enough to be implemented and even applied to livelihood insurance as well. See John H. Cochrane, "Time Consistent Health Insurance," *Journal of Political Economy* 103(3) (1995):445–73.

8. William Nowlan, "A Rational View of Insurance and Genetic Discrimination," *Science* 297(5579) (July 12, 2002):195–6.

9. Under the advocacy of Louis Kelso and Senator Russell Long, the Employee Stock Ownership Plan (ESOP) was created in the United States by the Employment Retirement Income Security Act (ERISA) of 1974. It offered certain tax advantages, amended by subsequent laws. Other forms of employee ownership plans include 401(K) plans and incentive options plans. Tax laws may have to be amended to provide encouragement to properly hedged employee ownership plans.

10. Regarding the Russian privatization program, Maxim Boycko, Andrei Shleifer, and Robert Vishny wrote that Russia's privatizers knew that "the Russian government did not really own the assets that needed to be privatized . . . various 'stakeholders,' including managers, employers and local governments, exercised substantial control over the allegedly public assets and could stop privatization if they chose to. . . . In designing the program, the privatizers consistently and generously recognized the stakeholders' claims, and thus ensured their eventual support of privatization." See Maxim Boycko, Andrei Shleifer, and Robert Vishny, *Privatizing Russia* (Cambridge: MIT Press, 1995), p. 13.

11. See, for example, Jeff Gates, *The Ownership Solution: Toward a Shared Capitalism for the 21st Century* (Vancouver, B.C.: Employee Share Ownership and Investment Association, 1998).

12. Some writers have seen the establishment of employee stock ownership plans as solving, in a capitalist framework, the problem of alienation of workers from their labor that was a strong motivation for Marxian communism. See Louis Kelso and Mortimer J. Adler, *The Capitalist Manifesto* (New York: Random House, 1958).

13. See Martin. J. Conyon and Richard B. Freeman, "Shared Modes of Compensation and Company Performance: UK Evidence," NBER Working Paper w8448, 2001; and Douglas Kruse and Joseph Blasi, "Employee Ownership, Employee Attitudes and Firm Performance," in Daniel J. B. Mitchell, David Lewin, and Mahummad Zaid, eds., *Handbook of Resource Management* (Greenwich, Conn.: JAI Press, 1997).

14. Shlomo Benartzi and Richard Thaler have conceived a "Sell More Tomorrow" (SMT) program to teach people the risks of holding their own company's stock and to encourage them to overcome psychological inhibitions against selling company stock by installing a program of gradual sales. Shlomo Benartzi and Richard Thaler. "Save More Tomorrow: An Easy Way to Increase Employee Saving," unpublished paper, University of Chicago, 2001.

15. The Southwest Home Equity Assurance Program in Chicago has had only ten claims since it began. The percent of the people in the area who are white has declined to only 20 percent, and yet the home values have risen steadily. In this sense, the program appears to have been a success.

16. We proposed "life-event-triggered" policies that would pay benefits to the insured for decline in the index value only if a specific life event, such as a move to a different city, occurs. We provided estimates of break-even policy premiums that take into account the frequency both of cancellation and of life events. See "Home Equity Insurance," NBER Working Paper w4860, 1994.

17. "Report of the Yale/NR Home Equity Project Group," December 14, 2001. The reasons for settling only on an index are described in Robert J. Shiller and Allan N. Weiss, "Moral Hazard and Home Equity Conversion," *Real Estate Economics* 28(1) (2000):1–31.

18. Other useful approaches to reducing the risks of homeownership include the shared appreciation mortgage (SAM), such as those issued by the Bank of Scotland and other banks in the 1990s under the direction of Sam Masucci who was then with UBS Warburg. With SAMs, mortgage lenders take on some of or all of the price appreciation of the home in lieu of mortgage interest. Certain kinds of reverse mortgages can also help homeowners deal with risks, see Ken Scholen, *Retirement Income on the House* (Apple Valley, Minn.: National Center for Home Equity Conversion Press, 1993). Yet another approach is the housing partnership, in which homeowners sell shares in their

home to institutional investors. See Andrew Caplin, Sewin Chan, Charles Freeman, and Joseph Tracy, *Housing Market Partnerships: A New Approach to a Market at a Crossroads* (Cambridge: MIT Press, 1997). A comparison of these various forms, with analysis of the associated moral hazard issues, can be found in Shiller and Weiss, "Moral Hazard and Home Equity Conversion."

CHAPTER NINE
MACRO MARKETS: TRADING THE BIGGEST RISKS

1. For evidence that risks are not fully shared around the world today, see Marianne Baxter and Urban Jermann, "The International Diversification Puzzle Is Worse Than You Think," *American Economic Review* 87 (1997):170–80; Maurice Obstfeld, "Risk-Taking, Global Diversification, and Growth," *American Economic Review* 84 (1994):1310–29; Xavier Sala-i-Martin and Jeffrey Sachs, "Fiscal Federalism and Optimum Currency Areas: Evidence for Europe and the United States," in M. B. Canzoneri et al., eds., *Establishing a Central Bank: Issues in Europe and Lessons for the United States* (Cambridge: Cambridge University Press, 1992); Linda L. Tesar, "Evaluating the Gains from International Risksharing," *Carnegie-Rochester Conference Series on Public Policy* 42 (1995):95–103; and Linda L. Tesar and Ingrid Werner, "Home Bias and High Turnover," *Journal of International Money and Finance* 14 (1995): 467–92.

2. Stock markets dividends or returns do not correlate well enough with the risks that countries face that stock markets would be very usable to hedge these larger risks. Evidence can be found in L. Bottazzi, P. Pesenti, and E. van Wincoop, "Wages, Profits, and the International Portfolio Puzzle," *European Economic Review* 40 (1996):219–54; see also my book *Macro Markets*.

3. The securities are warrants attached to collateralized thirty-year discount bonds, a US$1.865 billion issue, underwritten by Citibank N. A. They were created after Bulgaria sought a restructuring on their foreign debt, and were issued to their lenders as part of refinancing. The warrants pay out, as additional interest each year, one half of the growth rate of real GDP if Bulgarian real GDP, as reported by the World Bank, rises more than 25 percent above the 1993 level.

4. Perpetual futures resemble index-settled futures contracts that we have today, except that the daily settlement formula is different and they have no expiration date. Every day, the short pays the long the day's change in the futures market settlement price plus the one-day return on an alternative asset times the difference between the index for the day and the previous settlement price. The alternative asset could be a riskless government bill return. With such a perpetual future, I argued in *Macro Markets*, the short would essentially be swapping the risk of a long-term claim on the income index for the return on the alternative asset. The perpetual futures has a precedent of sorts in the Index Participations (IPs) traded briefly on the American Stock Exchange in 1989. For a further description of perpetual futures, and a comparison with

IPs, see *Macro Markets,* pp. 42–46. Perpetual futures are also discussed in Robert J. Shiller, "Measuring Asset Value for Cash Settlement in Derivative Markets: Hedonic Repeated Measures Indices and Perpetual Futures," *Journal of Finance* 68 (July 1993):911–31.

5. Allan Weiss, when he first arrived at this idea, originally named them *proxy assets.* Later, we called them *macro securities.* The macro securities are described in our patent, Allan N. Weiss and Robert J. Shiller, "Proxy Asset Data Processor," U.S. Patent No. 5,987,435, 1999.

Note the fundamental distinction between macro markets based on income indexes such as national income and macro markets based on price indexes such as real estate. In the latter case, the macro markets have somewhat different properties and economic functions. The macro markets based on indexes of prices of illiquid assets such as real estate serve the purpose of discovering something closer to the true market price of these assets, if the market were not so illiquid. For further discussion, see *Macro Markets.*

In 1999 Allan Weiss and I founded, originally under the auspices of Case Shiller Weiss, Inc., a new firm, Macro Securities Research, LLC, to pursue applications of these ideas. Mr. Sam Masucci is now Chief Operating Officer of this firm.

6. By some accounts, the Jubilee 2000 campaign secured a reduction of $18 billion out of $300 billion in debt of these countries. But these reductions might have happened anyway. See Nick Mathiason, "G7's Debt Relief Plan a 'Cruel Joke,'" *The Guardian,* December 30, 2001, p. 21.

7. See Stefano Athanasoulis and Robert J. Shiller, "The Significance of the Market Portfolio," *Review of Financial Studies* 13(2) (2000):301–29. See also Stefano Athanasoulis, "Essays in Risk Sharing, Derivatives Design, and Macroeconomic Policy," unpublished Ph.D. dissertation, Yale University, 1995; and Stefano Athanasoulis, Eric van Wincoop, and Robert J. Shiller, "Macro Markets and Financial Security," *Economic Policy Review* 5(1) (1999):21–39. An analogous proposal is for a "world currency unit," which is proportional to a basket of GDPs of major countries of the world. Bonds denominated in this unit would be analogous to the world securities proposed here. See Lok-Sang Ho, "Towards a New International Monetary Order: The World Currency and the Global Indexed Bond," *The World Economy* 23(7) (2000):939–50.

8. Stefano Athanasoulis and I have produced a mathematical derivation of the optimal markets to create in the context of a general equilibrium model of the world, and this derivation shows that unless risk aversions differ across people, there will always be better markets to create first than a world market. But when risk aversions do differ, there can be a strong reason to create such a market, even before other markets. Those people who are relatively less risk averse could hold the world security, thereby achieving greater expected return for bearing risk. Those people who are relatively more risk averse could take a short position in the market, thereby offsetting the world risk to their incomes. In any given country there might be relatively few people who differ enough in risk aversions that they would like to do these things, but the

world security is relevant to everyone in the world. Thus, there should be ample demand for it. Moreover, even if everyone has the same risk aversion, the world market will have important economic functions in the absence of some other markets. We may also argue, based on robustness and simplicity, for creating a market for the entire world. See Stefano Athanasoulis and Robert J. Shiller, op. cit. 2000; and "World Income Components: Measuring and Exploiting Risk Sharing Opportunities," *American Economic Review* 91(4) (2001):1031–54. A related theory appears in Gabrielle DeMange and Guy Laroque, "Optimality of Incomplete Markets," *Journal of Economic Theory* 65 (1995):218–32. See also Paul Willen, "Welfare, Financial Innovation and Self Insurance in Dynamic Incomplete Markets Models," unpublished working paper, Princeton University, 1999.

9. William Nordhaus and James Tobin, "Is Growth Obsolete?," in *Economic Growth: Fiftieth Anniversary Colloquium* (New York: National Bureau of Economic Research and Columbia University Press, 1972), pp. 1–80, reprinted in James Tobin, *Essays in Economics: Theory and Policy,* vol. 3 (Cambridge: MIT Press), pp. 360–450.

10. Richard B. Freeman, *The Market for College-Trained Manpower: A Study in the Economics of Career Choice* (Cambridge: Harvard University Press, 1971). A recent study has confirmed a similar mechanism in the pattern of physician incomes by specialty. See Sean Nicholson and Nicholas S. Souleles, "Physician Income Expectations and Specialty Choice," NBER Working Paper Number 8536, October 2001.

11. See the U.S. Bureau of Labor Statistics Occupational Outlook Handbook, http://stats.bls.gov/oco/.

12. The ability of market prices to incorporate information is somewhat compromised by market-generated price movements, booms and crashes, that have nothing to do with the information or that represent overreaction to information. But these events do not totally compromise the information-revealing character of prices. See Sanford J. Grossman, *The Informational Role of Prices* (Cambridge: MIT Press, 1989); and Franklin Allen, Stephen Morris, and Hyung Song Shin, "Beauty Contests, Bubbles, and Iterated Expectations in Asset Markets," unpublished paper, Yale University, April 2002.

13. These changes are computed using the Case Shiller Home Price Indexes, which are computed by our firm, Case Shiller Weiss, Inc. The price indexes are based on a repeat-sales econometric method that Karl Case and I developed. See Karl E. Case and Robert J. Shiller, "Prices of Single-Family Homes Since 1970: New Indexes for Four Cities," *New England Economic Review* (1987): 46–56, and "The Efficiency of the Market for Single Family Homes," *American Economic Review* 79(1) (1989):125–37.

14. See Case and Shiller, "The Efficiency of the Market for Single Family Homes," and "Forecasting Prices and Excess Returns in the Housing Market," *AREUEA Journal* 18(3) (1990):253–73.

15. See Case, Shiller, and Weiss, "Index-Based Futures and Options Trading in Real Estate."

16. See Matt Carroll, "Home-Equity Insurance Part of New Market Plan," *Boston Globe*, November 18, 1993, p. 45.

17. New Zealand economist Ronnie Horesh has proposed that governments issue "social policy bonds" whose payout is contingent on the achievement of some important long-term national objectives, such as the reduction of crime or the improvement of the environment. The payout of the bonds would depend on some predefined index of success in these objectives. Then, a business that can conceive a way to improve the situation as measured by one of these indexes, or even improve the outlook for improving the situation or increase the probability that the situation will be improved, can buy the bonds and hope to profit from their appreciation if their efforts are even a partial success. The creation of these social policy bonds, Horesh argues, creates a short-run financial incentive for many minds to seek out ways to contribute to the long-run implementation of the objectives. See Ronnie Horesh, "Injecting Incentives into Social Problems: Social Policy Bonds," *Economic Affairs* 20(3) (September 2000):39–42.

18. See my discussion of this potential problem in *Macro Markets*, pp. 202–7.

Chapter Ten
Income-Linked Loans: Reducing the Risks of Hardship and Bankruptcy

1. Milton Friedman, *Capitalism and Freedom* (Chicago: University of Chicago Press, 1982), p. 103.

2. Ibid.

3. If the income-indexed personal loans on individual incomes are bundled together as securities, then this means carrying forward the trend to securitization (the bundling of loans such as mortgages together so that investors can invest in the bundle as a security) to an individual income level. We now have securities that represent certain claims on individuals' future incomes: home mortgages, automobile loans, consumer loans, and other cash flows from individuals. But we do not have securities that represent a claim on a share of an individual's or family's future income itself. The bundled income-indexed personal loans might even resemble macro markets, and investors in these bundles might also use the macro markets to hedge their investments in the securitized income-linked personal loans.

4. This loan was also unusual in that it was arranged jointly by a bank and an insurance company.

5. See Eduardo Borensztein and Paulo Mauro, "Reviving the Case for GDP-Indexed Bonds," IMF Policy Discussion Paper, September 2002. The proposal for a sovereign debt restructuring mechanism (SDRM) made by Anne

Krueger at the International Monetary Fund might also, depending on how it is implemented, make loans effectively depend on income. Krueger asserts that "The objective of an SDRM is to facilitate the orderly, predictable, and rapid restructuring of unsustainable sovereign debt" and that "the mechanism would be invoked when there is no feasible set of sustainable macroeconomic policies that would enable the debtor to resolve the immediate crisis and restore medium-term viability." See Anne O. Krueger, *A New Approach to Sovereign Debt Restructuring* (Washington D.C.: International Monetary Fund, 2002), p. 4.

6. See William M. Bulkeley, "Old Blues: Some Alumni of Yale Realize That They Owe College a Lasting Debt," *Wall Street Journal,* February 23, 1999, p. A1, col. 1.

7. The Yale TPO plan implied that one's total payments ultimately depended on the incomes of the other students in the cohort. Thus, fluctuations in cohort income imposed a sort of unnecessary risk on each individual, unnecessary from the perspective of broader risk-sharing.

8. See Bret Ladine, " '70s Debt Program Finally Ending," *Yale Daily News,* March 27, 2001, p. 1.

9. The *Financial Times* quoted one banker: "Pullman's deals are cool, but they're not really worth it. . . . They are small. You can spend months putting them together and then the clients are pains in the butt." Issuing the bonds requires evaluating and extensively documenting the underlying assets. See Joshua Chaffin, "Man Who Sold the World Loves to Court Top Artists: David Pullman Created Bowie Bonds and He Likes to Litigate," *Financial Times,* August 16, 2001, p. 23.

10. See David A. Moss, *When All Else Fails: Government as the Ultimate Risk Manager* (Cambridge: Harvard Business School Press, 2002).

CHAPTER ELEVEN
INEQUALITY INSURANCE: PROTECTING THE DISTRIBUTION OF INCOME

1. The Gini coefficient is the area between the straight line and the Lorenz Curve as a percent of the total area below the straight line. The Gini coefficient can range from zero percent (meaning perfect equality) to 100 percent (meaning concentration of all the income in one person).

2. Basing our tax system on a consumption tax means allowing a new deduction against income for all increments to savings, so that only that portion of income that is actually consumed is taxed. There have been various versions of the consumption tax proposed, dating back to economist John Stuart Mill in the nineteenth century. Converting to a consumption tax was seriously debated in the U.S. Congress in the early 1920s. Recent examples are the Flat Tax of Robert Hall and Alvin Rabushka, and the U.S.A. Tax (so named for the term "unlimited savings allowance") introduced by Republican Senator Pete Domenici and Democratic Senator Sam Nunn in the mid 1990s.

The U.S.A. Tax proposal was particularly interesting in that it was posed as a modification of our existing income tax system that retains its progressivity. The proposal was a 100 percent income tax deduction for increments to investment accounts, that is, income added to savings vehicles. Their plan would possibly solve the problem faced by a person, say a novelist publishing a major book after many years working on it, experiencing one big income jump in a single year, since that person, knowing that the income would not continue, would probably save most of it, thereby getting such a tax allowance that the tax rate would not be high.

The proponents of a consumption tax weigh a number of elements in advocating this, others being the difficulty of taxing income from investments and the importance of simplification. The unlimited savings allowance would eliminate a lot of wasteful tax-reducing activity, as people try to shift income from one tax year to another to prevent the uneven application of the progressive tax system on their incomes. The consumption tax system also helps to encourage charity. Because charity is not consumption, the tax amounts to a 100 percent charitable deduction, without any of the limits that are in place in current law.

Against the progressive consumption tax one may argue that consumption may not be the gauge of lifetime income that economic theory suggests it is, since most people save little and are constrained from borrowing fully against future income. It would not solve the novelist's problem if the novelist went on a consumption splurge in that year. The progressive consumption tax could create problems as compared to a progressive income tax, if, for example, people with steady income from year to year had personal reasons (such as illness, divorce, remarriage, birth of children, or job change) to have unsteady consumption, which pushes them variably into higher and lower consumption tax brackets in different years.

There are difficulties defining what is consumption and what is investment. Consumption tax evaders would try to falsely reclassify some consumption as investment. Moreover, there are important problems in making a transition from an income tax to a consumption tax. Making that change can be unfair to people who saved a lot under the income tax.

Probably the problems with the pure consumption tax, and the entrenched interests against it, will prevent any major country from adopting a pure consumption tax in the near future. The United States could, however, probably move in the direction of a consumption tax, that is, in the direction of Europe which relies on a value added tax as well as an income tax, and there is some chance of its actually doing so.

For the present discussion of inequality insurance, it can be argued that whatever mix of consumption versus income taxation is finally chosen, the basic idea of inequality insurance can still be adopted, though some adjustments may need to be considered. If we are in an income tax regime, we should have income averaging and an income inequality insurance system. If we ever are in a consumption tax regime, we should have a consumption inequality insurance system.

3. According to some, income taxes are inherently inefficient, since, because of the double taxation of income when received and again on the interest on the income saved, an income tax is effectively a higher tax on future consumption than on current consumption. The theory of public finance, however, does not actually imply that pure consumption taxes, which would tax current and future consumption equally, are optimal, except under highly specific assumptions. See Anthony B. Atkinson and Joseph E. Stiglitz, *Lectures on Public Economics* (New York: McGraw-Hill, 1979); Martin Feldstein, "The Welfare Cost of Capital Income Taxation," *Journal of Political Economy* 86(2) (1978): S29–S51; and David F. Bradford, "The Case for a Personal Consumption Tax," in Joseph A. Pechman, ed., *What Should Be Taxed: Income or Expenditure?* (Washington, D.C.: Brookings Institution, 1980), pp. 75–113.

4. See Zick Rubin and Anne Peplau, "Belief in a Just World and Reactions to Another's Lot: A Study of Participants in the National Draft Lottery," *Journal of Social Issues* 29(4) (1973):73–93. Such experiments confirm a persistent human tendency to see moral justice in purely random outcomes. See Melvin J. Lerner, *The Belief in a Just World: A Fundamental Delusion* (New York: Plenum, 1980).

5. In this sense, the inequality insurance plan would resemble a plan proposed by Shlomo Benartzi and Richard Thaler, called "Save More Tomorrow." Employees of participating firms are offered a plan in which automatic payroll deductions are instituted that cause a large fraction of future income increases to be diverted to a savings account. They show through experimental adoptions of such a plan that the plan is able to cause major increases in savings. See Shlomo Benartzi and Richard Thaler, "Save More Tomorrow: An Easy Way to Increase Employee Saving," unpublished paper, University of Chicago, 2001.

6. See for example Wallace Oates and Robert Schwab, "Economic Competition Among Jurisdictions: Efficiency Enhancing or Distortion Inducing?" *Journal of Public Economics* 35 (1988):333–54, "The Theory of Regulatory Federalism: The Case of Environmental Regulation," in Wallace Oates, ed., *The Economics of Environmental Regulation* (Cheltenham, U.K.: Edward Elgar, 1996); Edward Glaeser, "The Incentive Effects of Property Taxes on Local Governments," *Public Choice* 37 (1996):93–111; and John P. Conley and Antonio Rangel, "Intergenerational Fiscal Constitutions: How to Protect Future Generations Using Land Taxes and Federalism," unpublished paper, University of Illinois, 2001.

7. It has been shown that, when comparing across countries, willingness to support social services for the poor depends on the public's opinions on why they are poor. One study found that in Denmark and The Netherlands only 11 percent and 12 percent, respectively, thought that poverty was due to personal characteristics such as laziness and lack of willpower, while in the United Kingdom and the United States over 40 percent thought so. Quoted in Alan Lewis, *The Psychology of Taxation* (New York: St. Martin's Press, 1982), p. 95.

8. Edward McCaffery, "Cognitive Theory and Tax" in Cass Sunstein, ed., *Behavioral Law and Economics* (Cambridge: Cambridge University Press, 2000).

9. There is evidence that migration does indeed tend to be towards areas with more generous welfare. See George J. Borjas, "Immigration and Welfare Magnets," *Journal of Labor Economics* 17(4) (October 1995):607–37.

10. There is evidence that immigration can harm the economic status of natives. See Joseph Altonji and David Card, "The Effects of Immigration on the Labor Market Outcomes of Natives," in John Abowd and Richard Freeman, eds., *Immigration, Trade, and Labor* (Chicago: National Bureau of Economic Research and University of Chicago Press, 1991); George J. Borjas, "The Economics of Immigration," *Journal of Economic Literature* 32(4) (1994): 1667–1717; and Rachel Friedberg and Jennifer Hunt, "The Impact of Immigrants on Host Country Wages, Employment and Growth," *Journal of Economic Perspectives* 9(2) (1995):23–44.

11. The U.S. Immigration Reform and Control Act of 1986 gave blanket amnesty to illegal immigrants who arrived before 1982. President George W. Bush has supported offering another amnesty. Other countries have given amnesty to illegal immigrants, for example, the United Kingdom in 1973, Italy in 1986, Argentina in 1993, and Malaysia in 1998.

12. The economist Julian Simon in 1986 proposed auctioning off a limited number of places for immigrants from LDCs. He also mentioned the idea that the price of immigration could be paid out of future income taxes. He pointed out then that other economists, Gary Becker, Barry Chiswick, Milton Friedman, and Melvin Reder, were also advocates of such a system. See Julian L. Simon, "Auction the Right to Be an Immigrant," *New York Times*, January 28, 1986, p. A25, col. 1.

13. A few countries have charged for immigration, and lists of these were compiled by newspapers in Hong Kong just before the return of Hong Kong to China in 1997, when many people were considering making a hasty exit. According to these accounts, one could buy one's way into Fiji for US$30,000 plus an additional US$100,000 placed in an investment account. Sierra Leone sold passports and citizenship for US$28,000, Peru sold passports for US$35,000, and Tonga sold passports for US$20,000. Canada gave landed immigrant status for investing C$250,000 in Canada. Moreover, the United States allowed ten thousand immigrants a year to buy their way in by investing US$1,000,000 in the United States in a business that creates at least ten jobs. The Canadian and the U.S. systems are indirect charges for immigration. The governments do not collect the money from immigrants but require immigrants to invest money in a way that is probably sub-optimal from the standpoint of their own investment criteria; in this sense it is a charge for immigration.

    Some countries also charge for exit visas. China and Cuba have both charged fees sufficiently large to provide a major obstacle to emigration. Recently Chinese students wishing an exit visa had to post a bond of 50,000 yuan (or about US$6000) to leave the country, refundable if they return. This is not a large sum of money compared to the present value of the increased earnings the applicant might expect to earn in many foreign countries, but, because of an inability to borrow against this foreign income, the bond represents a serious obstacle to emigration. Most countries apparently feel they cannot enforce such exit charges as China and Cuba do.

Countries also effectively charge to emigrate in the form of denying some retirement income to people who leave. Unfortunately, this form of charging is erratic in its impact. Young people are the most free to leave, since they have not yet accumulated retirement benefits, while elderly people may find it impossible to leave. The costs to leaving are not related to the relative advantages that the person offers to the releasing country and to the receiving country.

Some, but not all, countries have treaties to coordinate their social security systems for those who change countries. For example, the United States has social security treaties with only eighteen countries, mostly in Europe. Lacking sensible treaties, the individuals may be deterred from moving between countries. For example, there is no social security treaty between the United States and Japan.

14. See Lawrence Lindsey, "Individual Taxpayer Response to Tax Cuts 1982–84, with Implications for the Revenue-Maximizing Tax Rate," *Journal of Public Economics* 33(2) (July 1987):173–206. Other important studies that view the Reagan tax cuts as a "natural experiment" were Daniel Feenberg and James Poterba, "Income Inequality and the Incomes of Very High Income Taxpayers," in James Poterba, ed., *Tax Policy and the Economy* (Cambridge: MIT Press, 1992); and Martin Feldstein, "The Effect of Marginal Tax Rates on Taxable Income: A Panel Study of the 1986 Tax Reform Act," *Journal of Political Economy* 103(3) (June 1995):561–73.

15. See Austan Goolsby, "It's Not About the Money: Why Natural Experiments Don't Work on the Rich," in Joel Slemrod, ed., *Does Atlas Shrug? The Economic Consequences of Taxing the Rich* (Cambridge: Harvard University Press, 2000).

16. See Vickrey, "Measuring Marginal Utility by Reactions to Risk."

17. Festinger, "Wish, Expectation and Group Standards as Factors Influencing Level of Aspiration."

18. Robert H. Frank, *Luxury Fever: Money and Happiness in an Era of Excess* (Riverside, N.J.: The Free Press, 1999), and "Progressive Taxation and the Incentive Problem," in Joel H. Slemrod, ed., *Does Atlas Shrug?*, pp. 490–507.

19. These countries have not always been so egalitarian in their attitudes. A rise of egalitarian sentiment since the middle of the twentieth century, and then something of a decline in that sentiment recently, has been noted for both Canada and Sweden. For Canada, see Barbara Murphy, *The Ugly Canadian: The Rise and Fall of a Caring Society* (Winnipeg: J. Gordon Shillingford, 1999). For Sweden, see Nils-Eric Sandberg, *Vad Gick Snett I Sverige* (What

Went Wrong in Sweden?) (Timbro, Sweden, 1997). (The English translation is available at http://www.wrong-in-sweden.com.)

20. Business Council on National Issues, "Mediocrity Versus Excellence: The Choice Facing Canada." See http://www.bcni.com/memos/sep99.html, 1999, p. 5.

21. Sandberg, *Vad Gick Snett I Sverige*, p. 4.

22. Assar Lindbeck, "The Swedish Experiment," *Journal of Economic Literature* 35 (September 1997): 1273–1319, at 1297.

CHAPTER TWELVE
INTERGENERATIONAL SOCIAL SECURITY: SHARING RISKS
BETWEEN YOUNG AND OLD

1. World Bank, *Averting the Old Age Crisis* (Oxford: Oxford University Press, 1994).

2. Hannah Leslie has a nice account of this process of invention in the United Kingdom. See her *Inventing Retirement: The Development of Occupational Pensions in Britain* (Cambridge: Cambridge University Press, 1986).

3. The basic notion of intergenerational risk-sharing that is the foundation of this idea follows my paper, "Social Security and Institutions for Intergenerational, Intragenerational, and International Risk Sharing," *Carnegie Rochester Conference Series on Public Policy* 50 (1999):165–204. See also my paper "Social Security and Individual Accounts as Elements of Overall Risk Sharing," presented at the American Economic Association meetings, Washington, D.C., January 2003. A number of others have stressed that intergenerational risk sharing should be a prominent consideration in the design of social security. See Laurence Ball and N. Gregory Mankiw, "Intergenerational Risk Sharing in the Spirit of Arrow, Debreu and Rawls, with Applications to Social Security," NBER Working Paper w8270, 2001; Henning Bohn, "Social Security and Demographic Uncertainty: The Risk Sharing Properties of Alternative Policies," NBER Working Paper w7030, March 1999; Angus Deaton, Pierre-Olivier Gourinchas, and Christina Paxson, "Social Security and Inequality Over the Life Cycle," NBER Working Paper w7570, February 2000; and De-Mange and Laroque, "Social Security with Heterogeneous Populations Subject to Demographic Shocks," *Geneva Papers on Risk and Insurance Theory* 26(1) (2001):5–24.

4. The principal alternatives to the contributory systems with earnings-related benefits are systems that pay benefits related only to years of service or residence, and/or that pay only to people of limited means. Some countries have mandatory savings or mandatory private pensions. See U.S. Social Security System, Office of Research, Evaluation and Statistics, *Social Security Programs throughout the World 1999* (Washington: U.S. Government Printing Office, 1999), pp. xxxiv-xxxix.

5. See http://www.ssa.gov/pubs/10070.html for an explanation of the computation of social security benefits in the United States.

6. The example here comes, with some simplification, from my paper "Social Security and Institutions for Intergenerational, Intragenerational, and International Risk Sharing."

7. According to the U.S. Social Security Administration, thirty-one million retired persons and their dependents received benefits in 1999, 11 percent of the U.S. population then.

8. As for the individual financial account component of the Swedish social security system, the 2.5 percent of pensionable income, individuals can choose from among five hundred different funds to invest. See Ole Settergren, "The Automatic Balance Mechanism of the Swedish Pension System: A Non-Technical Introduction," Riksförsäkringsverket, The Swedish National Insurance Board, 2001, http://www.rfv.se/english/auto107.pdf.

9. Individual accounts might, however, be justified as offering diversification across investments, so long as this is achieved without compromising intergenerational risk sharing. See Peter A. Diamond and John Geanakoplos, "Social Security Investment in Equities." Cowles Foundation Discussion Paper No. 1214R, Yale University, 2002.

10. One study sought to find differences in risk aversion and to link these differences to differences in behaviors such as purchasing insurance or doing things that endanger the health. They had rather limited success in finding and linking these differences. See Robert Barsky, F. Thomas Juster, Myles S. Kimball, and Matthew D. Shapiro, "Preference Parameters and Behavioral Heterogeneity," *Quarterly Journal of Economics* (1997):537–79.

CHAPTER THIRTEEN
INTERNATIONAL AGREEMENTS FOR RISK CONTROL

1. These chain real GDP numbers, in 1996 US dollars, are from the Penn World Table, Mark 6.0, preliminary version, available at www.nber.org. By 1998, Korean real GDP *per capita* had risen to $13,247, while Argentina's had risen to $11,749, closing some of the gap. A severe economic crisis in Argentina starting in 2001, however, may reopen the gap.

2. Marek Weretka presents a model in which the welfare loss because of moral hazard is lower if international risk management contracts are arranged by governments rather than by macro markets. Marek Weretka, "Moral Hazard in Macro-Markets: Welfare Evaluation," unpublished paper, Yale University, 2002. A similar argument that governments might best control and limit the extent of risk sharing because of the potential for inefficiencies caused by moral hazard can be found in Wolf B. Wagner, *Risk Sharing under Incentive Constraints,* unpublished Ph.D. dissertation, Center for Economic Research, Tilburg University, The Netherlands, 2002. In both of these papers, the creation of macro markets can produce a sort of moral-hazard externality oper-

ating not directly through individuals but through individuals' control through their votes of government policy, policy that might show weakened resolve for economic growth once risk management policies are instituted. These papers are not arguments against international risk sharing, but arguments for government regulation of risk sharing.

3. Such limits might make it more plausible that the contract would in fact be honored by all parties. Since the limit is reached only if the country does exceptionally well relative to the expectations, the amount paid could still be a large fraction of the GDP of the receiving country which is performing less well. Economic models illustrating an equilibrium subject to such limits are discussed in Timothy J. Kehoe and David K. Levine, "Debt Constrained Markets," *Review of Economic Studies* 60 (1993):865–88; and Timothy J. Kehoe and David K. Levine, "Liquidity Constrained Markets versus Debt Constrained Markets," unpublished paper, University of Minnesota, Minneapolis, and Department of Economics, UCLA, 2001.

4. Our 2001 paper includes a formal analysis, maximizing the expected value of a social welfare function for the world, showing how the optimal contracts may be defined. See "World Income Components: Measuring and Exploiting Risk-Sharing Opportunities."

5. Athanasoulis and I described this as a private risk management contract between individuals within countries, however, the same idea can be used here for government agreements, and, indeed, as regards some developing countries where financial markets are less developed and less experimental in their orientation, it would seem that governmental agreements are the more likely form for such risk management. The analysis is in Athanasoulis and Shiller, "World Income Components: Measuring and Exploiting International Risk-Sharing Opportunities," table 3A. The working paper can be found on http://cowles.econ.yale.edu/P/au/d_shiller.htm, as Cowles Foundation Discussion Paper No. 1097. A revised version of this paper was published in the *American Economic Review* 91(4) (2001), but without table 3.

6. For a description of the parallel loan agreements of the 1970s, see John F. Marshall and Kenneth R. Kapner, *Understanding Swaps* (New York: Wiley Finance Editions, 1993); and Clifford W. Smith Jr., Charles W. Smithson, and D. Sykes Wilford, *Managing Financial Risk* (New York: Harper Business, 1990).

7. After the dissolution of the Soviet Union in 1991, there was some ambiguity in defining the actual amount of the roughly US$10 billion debt from India to the Soviet Union, since the debt was expressed in terms of a rupee-ruble protocol. Moreover, former-Soviet countries, who all created their own currencies, had difficulty agreeing on how repayments should be divided among them. India, however, did not take unfair advantage of the ambiguous situation.

8. That is, the mere creation of the contracts would have the same impact on expected utility, that is on "consumer surplus," of people living in India as would a gift to India over 10 percent of Indian GDP. To arrive at this estimate of consumer surplus created by the contract we had to make various

assumptions about coefficients of risk aversion, discount rates, and about the variance matrix of GDPs, and of course these assumptions could be questioned. See Robert J. Shiller and Stefano Athanasoulis, "World Income Components: Measuring and Exploiting International Risk Sharing Opportunities," NBER Working Paper w5095, April 1995, for a description of these assumptions.

9. See Alberto Alesino and David Dollar, "Who Gives Foreign Aid to Whom and Why?" NBER Working Paper w6612, Cambridge, Mass., June 1998).

10. Shiller and Athanasoulis, 1995.

11. For example, the International Conference on Financing for Development held at Monterrey, Mexico, March 18–22 2002, attended by most developing and developed countries as well as the International Monetary Fund, the World Bank, and the World Trade Organization, issued a statement, the "Monterrey Consensus," about financing development that made no unambiguous reference to sharing risks between countries. There was no hint of the idea that risk sharing can be beneficial both to developing and developed countries. There was only the vague statement that "We recognize the value of exploring innovative sources of finance, provided that these sources do not unduly burden developing countries."

CHAPTER FOURTEEN
GLOBAL RISK INFORMATION DATABASES

1. Such a system has been developed by the National Institute of Statistical Sciences. See Alan F. Karr and Ashish P. Sanil, "Web Systems that Disseminate Information but Protect Confidential Data," National Institute of Statistical Sciences, Research Triangle Park, North Carolina, 2001.

2. G. T. Duncan and R. B. Pearson, "Enhancing Access to Microdata while Protecting Confidentiality," *Statistical Science* 6 (1991):219–39

3. See Donald B. Rubin, "Discussion of Statistical Disclosure Limitation," *Journal of Official Statistics* 9 (1993):461–68; Stephen E. Fienberg, "Confidentiality and Data Protection through Disclosure Limitation: Evolving Principles and Technical Advances," *The Philippine Statistician,* 49 (2000): 1–12; and Arthur B. Kennickell, "Multiple Imputation and Disclosure Protection: The Case of the 1995 Survey of Consumer Finances," SCF Working Paper, 1997.

4. The U.S. Census Bureau, in collaboration with university economists, has been building a system integrating various databases about the income and employment of individuals and firms with its Longitudinal Employer-Household Dynamics (LEHD) program. Sophisticated masking techniques are under development so that the data can be made available to the public while preserving confidentiality. See John M. Abowd, "Unlocking the Information in Integrated Social Data," unpublished paper, Cornell University, 2002, forthcoming in *New Zealand Economic Papers.*

5. The importance of data sockets is described in Michael Dertouzos, *What Will Be: How the New World of Information Will Change Our Lives* (San Francisco: Harper Edge, 1998).

6. See William D. Nordhaus and James Tobin, "Is Growth Obsolete?" in *Economic Growth: Fiftieth Anniversary Colloquium* (New York: National Bureau of Economic Research and Columbia University Press, 1972), pp. 1–80.

7. These include the Household Income and Labour Dynamics in Australia (HILDA) Survey, the Belgian Socio-Economic Panel, Canada's Survey of Labor Income Dynamics (SLID), the French Household Panel, Germany's Socio-Economic Panel (SOEP), the Hungarian Household Panel, the Indonesia Family Life Survey, the Japanese Panel Survey on Consumers (JPSC), South Korea's Korean Labor and Income Panel Study (KLIPS), Luxembourg's Panel Socio-Economique "Liewen zu Letzebuerg" (PSELL), the Mexican Family Life Survey (MxFLS), the Dutch Socio-Economic Panel (SEP), the Polish Household Panel (PHP), the Russia Longitudinal Monitoring Survey (RLMS), Spain's Encuesta Continua de Presupuestos Familiares, the Swedish Panel Study Market and Nonmarket Activities (HUS), the Swiss Household Panel (SHP), Taiwan's Panel Study of Family Dynamics (PSF), and the British Household Panel Survey (BHPS). These various data panels are described on the PSID Web site, www.isr.umich.edu/src/psid/panelstudies.html.

8. See Robert J. Shiller and Ryan Schneider, "Labor Income Indices Designed for Use in Contracts Promoting Income Risk Management," *Review of Income and Wealth* 44 (June 1998):163–82.

9. Louis D. Brandeis, *Other People's Money* (New York: Augustus M. Kelley Publishers, Reprints of Economic Classics, 1971 [1914]), p. 92.

10. Ibid., p. 104.

11. In France, the *Commission des Opérations de Bourse* has organized a database with some company information, available via SOPHIE on www.cob.fr. In the United Kingdom the FSA has plans for an Edgar-like Web site. There is already a system of online company information for Europe at the European Business Register, www.ebr.org. Canada has a variant on EDGAR called the System for Electronic Document Analysis and Retrieval (SEDAR), available at www.sedar.com. In Japan, the government makes financial information available electronically at www.japanfinancials.com.

12. The U.S. Taxpayer Relief Act of 1997 restored the income averaging for farmers and ranchers, who have notoriously volatile incomes.

13. William Vickrey, "Averaging of Income for Tax Purposes," *Journal of Political Economy* 37(3) (June 1939):305–37.

14. The Roman satirist Juvenal (ca. 57–127 A.D.) wrote:

> No, no, I must live where there are no fires, no nightly alarms. Ucalgeon below is already shouting for water and shifting his chattels; smoke is pouring out of your third-floor attic above, but you know nothing of it; for if the alarm begins in the ground-floor, the last man to burn will

be he who has nothing to shelter him from the rain but the tiles, where the gentle doves lay their eggs. Codrus possessed a bed too small for the dwarf Procula, a marble slab adorned by six pipkins, with a small drinking cup, and a recumbent Chiron below, and an old chest containing Greek books whose divine lays were being gnawed by unlettered mice. Poor Codrus had nothing it is true: but he lost that nothing, which was his all; and the last straw in his heap of misery is this, that though he is destitute and begging for a bite, no one will help him with a meal, no one offers him board or shelter.

But if the grand house of Asturicus be destroyed, the matrons go disheveled, your great men put on mourning, the praetor adjourns his court: then indeed do we deplore the calamities of the city, and bewail its fires! Before the house has ceased to burn, up comes one with a gift of marble or of building materials, another offers nude and glistening statues, a third some notable work of Euphranor or Polyclitus, or bronzes that had been the glory of old Asian shrines. Others will offer books and bookcases, or a bust of Minerva, or a hundredweight of silver-plate. Thus does Persicus, that most sumptuous of childless men, replace what he has lost with more and better things, and with good reason incurs the suspicion of having set his own house on fire.

Juvenal Satire 3, in *Juvenal and Persius with an English Translation by G. G. Ramsay, LL.D., Lrrr.D.* (London: William Heinemann, 1928), pp. 47–49.

Marshall Sahlins has argued that pre-modern societies generally have a system of generalized reciprocity within kinship groups and to some extent even beyond kinship groups. See Marshall Sahlins, *Stone Age Economics* (Aldine De Gruyter, 1972). A survey of some primitive methods of risk-sharing can be found in Pranab Bardhan and Christopher R. Udry, *Development Microeconomics* (Oxford: Oxford University Press, 1999).

15. For an extreme example, one might devise certificates that people could buy to distribute to beggars that the beggar would insert into a cash machine to get cash. Assuming the cash machine employs personal identification systems, and assuming it is tied to a national database, the machine could refuse to pay if the beggar's other income were above a threshold. This would deal with the moral hazard of the "professional beggar" problem.

16. Ann E. Kaplan, ed., *Giving USA: The Annual Report on Philanthropy for the Year 1999* (New York: American Association of Fund-Raising Counsel, 2000).

Chapter Fifteen
New Units of Measurement and Electronic Money

1. See my paper "Why Do People Dislike Inflation?" in Christina Romer and David Romer, eds., *Reducing Inflation: Motivation and Strategy* (Chicago: National Bureau of Economic Research and University of Chicago Press, 1997).

2. The peso value of the UF is a daily interpolated lagged Chilean consumer price index. Since it is based on lagged data, it is slightly out of date. The newspapers show tomorrow's value as well as today's, but values are never known more than a month in advance since they will depend on later computations of the consumer price index.

3. See http://www.sii.cl/pagina/valores/uf/uf2002.htm.

4. I first made these proposals in a couple of working papers, "Indexed Units of Account: Theory and Assessment of Historical Experience," NBER Working Paper 6356, January 1998, forthcoming in Fernando Lefort and Klaus Schmidt-Hebbel, eds., *Indexation, Inflation, and Monetary Policy* (Santiago, Chile: Central Bank of Chile, 2002); and "Designing Indexed Units of Account," Cowles Foundation Discussion Paper 1179, Yale University, 1998, NBER Working Paper w7160, 1999.

5. Newcomb's discovery here reflected his profound interest in measurement. He noticed in 1881 that books of tables of logarithms in public libraries showed most heavy wear from use on the pages giving the logarithms for numbers beginning with the numeral 1, and least wear from use on the pages giving the logarithms for numbers beginning with the numeral 9. He concluded that people must most often encounter, when they measure things, numbers that begin with the numeral 1. His observation led to research that shows that numbers randomly chosen among those that people use to measure things tend to begin with 1 over six times as often as numbers that begin with 9. Why this should be so has puzzled mathematicians for over a century. See Ted Hill, "The First Digit Phenomenon," *American Scientist* 86 (July-August 1998):358–63.

6. Simon Newcomb, "The Standard of Value," *North American Review* (1879): 223–37.

7. Irving Fisher, *The Money Illusion* (New York: Adelphi, 1928).

8. See Robert Shiller, "Public Resistance to Indexation: A Puzzle," *Brookings Papers on Economic Activity* I (1997):159–211; and related work by Eldar Shafir, Peter Diamond, and Amos Tversky, "Money Illusion," *Quarterly Journal of Economics* 112 (May 1997):341–74.

9. Consider for example the Alternative Minimum Tax in the United States, which was enacted thirty years ago to help prevent wealthy people from evading taxes because they used many deductions and was not indexed to inflation. It impacts those making from $72,000 to $627,000, but has no impact on people whose incomes are above $627,000, the very group for which it was intended. Another example is the IRA limitation, which was set at $2000 in 1982, and remains there today.

10. See Jeremy J. Siegel, *Stocks for the Long Run: The Definitive Guide to Financial Market Returns and Long-Term Investment Strategies,* 3rd ed. (New York: McGraw-Hill, 2002), p. 33.

11. One of the most common adaptations to the extremely high inflation around 1981 was to switch to adjustable rate mortgages rather than fixed rate mortgages, since short term interest rates tended to be lower. But this did not re-

ally solve the problem, since it achieved a lowering of mortgage payments only by adding the risk that the homeowner would be forced to pay even higher rates in the future.

12. One of the guidelines for choosing a mortgage offered by Consumers Union (CU), the publisher of *Consumer Reports,* was "Don't go into the red." In fact, CU actively lobbied against fixed-real-payment mortgages: "Because it may not always be easy to match accumulating negative amortization with property values, CU has urged regulators to limit the amount of negative amortization that can accumulate." See "Can You Afford a Mortgage?" *Consumer Reports* 46(7) (July 1981):400–405, at 405.

13. "As attractive as the inflation-indexed notes appear, it may make sense to wait and watch instead of plunging right in." "Your Money: New Inflation-Proof Bonds Should They Be in Your Portfolio?" *Consumer Reports,* 62(4) (April 1997):88–89, at 89.

14. I checked whether this tendency is operative with the UF in Chile by counting the numbers of UF condominium prices by last digit (excluding trailing zeros) quoted in display advertisements (the larger advertisements, often including a photograph of an apartment building or graphic art) in the *Propriedades* (properties) section of the Sunday August 10, 1997, edition of the Santiago newspaper *El Mercurio.* There were twenty-six UF prices ending in 9, sixteen in 8, eleven in 7, nine in 6, sixteen in 5, four in 4, ten in 3, eight in 2, and six in 1.

15. Roger Bootle, *The Death of Inflation: Surviving and Thriving in the Zero Era* (London: Nicholas Brealey, 1997).

16. For example, within the last few years Japan, the European Community, and the United Kingdom have all taken steps to ensure the independence of their central banks. See Alan Blinder, *The Quiet Revolution: Central Banking Goes Modern* (New Haven: Yale University Press, 2003).

17. The essential point is that the *uncertainty* about inflation has been very high. If inflation were high but unvarying, people would probably largely grow accustomed to the steady high inflation and make adjustments for it so that it did not affect real quantities. But the uncertainty, as measured by the standard deviation of cumulated inflation over twenty-year intervals, has been very high. For Argentina, Brazil, Canada, Chile, France, Germany, India, Indonesia, Italy, Japan, South Korea, Mexico, Nigeria, Turkey, the United Kingdom, and the United States, the median such twenty-year standard deviation in the post war period (generally 1950–92) was 519 percent. The country with the lowest such standard deviation was Germany, at 19.2 percent, with the highest was Argentina, with 1.1×10^{12} percent. See Robert J. Shiller, "Public Resistance to Indexation: A Puzzle," *Brookings Papers on Economic Activity* 1 (1997):159–228.

18. Ibid., p. 188.

19. Márcio Garcia, a Brazilian economist, has documented that the lag in computing the consumer price index at a time of escalating inflation in Brazil caused indexed bonds there to lose much of their real value by 1990. Márcio G. P. Garcia, "The Fisher Effect in a Signal Extraction Framework: The Re-

cent Brazilian Experience," *Journal of Development Economics* 41(1) (June 1993):71–93.

20. Irving Fisher, "A Compensated Dollar," *Quarterly Journal of Economics* 27 (1913):213–35. For Newcomb's work, see "The Standard of Value." Different inventions that would have the effect of automatically maintaining the real value of the currency are discussed by Robert E. Hall, "Optimal Fiduciary Monetary Systems," *Journal of Monetary Economics* 12 (1983):33–50; and "Irving Fisher's Self-Stabilizing Money," *American Economic Review* 87 (1997):436–38.

21. For further discussion of his idea, see Robert J. Shiller, "Indexed Units of Account: Theory and Assessment of Historical Experience," NBER Working Paper 6356, 1998.

22. See for example the World Currency Unit, proposed by Lok-Sang Ho, "Toward a New International Monetary Order: the World Currency and the Global Indexed Bond," *The World Economy* 23(7) (2000):939–50.

23. We have already seen in chapter 9 the potential importance of a market for the entire world; this is set forth rigorously in Stefano Athanasoulis and Robert J. Shiller, "The Significance of the Market Portfolio," *Review of Financial Studies* 13(2) (2000):301–29.

24. George Akerlof, William Dickens, and George Perry, "The Macroeconomics of Low Inflation," *Brookings Papers on Economic Activity* I (1996):1–76.

25. Truman Bewley, *Why Wages Don't Fall During a Recession* (Cambridge: Harvard University Press, 2000).

CHAPTER SIXTEEN
MAKING THE IDEAS WORK: RESEARCH AND ADVOCACY

1. Robert J. Shiller and Ryan Schneider, "Labor Income Indices Designed for Use in Contracts Promoting Income Risk Management," *Review of Income and Wealth* 44 (June 1998):163–82.

2. The world shares that were described in chapter 9 would still have use because different people have different exposure to or sensitivity to world GDP.

3. The principal reference here is Athanasoulis and Shiller, "World Income Components: Measuring and Exploiting Risk-sharing Opportunities," *American Economic Review* 91(4) (2001):1031–54. See also Stefano Athanasoulis, "Essays in Risk-sharing, Derivatives Design, and Macroeconomic Policy," unpublished Ph.D. dissertation, Yale University, 1995; Stefano Athanasoulis, Eric van Wincoop, and Robert J. Shiller, "Macro Markets and Financial Security," *Economic Policy Review* 5(1) (1999):21–39; and Stefano Athanasoulis and Robert J. Shiller, "Defining Residual Risk-Sharing Opportunities: Pooling World Income Components," *Research in Economics* 56(1) (March 2002):61–84.

4. From the standpoint of our mathematical model, the optimal risk-sharing contracts are defined by the eigenvectors of the variance matrix of deviations of individual income from world-average income. The associated eigenvalue is an index of the welfare gain to sharing this risk. Therefore, we want to pick

the eigenvectors with the highest eigenvalues, and pursue the implied risk-sharing contracts. The fact that the unit eigenvector has a zero eigenvalue with this variance matrix indicates why a risk that is shared by everyone is the worst risk-sharing contract of all, and offers no welfare gain to society after all other risk-sharing opportunities are exploited. See Athanasoulis and Shiller, "World Income Components"; see also Athanasoulis, "Essays in Risk Sharing, Derivatives Design, and Macroeconomic Policy." An analogous result was derived independently by Gabrielle Demange and Guy Laroque, "Optimality of Incomplete Markets," *Journal of Economic Theory* 65 (1995):218–32.

In chapter 9 I advocate creating a market for the entire world, even though this market corresponds to a zero eigenvalue and is by our above theory the last market that should be created. However, even by the above theory, developing a market for world risk is valuable when not all other markets have been created, even though the world market is by that theory dominated by other potential new markets. Athanasoulis and I have developed variations on our basic mathematical model that we believe demonstrate the importance of creating a market for the entire world. See Stefano Athanasoulis and Robert J. Shiller, "The Significance of the Market Portfolio," *Review of Financial Studies* 13(2) (2000):301–29.

CHAPTER SEVENTEEN
LESSONS FROM MAJOR FINANCIAL INVENTIONS

1. The invention of coins was attributed in ancient times to Pheidon of Argos, Theseus of Athens, and others. The true origins are difficult to place: decorated gold disks resembling coins were found in Crete dating from a thousand years earlier, and it is impossible to tell when such things were first treated as money. See Robert A. Mundell, "The Birth of Coinage," Department of Economics, Columbia University, Discussion Paper No. 0102–08, February 2002.

2. Even though coins were cheap to make, it was difficult to counterfeit the coins using base metal. One could make a terra cotta mold of a silver coin, use it to cast a coin from copper or bronze, and then plate it with silver. But these counterfeits did not have quite the sharp and sparkling look of the original, and people could generally tell the difference. Still, some people would punch holes through coins to check for base metal inside.

3. "So far as we have any knowledge, they [the Lydians] were the first nation to introduce the use of gold and silver coins, and the first who sold goods by retail." Herodotus *The History*, George Rawlinson, trans. (Chicago: University of Chicago and Encyclopedia Britannica), bk. I, p. 22.

4. Metal plates were engraved by scratching a pattern on them by hand, with meticulous care by an engraver. Some of this hand work is still used in making modern paper money. Each such handmade metal plate is unique. It cannot be copied by any known process because it carries with it all the motions of the engraver's hand. The bills are printed by applying ink into the grooves of the plate and pressing a piece of paper onto the plate. The resulting note

shows all of the detail of the original hand-engraved plate, and shows as well a slight embossed or intaglio pattern that results from the three-dimensional nature of the plate. No counterfeiter can perfectly duplicate the appearance of the resulting bill, even today.

5. Technological advances from the fifteenth to the seventeenth centuries also made it increasingly possible for governments to make subsidiary coinage that could not be counterfeited. Subsidiary coins are made from base metals and have fixed exchange rates with precious metal coins. Subsidiary coins derive their value from the opportunity to exchange for precious metal coins, and so it is essential that they not be counterfeitable, even with the same base metal. The United Kingdom did not develop subsidiary coinage until the new technology was well in place in 1816, the United States not until 1853. See Thomas J. Sargent and François R. Velde, *The Big Problem of Small Change* (Princeton: Princeton University Press, 2001).

6. See Carlo M. Cippola, *Money, Prices and Civilization in the Mediterranean World: Fifth to Seventeenth Century* (New York: Gordian Press, 1956). Until the decimalization of the pound in 1971, the U. K. still used the symbol *d.*, for denarius, to refer to its penny coin.

7. The 1811 law said that shareholders "shall be individually responsible to the extent of their respective shares of stock in the said company, and no further." This seems quite clear; however, in 1826 a New York court ruled that this language meant double liability: Investors might be forced to come up with that value again. The 1811 law did effectively limit liability to twice the capital subscribed and set in motion the legal impetus for limited liability as we now know it in the United States. See David A. Moss, *When All Else Fails: Government as the Ultimate Risk Manager* (Cambridge: Harvard Business School Press, 2002), p. 57.

8. Ibid.

9. National limited liability laws were adopted in England in 1855, France in 1867, and Germany in 1870. See Tony Orhnial, *Limited Liability and the Corporation* (London: Croom Helm, 1982).

10. Kahneman and Tversky, "Prospect Theory: An Analysis of Decision under Risk."

11. Daily settlement of the margin credit was done in cash every day, and individuals did not have what we call margin accounts. The margin balances were traded with the contract. See Ulrike Schaede, "Forwards and Futures in Tokugawa-Period Japan: A New Perspective on the Dojima Rice Market," *Journal of Banking and Finance* 13 (1989):487–513.

12. For a comprehensive overview of the history of life insurance sales, see J. Owen Stalson, *Marketing Life Insurance: Its History in America* (Homewood, Ill.: Richard B. Irwin, 1969). Stalson remarks, in describing the importance of Robinson's success,

> Mutual life insurance, in spite of all its real merits, was hard to sell. Not that any damaging argument could be brought against the plan—or the practice—of the Mutual Life; the company was sound from its first day

of operations. The reason it did not prosper more fully from the start is explained by the simple fact that, regardless of how attractive mutual life insurance as a plan may be, yet it costs participants something to share in its benefits, and men prefer to spend their money for other things. A powerful and persistent program of selling is therefore needed to get the best life insurance to market. I mean, of course, in volume; there is always a small market for life insurance, even without the benefit of a selling program, since some men want protection even at high rates and minimum benefits. But the Mutual Life could not survive on a share of that small market. (p. 129)

13. See James E. Post, *Risk and Response: Management and Social Change in the American Insurance Industry* (Lexington, Mass.: Lexington Books, 1976). Whole life policies extend back at least to the Pennsylvania Company for Insurances on Lives and Granting Annuities, which was founded in 1812. See Stalson, *Marketing Life Insurance.*

14. John Alford Stevenson, Ph.D., *Selling Life Insurance* (New York: Harper & Brothers Publishers, 1922), p. 240.

15. Viviana A. Rotman Zelizer, *Morals and Markets: The Development of Life Insurance in the United States* (New York: Transaction Books, 1983), p. 132.

16. "In fact, the value of the survivors insurance you have under Social Security is probably more than the value of your individual life insurance," U.S. Social Security Administration, *Social Security Survivors Benefits,* Publication No. 05–10084, August 2000, p. 1. In the United States, the essential Social Security programs are summarized by the acronym OASDI, for old age, survivors, and disability insurance. Private insurance companies have never been very successful in selling disability insurance to the public; for some psychological reason most people are unreceptive to buying disability insurance, even though the risk of disability is very important and can wreak havoc on families' lives. Thus, the government's assuming of disability risk is another major risk management innovation in our society.

17. For a study that concludes that most people spend too little on life insurance, see Jegadeesh Gokhale and Laurence Kotlikoff, "The Adequacy of Life Insurance," Research Dialogue No. 71 (New York: TIAA-CREF Institute, 2002).

CHAPTER EIGHTEEN
LESSONS FROM MAJOR SOCIAL INSURANCE INVENTIONS

1. Traditional economies have long used a number of risk sharing devices that go beyond the tithe and zakat. Robert M. Townsend has shown that traditional villages in India effectively manage to pool a good fraction of their risks, and similar risk-sharing occurs in rural Thailand. See Robert M. Townsend, "Risk and Insurance in Village India," *Econometrica* 62 (1994):539–91, and "Financial Systems in Northern Thai Villages," *Quarterly Journal of Economics* 110(4) (November 1995):1011–46. Partial pooling occurs in very different primitive cul-

tures in Nigeria; see Christopher Udry, "Risk and Saving in Northern Nigeria," *American Economic Review* 85(5) (December 1995):1287–1300.

2. Adam Smith, *An Inquiry into the Nature and Causes of the Wealth of Nations* (London: Ward Lock, Bowden & Co., 1776), p. 690.

3. Ibid., p. 669.

4. John Stuart Mill, *Principles of Political Economy: With Some of their Applications to Social Philosophy* (Fairfield, N.J.: Augustus M. Kelley, 1976), book V, ch. 3, pp. 834–5.

5. Smith, *Wealth of Nations.*

6. The 1799 U.K. income tax is often described as the first true income tax, but earlier, if less influential precedents, appear in England for a short time after the Stuart Restoration (1660) to pay for a war with France, in France during the Terror of 1793, and in Holland in 1798 to pay for war expenses. See Carolyn Webber and Aaron Wildafsky, *A History of Taxation and Expenditure in the Western World* (New York: Simon and Schuster, 1986).

7. Letter "To the Editor of the Times," signed J. H., *The London Times,* March 5, 1816, p. 4, cols. 1 and 2.

8. U.S. Office of the Commissioner of Internal Revenue, *Report of the Commissioner of Internal Revenue on the Operations of the Internal Revenue System for the Year Ending June 30, 1867* (Washington, D.C.: U.S. Government Printing Office, 1867), p. XVII.

9. Ibid.

10. U.S. House 1871:1 January 23, 1871. Also quoted in *Sewanee Review* (August 1893), p. 472.

11. Henry George, *Progress and Poverty,* 4th ed. (New York: Henry George and Company, 1880), p. 288. George goes on to describe another problem with the income tax, "and finally, just in proportion as the tax accomplishes its effect, a lessening in the incentive to the accumulation of wealth, which is one of the strong forms of industrial progress." The problem with income taxes that he alludes to here can be remedied by allowing an unlimited savings allowance, that is, by transforming the income tax into a consumption tax. But appending an unlimited savings allowance to the income tax in his day would have required even more elaborate information technology.

12. The term "negative tax" was used by Augustin Cournot in 1838, but he does not argue for such a tax. See Augustin Cournot, *Researches into the Mathematical Principle of the Theory of Wealth,* trans. by Nathaniel Bacon from French original of 1938 (New York: Augustus M. Kelley Reprints of Economic Classics, 1960), p. 69.

13. Lady Juliet Rhys-Williams, D.B.E., in her privately circulated self-published pamphlet *Something to Look Forward To* (1942), as quoted in Lady Rhys-Williams, D.B.E., *Taxation and Incentives* (Oxford: Oxford University Press, 1953), pp. 121–22. Similar words can be found in her book *Something to Look Forward To* (London: MacDonald, 1943), which was derived from the pamphlet.

14. Rhys-Williams, *Something to Look Forward To.*

15. Ibid. (emphasis hers).

16. Robert Theobald, *Free Men and Free Markets* (New York: Clarkson N. Potter, 1963).

17. In *Fear of Falling: The Inner Life of the Middle Class* (New York: Pantheon Books, 1990), Barbara Ehrenreich details a number of different voices from the early 1960s for this theme of universal affluence.

18. Theobald, *Free Mean and Free Markets,* pp. 156–7.

19. Ibid., p. 151.

20. Daniel Patrick Moynihan, *The Politics of a Guaranteed Income: The Nixon Administration and the Family Assistance Plan* (New York: Random House, 1973).

21. In Italy and Spain, guaranteed minimum incomes exist only in certain localities. In Greece there is none at all. See "Commission Report to the Council, The European Parliament, and Social Committee of the Committee of the Regions on the Implementation of the Recommendation 92/441/EEC of June 23 1992 on Common Criteria Concerning Sufficient Resources and Social Insurance in Social Protection Systems., 1999."

22. Ibid.

23. See Anthony B. Atkinson, "The Case for Participation Income," *The Political Quarterly* 67 (1996):67–70.

24. See *First Report,* Special Issue of CESifo Forum, IFO (Munich: CESifo Council of Economic Experts, 2001).

25. The similarity of these plans across many countries can be easily gauged in U.S. Social Security Administration, *Social Security Programs Throughout the World—1999* (Washington D.C.: U.S. Government Printing Office, 2000).

26. "State Socialism in Germany," *The Times,* June 19, 1889, p. 15, cols. 2–3.

27. David Lloyd George, quoted in *The Daily News,* August 27, 1908. Quoted in E. P. Hennock, "The Origins of British National Insurance and The German Precedent 1880–1914," in W. J. Mommsen, ed., *The Emergence of the Welfare State in Britain and Germany* (London: Croom Helm, 1981), p. 87.

28. Gustav Schmoller, "Vier Briefe über Bismarcks sozialpolitische und volkswirtschaftliche Stellung und Bedeutung," in Gustav Schmoller, ed., *Charakterbilder* (Leipzig: Verlag von Duncker, 1913), p. 57.

29. Truman F. Bewley, *Why Wages Don't Fall in a Recession* (Cambridge: Harvard University Press, 2000).

30. Lujo Brentano, *Die Arbeitsversicherung Gemäss der Heutigen Wirtschaftsordnung* (Leipzig: Duncker & Humblot, 1879), p. 200.

31. The creation of unemployment insurance not only encourages individuals to take greater employment risks for higher wages, it also encourages firms to offer more high quality jobs that have greater employment risk. Thus, unemployment insurance has the potential to raise productivity. See Daron Acemoglu and Robert Shimer, "Efficient Unemployment Insurance," *Journal of Political Economy* 107 (October 1999):893–928.

References

Abowd, Gregory D., and Elizabeth Mynatt. "Charting Past, Present and Future in Ubiquitous Computing." *ACM Transactions on Computer-Human Interaction* 7(1) (March 2000):29–58.

Abowd, John M. "Unlocking the Information in Integrated Social Data." Unpublished paper, Cornell University, 2002; forthcoming in *New Zealand Economic Papers*.

Acemoglu, Daron, Simon Johnson, and James A. Robinson. "Reversal of Fortune: Geography and Institutions in the Making of the Modern World Income Distribution." NBER Working Paper w8460, September 2001.

Acemoglu, Daron, and Robert Shimer. "Efficient Unemployment Insurance." *Journal of Political Economy* 107 (October 1999):893–928

Ackerman, Bruce, and Anne Alstott. *The Stakeholder Society.* New Haven: Yale University Press, 1998.

Adler, Alfred. *Social Interest.* New York: Putnam, 1939.

———. *Understanding Human Nature.* Oxford: OneWorld, 1992.

Adler, Alfred, and J. S. Kounin. "Some Factors Operating at the Moment of Resumption of Interrupted Tasks." *Journal of Psychology* 7 (1939):355–67.

Aghion, Philippe. "Schumpeterian Growth Theory and the Dynamics of Income Distribution." *Econometrica* 70(3) (May 2002):855–83.

Aghion, Philippe, and Peter Howitt. "Technological Change and Wage Inequality." Unpublished paper prepared for Festschrift Conference for Ned Phelps, Columbia University, October 5 and 6, 2001

Ainslie, George W. "Specious Reward: A Behavioral Theory of Impulsiveness and Impulse Control." *Psychological Bulletin* 82 (1975):463–96.

Akerlof, George. "The Market for Lemons: Quality Uncertainty and the Market Mechanism." *Quarterly Journal of Economics* 84 (1970):488–500.

Akerlof, George, William Dickens, and George Perry. "The Macroeconomics of Low Inflation." *Brookings Papers on Economic Activity* I (1996):1–76.

Akerlof, George, and Rachel E. Kranton. "Economics and Identity." *Quarterly Journal of Economics* (2001).

Aldcroft, Derek H. *From Versailles to Wall Street 1919–1929.* Berkeley: University of California Press, 1977.

Alesino, Alberto, and David Dollar. "Who Gives Foreign Aid to Whom and Why?" NBER Working Paper w6612, June 1998.

Allen, Franklin, and Douglas Gale. *Financial Innovation and Risk Sharing.* Cambridge: MIT Press, 1994.

———. *Comparing Financial Systems.* Cambridge: MIT Press, 2000.

Allen, Franklin, Stephen Morris, and Hyung Song Shin. "Beauty Contests, Bubbles, and Iterated Expectations in Asset Markets." Unpublished paper, Yale University, April 2002.

REFERENCES

Allen, Frederick Lewis. "Who's Getting the Money?" *Harper's Magazine* 189(1129) (June 1944):1–10.

Almond, Gabriel, and Sidney Verba. *The Civic Culture: Political Attitudes and Democracy in Five Nations.* Princeton, N.J.: Princeton University Press, 1963.

Altonji, Joseph, and David Card. "The Effects of Immigration on the Labor Market Outcomes of Natives." In John Abowd and Richard Freeman (eds.), *Immigration, Trade and Labor.* Chicago: National Bureau of Economic Research and University of Chicago Press, 1991.

Altonji, Joseph, Fumio Hayashi, and Laurence Kotlikoff. "Risk-Sharing between and within Families." *Econometrica* 64(2) (1996):261–94.

Alvarez, Fernando, and Urban J. Jermann. "Efficiency, Equilibrium, and Asset Pricing with Risk of Default." *Econometrica* 68(4) (2000):775–97.

Ando, Netsuke. *Surrender, Occupation, and Private Property in International Law.* Oxford: The Clarendon Press, 1991.

Angrist, Joshua D. "Lifetime Earnings and the Vietnam-Era Draft Lottery: Evidence from Social Security Administration Records." *American Economic Review* 80 (June 1990):313–35.

Arrow, Kenneth J. "The Economic Foundations of Learning by Doing." *Review of Economic Studies* 29 (June 1962):153–73.

———. *Essays in the Theory of Risk Bearing.* Amsterdam: North Holland, 1974.

Aschinger, Gerhard. *Börsenkrach und Spekulation: Eine ökonomische Analyse.* München: Verlag Vahlen, 1995.

Athanasoulis, Stefano. "Essays in Risk Sharing, Derivatives Design, and Macroeconomic Policy." Ph.D. dissertation, Yale University, 1995.

Athanasoulis, Stefano, and Robert J. Shiller. "The Significance of the Market Portfolio." *Review of Financial Studies* 13(2) (2000):301–29.

———. "World Income Components: Measuring and Exploiting Risk Sharing Opportunities." *American Economic Review* 91(4) (2001):1031–54.

———. "Defining Residual Risk-Sharing Opportunities: Pooling World Income Components." *Research in Economics* 56(1) (March 2002):61–84.

Athanasoulis, Stefano, and Eric van Wincoop. "Growth, Uncertainty, and Risk Sharing." *Journal of Monetary Economics* 45(3) (2000):477–505.

Athanasoulis, Stefano, Eric van Wincoop, and Robert J. Shiller. "Macro Markets and Financial Security." *Economic Policy Review* 5(1) (1999):21–39.

Atkeson, A., and Robert E. Lucas. "Efficiency and Equality in a Simple Model of Efficient Unemployment Insurance." NBER Working Paper w4381, 1993.

Atkinson, Anthony B. "Income Maintenance and Social Insurance." In Alan J. Auerbach and Martin Feldstein (eds.), *Handbook of Public Economics.* Amsterdam: North Holland, 1987. Pp. 779–908.

———. "The Case for Participation Income." *The Political Quarterly* 67 (1996):67–70.

———. *Poverty in Europe.* Oxford: Blackwell, 1998.

Atkinson, Anthony B., and Joseph E. Stiglitz. *Lectures on Public Economics.* New York: McGraw Hill, 1979.

Attanasio, Orazio, James Banks, Costas Meghir, and Guglielmo Weber. "Humps and Bumps in Lifetime Consumption." NBER Working Paper w5350, November 1995.

Audretsch, David B., and Maryann P. Feldman. "R&D Spillovers and the Geography of Innovation and Production." *American Economic Review* 86(3) (June 1995):630–40.

Bagheri, Fathollah M., Nader Habibi, and Aygul Ozbafly. "Attitudes Towards Free Markets in Iran, Turkey, and the Former Soviet Union: A Survey Analysis." Unpublished paper, University of North Dakota, 1997.

Bailey, Martin J., Richard F. Muth, and Hugh O. Nourse. "A Regression Method for Real Estate Price Index Construction." *Journal of the American Statistical Association* 58 (1963):933–42.

Ball, Laurence, and N. Gregory Mankiw. "Intergenerational Risk Sharing in the Spirit of Arrow, Debreu and Rawls, with Applications to Social Security." NBER Working Paper w8270, 2001.

Baker, Guy E. *Why People Buy*, 4th ed. Newport Beach, Calif.: Standel Publishing, 2000.

Bardhan, Pranab, and Christopher R. Udry. *Development Microeconomics*. Oxford: Oxford University Press, 1999.

Barro, Robert J. "Unanticipated Money Growth and Unemployment in the United States." *American Economic Review* 67 (1977):101–15.

———. *Determinants of Economic Growth*. Cambridge: MIT Press, 1997.

Barro, Robert J., and Xavier Sala-i-Martin. *Economic Growth*. New York: McGraw-Hill, 1995.

Barsky, Robert, F. Thomas Juster, Miles S. Kimball, and Matthew D. Shapiro. "Preference Parameters and Behavioral Heterogeneity: An Experimental Approach in the Health and Retirement Study." *Quarterly Journal of Economics* (1997):537–79.

Baxter, Marianne, and Urban Jermann. "The International Diversification Puzzle Is Worse Than You Think." *American Economic Review* 87 (1997):170–80.

Baxter, Marianne, Urban Jermann, and Robert G. King. "Synthetic Returns on NIPA Assets: An International Comparison." *European Economic Review* 42 (1998):1141–72.

Becker, Lawrence, in J. Roland Pennock and John W. Chapman (eds.), *Property*. New York: New York University Press, 1980.

Beckmann, Johann. *A History of Inventions, Discoveries and Origins*, vol. 1. London: Henry G. Bohn, 1846.

Behm, G. "Über Alters- und Invalidencassen für Arbeiter." *Schriften des Vereins für Sozialpolitik* 5 (1874).

Bell, David E. "Regret in Decision Making Under Uncertainty." *Operations Research* 30(5) (1982):961–81.

Bellante, Don, and Gabriel Picone. "Fast Food and Unnatural Experiments: Another Perspective on the New Jersey Minimum Wage." *Journal of Labor Research* 20(4) (Fall 1999):463–77.

Benartzi, Shlomo, and Richard Thaler. "Save More Tomorrow: An Easy Way to Increase Employee Saving." Unpublished paper, University of Chicago, 2001.

Bernanke, Ben S. "Bankruptcy, Liquidity, and Recession." *American Economic Review* 71 (May 1981):155–59.

Bernheim, B. Douglas. "How Strong Are Bequest Motives? Evidence Based on Estimates of the Demand for Life Insurance." *Journal of Political Economy* 99(5) (1991):899–927.

Bernheim, B. Douglas, Andrei Shleifer, and Lawrence H. Summers. "The Strategic Bequest Motive." *Journal of Political Economy* 93 (1985):1045–76.

Bernstein, Peter L. *Against the Gods: The Remarkable Story of Risk.* New York: John Wiley, 1998.

Bewley, Truman. *Why Wages Don't Fall During a Recession.* Cambridge: Harvard University Press, 2000.

Bingham, Jonathan B. *Shirt-Sleeve Diplomacy: Point 4 in Action.* New York: The John Day Company, 1954.

Bisson, T. A. *Zaibatsu Dissolution in Japan.* Berkeley: University of California Press, 1954.

Bix, Amy Sue. *Inventing Ourselves Out of Jobs? America's Debate over Technological Unemployment.* Baltimore: The Johns Hopkins University Press, 2000.

Blinder, Alan. *The Quiet Revolution: Central Banking Goes Modern.* New Haven: Yale University Press, 2003.

Bohn, Henning. "Social Security and Demographic Uncertainty: The Risk Sharing Properties of Alternative Policies." NBER Working Paper w7030, March 1999.

Bootle, Roger. *The Death of Inflation: Surviving and Thriving in the Zero Era.* London: Nicholas Brealey, 1997.

Bordo, Michael D., and Finn E. Kydland. "The Gold Standard as a Rule: An Essay in Exploration." *Explorations in Economic History* 32 (October 1995):423–64.

Borensztein, Eduardo, and Paulo Mauro. "Reviving the Case for GDP-Indexed Bonds." IMF Policy Discussion Paper, September 2002.

Borjas, George J. "The Economics of Immigration." *Journal of Economic Literature* 32(4) (1994):1667–1717.

———. "Immigration and Welfare Magnets." *Journal of Labor Economics* 17(4) (October 1995):607–37.

———. *Heaven's Door: Immigration Policy and the American Economy.* Princeton, N.J.: Princeton University Press, 2001.

Borjas, George J., Richard B. Freeman, and Lawrence F. Katz. "How Much Do Immigration and Trade Affect Labor Market Outcomes." *Brookings Papers on Economic Activity* (1997):1–90.

Bottazzi, Laura, Paolo Pesenti, and Eric van Wincoop. "Wages, Profits, and the International Portfolio Puzzle." *European Economic Review* 40 (1996):219–54.

Boulding, Kenneth E. "The Balance of Peace." *Papers, Peace Research Society* 13 (1970):59–65. Reprinted in Kenneth E. Boulding, *Collected Papers.* Boulder: Colorado Associated University Press, 1975.

Bowles, Samuel, Herbert Gintis, and Melissa Osborne. "The Determinants of Earnings: A Behavioral Approach." *Journal of Economic Literature* 39(4) (December 2001):1137–76.

Boycko, Maxim, Andrei Shleifer, and Robert Vishny. *Privatizing Russia.* Cambridge: MIT Press, 1995.

Bradford, David F. "The Case for a Personal Consumption Tax." In Joseph A. Pechman (ed.), *What Should Be Taxed: Income or Expenditure?* Washington, D.C.: The Brookings Institution, 1980, pp. 75–113.

———. *Untangling the Income Tax.* Cambridge: Harvard University Press, 1986.

———. *Distributional Analysis of Tax Policy.* Washington, D.C.: AEI Press, 1995.

Brainard, William C., and F. Trenery Dolbear. "Social Risks in Financial Markets." *American Economic Review* 61 (1971):360–70.

Brandeis, Louis D. *Other People's Money.* New York: Augustus M. Kelley, 1971 [1914].

Brentano, Lujo. *Die Arbeitsversicherung Gemäss der Heutigen Wirtschaftsordnung.* Leipzig: Duncker & Humblot, 1879.

Brown, Charles. "Minimum Wages, Employment, and the Distribution of Income." *Handbook of Labor Economics.* Amsterdam: North Holland, 1999.

Buck, Fred S. *Horse Race Betting: A Comprehensive Account of Pari-Mutuel, Off-Track Betting and Bookmaking Operations,* 4th ed. New York: ARCO, 1978.

Buckley, Robert, Barbara Lipman, and Thakoor Persaud. "Mortgage Design under Inflation and Real Wage Uncertainty: The Use of a Dual Index Instrument." *World Development* 21(3) (1993):455–64.

Bulkeley, William M. "Old Blues: Some Alumni of Yale Realize That They Owe College a Lasting Debt." *Wall Street Journal,* February 23, 1999, page A1 col. 1.

Butler, Frank O. *The Story of Paper-Making: An Account of Paper-Making from Its Earliest Known Record Down to the Present Time.* Chicago: J. W. Butler Paper Co., 1901.

Camerer, Colin, and Howard Kunreuther. "Experimental Markets for Insurance." *Journal of Risk and Uncertainty* 2 (1989):265–300.

Campbell, John Y., and N. Gregory Mankiw. "Permanent and Transitory Components of Macroeconomic Fluctuations." *American Economic Review* 77 (May 1987):111–17.

Campbell, John Y., Andrew W. Lo, and A. Craig MacKinlay. *The Econometrics of Financial Markets.* Princeton, N.J.: Princeton University Press, 1996.

Campbell, John Y., and Luis M. Viceira. *Strategic Asset Allocation: Portfolio Choice for Long-Term Investors.* Oxford: Oxford University Press, 2002.

Campbell, Karl, and Kunal Kamlani. "The Reasons for Wage Rigidity: Evidence from a Survey of Firms." Unpublished paper, Dartmouth College, 1996.

Caplin, Andrew, Sewin Chan, Charles Freeman, and Joseph Tracy. *Housing Market Partnerships: A New Approach to a Market at a Crossroads.* Cambridge: MIT Press, 1997.

Card, David, and Dean Hyslop. "Does Inflation Grease the Wheels of the Labor Market." NBER Working Paper w5538, 1996. Reprinted in Christina Romer and David Romer (eds.), *Reducing Inflation: Motivation and Strategy.* Chicago: National Bureau of Economic Research and University of Chicago Press, 1997. Pp. 71–121.

Card, David, and Alan Krueger. *Myth and Measurement: The New Economics of the Minimum Wage.* Princeton, N.J.: Princeton University Press, 1995.

Card, James. *Seductive Cinema: The Art of Silent Film.* New York: Alfred A. Knopf, 1994.

Carroll, Christopher D. "The Buffer Stock Theory of Saving." *Brookings Papers on Economic Activity* 2 (1992):61–156.

Carroll, Christopher, and Lawrence H. Summers. "Consumption Growth Parallels Income Growth: Some New Evidence." NBER Working Paper w3090, 1989. Reprinted in B. Douglas Bernheim and John Shoven (eds.), *National Saving and Economic Performance.* Chicago: University of Chicago Press, 1991.

Carroll, Matt. "Home-Equity Insurance Part of New Market Plan." *Boston Globe,* November 18, 1993, p. 45.

Case, Karl E. "The Market for Single-Family Homes in Boston." *New England Economic Review* (May/June 1986):38–48.

Case, Karl E., and Robert J. Shiller. "Prices of Single-Family Homes Since 1970: New Indexes for Four Cities." *New England Economic Review* (September/October 1987):46–56.

———. "The Behavior of Home Buyers in Boom and Post-Boom Markets." *New England Economic Review* (1988):29–46.

———. "The Efficiency of the Market for Single Family Homes." *American Economic Review* 79(1) (1989):125–37.

———. "Forecasting Prices and Excess Returns in the Housing Market." *AREUEA Journal* 18(3) (1990):253–73.

Case, Karl E., Robert J. Shiller, and Allan N. Weiss. "Index-Based Futures and Options Markets in Real Estate." *Journal of Portfolio Management* (Winter 1993):83–92.

CESifo Council of Economic Experts. *First Report* (Special Issue of CESifo Forum). Munich: IFO, 2001.

Champernowne, D. G, and F. A. Cowell. *Economic Inequality and Income Distribution.* Cambridge: Cambridge University Press, 1998.

Chwe, Michael Suk-Young. *Rational Ritual: Culture, Coordination, and Common Knowledge.* Princeton, N.J.: Princeton University Press, 2001.

Cialdini, Robert B., *Influence: Science and Practice.* Needham Heights, Mass.: Allyn & Bacon, 2001.

Cioffi, D. and R. Garner. "On Doing the Decision: The Effects of Active versus Passive Choice on Commitment and Self Perception." *Personality and Social Psychology Bulletin* 22 (1996):133–47.

Cippola, Carlo M. *Money, Prices and Civilization in the Mediterranean World: Fifth to Seventeenth Century.* New York: Gordian Press, 1956.

Cochrane, John H. "A Simple Test of Consumption Insurance." *Journal of Political Economy* 99 (1991):957–76.

———. "Time Consistent Health Insurance." *Journal of Political Economy* 103(3) (1995):445–73.

Cole, Harold L., and Maurice Obstfeld. "Commodity Trade and International Risksharing: How Much Do Financial Markets Matter?" *Journal of Monetary Economics* 28 (1994):3–24.

Cole, Harold L., and Lee Ohanian. "New Deal Policies and the Persistence of the Great Depression." Unpublished paper, UCLA, 2001.

Coleman, James S. "Social Capital in the Creation of Human Capital." *American Journal of Sociology* Supplement 94 (1988):S95–S120.

Combs, B., and P. Slovic. "Causes of Death: Biased Newspaper Coverage and Biased Judgments." *Journalism Quarterly* 56 (1979):837–43.

Conley, John P., and Antonio Rangel. "Intergenerational Fiscal Constitutions: How to Protect Future Generations Using Land Taxes and Federalism." Unpublished paper, Department of Economics, University of Illinois, June 2001.

Connor, Robert A. "More than Risk Reduction: The Investment Appeal of Insurance." *Journal of Economic Psychology* 17 (1996):39–54.

Conyon, Martin J., and Richard B. Freeman. "Shared Modes of Compensation and Company Peformance: UK Evidence." NBER Working Paper w8448, 2001.

Cooper, Richard N. "Growth and Inequality: The Role of Foreign Trade and Investment." Paper presented at William Brainard Festschrift Conference, Yale University, October 27, 2001.

Cournot, Augustin. *Researches into the Mathematical Principles of the Theory of Wealth.* Translated by Nathaniel Bacon from French original of 1838. New York: Augustus M. Kelley Reprints of Economic Classics, 1960.

Cowles, Alfred. *Common Stock Indexes,* 2nd ed. Bloomington Indiana: Principia Press, 1939.

Coyle, Diane. *Paradoxes of Prosperity: Why New Capitalism Benefits All.* New York: Texere, 2001.

Damasio, Antonio R. *Descartes' Error: Emotion, Reason and the Human Brain.* New York: G.P. Putnam, 1994.

Davis, Steven J., Jeremy Nalewaik, and Paul Willen. "On the Gains to International Trade in Risky Financial Assets." NBER Working Paper w7796, July 2000.

Deaton, Angus. *Understanding Consumption.* Oxford: Oxford University Press, 1992.

Deaton, Angus, Pierre-Olivier Gourinchas, and Christina Paxson. "Social Security and Inequality Over the Life Cycle." NBER Working Paper w7570, February 2000.

DeMange, Gabrielle, and Guy Laroque. "Optimality of Incomplete Markets." *Journal of Economic Theory* 65 (1995):218–32.

———. "Social Security with Heterogeneous Populations Subject to Demographic Shocks." *Geneva Papers on Risk and Insurance Theory* 26(1) (2001):5–24.

Denison, Edward F. *Why Growth Rates Differ.* Washington D.C.: The Brookings Institution, 1967.

Dertouzos, Michael. *What Will Be: How the New World of Information Will Change Our Lives.* San Francisco: Harper Edge, 1998.

De Soto, Hernando. *The Mystery of Capital: Why Capitalism Triumphs in the West and Fails Everywhere Else.* New York: Basic Books, 2000.

Diamond, Peter. "Optimal Income Taxation: An Example with a U-Shaped Pattern of Optimal Marginal Tax Rates." *American Economic Review* 88 (1998):83–95.

Diamond, Peter A., and John Geanakoplos. "Social Security Investment in Equities." Cowles Foundation Discussion paper 1214R, Yale University, 2002.

Dixit, Avinash, and Joseph Stiglitz. "Monopolistic Competition and Optimum Product Diversity." *American Economic Review* 67 (1977):297–308.

Dollar, David, and Aart Kraay. "Growth is Good for the Poor." Washington, D.C.: World Bank, 2000.

REFERENCES

Dougherty, Peter J. *Who's Afraid of Adam Smith? How the Market Got Its Soul*. Hoboken, N.J.: John Wiley & Sons, 2002.

Duncan, G. T., and R. B. Pearson. "Enhancing Access to Microdata while Protecting Confidentiality." *Statistical Science* 6 (1991):219–39.

Dynan, Karen E. "How Prudent Are Consumers?" *Journal of Political Economy* 101 (1993):1104–13.

Easterlin, Richard. "Does Economic Growth Improve the Human Lot?" In Paul A. David and Melvin W. Reder (eds.), *Nations and Households in Economic Growth*. New York: Academic Press, 1974.

Ehrenreich, Barbara. *Fear of Falling: The Inner Life of the Middle Class*. New York: Pantheon, 1989.

———. *Nickel and Dimed: On (Not) Getting by in America*. New York: Metropolitan Books, 2001.

Eisner, Robert, and Robert H. Strotz. "Flight Insurance and the Theory of Choice." *Journal of Political Economy* 69 (1961):355–68.

Engel, Eduardo, Alexander Galetovic, and Claudio E. Raddatz. "Tax and Income Distribution in Chile: Some Unpleasant Redistributive Arithmetic." *Journal of Development Economics* 59 (June 1999):155–92.

Fair, Ray C. "Sources of Output and Price Variability in a Macroeconometric Model." Cowles Foundation Working Paper 815, Yale University, 1987.

Farmer, Roger E. A. *Macroeconomics of Self-fulfilling Prophecies*. Cambridge: MIT Press, 1999.

Feenberg, Daniel, and James Poterba. "Income Inequality and the Incomes of Very-High-Income Taxpayers." In James Poterba (ed.), *Tax Policy and the Economy*, vol. 7. Cambridge: MIT Press, 1993.

Fehr, Ernst, and Urs Fischbacher. "Why Social Preferences Matter—The Impact of Non-Selfish Motives on Competition, Cooperation and Incentives." Unpublished paper, University of Zurich, Switzerland, 2001, presented at Nobel Symposium on Behavioral and Experimental Economics, 2001.

Feldstein, Martin. "The Effect of Unemployment Insurance on Temporary Layoff Unemployment." *American Economic Review* 68 (1978):834–46.

———. "The Welfare Cost of Capital Income Taxation." *Journal of Political Economy* 86(2) (1978):S29–S51.

———. *The Risk of Economic Crisis*. Cambridge: National Bureau of Economic Research, 1991.

———. "The Effect of Marginal Tax Rates on Taxable Income: A Panel Study of the 1986 Tax Reform Act." *Journal of Political Economy*, 103(3) (June 1995):561–73.

Ferguson, Niall. *Virtual History: Alternatives and Counterfactuals*. New York: Basic Books, 2000.

Festinger, Leon. "Wish, Expectation and Group Standards as Factors Influencing Level of Aspiration." *Journal of Abnormal Psychology* 37 (1942):184–200.

———. *A Theory of Cognitive Dissonance*. Stanford: Stanford University Press, 1957.

Fienberg, Stephen E. "Confidentiality and Data Protection through Disclosure Limitation: Evolving Principles and Technical Advances." *The Philippine Statistician* 49 (2000):1–12.

Fischer, Stanley, and Franco Modigliani. "Towards an Understanding of the Real Effects and Costs of Inflation." *Weltwirtschaftliches Archiv* 114(4) (1978): 810–33.

Fisher, Irving. "A Compensated Dollar." *Quarterly Journal of Economics,* 27 (1913): 213–35.

——. *The Money Illusion.* New York: Adelphi, 1928.

——. "The Debt-Deflation Theory of Great Depressions." *Econometrica* I (1933): 337–57.

Fisher, Willard C. "The Tabular Standard in Massachusetts History." *Quarterly Journal of Economics* 27 (1913):417–51.

Frank, Robert H. "Are Workers Paid their Marginal Products?" *American Economic Review* 74(4) (September 1984):549–71.

——. *Luxury Fever: Money and Happiness in an Era of Excess.* New York: Free Press, 1999.

——. "Progressive Taxation and the Incentive Problem." In Joel H. Slemrod (ed.), *Does Atlas Shrug? The Economic Consequences of Taxing the Rich.* Cambridge: Russell Sage Foundation and Harvard University Press, 2000. Pp. 490–507.

Frank, Robert H., and Philip J. Cook, *The Winner-Take-All Society: How more and more Americans compete for ever fewer and bigger prizes, encouraging economic waste, income inequality, and an impoverished cultural life.* New York: Martin Kessler, 1995.

Frederick, Shane, George Lowenstein, and Ted O'Donoghue. "Time Discounting: A Critical Review." Unpublished paper, Massachusetts Institute of Technology, 2001.

Freedberg, Rachel, and Jennifer Hunt. "The Impact of Immigrants on Host Country Wages, Employment and Growth." *Journal of Economic Perspectives* 9(2) (1995):23–44.

Freedman, Jonathan L., and Scott C. Fraser. "Compliance without Pressure: The Foot in the Door Technique." *Journal of Personality and Social Psychology* 4(2) (1966):195–202.

Freeland, Chrystia. *Sale of the Century: Russia's Wild Ride from Communism to Capitalism.* New York: Crown Business, 2000.

Freeman, Richard B. *The Market for College-Trained Manpower: A Study in the Economics of Career Choice.* Cambridge: Harvard University Press, 1971.

Freeman, Richard B., and Remco H. Oostendorp. "Wages around the World: Pay Across Occupations and Countries." NBER Working Paper w8058, December 2000.

Freeman, Richard B., Eric Weinstein, Elizabeth Marincola, Janet Rosenbaum, and Frank Solomon. "Competition and Careers in Biosciences." *Science* 294 (December 14, 2001):2293–4.

Friedman, Milton. "Lerner on the Economics of Control." *Journal of Political Economy* 55(5) (1947):405–16.

——. "Choice, Chance, and the Personal Distribution of Income." *Journal of Political Economy,* 41 (1953):277–90.

Friedman, Milton, with the assistance of Rose D. Friedman. *Capitalism and Freedom*. Chicago: University of Chicago Press, 1962.

Friedman, Milton, and Anna J. Schwartz. *A Monetary History of the United States, 1867–1960*. Princeton, N.J.: Princeton University Press, 1963.

Froot, Kenneth A. (ed.). *The Financing of Catastrophe Risk*. Chicago: National Bureau of Economic Research and University of Chicago Press, 1999.

Fukayama, Francis. *Trust*. New York: Free Press, 1995.

Galbraith, John Kenneth. *The Affluent Society*. Boston: Riverside Press, 1958.

Gale, Douglas. "The Efficient Design of Public Debt." In Rudiger Dornbusch (ed.), *Public Debt Management: Theory and History*. Cambridge: Cambridge University Press, 1990; reprinted in Franklin Allen and Douglas Gale (eds.), *Financial Innovation and Risk Sharing*. Cambridge: MIT Press, 1994.

———. "Standard Securities." *Review of Economic Studies*, 59 (1992):731–55; reprinted in Franklin Allen and Douglas Gale (eds.), *Financial Innovation and Risk Sharing*. Cambridge: MIT Press, 1994.

Gamson, William A., and André Modigliani. "The Changing Culture of Affirmative Action." *Research in Political Sociology* 2 (1987):137–77.

Garcia, Márcio G. P. "The Fisher Effect in a Signal Extraction Framework: The Recent Brazilian Experience." *Journal of Development Economics* 41(1) (June 1993): 71–93.

Gaspar, Jess, and Edward L. Glaeser. "Information Technology and the Future of Cities." *Journal of Urban Economics* 43 (January 1998):136–56.

Gates, Jeff. *The Ownership Solution: Toward a Shared Capitalism for the 21st Century*. Vancouver, B.C.: Employee Share Ownership and Investment Association, 1998.

Geanakoplos, John. "Common Knowledge." *Journal of Economic Perspectives* 6 (1992):53–82.

Geanakoplos, John, and Martin Shubik. "The Capital Asset Pricing Model as a General Equilibrium with Incomplete Markets." *The Geneva Papers on Risk and Insurance Theory* 15(1) (1990):55–71.

Geanakoplos, John, Olivia S. Mitchell, and Stephen P. Zeldes. "Social Security Money's Worth." In Robert J. Myers and Howard Young (eds.), *Prospects for Social Security Reform*. Philadelphia: Pension Research Council Publications and University of Pennsylvania Press, 1999.

Geduld, Harry. *The Birth of the Talkies*. Bloomington: Indiana University Press, 1975.

George, Henry. *Progress and Poverty*, 4th ed. New York: Henry George and Company, 1880.

Gertler, Marc. "Financial Structure and Aggregate Economic Activity: An Overview." *Journal of Money, Credit and Banking* 20(2) (1988):559–88.

Glaeser, Edward. "The Incentive Effects of Property Taxes on Local Governments." *Public Choice* 37 (1996):93–111.

Gohman, Stephen E. "Age-Earnings Profile Estimates for Older Persons in Wrongful Death and Injury Cases." *Journal of Risk and Insurance* 59(1) (1992):124–35.

Gokhale, Jegadeesh, and Laurence Kotlikoff. "The Adequacy of Life Insurance." *Research Dialogue* no. 72. New York: TIAA-CREF Institute, 2002.

Goode, Richard. "Long-Term Averaging of Income for Tax Purposes." In Henry J. Aaron and Michael J. Boskin (eds.), *The Economics of Taxation*. Washington, D.C.: The Brookings Institution, 1980.

———. "The Superiority of the Income Tax." In Joseph A. Pechman (ed.), *What Should Be Taxed: Income or Expenditure?* Washington, D.C.: The Brookings Institution, 1980. Pp. 49–73.

Goolsby, Austan. "It's Not About the Money: Why Natural Experiments Don't Work on the Rich." In Joel Slemrod (ed.), *Does Atlas Shrug? The Economic Consequences of Taxing the Rich*. Cambridge: Russell Sage Foundation and Harvard University Press, 2000. Pp. 141–58.

Graetz, Michael J. *The Decline (and Fall?) of the Income Tax*. New York: W.W. Norton, 1997.

Green, Francis, Stephen Machin, and Alan Manning. "The Employer Size-Wage Effect: Can Dynamic Monopsony Provide an Explanation?" *Oxford Economic Papers* 48(3) (July 1996):433–55.

Grossman, Sanford J. *The Informational Role of Prices*. Cambridge: MIT Press, 1989.

Gustman, Alan L., and Thomas L. Steinmeier. "The Effect of Partial Retirement on the Wage Profile of Older Workers." *Industrial Relations* 24 (1985):257–65.

Güth, Werner, Rolf Schmittberger, and Bernd Schwarze. "An Experimental Analysis of Ultimatum Bargaining." *Journal of Economic Behavior and Organization* 3 (1982):367–88.

Hacking, Ian. *The Emergence of Probability: A Philosophical Study of Early Ideas about Probability, Induction, and Statistical Inference*. London: Cambridge University Press, 1975.

Hakansson, Nils H. "Welfare Aspects of Options and Supershares." *Journal of Finance* 33 (June 1978):754–76.

Hall, Robert E. "The Importance of Lifetime Jobs in the U.S. Economy." *American Economic Review* 72(4) (1982):716–24.

———. "Optimal Fiduciary Monetary Systems." *Journal of Monetary Economics* 12 (1983):33–50.

———. "The Role of Consumption in Economic Fluctuations." In Robert J. Gordon (ed.), *The American Business Cycle: Continuity and Change*. Chicago: National Bureau of Economic Research and University of Chicago Press, 1986.

———. "Irving Fisher's Self-Stabilizing Money." *American Economic Review* 87 (1997):436–38.

Hall, Robert E., and Alvin Rabushka. *The Flat Tax,* 2nd ed. Stanford: Hoover Institution, 1995.

Halle, Fritz, D. Zillmer, L. F. Ludwig-Wolf, F. Hiltrop, and G. Behm. "Über Alters- und Invalidencassen für Arbeiter." *Schriften des Vereins für Socialpolitik* 1 (1874).

Hamilton, James D. "Oil and the Macroeconomy since World War II." *Journal of Political Economy* 91 (April 1983):228–48.

Hannah, Leslie. *Inventing Retirement: The Development of Occupational Pensions in Britain*. Cambridge: Cambridge University Press, 1986.

Hansmann, Henry. *The Ownership of Enterprise*. Cambridge: The Belknap Press of Harvard University Press, 1996.

Harrington, Michael. *The Other America*. New York: Macmillan, 1962.

Harsanyi, John C. "Cardinal Utility in Welfare Economics and in the Theory of Risk-Taking." *Journal of Political Economy* 61 (1953):434–35.

———. "Cardinal Welfare, Individualist Ethics, and Interpersonal Comparisons of Utility." *Journal of Political Economy,* 63 (1955):309–21.

———. "Can the Maximin Principle Serve as a Basis for Morality? A Critique of John Rawls's Theory." *American Political Science Review* 69 (1975):594–606.

Heaton, John, and Deborah Lucas. "Evaluating the Effects of Incomplete Markets on Risk Sharing and Asset Pricing." *Journal of Political Economy* 104(3) (1996): 443–87.

Helliwell, John F. "Do Borders Matter for Social Capital? Economic Growth and Civic Culture in U.S. States and Canadian Provinces." NBER Working Paper w5863, December 1996.

Helliwell, John F., and Robert D. Putnam. "Economic Growth and Social Capital in Italy." *Eastern Economic Journal* 21(3) (1995):295–307.

Hennock, E. P. "The Origins of British National Insurance and The German Precedent 1880–1914." In W. J. Mommsen (ed.), *The Emergence of the Welfare State in Britain and Germany.* London: Croom Helm, 1981. Pp. 84–106.

Hill, Ted. "The First Digit Phenomenon." *American Scientist* 86 (July-August 1998):358–63.

Hirschman, Albert O. *Getting Ahead Collectively: Grassroots Experiences in Latin America*. Elmsford, N.Y.: Pergamon, 1984.

Ho, Lok-Sang. "Towards a New International Monetary Order: the World Currency and the Global Indexed Bond." *The World Economy* 23(7) (2000): 939–50.

Holmström, Bengt, and Jean Tirole. "Private and Public Supply of Liquidity." *Journal of Political Economy* 106(1) (1998):1–40.

Hoover, Kevin D., James E. Hartley, and Kevy Salyer. *Real Business Cycles: A Reader*. New York: Routledge, 1998.

Horesh, Ronnie. "Injecting Incentives into Social Problems: Social Policy Bonds." *Economic Affairs* 20(3).

Hunt, Robert M. "Can You Patent That? Are Patents on Computer Programs and Business Methods Good for the New Economy?" *Business Review,* Federal Reserve Bank of Philadelphia, Q1 2001, pp. 5–14.

James, William. *Principles of Psychology,* vol. 1. New York: Henry Holt and Company, 1890.

Jevons, William Stanley. *Money and the Mechanism of Exchange*. New York: D. Appleton & Co., 1875.

Johnson, Bryan. "U.S. Foreign Aid and United Nations Voting Records." Backgrounder #1186, Heritage Foundation, June 1998.

Jung, Jeeman, and Robert J. Shiller. "One Simple Test of Samuelson's Dictum for the Stock Market." Cowles Foundation Discussion Paper 1386, Yale University, 2002.

Kagansky, Nina, *Titra Film: Une Chronique cinématographique et familiale*. N. Kagansky, 21–Quétigny, Impr. Darantière, 1995.

Kahneman, Daniel. "Experienced Utility and Objective Happiness: A Moment-Based Approach." In Daniel Kahneman and Amos Tversky (eds.), *Choices, Values and Frames*. Cambridge: Cambridge University Press, 2000.

———. "Alternative Conceptions of Utility." Unpublished paper, presented at the Nobel Symposium on Behavioral and Experimental Economics, Stockholm, 2001.

Kahneman, Daniel, and Amos Tversky. "Prospect Theory: An Analysis of Decision under Risk." *Econometrica* 47(2) (1979):263–91.

Kahneman, Daniel, Jack L. Knetsch, and Richard Thaler. "Fairness as a Constraint on Profit Seeking." *American Economic Review* 76(4) (1986):728–41.

———. "Experimental Tests of the Endowment Effect and the Coase Theorem." *Journal of Political Economy* 98 (1990):1325–48.

Kakwani, Nanak. "Applications of Concentration Curves to Optimal Negative Income Taxation." *Journal of Quantitative Economics* 1(2) (1985):165–86.

Kaplan, Ann E. (ed.). *Giving USA: The Annual Report on Philanthropy for the Year 1999*. New York: American Association of Fund-Raising Counsel, 2000.

Karr Alan F., and Ashish P. Sanil. "Web Systems that Disseminate Information but Protect Confidential Data." National Institute of Statistical Sciences, Research Triangle Park, North Carolina, 2001.

Katona, George. *Psychology of Economics*. New York: Elsevier, 1965.

Kehoe, Timothy J., and David K. Levine. "Debt Constrained Markets." *Review of Economic Studies* 60 (1993):865–88.

———. "Liquidity Constrained Markets versus Debt Constrained Markets." Unpublished paper, University of Minnesota, Minneapolis, 2000.

Kelso, Louis, and Mortimer J. Adler. *The Capitalist Manifesto*. New York: Random House, 1958.

Kennickell, Arthur B. "Multiple Imputation and Disclosure Protection: The Case of the 1995 Survey of Consumer Finances." SCF Working Paper, 1997.

Keynes, John Maynard. *The Economic Consequences of the Peace. The Collected Writings of John Maynard Keynes Volume II*. London: Macmillan, 1971 [1919].

Khurana, Rakesh. *Searching for a Corporate Savior*. Princeton, N.J.: Princeton University Press, 2002.

Knetsch, Jack L., and J. A. Sinden. "Willingness to Pay and Compensation Demanded: Experimental Evidence of an Unexpected Disparity in Measures of Value." *Quarterly Journal of Economics* 99 (1984):507–21.

Kocherlakota, Narayana R. "Implications of Efficient Risk Sharing without Commitment." *Review of Economic Studies* 63 (1996):595–609.

Kocka, Jürgen. *Industrial Culture & Bourgeois Society: Business, Labor, and Bureaucracy in Modern Germany*. New York: Berghahn Books, 1999.

Köhler, Peter A. "Historical Context and Origins of Social Security." In B. von Maydell and E. M. Hohnerlein (eds.), *The Transformation of Social Security Systems in Central and Eastern Europe*. Leuven: Peters Press, 1994. Pp. 19–34.

REFERENCES

Kokh, Alfred. *The Selling of the Soviet Empire: Politics and Economics of Russia's Privatization—Revelations of the Principal Insider.* New York: SPI Books, 1998.

Kotlikoff, Laurence. "Intergenerational Transfers and Savings." *Journal of Economic Perspectives* 2 (1988):41–58.

———. *Generational Accounting: Knowing Who Pays, and When, for What We Spend.* New York: The Free Press, 1992.

Kotlikoff, Laurence J., and Lawrence H. Summers. "The Role of Intergenerational Transfers in Aggregate Capital Formation." *Journal of Political Economy* 89 (1981):706–32.

———. "Tax Incidence." In Alan Auerbach and Martin J. Feldstein (eds.), *Handbook of Public Economics.* Amsterdam: North Holland, 1987. Pp. 1043–94

Kremer, Michael. "Population Growth and Technological Change: One Million B.C. to 1990." *Quarterly Journal of Ecomomics* 108 (August 1993):681–716.

———. "Patent Buyouts: A Mechanism for Encouraging Invention." *Quarterly Journal of Economics* 113(4) (1998):1137–68.

Krueger, Anne O. *A New Approach to Sovereign Debt Restructuring.* Washington, D.C.: International Monetary Fund, 2002.

Krugman, Paul. *Rethinking International Trade.* Cambridge: MIT Press, 1994.

Kruse, Douglas, and Joseph Blasi. "Employee Ownership, Employee Attitudes and Firm Performance." NBER Working Paper w5277, September 1995; reprinted in Daniel J. B. Mitchell, David Lewin, and Mahummad Zaidi (eds.), *Handbook of Resource Management.* Greenwich, Conn.: JAI Press, 1997.

Kydland, Finn, and Edward C. Prescott. "Time to Build and Aggregate Fluctuations." *Econometrica* 50 (1982):1345–70.

Ladine, Bret. "'70s Debt Program Finally Ending." *Yale Daily News,* March 27, 2001, p. 1.

Laibson, David I. "Golden Eggs and Hyperbolic Discounting." *Quarterly Journal of Economics* 62(2) (1997):443–78.

Laibson, David, Andrea Repetto, and Jeremy Tobacman. "Self-Control and Retirement Savings." National Bureau of Economic Research Summer Institute, 1998.

Lange, Jeffrey, and Nick Economides. "A Parimutuel Market Microstructure for Contingent Claims Trading." Unpublished paper, Longitude, Inc., New York, 2001.

LaPorta, Rafael, Florencio Lopez-de-Silanes, Andrei Shleifer, and Robert W. Vishny. "Trust in Large Organizations." NBER Working Paper w5864, December 1996.

Leahy, John, and Andrew Caplin. "Anticipation, Uncertainty and Time Inconsistency." Unpublished paper, Boston University, 1998.

Lee, David S. "Wage Inequality in the United States during the 1980s: Rising Dispersion or Falling Minimum Wage?" *Quarterly Journal of Economics* 114(3) (1999):941–1024.

Leland, Hayne E. "Who Should Buy Portfolio Insurance." *Journal of Finance* 75(2) (May 1980):581–94.

Lerner, Melvin J. *Belief in a Just World: A Fundamental Delusion.* New York: Plenum Books, 1980.

Lesard, Donald, and Franco Modigliani. *New Mortgage Designs for an Inflationary Environment: Proceedings of a Conference Held at Cambridge, MA, January 1995.* Boston: Federal Reserve Bank of Boston, 1975.

Leuchtenberg, William E. *Franklin Roosevelt and the New Deal, 1932–1940.* New York: Harper & Row, 1963.

Lewis, Alan. *The Psychology of Taxation.* New York: St. Martin's Press, 1982.

Lilien, David M. "Sectoral Shifts and Cyclical Employment." *Journal of Political Economy* 90(3) (1982):777–93.

Lindbeck, Assar. *Unemployment and Macroeconomics.* Cambridge: Cambridge University Press, 1993.

———. "The Swedish Experiment." *Journal of Economic Literature* 35 (September 1997):1273–1319.

Lindert, Peter H., and Jeffrey G. Williamson. "Does Globalization Make the World More Unequal?" NBER Working Paper w8228, April 2001.

Lindsey, Lawrence. "Individual Taxpayer Response to Rate Cuts, 1982–84, with Implications for the Revenue Maximizing Tax Rate." *Journal of Public Economics* 33(2) (July 1987):173–206.

Linton, David. "The Luddites: How Did They Get That Bad Reputation?" *Labor History* 33(4) (1992):529–37.

Locke, Edwin A., and Gary P. Latham. "Building a Practically Useful Theory of Goal Setting and Task Motivation: A 35-Year Odyssey." *American Psychologist* 52(9) (September 2002):705–17.

Loewenstein, George F., Christopher K. Hsee, Elke U. Weber, and Ned Welch. "Risk as Feelings." *Psychological Bulletin* 127(2) (2001):267–86.

Loomis, Graham, and Robert Sugden. "Regret Theory: An Alternative Theory of Rational Choice Under Uncertainty," *The Economic Journal* (1982) 92: 805–24.

Lucas, Robert E. "On the Mechanics of Economic Development." *Journal of Monetary Economics* 22 (July 1988):30–42.

Lustig, Hanno. "The Market Price of Aggregate Risk and the Wealth Distribution." Unpublished paper, Stanford University, 2002.

MacLean, F. J. *The Human Side of Insurance.* London: Sampson Low, Marston & Co., Ltd, 1931.

Maddison, Angus. *Monitoring the World Economy 1820–1992.* Paris: Development Centre Studies, Organization for Economic Co-operation and Development, 1995.

Mandel, Michael. *The High Risk Society: Peril and Promise in the New Economy.* New York: Times Business, 1996.

Mankiw, N. Gregory, David Romer, and David N. Weil. "A Contribution to the Empirics of Economic Growth." *Quarterly Journal of Economics* 107 (May 1992):407–37.

Mantoux, Etienne. *The Carthaginian Peace, or the Economic Consequences of Mr. Keynes.* Pittsburgh: University of Pittsburgh Press, 1952.

Marshall, John F., and Kenneth R. Kapner. *Understanding Swaps.* New York: Wiley Finance Editions, 1993.

Marshall, J. F., V. Bansal, A. F. Herbst, and A. L. Tucker. "Hedging Business Cycle Risk with Macro Swaps and Options." *Continental Bank Journal of Applied Corporate Finance* 4(1) (1992):103–8.

Marshall, Ray. *Back to Shared Prosperity: The Growing Inequality of Wealth and Income in America*. Armonk, N.Y.: Sharpe, 2000.

Marx, Karl. *Das Kapital: Kritik der politischen Ökonomie*. Hamburg: Otto Meissner, 1883.

McCaffery, Edward. "Cognitive Theory and Tax." In Cass Sunstein (ed.), *Behavioral Law and Economics*. Cambridge: Cambridge University Press, 2000.

Mehrling, Perry. "The Social Mutual Fund: A Proposal for Social Security Reform." Unpublished paper, Barnard College, New York, 1998.

Mendelsohn, Robert. *Global Warming and the American Economy: A Regional Assessment of Climate Change Impacts*. London: Edward Elgar, 2002.

Merton, Robert C. "On Consumption-Indexed Public Pension Plans." In Zvi Bodie and John Shoven (eds.), *Financial Aspects of the United States Pension System*. Chicago: National Bureau of Economic Research and University of Chicago Press, 1983. Pp. 259–90.

Milgrom, Paul. *Auction Theory for Privatization*. Cambridge: Cambridge University Press, 2001.

Mill, John Stuart. *Principles of Political Economy: With Some of their Applications to Social Philosophy*. Fairfield, N.J.: Augustus M. Kelley, 1976.

Mirrlees, James. "An Exploration in the Theory of Optimal Income Taxation." *Review of Economic Studies* 38(114) (1971):175–208.

———. "The Optimal Structure of Incentives and Authority within an Organization." *The Bell Journal of Economics* 7(1) (1976):103–31.

Mishkin, Frederic. "Understanding Financial Crises: A Developing Country Perspective." NBER Working Paper w5600, May 1996.

Mishkin, Frederic, and Philip E. Strahan. "What Will Technology Do to Financial Structure?" Brookings-Wharton Papers on Financial Services, 1999.

Modigliani, Franco. "The Role of Intergenerational Transfers and Life Cycle Saving in the Accumulation of Wealth." *Journal of Economic Perspectives* (1988).

Mokyr, Joel. *Lever of Riches: Technological Creativity and Economic Progress*. New York: Oxford University Press, 1990.

Moskowitz, Gordon B. "Preconscious Effects of Temporary Goals on Attention." *Journal of Experimental Social Psychology* 38(4) (July 2002):397–404.

Moss, David A. *When All Else Fails: Government as the Ultimate Risk Manager*. Cambridge: Harvard Business School Press, 2002.

Mowery, David C., and Nathan Rosenberg. *Paths of Innovation: Technological Change in 20th Century America*. Cambridge: Cambridge University Press, 1998.

Moynihan, Daniel Patrick. *The Politics of a Guaranteed Income: The Nixon Administration and the Family Assistance Plan*. New York: Random House, 1973.

Mueller, Eva. "Public Attitudes toward Fiscal Programs." *Quarterly Journal of Economics* 77(2) (1963):210–35.

Mueller, Hans-Eberhard. *Bureaucracy, Education and Monopoly: Civil Service Reforms in Prussia and England*. Berkeley: University of California Press, 1984.

Mundell, Robert A. "The Birth of Coinage." Discussion Paper No. 0102-08, Department of Economics, Columbia University, February 2002.

Munsell, J. *Chronology of Paper and Paper-Making.* Albany: J. Munsell, 1864.

Murphy, Barbara. *The Ugly Canadian: The Rise and Fall of a Caring Society.* Winnipeg: J. Gordon Shillingford, 1999.

Murphy, Kevin M., and Finis Welch. "Empirical Age-Earnings Profiles." *Journal of Labor Economics* 8 (1990):202–29.

Murray, Christopher J., and Alan D. Lopez (eds.). *The Global Burden of Disease.* Cambridge: Harvard School of Public Health and Harvard University Press, 1996.

Musgrave, Richard A. *The Theory of Public Finance: A Study in Public Economy.* New York: McGraw-Hill, 1959.

Naisbitt, John. *The Global Paradox: The Bigger the World Economy, the More Powerful Its Smallest Players.* New York: W. Morrow, 1994.

National Association of Manufacturers. *Unemployment Insurance Handbook: A Reference Book for the Use of Legislators, Business Executives, Teachers and Students.* New York: National Association of Manufacturers, 1933.

National Research Council. *Trends in the Early Careers of Life Scientists.* Washington, D.C.: National Academy Press, 1998. Available at http://www.nap.edu/html/trends/.

Neal, Larry. "The Integration and Efficiency of the London and Amsterdam Stock Markets in the Eighteenth Century." *Journal of Economic History* 47(1) (1987): 97–115.

Nelli, Humberto O. "The Earliest Insurance Contract: A New Discovery." *Journal of Risk and Insurance* 39 (September 1972):215–20.

Nelson, Thomas E., and Donald R. Kinder. "Issue Frames and Group-Centrism in American Public Opinion." *Journal of Politics* 58 (1996):1055–78.

Nelson, Thomas E., Zoe M. Oxley, and Rosalee Clawson. "Toward a Psychology of Framing Effects." *Political Behavior* 19(3) (1997):221–46.

Neumark, David, and William Wascher. "Using the EITC to Help Poor Famlies: New Evidence and Comparison with the Minimum Wage." *National Tax Journal* 54(2) (June 2001):281–317.

Newcomb, Simon. "The Standard of Value." *North American Review* (1879):223–37.

Newman, Katherine S., *Falling from Grace: The Experience of Downward Mobility in the American Middle Class.* New York: Free Press, 1988.

Nicholson, Sean, and Nicholas S. Souleles. "Physician Income Expectations and Specialty Choice." NBER Working Paper w8536, October 2001.

Noble, David F. *Progress Without People: New Technology, Unemployment, and the Message of Resistance.* Toronto: Between the Lines, 1995.

Nordhaus, William D. "Expert Opinion on Climactic Change." *American Scientist* (1994):45–51.

———. "Do Real-Output and Real-Wage Measures Capture Reality? The History of Lighting Suggests Not." In Timothy F. Breshahan and Robert J. Gordon (eds.), *The Economics of New Goods,* vol. 58. Chicago: University of Chicago Press, 1997. Pp. 29–66.

Nordhaus, William D. "The Health of Nations: Irving Fisher and the Contribution of Improved Longevity to Living Standards." Unpublished paper, Yale University, May 1998.

———. "The Progress of Computing." Cowles Foundation Discussion Paper 1324, Yale University, September 2001.

Nordhaus, William, and James Tobin. "Is Growth Obsolete?." In *Economic Growth: Fiftieth Anniversary Colloquium*. New York: National Bureau of Economic Research and Columbia University Press, 1972. Pp. 1–80. Reprinted in James Tobin, *Essays in Economics: Theory and Policy*, vol. 3. Cambridge: MIT Press. Pp. 360–450.

Nordhaus, William D., and Zili Yang. "A Regional Dynamic General-Equilibrium Model of Alternative Climate-Change Strategies." *American Economic Review* 86 (1996):741–65.

Northcraft, G. B., and M. A. Neale. "Experts, Amateurs, and Real Estate: An Anchoring-and-Adjustment Perspective on Property Pricing Decisions." *Organizational Behavior and Human Decision Processes* 39 (1987):84–97.

Nowland, William. "A Rational View of Insurance and Genetic Discrimination." *Science* 297(5579) (July 12, 2002):195–6.

Oates, Wallace, and Robert Schwab. "Economic Competition Among Jurisdictions: Efficiency Enhancing or Distortion Inducing?" *Journal of Public Economics* 35 (1988):333–54.

———. "The Theory of Regulatory Federalism: The Case of Environmental Management." In Wallace Oates (ed.), *The Economics of Environmental Regulation*. Cheltenham, U.K.: Edward Elgar, 1996.

Obstfeld, Maurice. "Risk-Taking, Global Diversification, and Growth." *American Economic Review* 84 (1994):1310–29.

O'Hara, Maureen. *Market Microstructure Theory*. London: Basil Blackwell, 1997.

Ohmae, Kenichi. *The End of the Nation State: The Rise of Regional Economies*. New York: Free Press, 1996.

Orhnial, Tony. *Limited Liability and the Corporation*. London: Croom Helm, 1982.

Orwell, George. *Down and Out in Paris and London*. New York: Harcourt Brace Jovanovich, 1961.

Palme, Mårten, and Ingemar Svensson. "Social Security, Occupational Pensions, and Retirement in Sweden." In Jonathan Gruber and David A. Wise (eds.), *Social Security and Retirement around the World*. Chicago: National Bureau of Economic Research and University of Chicago Press, 1999. Pp. 355–402.

Persson, Torsten, and Guido Tabellini. "Federal Fiscal Constitutions: Risk Sharing and Redistribution." *Journal of Political Economy* 104(5) (1996):979–1009.

Phelps, E. S., and Robert A. Pollak. "On the Second-Best National Saving and Game-Equilibrium Growth." *Review of Economic Studies* 35 (1968):185–99.

Post, James R. *Risk and Response: Management and Social Change in the American Insurance Industry*. Lexington, Mass.: Lexington Books, 1976.

Poterba, James M. "The History of Annuities in the United States." NBER Working Paper w6001, April 1997.

———. "The Rate of Return to Corporate Capital and Factor Shares: New Estimates Using Revised National Income Accounts and Capital Stock." *Carnegie-Rochester Conference Series on Public Policy* 48 (1998):211–46.

Putnam, Robert D. *Making Democracy Work: Civic Traditions in Modern Italy.* Princeton, N.J.: Princeton University Press, 1993.

———. "Bowling Alone: America's Declining Social Capital." *Journal of Democracy* (1995):65–78.

———. *Bowling Alone: The Collapse and Revival of American Community.* New York: Simon & Schuster, 2000.

Rabin, Matthew. "Incorporating Fairness into Game Theory." *American Economic Review* 83 (1993):1281–1302.

Rabin, Matthew, and Richard Thaler. "Anomalies: Risk Aversion." *Journal of Economic Perspectives* 15(1) (2001):219–22.

Radelet, Steven, and Jeffrey Sachs. "The Onset of the East Asian Financial Crisis." Reproduced, Harvard Institute for International Development, 1998.

Rahnema, Saeed, and Sohrab Behdad. *Iran: After the Revolution.* London: I. B. Tauris and St. Martin's Press, 1995.

Rassenti, Stephen, Vernon L. Smith, and Bart J. Wilson. "Controlling Market Power and Price Spikes in Electricity Networks: Demand-Side Bidding." Unpublished paper, Interdisciplinary Center for Economic Science, George Mason University, 2001.

Raven, Peter H. "Science, Sustainability and the Human Prospect." *Science* 297(5583) (9 August 2002):954–58.

Rawls, John. *Theory of Justice.* Cambridge: Harvard University Press, 1971.

———. "Some Reasons for the Maximin Criterion." *American Economic Review Papers and Proceedings* 64 (1974):141–66.

Reich, Robert. *The Work of Nations.* New York: Vintage Books, 1991.

Rhys-Williams, Lady Juliet. *Something to Look Forward To.* London: MacDonald, 1943.

———. *Taxation and Incentive.* London: W. Hodge, 1953.

Ritter, Gerhard A. *Social Welfare in Germany and Britain: Origins and Development.* Translated by Kim Traymor. Berg: Learnington Spa / New York, 1983.

Rodgers, Daniel T. *Atlantic Crossings: Social Politics in a Progressive Age.* Cambridge: Belknap Press of Harvard University Press, 1998.

Rodgers, James D., Michael Brookshire, and Robert J. Thornton. "Forecasting Earnings Using Age-Earnings Profiles in Longitudinal Data." *Journal of Forensic Economics* 9(2) (1996):169–200.

Roemer, John. "Egalitarianism Against the Veil of Ignorance." Cowles Foundation Discussion Paper 1328, Yale University, April 18, 2001.

Rogers, Dann. "'Citizenship for Sale' Programme Criticism Grows." *South China Morning Post,* September 30, 1993, p. 4.

Romer, Christina. "The Great Crash and the Onset of the Great Depression." *Quarterly Journal of Economics* 105(3) (1990):597–624.

Romer, Paul. "A Taste for Violence." Unpublished working paper, Stanford University.

Rosen, Sherwin. "The Economics of Superstars." *American Economic Review* 71 (December 1981):845–68.

Ross, Lee. "The Problem of Construal in Social Inference and Social Psychology." In N. Grunberg, R. E. Nisbett, and J. Singer (eds.), *A Distinctive Approach to Psychological Research: The Influence of Stanley Schachter.* Hillsdale, N.J.: Erlbaum, 1987.

Ross, Lee, and Steven M. Samuels. "The Predictive Power of Personal Reputation vs. Labels and Construal in the Prisoner's Dilemma Game." Unpublished manuscript, Stanford University, 1993.

Ross, Lee, and Andrew Ward. "Naive Realism in Everyday Life: Implications for Social Conflict and Misunderstanding." In Edward S. Reed, Elliot Turiel, and Terrance Brown (eds.), *Values and Knowledge.* Mahwah, N.J.: Lawrence Erlbaum Associates, 1996.

Rotemberg, Julio, and Garth Saloner. "A Supergame-Theoretic Model of Price Wars during Booms." *American Economic Review* 76 (June 1986):390–407.

Roth, Alvin E. "The Economist as Engineer: Game Theory, Experimental Economics and Computation as Tools of Design Economics." *Econometrica* 70 (July 2001):1341–78.

Rubin, Donald B. "Discussion of Statistical Disclosure Limitation." *Journal of Official Statistics* 9 (1993):461–68.

Rubin, Zick, and Anne Peplau. "Belief in a Just World and Reactions to Another's Lot: A Study of Participants in the National Draft Lottery." *Journal of Social Issues* 29(4) (1973):73–93.

Sahlins, Marshall. *Stone Age Economics.* Amsterdam: Aldine De Gruyter, 1972.

Sale, Kirkpatrick. *Rebels Against the Future: The Luddites and their War on the Industrial Revolution.* Reading, Mass.: Addison Wesley, 1995.

Samuelson, Paul A. "A Note on Measurement of Utility." *Review of Economic Studies* 4 (1937):155–61.

Sandberg, Nils-Eric. *Vad Gick Snett I Sverige (What Went Wrong in Sweden?).* Timbro, Sweden, 1997 (English translation available at http://www.wrong-in-sweden.com).

Sargent, Thomas J., and François R. Velde. *The Big Problem of Small Change.* Princeton, N.J.: Princeton University Press, 2002.

Schaede, Ulrike. "Forwards and Futures in Tokugawa-Period Japan: A New Perspective on the Dojima Rice Market." *Journal of Banking and Finance* 13 (1989):487–513.

Schieber, Sylvester J., and John B. Shoven. *The Real Deal: The History and Future of Social Security.* New Haven: Yale University Press, 1999.

Schloss, Glenn. "Passport Trade Worth Billions." *South China Morning Post,* August 19, 1996, p. 3.

———. "Fiji Backs Plan to Lure Rich Migrants." *South China Morning Post,* September 29, 1996, p. 4.

Schmidt, John C. *Win Place Show: A Biography of Harry Strauss The Man Who Gave America the Tote.* Baltimore: The Johns Hopkins University, 1989. Published with the assistance of the G.W.C. Whiting School of Engineering.

Schmoller, Gustav. *Die Entwicklung der deutschen Volkswirtschaftslehre im neunzehnten Jahrhundert.* Leipzig: Duncker & Humboldt, 1908.

———. "Vier Briefe über Bismarcks sozialpolitische und volkswirtschaftliche Stellung und Bedeutung." In *Charakterbilder.* Munich: Verlag von Duncker & Humblot, 1913.

Schneider, Friedrich, and Dominik H. Enste. "Shadow Economies: Size, Causes, and Consequences." *Journal of Economic Literature* 38 (March 2000):77–114.

Scholen, Ken. *Retirement Income on the House.* Apple Valley, Minn.: National Center for Home Equity Conversion Press, 1993.

Schwartz, Evan I. "Digital Cash Payoff," *Technology Review* 361(8247) (2001): 62–68.

Sen, Amartya. "Rational Fools: A Critique of the Behavioral Foundations of Economic Theory." *Philosophy and Public Affairs* (1977).

———. *On Economic Inequality.* Oxford: Clarendon Press, 1997.

Shafir, Eldar, Peter Diamond, and Amos Tversky. "Money Illusion." *Quarterly Journal of Economics* 112(2) (May 1997):341–74.

Shapiro, Ian. *The Evolution of Rights in Liberal Theory.* Cambridge: Cambridge University Press, 1986.

Shapley, Lloyd S., and Martin Shubik. "Trade Using One Commodity as a Means of Payment." *Journal of Political Economy* 85(5) (1977):937–68.

Shavell, Steven, and Tanguy van Ypserle. "Rewards versus Intellectual Property Rights." Reproduced, Harvard Law School, 1998.

Shefrin, Hersch M., and Richard H. Thaler. "An Economic Theory of Self Control." *Journal of Political Economy* 89(2) (1981):392–406.

Sherman, Steven J. "On the Self-Erasing Nature of Errors of Prediction." *Journal of Personality and Social Psychology* 39(2) (1980):211–21.

Sheshinski, Eytan. "The Optimal Linear Income Tax." *Review of Economic Studies* 39(119) (1972):297–302.

Shiller, Robert J. *Market Volatility.* Cambridge: MIT Press, 1989.

———. "Arithmetic Repeat Sales Price Estimators." *Journal of Housing Economics* 1 (1991):110–26.

———. *Macro Markets: Creating Institutions for Managing Society's Largest Economic Risks* (Clarendon Series). Oxford: Oxford University Press, 1993.

———. "Measuring Asset Value for Cash Settlement in Derivative Markets: Hedonic Repeated Measures Indices and Perpetual Futures." *Journal of Finance* 68 (July 1993):911–31.

———. "Public Resistance to Indexation: A Puzzle." *Brookings Papers on Economic Activity* 1 (1997):159–211.

———. "Why Do People Dislike Inflation?" In Christina Romer and David Romer, (eds.), *Reducing Inflation: Motivation and Strategy.* Chicago: National Bureau of Economic Research and University of Chicago Press, 1997.

———. "Designing Indexed Units of Account." Cowles Foundation Working Paper 1179, Yale University, May 1998; and NBER Working Paper w7160, 1999.

———. "Social Security and Institutions for Intergenerational, Intragenerational, and International Risk Sharing." *Carnegie Rochester Conference Series on Public Policy* 50 (1999):165–204.

Shiller, Robert J. *Irrational Exuberance*. Princeton, N.J.: Princeton University Press, 2000.

———. "Indexed Units of Account: Theory and Assessment of Historical Experience." NBER Working Paper w6356, January 1998; forthcoming in Fernando Lefort and Klaus Schmidt-Hebbel (eds.), *Indexation, Inflation, and Monetary Policy*. Santiago, Chile: Central Bank of Chile, 2002.

———. "Social Security and Individual Accounts as Elements of Overall Risk Sharing." Paper presented at American Economic Associations meetings, Washington, D.C., January 2003.

Shiller, Robert J., and Stefano Athanasoulis. "World Income Components: Measuring and Exploiting International Risk Sharing Opportunities." NBER Working Paper w5095, April 1995.

Shiller, Robert J., and Ryan Schneider. "Labor Income Indices Designed for Use in Contracts Promoting Income Risk Management." *Review of Income and Wealth* 44(2) (June 1998):163–82.

Shiller, Robert J., and Allan Weiss. "Home Equity Insurance." NBER Working Paper w4860, 1994.

———. "Evaluating Real Estate Valuation Systems." *Journal of Real Estate Finance and Economics* 18(2) (1999):147–61.

———. "Home Equity Insurance." *Journal of Real Estate Finance and Economics* 19(1) (1999):21–47.

———. "Moral Hazard and Home Equity Conversion." *Real Estate Economics* 28(1) (2000).

Shiller, Robert J., Maxim Boycko, and Vladimir Korobov. "Popular Attitudes Toward Free Markets: The Soviet Union and the United States Compared." *American Economic Review* 81(3) (1991):385–400.

———. "Hunting for Homo Sovieticus: Situational versus Attitudinal Factors in Economic Behavior." *Brookings Papers on Economic Activity* 1 (1992): 127–194.

Shoven, John B., and David A. Wise. "The Taxation of Pensions: A Shelter Can Become a Trap." NBER Working Paper w5815, November 1996.

Shubik, Martin. "Terrorism, Technology, and the Socioeconomics of Death." *Comparative Strategy* 16 (1997):399–414.

Siegel, Jeremy J. *Stocks for the Long Run: The Definitive Guide to Financial Market Returns and Long-Term Investment Strategies*, 3rd ed. New York: McGraw-Hill, 2002.

Sims, Christopher A. "Macroeconomics and Reality." *Econometrica* 48(1) (January 1980):1–48.

Sims, George R. *How the Poor Live*. London: Chatto & Windus, 1889.

Slovic, Paul. "Rational Actors and Rational Fools: Implications of the Affect Heuristic for Behavioral Economics." Unpublished paper, University of Oregon, 2001.

Smith, Adam. *An Inquiry into the Nature and Causes of the Wealth of Nations*. London: Ward Lock, Bowden & Co,. 1776.

Smith, Clifford W., Jr., Charles W. Smithson, and D. Sykes Wilford. *Managing Financial Risk*. New York: Harper Business, 1990.

Soltow, Lee. "America's First Progressive Tax." *National Tax Journal* 30(1) (1977):53–58.

Srinivasan, T. N. "Development in the Context of Rapid Population Growth: An Overall Assessment." Population Growth and Demographic Structure: Proceedings of the United Nations Expert Group Meeting on Population Growth and Demographic Structure, ST/ESA/SER.R/132. New York: United Nations, 1994.

Stalson, Owen J. *Marketing Life Insurance: Its History in America*. Homewood, Ill.: Richard B. Irwin, 1969.

Stavins, Robert N. "Policy Instruments for Climate Change: How Can National Governments Address a Global Problem?" *The University of Chicago Legal Forum* (1977):293–329.

Steinmo, Sven. *Taxation and Democracy*, New Haven: Yale University Press, 1993.

Stiglitz, Joseph. *Economics of the Public Sector*, 2nd ed. New York: W.W. Norton, 1988.

Stiglitz, Joseph, and Andrew Weiss. "Incentive Effects of Termination: Applications to Credit and Labor Markets." *American Economic Review* 73 (1983): 912–27.

Stone, Richard. *Input-Output and National Accounts*. Paris: Organization for Economic Cooperation and Development, 1961.

Stone, Richard, and Giovanna Stone. *National Income and Expenditure*. Chicago: Quadrangle Books, 1962 [1944].

Strotz, Robert H. "Myopia and Inconsistency in Dynamic Utility Maximization." *Review of Economic Studies* 23(3) (1955):165–80.

Suls, Jerry M. "Social Comparison Theory and Research: An Overview from 1954." In Jerry M. Suls and Richard L. Miller (eds.), *Social Comparison Processes*. New York: Hemisphere Publishing Company and John Wiley & Sons, 1977. Pp. 1–19.

Taleb, Nassim Nicholas. *Fooled by Randomness: The Hidden Role of Chance in Markets and Life*. New York: Texere, 2001.

Tesar, Linda L. "Evaluating the Gains from International Risksharing." *Carnegie-Rochester Conference Series on Public Policy* 42 (1995):95–103.

Tesar, Linda L., and Ingrid Werner. "Home Bias and High Turnover." *Journal of International Money and Finance* 14 (1995):467–92.

Theobald, Robert. *Free Man and Free Markets*. New York: C. N. Potter, 1963.

Thomas, Malcolm I. *The Luddites: Machine Breaking in Regency England*. Newton Abbot, Devon, U.K.: David & Charles Archon, 1970.

Tobin, James. "Raising the Incomes of the Poor." In Kermit Gordon (ed.), *Agenda for the Nation*. Washington: Brookings Institution, 1968. Pp. 77–116.

Tobin, James, Joseph Pechman, and Peter Mieszkowski. "Is a Negative Income Tax Practical?" *Yale Law Journal* 77 (1967):1–27.

Toffler, Alvin. *The Third Wave*. New York: Morrow, 1980.

Townsend, Robert M. "Risk and Insurance in Village India." *Econometrica* 62 (1994):539–91.

———. "Financial Systems in Northern Thai Villages." *Quarterly Journal of Economics* 110(4) (November 1995):1011–46.

Townsend, Robert M., and Rolf A. E. Mueller. "Mechanism Design and Village Economies: From Credit to Tenancy to Cropping Groups." *Review of Economic Dynamics* 1(1) (January 1998):119–72.

Trenerry, C. F. *The Origin and Early History of Insurance*. London: P. S. King & Son Ltd., 1926.

Tuomala, M. *Optimal Income Tax and Redistribution*. Oxford: The Clarendon Press, 1990.

Tversky, Amos, and Daniel Kahneman. "Judgment under Uncertainty: Heuristics and Biases." *Science* 185(4157) (1974):1124–31.

———. "The Framing of Decisions and the Psychology of Choice." *Science* 211(4481) (1981):453–58.

Udry, Christopher. "Risk and Saving in Northern Nigeria." *American Economic Review* 85(5) (December 1995):1287–1300.

United Nations Development Program. *The Human Development Report*. New York: UNDP 1992.

U.S. Congress, Congressional Budget Office. "Estimates of Federal Tax Liabilities for Individuals and Families by Income Category and Family Type for 1995 and 1999," Washington, D.C.: Government Printing Office, May 1998. Available at http://www.cbo.gov/showdoc.cfm?index=527&sequence=0&from=5.

———. "Estimates of Federal Tax Liabilities for Individuals and Families by Income Category and Family Type for 1995 and 1999." Washington, D.C.: Government Printing Office, 1999. Available at http://www.cbo.gov/showdoc.

U.S. House of Representatives, Committee on Ways and Means. "Hearings on the Legal Status of OASI Benefits" (Part 6). November 27, 1953.

U.S. Office of the Commissioner of Internal Revenue. *Report on the Operations of the Internal Revenue System for the Year Ending June 30, 1867*. Washington, D.C.: Government Printing Office, 1867.

U.S. Social Security Administration. *Social Security Programs Throughout the World—1999*. SSA Publication No. 13-11805. Washington, D.C.: Government Printing Office, August 1999.

———. *Social Security Survivors Benefits*, Publication No. 05-10084. Washington, D.C.: Government Printing Office, August 2000.

U.S. Subcommittee on Ways and Means. *Analysis of the Social Security System: Hearings before a Subcommittee of the Committee on Ways and Means House of Representatives, Eighty-Third Congress on Legal Status of OASI Benefits, Part 6*. Washington, D.C.: Government Printing Office, 1953.

van der Veen, Robert, and Loek Groot (eds.). *Basic Income on the Agenda*. Amsterdam: Amsterdam University Press, 2000.

van Wincoop, Eric. "Welfare Gains from International Risksharing." *Journal of Monetary Economics* 34 (1994):175–200.

———. "How Big are Potential Welfare Gains from International Risksharing?" *Journal of International Economics* 47 (1999):109–35.

Varian, Hal R. "Redistributive Taxation as Social Insurance." *Journal of Public Economics* 14 (1980):49–68.

Veblen, Thorstein. *The Theory of the Leisure Class: An Economic Study of Institutions.* New York: Vanguard Press, 1922.

Venti, Steven F., and David A. Wise. "Choice, Chance and Wealth Dispersion at Retirement." Prepared for the Joint JCER-NBER Conference on the Economics of Aging, Kyoto, Japan, May 8 and 9, 1997.

———. "Aging and Housing Equity: Another Look." NBER Working Paper w8608, November 2001.

Vickrey, William. "Averaging of Income for Tax Purposes." *Journal of Political Economy* 37(3) (June 1939):305–37.

———. "Measuring Marginal Utility by Reactions to Risk." *Econometrica* 13(4) (1945):319–33.

de Voogd, J., J. de Konig, M. M. J. Leenders, A. Gelderblom, and N. Mahieu. *Guaranteed Minimum Income Arrangements in the Netherlands, Belgium, Denmark, France, Germany and Great Britain.* Sociale Zekerheid, Dutch Ministry of Social Affairs and Employment, Department of Labour-Market and Education, 1992.

Vuolteenaho, Tuomo. "What Drives Firm-Level Stock Returns?" *Journal of Finance* 67 (2002):233–64.

Wagner, Wolf B. *Risk Sharing under Incentive Constraints.* Ph.D. dissertation, Center for Economic Research, Tilburg University, Netherlands, 2002.

Webber, Carolyn, and Aaron Wildafsky. *A History of Taxation and Expenditure in the Western World.* New York: Simon and Schuster, 1986.

Weiss, Allan N., and Robert J. Shiller. *Proxy Asset Data processor.* U.S. Patent No. 5,987,435, 1999.

Weretka, Marek. "Moral Hazard in Macro Markets: Welfare Evaluation." Unpublished paper, Yale University, 2002.

Wiener, Norbert. *Cybernetics, Or Control and Communication in the Animal and the Machine.* New York: John Wiley, 1948.

Willen, Paul. "Welfare, Financial Innovation and Self Insurance in Dynamic Incomplete Market Models." Working Paper, Princeton University, 1999.

Williams, C. Arthur. *An International Comparison of Workers' Compensation.* Boston: Kluwer Academic Publishers, 1991.

Wilmoth, John R. "The Future of Human Longevity: A Demographic Perspective." *Science* 280 (1998):395–97.

Wilson, E. O. *On Human Nature.* Toronto: Bantam Books, 1990 [1978].

Wilson, Gail. "Money and Independence in Old Age." In Sara Arber and Maria Evandrou (eds.), *Ageing, Independence and the Life Course.* London: Jessica Kingsley, 1993.

Woodford, Michael. "Self-Fulfilling Expectations and Business Cycles." *American Economic Review Papers and Proceedings* 77 (May 1987):93–98.

World Bank. *Averting the Old Age Crisis.* Oxford: Oxford University Press, 1994.

REFERENCES

Yates, Jo Anne. *Control Through Communication: The Rise of System in American Management.* Baltimore: The Johns Hopkins University Press, 1989.

Yellen, Janet. "Efficiency Wage Models of Unemployment" *American Economic Review* 74 (May 1984):200–5.

Zeldes, Stephen P. "Consumption and Liquidity Constraints: An Empirical Investigation." *Journal of Political Economy* 97 (1989):305–46.

Zelizer, Viviana A. Rotman. *Morals and Markets: The Development of Life Insurance in the United States.* New York: Transaction Books, 1983.

Index